When Peacekeeping Missions Collide

Advance Praise for *When Peacekeeping Missions Collide*

"This important new book, written by renowned experts, takes a look under the bonnet of UN peacekeeping to examine how the different tasks peacekeepers are given interact with one another and influence the overall effectiveness of UN operations. Combining detailed case studies with rigorous social scientific analysis, this book takes a giant leap in thought and understanding. The results are so compelling that readers—academics, students, and practitioners alike—won't look at peacekeeping in the same way again."

—Alex Bellamy, Professor of Peace and Conflict Studies,
University of Queensland, Australia

"Not always, but on average, peacekeeping works. This insightful book asks how and why peacekeeping is asked to work in ever more complex ways, with 'Christmas trees' of ambitions. Then it develops evidence-based principles for priority setting. 'Security first' is not a surprising finding. When a peace operation fails to stem the bloodshed and rape, subsequent goals, like moving on to a post-conflict election, likely will have limited success. A surprise, on the other hand, is that accomplishing 'democracy' with peace operation support is mostly not a gateway to further mission accomplishments. This is thoughtful, helpful research by greats of peacekeeping research on matters of importance."

—John Braithwaite, Distinguished Emeritus Professor,
Australian National University

"Diehl, Druckman, and Mueller add a valuable perspective on our understanding of peace operations success (and failure) by focusing on a neglected factor: missions' interdependencies. The book offers novel insights on how to define and assess compatibility between simultaneous or sequential missions, and implications for success. The conceptualization and operationalization of compatibility is followed by a clear set of empirical expectations tested across five in-depth case studies, which include some of the most prominent peacekeeping missions. This book is a major contribution given that a significant number of missions do not operate in isolation, and the UN has committed to a sequenced approach for future peacekeeping missions. Academic rigor and policy relevance make the book a must-read for those interested in the study and practice of peace operations."

—Jessica Di Salvatore, Associate Professor in Political Science and Peace Studies, University of Warwick

"Peacekeeping operations are tasked with many 'missions', some of which overlap, are contradictory, or have varying effects on one another. The authors build a novel quantitative dataset, while employing qualitative cases studies, in order to evaluate the extent to which one mission, say, promoting democratic elections, might reinforce or undermine other missions like providing security. In this way, the authors fill an important 'middle-level' theoretical and empirical gap in the literature. A must-read for peacekeeping scholars, students, and practitioners."

—Lise Howard, Professor of Government and Foreign Service, Georgetown University, and President of the Academic Council on the United Nations System

"This book provides an excellent guide to understanding the complexity of UN peacekeeping. Diehl, Druckman, and Mueller advance the field by conceptualizing and categorizing the overall goals of UN peacekeeping operations. Their rich empirical analysis generates new insights into the highly policy-relevant question of how to sequence and combine different missions that the UN seeks to accomplish. *When Peacekeeping Missions Collide* will enrich both scholarship and policy discussions on the future of peacekeeping."

—Lisa Hultman, Professor of Peace and Conflict Research, Uppsala University

"The complexity of peacekeeping missions and their effectiveness have outpaced our understanding of them. In this nuanced book, Diehl, Druckman, and Mueller offer a clear framework for understanding the different missions involved in peace operations, the ways in which they interact, and the effects of these dynamics on success. This is the much-needed advancement we have been waiting for."

—Barbara Walter, Rohr Professor of International Affairs, University of California, San Diego

When Peacekeeping Missions Collide

Balancing Multiple Roles in Peace Operations

PAUL F. DIEHL, DANIEL DRUCKMAN, AND
GRACE B. MUELLER

OXFORD
UNIVERSITY PRESS

OXFORD
UNIVERSITY PRESS

Oxford University Press is a department of the University of Oxford. It furthers
the University's objective of excellence in research, scholarship, and education
by publishing worldwide. Oxford is a registered trade mark of Oxford University
Press in the UK and certain other countries.

Published in the United States of America by Oxford University Press
198 Madison Avenue, New York, NY 10016, United States of America.

Library of Congress Cataloging-in-Publication Data
Names: Diehl, Paul F. (Paul Francis), author. | Druckman, Daniel, 1939–
author. | Mueller, Grace B., author.
Title: When peacekeeping missions collide : balancing multiple roles in
peace operations / Paul F. Diehl, Daniel Druckman, and Grace B. Mueller.
Description: New York, NY : Oxford University Press, [2024] |
Includes bibliographical references and index.
Identifiers: LCCN 2023011431 (print) | LCCN 2023011432 (ebook) |
ISBN 9780197696859 (paperback) | ISBN 9780197696842 (hardback) |
ISBN 9780197696866 (epub)
Subjects: LCSH: United Nations—Peacekeeping forces—Case studies. |
Strategy—Case studies. | Conflict management—Case studies.
Classification: LCC JZ6374 .D54 2024 (print) | LCC JZ6374 (ebook) |
DDC 355.3/57—dc23/eng/20230515
LC record available at https://lccn.loc.gov/2023011431
LC ebook record available at https://lccn.loc.gov/2023011432

DOI: 10.1093/oso/9780197696842.001.0001

Paperback printed by Marquis Book Printing, Canada
Hardback printed by Bridgeport National Bindery, Inc., United States of America

Contents

Illustrations

Figures

Tables

Acknowledgments

Writing a book is not something done in isolation, and we have benefitted greatly from feedback from colleagues in multiple settings and at different stages of our project. Most critical were the comments and suggestions from three anonymous reviewers who assessed this manuscript for Oxford University Press; we have sought to address issues raised by those individuals, and we believe that the final product is stronger and clearer as a result. In addition, we benefitted from feedback from audience members at numerous institutions where various parts of the project were presented: American University, University of Texas-Dallas, University of Illinois, Drexel University, University of Oklahoma, University of Georgia, Southern Methodist University, University of North Texas, Texas Tech University, Peoples' Friendship University of Russia (RUDN 2021), University of Genoa and Folke Bernadotte Academy, the Military Operations Research Society, and the Brute Krulak Center for Innovation and Future Warfare, Marine Corps University.

Research assistance was provided through the Ashbel Smith Professor Fund at the University of Texas-Dallas. The authors would like to thank Jacqueline Doan and Yahve Gallegos for their assistance in research and coding of peace operation missions early in the project. In addition, the authors appreciated theoretical advice from Gary Goertz and Alex Bellamy and sharing of data by Robert Blair.

1

The Puzzle of Multiple Missions

Introduction

The modern world of international relations is beset with a wide variety of conflicts without historical precedent. National borders are porous, state relationships change, and non-state actors play a substantial role in fomenting and sustaining deadly conflicts within and between countries. Peacekeepers are part of this new world. The traditional peacekeeping mission of sustaining a cease-fire during or after peace negotiations hardly captures the variety of challenges that they now face. These challenges thrust them into the unconventional roles of monitoring elections, facilitating transitions to the rule of law, distributing humanitarian aid, and resolving conflicts in civil societies that are undergoing transformation. No longer are military skills sufficient to meet these challenges. Those skills must be supplemented with a variety of others shared with civilians in governmental and nongovernmental organizations. Training programs need to be more robust and performance assessments more complex. This is the context for understanding the activities of modern-day peacekeepers. It is this kind of understanding that we hope to convey in this book. We do this through both conceptual and case-study lenses.

The book is written for both scholars and practitioners. For scholars, we build on and contribute new knowledge to the research literature on peacekeeping. Focusing attention on missions within peace operations,[1] we distinguish among different kinds of missions in terms of their functions and tasks. Compiling a data set of seventy UN peace operations, we discover aspects of missions that influence operational outcomes. In addition, we impose our theoretical lens on several cases to explain how the peace operations unfolded through time. By blending theoretical expectations with empirical analyses, we contribute to the state of the art (or science) on the brave new

---

[1] See a later section in this chapter on terminology, including definitions of peace operations and missions, respectively.

When Peacekeeping Missions Collide. Paul F. Diehl, Daniel Druckman, and Grace B. Mueller, Oxford University Press. © Oxford University Press 2024. DOI: 10.1093/oso/9780197696842.003.0001

world of peace operations. For practitioners, we provide guidance about how missions within peace operations can be configured. The analyses of compatibility suggest more and less useful ways of combining and sequencing missions. The case studies offer lessons learned for the design of operations in other contexts. More broadly, this book takes a lid off of peace operations by looking more deeply into how they are structured and the ways that current-day peacekeepers operate.

From Monitoring Cease-Fires to Peacebuilding

During the Cold War era, many peace operations traditionally performed cease-fire monitoring. With the development of peacebuilding operations, however, peacekeepers have undertaken a variety of other missions. Cease-fire monitoring and associated tasks remain a core mission, but peace operations also supervise elections, assist in building the rule of law, deliver humanitarian assistance, and protect threatened populations from human rights abuses, among other missions. For example, the United Nations Mission in Sudan (UNMIS, 2005–2011) included a wide range of missions, among them election supervision, humanitarian assistance, and disarmament, demobilization, and reintegration (DDR). Overall, more than 80 percent of modern UN peace operations have included more than one mission. As Bellamy and Williams (2012:281) note: "Such overlapping mandates and complex partnerships are becoming a more common feature of UN peace operations. Accounting for these in the evaluation of missions is one of the key challenges for the future." A similar call for study is made by Leib and Ruppel (2021). We take on these challenges in this book, by building on and extending our earlier research (Diehl, Druckman, and Wall, 1998; Diehl and Druckman, 2010).

We focus on the integrated dynamics of peace operations with an emphasis on the way that multiple missions interact. The increasing frequency of multiple missions in peace operations (Diehl and Druckman, 2018) makes it important to take them into account in research on peace operation effectiveness. If analysts largely ignore missions other than to monitor cease-fires and protect civilians, they miss other outcomes and make myopic, and perhaps misleading, conclusions about peace operations and the conditions that promote success and failure. Indeed, declaring victory because of success in supervising elections in the Congo misses failures in terms of reconciliation in the long run. Only by considering all missions, even across multiple studies and reports, does one get a full picture of a peace operation.

Our central concern is that success or failure in one mission might have implications for the outcomes of other missions. Concluding that the size of a peacekeeping force alone is critical in protecting civilians (e.g., Hultman, Kathman, and Shannon, 2020) might be incomplete if successful DDR efforts enhanced this effect. UN forces in Somalia (e.g., UNOSOM II) were much larger than average, but the ongoing presence of well-armed groups undermined the ability of the peace operations to provide security for the local population. In contrast, effective peacebuilding in the form of security sector reform lays the groundwork for establishing the rule of law in post-conflict societies. Moving beyond the analysis of traditional peacekeeping missions allows one to investigate these dynamic, interrelated relationships.

Terminology

There has been an unfortunate tendency in discourse about peace-keeping to use the same terms for different phenomena, or conversely different terms for the same phenomena. There is still some confusion about how encompassing the term "peacekeeping" is and what falls within its parameters, although there appears to be some consensus, at least in practice. *Peacekeeping* is an umbrella term that includes a variety of actions including those in the subcategory of peacebuilding (for a discussion of peacekeeping concepts, see Diehl, 2022b). Our concern is with a set of terms—peace operation, mandate, mission, and tasks—that are used in multiple ways, often to the confusion of readers and analysts. Indeed, the UN itself is guilty of this transgression, titling some of its peacekeeping actions as "operations" and others as "missions" without recognizing differences between these terms. We define the terms used in this study for the purposes of clearing up some of this muddling and because we do not always follow the convention in some scholarly or policy circles.

By *peace operations*, we refer to the general peacekeeping efforts performed in a given state(s) during a designated time period; such operations are authorized by the UN and appear as separate entities on the UN website.[2] This

---

[2] https://peacekeeping.un.org/en/department-of-peace-operations (last accessed November 23, 2022).

is consistent with UN classification, which places these under its Department of Peace *Operations* (emphasis added). Peace operations then represent organizational structures that encompass all that those entities are asked to do. Thus, operations deployed in the same region with the same disputants are treated as individual operations if they were authorized separately (e.g., UNOSOM I and II in Somalia or the several operations in Haiti). Here, for our purposes, we focus exclusively on UN operations, recognizing that other operations by different agents (e.g., African Union, European Union) might also have peace operations deployed to the conflict and some activities might be carried out jointly or separately by those agents. The history of UN peace operations provides a wealth of experience for analysis, both chronologically and with respect to multiple regions of the world including the varied types of conflicts that have occurred in those regions. Implications drawn from the UN experiences can be applied to other sponsoring organizations.

Mandates generally correspond to the goals of a given operation and are initially specified in UN resolutions that create and reauthorize peace operations. Peacekeeping mandates also specify the size, duration, and tasks of peacekeeping operations (Di Salvatore, Lundgren, Oksamytna, and Smidt, 2022). The protection of civilians, an increasingly common charge given to peacekeepers, is an example of a mandate. Mandates are often vague—"restore government authority"—a reflection of the political processes and compromises necessary to find common ground between the differing perspectives and priorities of the UN Secretariat and the UN Security Council (Oksamytna and Lundgrun, 2021), the latter being the authorizing body of peace operations and whose resolutions specify mandates.

Tasks are typically individual activities designed to fulfill goals within mandates. These can be described at the micro-level and be as specific as delivery of medical supplies to refugee camps. In other cases, they can be aggregated into categories reflecting common goals or mandates; for example, public health and border control are sets of tasks within one data set on UN peacekeeping mandates (Di Salvatore et al., 2022; see also Lloyd, 2021).

Our focus is on *missions*, classified as subsumed under operations rather than being treated as synonymous with them. Missions involve coherent categories of tasks designed to achieve broad goals or mandates. They are akin to what others have called "performance areas" (de Coning and Brusset, 2018). Thus, missions are of a higher order than tasks or activities; missions often involve multiple activities and the same tasks might be used to support different missions (e.g., monitoring).[3] For example, we treat election super-vision and promoting democracy together as one mission; this could involve tasks such as supervising the voter registration process and monitoring polling sites on election day respectively. Missions might also serve more than one mandate or goal (e.g., protection of civilians and repatriation of refugees under Human Rights) and place together a series of mandate task sets (e.g., police, military, and judicial sector reform under Rule of Law). We do so, as noted in the next chapter, because a mission includes activities that share common goals and characteristics, and those differ from other missions. This conceptualization serves our research needs to analyze interactions of activities within operations.

The knowledge gap filled by this book is the incomplete understanding of peace operations largely from a lack of frameworks or research designs that allow for probing the ways that missions interact. In part, this has been the consequence of failures by peacekeeping researchers to recognize the importance of multiple missions. As a result, there are few attempts to dig more deeply into the ways that peace operations operate over time and how their dynamics produce outcomes. By doing so, we hope to contribute to the development of understanding relationships between processes and outcomes as well as to improved designs of the field operations.

Past Research

We begin with the question: what have we learned from previous research? Peace operation studies have been most often concerned with success/failure as compared to any other foci (e.g., see the reviews by Di Salvatore and Ruggeri, 2017; Sandler, 2017; Walter, Howard, and Fortna, 2021; and the overviews of Dorussen, 2022, and Williams and Sterio, 2020). In doing so, however, there has been a tendency to concentrate on a single outcome represented by a single indicator. Most commonly, scholars have looked at the ability of missions to "keep the peace," namely preventing the recurrence of widespread violence or war. This is often indicated by "peace duration," the time elapsed from the onset of a cease-fire to the renewal of violence (e.g., Fortna, 2008) or alternatively by battle deaths. On the one hand, these

[3] See Table 1 of Di Salvatore et al. (2022) for a comparison of their mandate data set and an earlier version of our mission taxonomy described in Chapter 2.

indicators are appropriate because most peace operations have been assigned this core function, and all ultimately have it as a goal. At the same time, any other elements of the mandate or missions assigned to the peace operation are often ignored. Thus, even if one has designs on performing a holistic assessment, many other elements of modern peace operations are usually not considered.

More recently, peacekeeping research has expanded to look at other outcomes beyond the renewal of violence, thereby addressing different missions. In their reviews of peacekeeping effectiveness research, Di Salvatore and Ruggeri (2017) and Dorussen (2022) identify several new strands of research. These consider several different effects from peacekeeping, including human rights, democracy, rule of law (Blair, 2020), and economic development, among others; these match some of the liberal peacebuilding missions assigned to some operations. Other outcome foci fall into the category of "unintended consequences" (Aoi et al., 2007), which consist of those impacts that are not tied to a mandate or mission, but nonetheless result, at least in part, from the deployment of a peacekeeping operation. Such outcomes include sexual exploitation, environmental impacts (Maertens, 2019), and market distortions. Unintended consequences tend to focus on negative outcomes, but there is emerging research on prospective positive externalities from peacekeeping, including educational attainment (Reeder and Polizzi, 2021), nonviolent protests (Belgioioso, Di Salvatore, and Pinckney, 2021), and environmental quality (Bakaki and Bohmelt, 2021). As welcome as this research expansion might be, however, these studies tend to look only at one of those foci or outcomes at a time, thereby ignoring the intersection of different missions.

The above limitations are evident when we attempt to analyze a peacekeeping system with moving parts. There are no shortcuts in performing these analyses. A first step involves addressing the decision-making processes that lead to authorizing the shape and scope of operations, including the way peacekeepers are distributed among different missions and the way the missions are sequenced. A second step is to describe the way the assigned missions interact in the field. Foremost in this phase is to gauge the compatibility of the different types of missions. A third step consists of developing indicators of progress through the course of a peace operation. These assessments include mission-by-mission evaluations (the parts) as well as the interactions among them (the whole). A fourth step is to judge outcomes at the time of departure or at transition points such as the signing of peace agreements and the onset of a period of stability. Taken together, these steps expand the analyst's purview from single or few to many interacting dimensions of an operation.

Multiple missions necessitate substantial differentiation in terms of the indicators of success. That is, indicators for success for one mission are unlikely to be measures of progress for other missions. Diehl and Druckman (2010) identify 140 possible indicators of success across fourteen prospective missions. There is some overlap between missions, which have similar indicators for success or failure; for example, pre-election violence for election supervision missions is related to the number of violent incidents or attacks in traditional peacekeeping missions. Nevertheless, most success indicators are unique to the mission at hand, such as the percentage of people for whom legal services are available in rule of law missions and reductions in epidemics for humanitarian assistance missions. Considering only a single outcome measure ignores other missions and, in most cases, that one indicator is not applicable beyond the particular mission studied.

Some work makes separate evaluations with associated indicators using a multiple-mission framework as a lens for analyzing specific peace operations. Applying a common framework, the authors in Druckman and Diehl (2012) evaluated their cases in the multiple and different missions undertaken. In her analysis of the United Nations Transitional Authority (UNTAC), Whalan (2012) heralded the value of a disaggregated evaluation for distinguishing between mission goals that succeeded (conflict containment, repatriation), failed (violence abatement, DDR, and democratization), or had mixed results (human rights protection, humanitarian assistance). In their evaluation of United Nations Operation in Côte d'Ivoire (UNOCI), Bellamy and Williams (2012) also distinguished among missions that succeeded and those that failed.

A similar assessment was conducted by Braithwaite (2012) on the peacekeeping operations in East Timor. He also found combinations of successes and failures on practically all of the missions. He took the analysis further, however, by examining interactions and sequencing among the missions, something unprecedented at the time in scholarly analyses. These included the relationship between the core goals of violence abatement and conflict settlement, the relationship between democratization and violence abatement, and the temporal order of newer missions. In his assessment of the peace operation in Liberia, Farrall (2012) considered whether the various mission goals should be prioritized, and the matter of sequencing such as the order in which electoral reform, security sector reform, and constitution development occur. Blair, Di Salvatore, and Smidt (2021) note that peace operation mandates are increasingly fragmented and that, as a result, several mandates and associated tasks are not implemented in practice even as they are prescribed in UN authorizing resolutions.

In statistical studies of peacekeeping, multiple missions are sometimes introduced in equations as "control" variables rather than as a part of the central theoretical argument (e.g., Fortna, 2008). That is, multiple missions are thought to affect the outcome under study, but they are included primarily only to isolate the effects of other factors. Control variables often lack the detailed theoretical explanation that accompanies the main theoretical variables of interest. Thus, even if the factor is found to be statistically significant, we often do not have an in-depth understanding of why or how such an impact has occurred. Multiple missions are typically represented in statistical analyses by a single dichotomous measure (yes/no) indicating whether the operation was multidimensional or not (e.g., Doyle and Sambanis, 2006);[4] a variation is designating the type as "transformational," combining multidimensional and enforcement operations (e.g., Hegre, Hultman, and Nygard, 2019). This has several pernicious effects. First, it combines operations that have a varying number of different missions (empirically 2–11). One might anticipate that the greater the number of missions, the greater the effects on the outcome, but such distinctions are obscured with a binary measure. There might be an optimal "carrying capacity" of missions for operations, with implications for force size, but this cannot be determined by such a crude measure.

Second, the dichotomous measure makes no distinction between the different kinds of missions incorporated by the operation, only that more than one mission is included. For example, coercive or "robust" missions might be coded or regarded similarly as humanitarian relief or various peacebuilding missions. One might anticipate that these have different effects on outcomes, but this cannot be determined if they are lumped together; indeed, if they have opposite effects, these might cancel each other out, leading to the wrong conclusion that multiple missions have no effect. For example, the United Nations Operation in Somalia (UNISOM I) can be regarded as relatively successful in its humanitarian mission, but a failure in promoting a cease-fire.

---

[4] Or simply one among several categorical variables, as in Fortna (2003).

Some research has explored specific multiple missions within the same peacekeeping operation, even if that was not the explicit focus. In multiple studies, Hultman and colleagues (2013, 2014, 2020) demonstrate that a common factor—peacekeeping force size—affects two different missions in peace operations: reducing violence (measured as battle deaths) between disputants and protecting civilians. This suggests that both mission outcomes and the factors influencing those outcomes may be related. Such synergies have implications for peacekeeping theory as well as policy planning.

Most studies do not consider how multiple missions might interact to have reinforcing or countervailing effects on each—reinforcing effects are additive, countervailing effects are subtractive. Diehl and Druckman (2010) postulate a series of largely positive effects between missions, but there is no empirical examination of their claims. Without taking these into account, scholars run the risk of ignoring some of the correlates of particular mission success and in describing the process that led to that success (or failure).

Previous work is suggestive of connections between missions. Doyle and Sambanis (2006) examine the impact of peacekeeping on the prevention of armed conflict renewal, progress toward democratization, and postwar economic growth, although it is not clear that the last outcome is an explicit mission of peace operations. The reported positive associations suggest reinforcing effects, but such interactions are not evaluated. Paris (2004) addresses some similar concerns and raises the issue of sequencing, noting that efforts at early elections might be counterproductive unless economic and political stability are established first; such an argument implicitly connects the timing of different missions with their outcomes.

In summary, past studies suggest that multiple missions might be connected to one another in various ways, not the least of which is how the outcomes of one mission are related to those of other missions. Nevertheless, they stop short of engaging with those concerns. Accordingly, a set of critical questions are unexplored. Can a peace operation be effective in limiting violence, but not be well suited to promote DDR? Might missions such as promoting the rule of law have a feedback mechanism to reinforce democratic processes? Overall, the interconnection of peacekeeping missions is underspecified theoretically and understudied empirically. Thus, there is substantial room to make contributions to our understanding of the integrated dynamics of peacekeeping. Progress in this direction is evident in the articles written for the Druckman and Diehl (2012) special issue. We move this needle forward by delving more deeply into the way different missions interact, with specific research questions, theoretically driven expectations, and empirical explorations.

Research Questions

Fundamentally, this book is concerned with how different peacekeeping missions intersect with one another. Our initial research concerns are largely descriptive ones. How frequently do UN peace operations undertake multiple missions? This determines the scope of the prospective multiple mission problems. How has the adoption of multiple missions changed over time? Our suspicion noted above, and reflected in many other commentaries, has been that UN peacekeeping has assumed more missions since the end of the Cold War. Nevertheless, the extent of that increase has not been systematically documented, something that we do before any analysis of implications. Our analysis also considers some correlates of those trends. Still in the descriptive mode, we also document the patterns of different combinations of missions present in UN operations. Are there distinct patterns in which certain missions regularly go together or are rarely assigned to the same operation? Or is the distribution of missions across UN peacekeeping operations random, and therefore seemingly non-purposive?

Understanding the frequency and configuration of multiple missions lays the groundwork for exploring their implications. We concentrate on peacekeeping mission outcomes, specifically success and failure, which have been the primary focal points of peacekeeping research and policy deliberations over the past decades. Our intention is not to undertake a comprehensive assessment of all the different factors that influence peacekeeping success (something beyond the scope of any single study). Rather, we limit our attention to the way that multiple missions interact during the course of an operation. We further break down that success (or failure) according to individual missions within cases. The overarching question is: How do individual peacekeeping missions affect the outcomes of other missions within the same operation?

Within the parameters of our concerns, we explore several elements of mission interdependence. First, we consider whether outcomes in some missions influence the results of other missions. This research concern includes several elements. One is that we do not necessarily assume that all missions affect every other mission in the same way. That is, some missions might be more important than others, and thereby exercise a broader impact than other missions. In particular, we examine whether certain security-related missions or tasks (cease-fire monitoring, DDR) play this role. Another is that the sequence of different missions affects outcomes, something that has been a repeated concern of policymakers (International Peace Institute, 2019a, 2019b; see also the priority of sequencing in the Action for Peacekeeping plan—United Nations Security-General, 2018). That is, the influence of some peacekeeping missions on others might depend on their successful completion before other missions can even be attempted. It might also be the case that ongoing success throughout the life of an operation might be needed for other missions to fulfill their goals. Thus, a key research question is: What are the impacts of different sequences of missions on the interaction effects explored above?

Second, we ask whether the compatibility of different missions affects the outcomes of each. A priori, one expects that compatibility enhances success for all "similar" missions. In contrast, incompatible missions are assumed to create problems for UN peacekeepers. To address research concerns associated with mission compatibility, we first must provide answers to several questions about compatibility. What makes peacekeeping missions compatible or incompatible? Based on that, to what extent are different missions compatible or incompatible with one another, and to what degree? Answering these questions allows us to determine how (in)compatibility affects the way that peacekeeping missions interact.

Collectively, the set of research questions outlined in this section set the stage for analyses of peace operation dynamics. They also reflect the different contributions made by this book, including descriptive insights on compatibility issues. These are evident in the chapters that follow.

Theoretical Implications

Early peacekeeping studies tended to be single-case descriptions and recollections by former peacekeeping personnel. These did not aspire to broader generalizations, although there was often a "lessons learned" orientation directed toward the military and operational aspects of operations. In large part, this is what led Fetherston (1994) to decry the lack of theory in peacekeeping studies, often deriving from the so-called problem-solving orientation common in those analyses (Paris, 2000). In the last several decades, this lacuna has been filled to some extent, but most of the theoretical formulations have been borrowed from studies of war and in any case are inapplicable to the research questions here.

Within statistical studies, the most common theoretical formulations have been based on the bargaining model of war (Fearon, 1995; Walter, 1997, 2009), which has its roots in rational choice theory (see Smith and Stam, 2004, for a peacekeeping application). The central points of such applications are that peacekeeping forces provide a "credible commitment" for guaranteeing cease-fires, preventing surprise attacks, and lessening the flow of information about each side's resolve, making peaceful resolution more attractive (see, e.g., Fortna, 2008). This is the underlying rationale for why, for example, peacekeeping lowers civilian casualties after deployment (Hultman et al., 2020).

Generally, and specifically for our purposes, there are several limitations to these and related ideas. First, they are based on theories of war and not peace or peacekeeping per se. That is, they focus on the willingness of the disputants to use military force, and not on peacekeeping forces. Second, the theories rely on the incentives and behavior of the disputants, and not on the peacekeeping operation. That is, peacekeepers are an intervening variable in the calculus of disputants, and outcomes remain in the hands of the protagonists. Third, putting all this together, bargaining theory, at best, deals with the traditional peacekeeping mission that seeks violence abatement through cease-fire monitoring. Because it focuses on disputant incentives to use military force, it has little directly to say about other missions such as humanitarian aid delivery or promoting the rule of law, except as renewed violence might affect those missions. This is not to say that cease-fire maintenance and preventing killing are unimportant, but rather that the bargaining model has little purchase beyond that and does not address the interaction of, or even recognize, different missions. The narrow security focus of these studies and related approaches precludes insights about the dynamic complexities of peacekeeping operations.

On the other side of the epistemological coin are critical theory studies. These works have engaged with peacekeeping's many missions, moving beyond traditional security matters (see Pugh, 2004, for an agenda, and for an overview, see Diehl and Richmond, 2022). The centerpiece of these works is the "liberal peacebuilding model" that emphasizes the promotion of democracy, Western styles of government, and open markets. These concerns deal with a variety of peacekeeping missions, including promoting democracy, local governance, and the like. The main thrust of critical theory works is that the liberal peacebuilding model is ill-conceived and inappropriate for the needs of the local population (e.g., Zanotti, 2011; Richmond and McGinty, 2013; Chandler, 2017). Although frequently insightful, these works are more normative critiques than theoretical explanations in the conventional sense, something characteristic of critical theory more broadly. In addition, critical theorists do not engage with how different missions influence one another, except to the extent that they flow from the same liberal world order.

Understanding multiple mission interdependence entails a focus on the peacekeeping force itself and those missions as agents of change rather than primarily on the disputants. This means taking into account that the UN, or any agent of peacekeeping, has an impact on outcomes. Older studies of international organizations (IOs) saw them as little more than pawns of state members, typically major powers (see Mearsheimer, 1994–1995). Only more recently has the idea that international organizations have some autonomy (Barnett and Finnemore, 2004) given rise to the ideas that IOs do more than what they are directed to do. In terms of peacekeeping studies, this has meant looking internally at processes and strategies of the organization. Howard (2008) focuses on organizational learning in the sponsoring organization as a partial cause of success and failure in multidimensional peacekeeping operations. She (Howard, 2019) lays out how peacekeepers exercise power to influence outcomes. Consistent with this are constructivist arguments based on the norms and cultures of organizations carrying out peacekeeping missions as they relate to, and are mismatched with, the needs of the local population (Autesserre, 2014, 2021).

Our theoretical approach, and therefore our contribution, does not dismiss the value of these approaches, but rather brings into play what peacekeepers *do* rather than primarily where they *go* and how disputants influence their outcomes. In doing so, we develop theoretical arguments on multi-mission peacekeeping that rely on their functions and how they go together in affecting mission outcomes. Thus, this is a form of what has been referred to as middle-level peacekeeping theory (as opposed to grand theory in international relations), and we believe that it addresses aspects of peacekeeping that have been ignored.[5]

---

[5] For an early discussion on middle-range theory in international relations, see Mahoney and Druckman (1975).

As will be evident in subsequent chapters, our analysis focuses substantially, albeit not exclusively, on the concept of mission *compatibility*. As an original contribution, we develop this notion in the peacekeeping context and use it to generate predictions about outcomes in peace operations. Methodologically, we provide multiple indicators of mission compatibility, each representing a different theoretical logic, that inform our analysis and provide data for use in other projects.

Consistent with this theoretical contribution, the findings of our study provide empirical value added to our understanding of peacekeeping success. As is evident from our brief review of past work, peacekeeping studies rarely look at multiple missions and do not account for the way multiple missions interact. Those that do are suggestive of some patterns of integrated dynamics, but have not fully engaged with the phenomena. Looking at multiple missions might lead to a re-evaluation of existing studies of individual mission success. This does not mean that judgments about the success of those missions would change, but rather that part of the explanation for success or failure might change. Multiple missions could be an important factor contributing to and modifying existing explanations.

Findings from our study also provide insights into some of the missions and peacekeeping outcomes that are understudied, whether tied to mission interdependence or not. These include missions that go beyond cease-fire monitoring and civilian protection, to include security sector reform and long-term goals such as reconciliation.

Policy Implications

The expansion of UN peace operation activities has received extensive attention as part of UN debates. Most notably, peace operations have been compared to a "Christmas tree" with a wide variety of "ornaments" designed to enhance the appearance of the operation. This is meant as a derisive term, suggesting that UN peace operations are attempting to do too much and prompting UN Secretary-General António Guterres to declare that "Christmas is over." Indicative is the UN Mission in South Sudan (UNMISS) that was assigned 209 different tasks (Bellamy and Hunt, 2019). Nevertheless, there is no consensus over what peace operations should be doing, with different priorities reflected in Security Council vis-à-vis UN Secretariat preferences, especially with respect to peacebuilding activities (for an analysis, see Oksamytna and Lundgrun, 2021). It might be that UN peacekeeping is not doing too much, but too little. Or UN operations need to consider not merely the *number* of missions and associated tasks, but how they go together (or not) and what might be optimal configurations.

Although our study is not designed specifically for making policy recommendations, we aver that understanding how multiple missions interact is an imperative for policymakers. Unlike the contextual factors (e.g., geography, competing ethnic groups) that peace operations face, the number and types of missions performed by peacekeepers are directly and explicitly chosen by decision makers. Thus, these policymakers are in a unique position to decide what missions are performed, in what combination, and in what order. Optimal choices, however, require knowledge about the likely implications of the selected policies. This study provides some of that information. There are several specific concerns.

Historically, peace operations are suboptimal in size relative to the basic task of cease-fire supervision and the geographic area covered. For example, the initial authorization for the United Nations Organization Mission in the Democratic Republic of the Congo (MONUC) provided fewer than 6,000 troops for a very large country with armed conflict in multiple locations. Do simultaneous and multiple missions exacerbate these problems? In addition, many of the peacebuilding missions, such as local governance, involve coordination with other actors. Does this add a burden to the peace operation that interferes with its performance of other missions? As the number of missions increases, so do the peacekeeping troops deployed, but it is less clear whether the number of personnel are sufficient to perform the additional missions. The multi-mission perspective encourages peacekeeping planners and field commanders to take into account the resource and personnel requirements needed to accomplish those missions.

The focus on mission compatibility could allow policymakers to ascertain when different peacekeeping missions are incompatible and therefore problematic. Should decision makers be reluctant to charge UN peace operations with multiple missions for fear of compromising some or all of them? For example, the attempt to combine pacification efforts with humanitarian assistance efforts in Somalia is illustrative of such incompatibility of functions, at least when performed by the same operation; peacekeepers were asked to take robust military action against certain groups while depending on their cooperation to deliver food and medical supplies to internally displaced populations. This might complicate the ability to achieve goals associated with the delivery of supplies. One policy implication from our framework might be that divergent missions are best handled by different sets of personnel or separate operations. In the cases of more coercive activities and humanitarian assistance, a prominent role for traditional military forces in the former and NGOs in the latter, with appropriate coordination between the two, would be preferable to having peacekeepers attempt both roles simultaneously.

If incompatibility inhibits success, can this be redressed by a proper sequencing of missions so that overlap is limited? Might some combinations of missions be better than others, even to the point of enhancing success for all missions involved? This might suggest expanding missions that are compatible and as needed. At a minimum, this would do no harm and could even improve performance for all involved.

Beyond the implications above, others relate to how peacekeeping soldiers are trained for their missions (Diehl, Druckman, and Wall, 1998). Some missions that place peacekeepers as primary parties in a conflict will require them to exercise negotiating skills suitable for competitive situations. These include such tactics as presenting evidence indicating unalterable commitments to a position, making it easy for an opponent to concede, proposing deadlines to force actions, and developing attractive alternatives to proposals on the table. Other missions require such problem-solving and communication skills as searching for information that reveals underlying interests and needs, developing trust, and identifying solutions that avoid concessions. More coercive missions emphasize primarily combat skills. Other, less coercive, missions depend for their effectiveness on a complex set of contact skills. For example, missions whose primary purpose is monitoring call for observational and analytical skills. Those that attempt to restore countries to functioning civil societies require a much broader range of skills, including interpersonal and intergroup relations, coordination, communication, negotiation, and, in the case of military operations, a mix of combat and political skills. Organizational skills are needed for missions intended to limit damage, such as humanitarian assistance. The actual skills needed for any particular operation, however, depend on the mix of functions being served as well as the stage of the conflict at the time of intervention.

As a consequence of the different missions, to perform many of the missions effectively, peacekeepers need contact as well as combat skills. They should not be expected to adapt from a combat orientation, such as neutralizing the opponent's warfare capabilities, to a contact orientation, such as negotiating with a party to find a viable solution, any more than they should be expected to adapt in the opposite direction. Rather, they should be trained in all relevant skills so that they can handle assignments to many types of missions. There are other training implications that flow from a conflict management approach to peacekeeping. One issue is whether a given soldier can master all the skills and behaviors outlined above, assuming that present or expanded training regimens could accommodate them. Will training in one approach undermine the training required in another approach? Can national militaries train their soldiers for all these peace operation missions?

These questions deal with the challenge of switching from one type of skill to another, often quickly. More needs to be learned about this challenge. One extension of our study would be to develop a typology of the skill combinations needed in the different types of missions. This is best done with training teams that include peacekeepers with a variety of types of field experiences.

Mission choices are not a single-shot process. UN peacekeeping operations have been typically authorized by the Security Council in six-month increments, and these historically were renewed with the same mandate, and therefore with mission(s) unchanged. This has evolved over time as the situation on the ground changed; thus, mandates changed and additional missions have been added. Such changes represent opportunities to understand strategic adaptations and their outcomes. For example, MONUSCO (United Nations Organization Stabilization Mission in the Democratic Republic of the Congo) has seen its mandate evolve several times based on conditions on the ground and the performance of earlier missions. Understanding mission interdependence could mean expanding missions, waiting for some missions to be finished, such as election supervision, before adding another mission, such as the rule of law, or tying new missions to the success of other missions whose success serves as necessary conditions for others.

Finally, policy implications could extend beyond the realm of peacekeeping. Although we take some insights from aforementioned literatures on multitasking and compatibility, we also aspire to develop conclusions and lessons for organizations outside of the UN and peacekeeping. Ideally, one of our broader contributions is about when and why different roles and tasks are successful (or not) in large organizations and how organizational design or implementation might be modified accordingly. For example, is it better for a government agency to take on new, but very different, responsibilities versus creating a new, specialized agency to perform said tasks? Our findings could be suggestive and point to the directions for future research.

Overview of the Book

The remainder of the book is dedicated to addressing the questions and making the contributions specified in previous sections. Chapter 2 provides several foundations for those ends. We develop a taxonomy of eleven different UN peacekeeping missions, with a description and example for each. These are largely conceptual, although they are informed by actual missions in past peace operations. We examine the frequency of seventy UN peace operations over the 1948–2016 period and identify which missions took place in which operations. This is used for our later analysis of individual operations and their missions. In this chapter, however, we also present a series of empirical patterns about those missions and how they vary across time and other contexts, as well as in relation to one another.

Chapter 2 also includes a specification of twelve dimensions along which peace operations can be compared for similarity and ultimately compatibility. We use these dimensions to develop three quantitative indicators of compatibility, each having a different underlying theoretical logic, for peace operations given their particular portfolios of missions. Scores are given for all seventy UN operations across those three indicators, and our analyses also permit compatibility assessments between individual or groups of missions. This chapter also lays out our theoretical expectations about how the sequencing and interactions of different missions affect the outcomes of those missions. We develop eight different expectations for these effects, based on logics dealing with sequencing/simultaneity and compatibility respectively.

Chapter 3 details the research plan for this study. Initially, we select five cases of peace operations as case studies: United Nations Protection Force or UNPROFOR (Bosnia); United Nations Operation in the Congo or ONUC (Congo); United Nations Transitional Administration in East Timor or UNTAET (East Timor); United Nations Organization Mission in the Democratic Republic of the Congo or MONUC (Congo); and the United Nations Mission in Sierra Leone or UNAMSIL (Sierra Leone). This is followed by a discussion of the issues involved in making inferences and establishing valid baselines for assessment. The chapter then summarizes the bases and associated information sources used to make judgments about the outcomes of the missions embedded in those operations.

Chapters 4, 5, and 6 contain the individual case studies of multiple missions in peace operations. For each operation, we provide a brief overview of the conflict background and the key elements in the timeline for the operations. The core of the analysis is an assessment of the outcomes for each of the missions in the operation, with an eye to how they are interconnected in ways laid out by our expectations (or not). We begin in Chapter 4 with the two operations—ONUC and UNPROFOR—that are the oldest ones in our set and involve the fewest number of missions. Chapter 5 examines the more complex operations of UNTAET and MONUC, which include more and different combinations of missions. Chapter 6 is the last case study, namely UNAMSIL, with the full number and range of missions covered in the expectations and compatibility indicators.

Chapter 7 is the concluding one, and it first takes stock of how well our theoretical expectations comported with the collective results of the case studies. We then provide a framework for organizing the various parts and stages of a peace operation, many of which are treated in this book. It offers the scholar and policymaker a broader vision of how peace operations unfold from preparations through processes and situational changes to post-operation developments. In the context of the framework, we return to many of the policy-relevant questions posed above. We end the book with a discussion of a future research agenda addressing unanswered or suggestive questions from our study, and what new missions for peace operations might mean for compatibility and effectiveness.

2

Patterns in Multi-Mission Peace Operations and Theoretical Expectations

Introduction

In this chapter, we document the frequency of multiple missions in peace operations. We also explore patterns among missions in terms of a key concept in this book—compatibility. The net results are that peace operations increasingly involve multiple and diverse missions, and that these missions exhibit varying degrees of compatibility with one another. These results demonstrate the empirical importance of multiple missions and their compatibility, and this serves as a prelude to the final section the chapter in which we present a theoretical perspective that suggests expectations about mission interdependence.

The first step in understanding how multiple peacekeeping missions interact is specifying the range and types of those missions. This involves laying out the potential tasks and actions that operations might be asked to perform. We offer a taxonomy of the dimensions of peacekeeping missions, and then consider how common they are in practice both individually and in combination.

We then address the concept of mission compatibility and develop twelve continua along which peace operations might differ. A statistical technique using those characteristics allows us to array the missions in a multidimensional space in order to understand how missions are similar or different from one another. Yet in practice, peace operations encompass various combinations of those missions. Accordingly, we combine the empirical patterns of missions in peace operations with our spatial analysis to produce three different indicators of compatibility as reflected in seventy UN peace operations in the 1948–2016 time frame.

In the concluding section of this chapter, we develop eight expectations about how different peacekeeping missions interact with one another, clustered within two theoretical sets: (1) Sequencing, Simultaneity, and

When Peacekeeping Missions Collide. Paul F. Diehl, Daniel Druckman, and Grace B. Mueller, Oxford University Press.
© Oxford University Press 2024. DOI: 10.1093/oso/9780197696842.003.0002

Prerequisites; and (2) Compatibility. These are derived from our original theorizing about different missions, previous work on peacekeeping and other literatures, assumptions underlying policy choices and models (e.g., the liberal model of peacebuilding), and the compatibility analyses earlier in the chapter. These expectations guide the development of our research plans in Chapter 3 as well as the case study narratives in the subsequent three chapters.

Peacekeeping Missions: A Taxonomy

Given our definitions of missions and mandates in Chapter 1, we have chosen to focus on the specific actions and associated goals that peacekeepers are asked to perform rather than a taxonomy based on the general purposes of the operation, as reflected in, for example, Williams and Bellamy (2021). We build on several works that introduce various lists of functions or missions. The review in this section places our taxonomy in the context of the relevant literature.

Diehl, Druckman, and Wall (1998) were perhaps the first to develop a peacekeeping taxonomy, largely in response to new roles for national militaries in peacekeeping operations. They provided a set of sixteen different missions. Nevertheless, a number of these were hypothetical or proposed ideas for peacekeepers at the time and as such did not reflect contemporaneous practice. Indeed, several of them were ones that have not been carried out by peacekeepers: drug eradication and disaster relief, to name a few. That list was constructed in the 1990s when peacekeeping was expanding in number and scope but does not represent what peace operations have done in the decades since. The listing also reflected some of the concerns specific to the US Army, a sponsor of the original research, and not necessarily reflective of UN planning or practice in peacekeeping.

Other efforts are informative, but somewhat limited. Franke and Warnecke (2009) provide an inventory of the different missions within UN operations, but their general categorizations are broad (e.g., peacebuilding, peacekeeping, multidimensional peacebuilding). Most useful in this work are the heuristics one gets by looking at the specific contributions to four categories: (1) security and public order; (2) socioeconomic wellbeing; (3) governance and participation; and (4) justice and reconciliation. More precise is Mullenbach's (2013) taxonomy, but this is also a limited conceptualization of missions, including only six categories—law and order, humanitarian assistance, DDR (Disarmament, Demobilization, and Reintegration), providing security, maintaining a buffer zone, and cease-fire monitoring. It is not clear that some of these categories are conceptually and empirically distinct from one another—for example, maintaining a buffer zone is a means to facilitate cease-fire monitoring rather than a goal in itself.

Di Salvatore et al. (2022) focus on peacekeeping "mandates," or that which peace operations are formally charged with doing in authorizing resolutions. Data were collected for twenty-seven African peacekeeping operations from 1991 to 2017 in their Peacekeeping Mandates (PEMA) Dataset. Their focus is on the activities used to fulfill those mandates, specifically forty-one different activities and the level of engagement associated with them: (1) monitoring; (2) assisting (e.g., through training); and (3) securing (see also Blair, Di Salvatore, and Smidt, 2021; Helms, 2022; Benson and Tucker, 2019).

Similarly, Lloyd (2021) identifies fifty tasks associated with UN peace operations from 1948 to 2015 in her Tasks Assigned to Missions in their Mandates (TAMM) data set. These tasks are subsumed under some of the categories of what we define above and identify below as missions: (1) peace agreement/cease-fire; (2) human security; (3) territorial integrity; (4) authorization under Chapter VII of the UN Charter; (5) elections; (6) statebuilding; (7) transitional justice; (8) Disarmament, Demobilization, and Reintegration, or DDR; and (9) public information.

Data sets on mandates employ a unit of analysis that is more akin to tasks (actions performed to achieve missions) rather than missions themselves. Although these data sets are valuable for a number of analyses, our concern is with the broader goals of peace operations represented by missions rather than the individual activities used to achieve those goals, even as the form and application of those tasks might be associated with particular goal achievements (or lack thereof).

Informed by these previous works, we began with the set of missions described in Diehl and Druckman (2010). They have twelve different missions arrayed across three general categories: core peacekeeping goals, nontraditional peacekeeping goals, and post-conflict peacebuilding, respectively. These are similar to the different kinds of mandates that are identified by Di Salvatore and Ruggeri (2017). Using these sources and our own formulations, we have revised our list to the eleven described in Table 2.1.

Traditional Peacekeeping might be considered the baseline mission, and it encompasses several core goals of monitoring cease-fires, abating

Table 2.1 Peace operation mission types

Traditional Peacekeeping: The stationing of troops as an interposition force following a cease-fire to separate combatants and promote an environment suitable for conflict resolution. This mission is also designed to prevent the spread of conflict in terms of geographic area or the number of actors involved.

Humanitarian Assistance: The transportation and distribution of life-sustaining food and medical supplies, in coordination with local and international nongovernmental organizations (NGOs), to provide for the basic needs of threatened populations and internally displaced individuals and groups.

Election Supervision/Promotion of Democracy: The observation and monitoring of a democratic election following a peace agreement among previously warring internal groups and/or institution building and promoting political participation and democratic culture.

Preventive Deployment: The stationing of troops in an area that has not yet experienced violence to deter the onset or prevent the spread of violent conflict from other areas.

Disarmament, Demobilization, and Reintegration (DDR): Some or all of three sets of activities, including the collection, documentation, control, and disposal of small arms, ammunition, explosives and light and heavy weapons from combatants and often from the civilian population and/or the supervision of troop withdrawals; the formal and controlled discharge of active combatants from armed forces and groups; and the process by which ex-combatants acquire civilian status and gain sustainable employment and income. Generally, this is done following a peace agreement ending a civil war, or in other cases by agreement between the disputants.

Pacification: Quelling civil disturbances, defeating local armed groups, and forcibly separating belligerents through the proactive use of military force to establish or re-establish "peace."

Human Rights: The establishment of safe havens, "no-fly" zones, and guaranteed freedom of movement for the purpose of protecting or denying hostile access to threatened civilian populations or areas of a state, as well as specifically protecting designated groups from attack or human rights abuses.

Security Sector Reform (SSR): The establishment and maintenance of law and order in cities and towns, including the physical protection of civilians in their everyday activities and policing of those areas, sometimes in conjunction with indigenous forces. This also can include the organization and training of local and national police and military forces to assume responsibility for maintaining law and order.

Rule of Law: Assisting in the establishment of legal processes and institutions for the maintenance of order and the peaceful resolution of disputes and/or the creation or encouragement of nongovernmental organizations that promote dialogue and input for citizenry in government functions.

Local Governance: The provision of standard government services and facilitation of indigenous government institutions to provide such services, and assistance in building local capacity to assume such responsibilities.

Reconciliation: The provision of mechanisms and processes for changing attitudes among former disputants, redressing past grievances and crimes in the pursuit of justice, and for enhancing cooperation among former enemies.

violence, preventing its spread from current geographic areas to new ones, and inhibiting additional actors from joining the conflict. This mission is the one that is most associated with peace operations and traces its origins to the early peace observation missions and then the first full-fledged peacekeeping operation—the United Nations Emergency Force (UNEF I)—in 1956 (Diehl, 2015). This mission is also the one that has received the most attention from scholars and is a priority of UN decision makers, force commanders, and diplomats in national capitals around the world.

With more peace operations occurring in post–civil war contexts, Disarmament, Demobilization, and Reintegration (DDR) has become important for sustaining peace (see Herrera and Pena, 2022). This mission is composed of three different sets of activities, some or all of which might be carried out by peacekeepers. The disarmament component consists of former combatants surrendering weapons, often as part of a cease-fire or more likely a peace agreement ending a war. Peacekeepers monitor and document this process, given that disputants cannot trust one another to fulfill disarmament pledges. Disarmament might also include withdrawal of troops from certain regions, the establishment of weapons-free zones, and no-fly zones that restrict the use of airpower in some areas. In Namibia, the United Nations Transition Assistance Group (UNTAG) ensured that military forces were confined to bases. Demobilization occurs when organized military groupings (e.g., rebel forces, militias, foreign troops) are disbanded and therefore become incapable of fighting as organized entities. For example, the United Nations Angola Verification Mission (UNAVEM) I was assigned to monitor the withdrawal of Cuban troops from that civil war. Reintegration, which is predicated on disarmament and demobilization, involves converting ex-combatants to civilian status and assisting them in the transition into civil society. This tends to be a longer process than the other two components (Knight, 2008). Among the duties of the United Nations Operation in Burundi (ONUB) was to assist in the rehabilitation of former child soldiers. In our analyses, we label Traditional Peacekeeping and DDR as "basic security missions."

Beyond these security missions are a series of other missions that have become more visible since the end of the Cold War and usually have shorter-term orientations; that is, they are designed to facilitate results that address immediate or interim problems during peace operation deployment rather than necessarily influencing the long-term trajectory of the host country. These include Humanitarian Assistance, Human Rights, and Election

Supervision/Promotion of Democracy. As noted below, these missions share some similarities with basic security roles in that they involve monitoring functions and, in particular, are similar in some instances to Traditional Peacekeeping assignments.

During active conflict or in its immediate aftermath, there are numerous human security problems. These can include large numbers of internally displaced persons who have fled the fighting, as well as those injured or ill because of the violence. They are in need of immediate food and medical aid. Nevertheless, the violence has, in many cases, destroyed or disrupted the supply lines and the infrastructure needed to provide such services and materials. In the Humanitarian Assistance mission, peacekeepers work with the UN and various actors (UN agencies, NGOs, and regional organizations) either to distribute that aid directly and/or to provide the security needed to transport and deliver the aid. The United Nations Multidimensional Integrated Stabilization Mission in the Central African Republic (MINUSCA) had several purposes, but humanitarian assistance was one of its missions in pursuit of establishing stability and security in that country and providing aid to the civilian population. This is designed to have both short- and long-term effects on health and human security (Dallas and Beckelman, 2020).

Peacekeepers are not responsible for ensuring that all international human rights standards are observed. Nevertheless, peace operations are sometimes charged with protecting certain groups who are under threat of displacement, violence, or even genocide. More generally, peace operations have been assigned the responsibility to protect civilians, especially when the operation is deployed prior to a peace agreement. As an illustration, the United Nations–African Union Hybrid Operation in Darfur (UNAMID) was specifically charged with protecting civilians in a conflict that had previously experienced what many labeled as genocide.

Election Supervision/Promotion of Democracy, at the most fundamental level, involves assistance in and the monitoring of the election process in a given country (see Smidt, 2022). This could involve helping with voter registration as well as the conventional supervision of an election itself on a given day(s), as well as an extended campaign period preceding the actual election. The purpose in any case is ensuring that the election is free and fair, something the third-party peacekeepers can certify with more credibility than the extant government or other internal and interested political groups. This mission can also involve activities that enhance democratic culture and attitudes associated with elections and beyond, such as facilitating participation in political processes by internal NGOs. The United Nations Observation Mission in El Salvador (ONUSAL) is an example of a peace operation performing this mission.

Other missions fall more comfortably under the peacebuilding rubric (Jenkins, 2013): Rule of Law, Local Governance, Security Sector Reform (SSR), and Reconciliation. These tend to be those that have longer-term orientations, and thereby promote conflict resolution, removing the underlying bases of conflict, rather than merely conflict management (Boutros-Ghali, 1992). They involve much more than conventional military roles for soldiers, adopting more holistic goals for dealing with conflict, especially those in civil war and post–civil war contexts. These missions usually follow peace agreements. Peacekeepers are more likely to work with local government authorities, NGOs, and other actors that specialize in setting the stage for durable peace, particularly with regard to reconciliation. Although they are often aggregated under the term "peacebuilding" or "statebuilding," because of these shared characteristics, they are, in fact, distinct missions and can have different outcomes (i.e., success in some, but failure in others).

Promoting the Rule of Law is not the imposition of law and order (that is part of SSR, although closely related) but rather assisting in the creation of rules, institutions, and processes that provide for the peaceful resolution of disputes as opposed to violent mechanisms for handling disagreements (see Blair, 2022). This involves working with local and international partners. An example of a rule of law mechanism is judicial independence, which serves as a check on executive and legislative power. For example, the United Nations Stabilization Mission in Haiti (MINUSTAH) entered a context characterized by the breakdown of judicial authority and the latitude for some individuals and groups to act with impunity.

The post-conflict context for states coming out of, or in some cases still experiencing, civil war often involves the absence or the significant weakening of government authority. Peacebuilding necessitates that such basic services as water and roads be supplied to the local populations. This means that government structures must be in place to do so, and government authority and capability need to extend to all areas of the state—the Local Governance mission. Peacekeepers might need to provide services in the short term, but also can be charged with assisting the (re)development of indigenous contributions in the longer term. The United Nations Mission in

Liberia (UNMIL) was charged with assisting the transitional government in extending government authority to all areas.

Security Sector Reform (SSR) involves two interrelated sets of activities for peacekeepers. On the one hand, peacekeepers, often in the form of civilian police, can be responsible for (re)establishing law and order during active conflict or for post-conflict states. This comes in the form of everyday policing and providing a secure environment for the local population to return to "normal" activities such as shopping at local markets and freedom of movement throughout areas. This is distinct from cease-fire monitoring involving armed forces of opposing sides in a civil conflict. SSR is dedicated to helping create and/or improve local and national capacities to perform these same functions. This frequently involves UN personnel conducting training of local and national police and advising on how the government can develop its own security capabilities. This can take many forms beyond the most obvious of policing in an urban area. For example, maritime security was the focus of UN efforts in Mali (United Nations Multidimensional Integrated Stabilization Mission in Mali [MINUSMA]) and defense sector reform in the Central African Republic (United Nations Multidimensional Integrated Stabilization Mission in the Central African Republic [MINUSCA]).

Reconciliation is a mission that is conceived of as occurring toward the end of a peace operation, but there are instances in which such efforts began earlier in the post-conflict process. This mission involves less tangible and less observable outcomes than other missions. Here, the goal is to change the attitudes of individuals and groups who were recently at war with one another. Although peacekeepers can sometimes be met with resistance, this can be achieved by providing mechanisms for transitional justice, such as war crimes tribunals, as well as those promoting healing through truth and reconciliation commissions. For example, the Sierra Leone Truth and Reconciliation Commission was part of the Lomé Peace Accord that ushered in the United Nations Mission in Sierra Leone (UNAMSIL) operation.

Finally, two other missions, Preventive Deployment and Pacification, are widely discussed as roles for peacekeepers, although they might not be reflected as frequently in practice. Pacification involves an explicit relaxation, if not outright violation, of the "holy trinity" principle of using limited military force and only in self-defense.[1] In this mission, peacekeepers use offensive

---

[1] The "holy trinity" refers to the core principles of traditional UN peacekeeping doctrine. Beyond the use of force only in self-defense, the other legs of the triad are host state consent and impartiality, respectively.

military force to defeat armed groups, and thereby most closely resemble standard military operations in terms of actions and tactics. This became an explicit mission of the United Nations Operation in the Congo (ONUC).

The other peacekeeping missions are predicated on violent conflict already having occurred or is ongoing. Preventive Deployment is designed for peacekeepers to be deployed *prior to* the onset of armed conflict in order to discourage or deter its formation; this can be with respect to "new" conflict or the spread of existing conflict to a different country. The United Nations Preventive Deployment Force (UNPREDEP) in Macedonia was intended to ensure that the civil conflict in other parts of the Balkans during the Yugoslav Wars did not spread there.

The missions listed in Table 2.1 provide the basis for our exploration of multiple mission interdependence. This is not to say that peacekeepers have not or could not perform other missions. In the course of deployment, peacekeeping forces might carry out other functions that do not fit neatly into any of the mission categories; for example, they might assist in economic development efforts by building roads or other infrastructure. Indeed, we address so-called new or prospective missions in the concluding chapter. Nevertheless, our taxonomy covers the explicit and primary missions carried out in operations. The next step is to examine how often these missions are assigned and in what combinations. In the next section, we investigate UN peace operations over a long-time frame to determine these patterns.

Peacekeeping Missions in UN Operations

The UN was historically the primary purveyor of peace operations, and remains the agent for a plurality of operations even when peace operations are defined in the broadest sense (Diehl and Balas, 2014) to include so-called political missions.[2] In addition to this central role, as well as consistency with past studies and informational concerns, we focus on UN peace operations, as identified by the UN itself.[3] Accordingly, we examined all UN peace

---

[2] If one includes so-called political missions and related operations, the number of operations swells to over 200, but the UN is still the organizing agent for more than 40 percent of these.

[3] https://peacekeeping.un.org/en/department-of-peace-operations (last accessed September 18, 2022).

operations in the period 1948–2016; seventy operations qualify as being deployed sometime during this period.[4]

For each of the seventy operations, we considered whether the peacekeeping force was formally charged with and/or operationally performed each of the missions listed in Table 2.1 at any time during their deployment; the number and types of missions assigned to a given operation occasionally change over time by UN resolution. These coding decisions were made by reference to a number of sources. Most notable was the original authorizing resolutions of the Security Council, reauthorization resolutions, and information provided by the United Nations.[5] Historical narratives and accounts of individual missions provided additional information (see, e.g., the chapters in Koops et al., 2015). Finally, we cross-referenced our coding decisions against the descriptions of missions provided by Franke and Warnecke (2009) and the data set compiled by Mullenbach (2013). A listing of all seventy UN operations and their associated missions in the period studied is given in Table 2A.1.

There is considerable variation in the number of missions. Table 2.2 charts the number of missions that individual peace operations have undertaken. Only twelve (or about 17%) peace operations are confined to one mission; indicative of these is the UN Truce Supervision Organization (UNTSO), the oldest peace operation, put in place in 1948 to monitor the cease-fire after the first of the Arab-Israeli wars. Looking at the data from another perspective, almost 83 percent of peace operations are tasked with more than one mission, even as scholars tend to focus on a single element. The mean number of missions is 4.17, and therefore peace operations are being assigned multiple roles in achieving the goals of promoting international peace and security. A small set of operations are even asked to do a majority of the missions on the list. An example is UNAMSIL, first deployed in 1999, with nine missions.

More numerous missions per operation have other implications for peace operations. One is the number of troops required to carry out those missions. The number of troops adds to the cost of missions, but it also has been associated with a greater ability to protect civilians during conflict and reduce battlefield deaths (Hultman, Kathman, and Shannon, 2020). Using data from

---

[4] As of the end of 2022, only one operation had been authorized since 2016—United Nations Mission for Justice Support in Haiti (MINUJUSTH) in 2017.

[5] https://peacekeeping.un.org/en/department-of-peace-operations (last accessed September 18, 2022).

Table 2.2 Frequency of multiple missions
in peace operations, 1948–2016

Number of missions	Count	% Total
1	12	17.14
2	12	17.14
3	10	14.29
4	7	10.00
5	8	11.43
6	3	4.29
7	8	11.43
8	7	10.00
9	2	2.86
10	1	1.43

the IPI Data Base and the United Nations on troop levels,[6] we ran correlations with the number of missions performed. The number of troops was modestly correlated with the number of missions ($r = .40$).[7] Thus, independent of other requirements that go with an increased number of missions, greater costs are incurred and more resources, ceteris paribus, are needed.

Are there particular patterns to the variation in mission numbers? Peacekeeping is purported to have changed dramatically with the end of the Cold War, most notably by the increase in the number of operations authorized by the Security Council. Our results reveal that accompanying this is a 130 percent increase in the number of missions assigned to peace operations. In the Cold War period (operations initially authorized before 1991), peace operations had an average of 2.11 missions, whereas post–Cold War operations (authorized in 1991 and thereafter) had a mean of 4.88 missions.

The dramatic increase in post–Cold War missions identifies a temporal pattern, but that does not in itself provide an explanation for that pattern.

[6] International Peace Institute, *Providing for Peacekeeping*, http://www.providingforpeacekeeping.org/contributions/, and https://peacekeeping.un.org/en/list-of-past-peacekeeping-operations (both last accessed on July 15, 2021) and United Nations, *United Nations Peacekeeping* (last accessed July 15, 2021). As troop size and configuration varied over time, we took the maximum of troops deployed at any time during the operations and included associated police forces as well.
[7] As the distribution of troop data is skewed, we reran the analysis with the log of troop size, but the correlation was only slightly greater ($r = .44$).

One possibility is that operations are being placed in different conflict contexts that necessitate a wider set of missions. Peace operations in certain post–Cold War contexts, mostly civil and internationalized civil conflicts, have increased over time, whereas Cold War operations tended to be concentrated in interstate disputes. The former offer a broad set of problems (e.g., refugees, democratization) that might be addressed by newer missions. The latter occurred during cease-fire periods and often only required peace operations to monitor those cease-fires. Even the United Nations Mission in Ethiopia and Eritrea (UNMEE) operation, launched after the Cold War in 2000, had only a single traditional peacekeeping mission, and it was deployed to an interstate conflict. To investigate whether the kind of conflict influences the number of missions, we used classifications for interstate war, civil war, and internationalized civil war from the Uppsala Conflict Data Project[8] and matched these to the kind of conflict that occurred at the outset of individual peace operation deployments. As expected, operations deployed in interstate conflicts (e.g., United Nations Emergency Force [UNEF I and II] separating Egypt and Israel) had 1.73 missions on average, whereas those with a civil conflict component averaged more than double that: 4.84 missions for civil wars and 4.00 missions for internationalized civil wars (e.g., United Nations Organization Mission in the Democratic Republic of the Congo [MONUC]), respectively.

Turning to the frequency of different missions and various combinations thereof, there is perhaps no single typical mission profile. Table 2.3 indicates that Traditional Peacekeeping missions involving observation and monitoring of cease-fires remain the most common, present in almost 80 percent of peace operations (e.g., United Nations Observation Group in Lebanon [UNOGIL]). Nevertheless, most other missions appear one-fourth to one-half of the time, suggesting that these missions deserve more analytical attention. Only Preventive Deployment and Pacification missions are rare. The former does not occur because of the difficulties associated with early warning systems in the United Nations, whereas the latter mission goes beyond "robust" peacekeeping and is more often taken by multilateral or unilateral national military forces rather than peacekeepers.

To detect patterns among multiple mission configurations further, we calculated correlations between all pairs of missions, as well as between the

___

[8] http://www.ucdp.uu.se, Uppsala University (last accessed July 15 2021).

Table 2.3 Distribution of peace operation mission types, 1948–2016

Mission type	Count	% Total
Traditional Peacekeeping	55	78.57
Humanitarian Assistance	36	51.43
Election Supervision/Democracy	32	45.71
Preventive Deployment	1	1.43
DDR	39	55.71
Pacification	2	2.86
Human Rights	25	35.71
SSR	38	54.29
Rule of Law	22	31.43
Local Governance	18	25.71
Reconciliation	24	34.29

missions and the other variables (Cold War, War Type, Troops, and Total Number of Missions); the result is a fifteen-variable correlation matrix consisting of 105 bivariate correlations. Looking at bilateral combinations of missions, only five of the fifty-five possible combinations involve moderately high correlations (r) > .50: (1) Human Rights–Humanitarian Assistance; (2) Human Rights–Election Supervision/Democracy; (3) Election Supervision/Democracy–Local Governance; (4) Election Supervision/Democracy–Reconciliation: and (5) Human Rights–Reconciliation, respectively. The lack of a common set of mission combinations suggests that UN planners and Security Council members do not have standard packages that they apply to conflicts as they arise, at least with respect to sets of missions. It might be that the decisions to launch certain missions are largely reactive to the particular conflict context and subject to change after initial deployment as conditions change. It also suggests that the organization and its members do not have a sense of which missions are best performed together or avoided. The centrality of the Human Rights mission to the configurations that do exist reflects the priority given to civilian protection in UN mandates, especially in more recent operations.

A factor analysis of the correlation matrix showed that four mission types—Traditional, Preventive Deployment, DDR, and Pacification—were isolated from the other seven missions; that is, they were associated with different factors. Those other missions had strong loadings on the first factor, which explained the most variance (35%); the Total Number of Missions and the Cold War variables also had very strong loadings on that factor. The negative loading for Cold War indicates that these missions occurred frequently during the post–Cold War years. Thus, post–Cold War operations not only had larger numbers of missions than pre–Cold War operations, but they also have more missions associated with post-conflict peacebuilding: Humanitarian Assistance, Election Supervision/Democracy, Human Rights, SSR, Rule of Law, Local Governance, and Reconciliation.[9]

Dimensions of Comparison for Peace Operation Missions

We now have a list of UN peace operations and their associated missions. The next step is to identify a series of dimensions along with those missions can be compared, and these comparisons form the basis for our subsequent expectations and analyses of compatibility.

The analysis of compatibility begins with the assumptions that different missions involved different behaviors, skill sets, and processes. Broadly, Howard (2019) has documented how modern peace operations exercise power and influence actors in different ways. "Coercive" power is most evident in the traditional cease-fire activities, but it might also appear in actions designed to protect civilians in the Human Rights mission. "Inducement" is found in a series of different missions, including DDR, when former combatants are offered payments for turning in weapons and opportunities for employment in society. Humanitarian aid is also related to inducement, and Howard (2019) also classifies institution building—a key part of peacebuilding missions of Local Governance, Rule of Law, and SSR—as part of the inducement form of power. Finally, "persuasion" power is found in election supervision and human rights monitoring. Thus, prima facie, the way that peace operations can affect outcomes varies, and to some extent this is different across missions.

In what ways do missions differ and which suggest (in)compatibility? We identified a series of characteristics upon which different missions could be compared. These are drawn broadly from the literature on conflict management[10] as well as from various analyses of peace operations

---

[9] This finding corresponds with the distinctions between Core Peacekeeping Goals and Post-Conflict Peacebuilding made by Diehl and Druckman (2010).
[10] We began with an early version specified in Diehl et al. (1998).

Table 2.4 Dimensions for comparison of mission compatibility

Mission characteristic	Left continuum point (1)	Middle point (2)	Right continuum point (3)
Role Orientation	Primary Party	Mixed	Third Party
Conflict Management Process	Integrative	Mixed	Distributive
Local Population Focus	High	Medium	Low
Impartiality	High	Medium	Low/Biased
Ease of Exit	Easy	Mixed	Hard
Mission Creep Potential	Low	Medium	High
Coordination with IOs	Low	Medium	High
Coordination with Government	Low	Medium	High
Control over Mission	High	Medium	Low
Cost	Low	Medium	High
Temporal Orientation	Short-Term	Medium-Term	Long-Term
Institutional Change	Limited	Moderate	Extensive

as they took on more peacebuilding tasks. We consider this set to encompass the key features of any peace operation including aspects of actors, organization, local populations, constraints, and goals. Each dimension is conceptualized along an ordinal continuum with three categories, as shown in Table 2.4. Although not including all considerations, this set does capture a broad variety of characteristics suitable for the analyses of multiple missions (see Diehl et al., 1998 for the rationale underlying many of these dimensions).

Most of the dimensions capture our appraisal of the essential concerns of peacekeeping missions. Three of them are drawn from conflict resolution studies. The first is the classic role orientation distinction between entry into a conflict as a primary versus third party. This distinction captures the difference between direct and indirect involvement in a conflict management process, and indeed the conflict itself (see Druckman and Wall, 2017, for examples of settings in which one or the other role is emphasized). For example, peacekeepers take primary roles in such missions as Human Rights (e.g., protecting threatened populations) and SSR (especially in providing local security). They take third-party roles in such missions as Traditional Peacekeeping (especially cease-fire monitoring) and supervising elections.

The distinction between integrative and distributive processes has been a centerpiece of the conflict management literature since Walton and McKersie (1965) introduced it in the context of labor negotiations (see also Hopmann, 1995, for an application to international negotiations). Generally, this refers to the extent that the actions of the peacekeepers produce benefits to all the parties in the sense of a win-win, public good, or "expand-the-pie" outcome (thus "integrative"). In contrast, distributive processes are those in which fixed goods are divided between the parties involved, and thus the outcomes are conceived in more of a zero-sum fashion, referred to also as a fixed-pie solution (Harinck, De Dreu, and Van Vianen, 2000). Reconciliation activities are clearly integrative, whereas Humanitarian Assistance is fixed and is distributive.

The idea of impartiality has been debated for decades, with a turn in more recent years to the impacts of biased third-party involvement (e.g., see Svensson, 2009). Impartiality refers to the extent to which a peacekeeper acts intentionally to favor one or more sides in a conflict. This does not mean that the outcomes might not benefit one side over others, but rather that the peacekeepers will take action against whatever disputant is required to fulfill the mission; for example, cease-fire monitoring applies to all sides equally and peacekeeping responses will be directed toward any violator without partisanship. Biased missions might tilt toward the interests of one disputant over another; conventional military intervention on the side of an ally is an example. With respect to peace operations, Local Governance favors the interests of those currently in political power.

The other nine dimensions are divided between those that focus on the peace operation—local population, control over mission, ease of exit, mission creep, and temporal orientation—and those that involve broader policy concerns as part of the operational context—coordination with international organizations, coordination with government, cost, and institutional change. The degree to which peacekeepers interact with the local population was lower in Traditional Peacekeeping when armed forces were much of the focus of cease-fire monitoring, as opposed to newer missions such as Human Rights whose exclusive concentration is on civilians. In addition, peacekeeping missions also vary considerably in the degree of control by the organizations conducting the peace operations. Less autonomy is evident when peacekeepers must coordinate with other actors, as in the case of Humanitarian Assistance versus when full responsibility of mission is in their hands—cease-fire monitoring in Traditional Peacekeeping.

Peacekeepers are also constrained by the control over outcomes that they share with other actors. Some missions are easier to terminate than others—at the discretion of the agency authorizing the mission. Humanitarian Assistance can be turned on and off in a spigot-like fashion, but other missions are more ambiguous or contain termination conditions that are not fixed points. For example, Election Supervision ends when the election is over or shortly thereafter, but Promotion of Democracy is a more complex process without necessarily having a defined endpoint. The prospect for mission creep, or the potential that one mission will lead to expansion of actions into other missions, may not be envisioned at the time of the original mandate. There is probably some risk of mandate expansion for every peacekeeping mission that we identify. Nevertheless, peacebuilding missions are especially vulnerable given the strong interconnection between them—for example, the Rule of Law might require SSR and accompanying Local Governance in order to guarantee it.

The timeline for implementation and for the purposes of missions range from relatively short to long term. Cease-fire monitoring in Traditional Peacekeeping, which is, by definition, temporary until a peace agreement is achieved or the situation is stable, is a day-to-day concern, as is Humanitarian Assistance, which is not intended to provide a permanent solution to needs. In contrast, the Rule of Law, Local Governance, and Reconciliation are missions predicated on achieving long-lasting impacts.

The costs of a peace operation are salient concerns to the United Nations and the member states who foot the bill. Costs are often evaluated on a year-to-year basis as the actual lengths of operations are uncertain even as they might be authorized for fixed time periods.[11] Nevertheless, we consider costs in terms of prospective total costs. None of the missions is inexpensive, as even some Traditional Peacekeeping missions with small numbers of personnel have lasted for decades. SSR and democracy efforts can be costly. Costs are likely to increase as the conflict management processes move from settling the conflict to implementing the settlement to sustaining the peace. These costs include the need for a larger variety of professional organizations as the process transitions from one phase to another.

Missions vary in terms of how much interaction and coordination is required with other actors. Among the most critical are the interactions with

---

[11] Note that even as operations might be authorized for typical six-month periods, they are often renewed repeatedly and in many recent cases the mandates are adjusted over time.

the local government. The peacebuilding missions of Rule of Law and Local Governance are at the high end, as these involve developing capacity that national and local governments will ultimately assume; those actors are often partners with the peace operation in that development. The basic security missions, especially Traditional Peacekeeping, are at the lower end, as peacekeepers are third-party guarantors of government in the missions. Some missions work side by side with international organizations. These can be governmental organizations (IGOs) such as the UN or World Bank in peacebuilding activities or nongovernmental organizations (NGOs) such as the many charitable entities that assist in the delivery of Humanitarian Assistance (Bartolli, 2013).

Finally, peacekeeping missions vary, often dramatically, in how much institutional change is needed in the host country in order to be successful. Election Supervision/Promotion of Democracy and some peacebuilding actions require substantial change, some aspects of DDR require a moderate amount, and virtually none at all is required for Traditional Peacekeeping.

Mission Compatibility

With the peace operation missions and their characteristics specified, the next step is to consider their compatibility vis-à-vis each other. We consider compatibility to be a critical aspect of peace operations, contributing vitally to the success of the operation. For this reason, we analyze it in some detail. Although the specific elements of compatibility vary from one context to another (e.g., marriage, software, sports teams), there is a commonality shared across settings: namely, two or more elements of a system, process, or unit that are able to function effectively together. This can boost performance, but at a minimum it means not inhibiting or preventing successful outcomes. For example, software compatible with a computer operating system allows programs to run smoothly. In contrast, incompatible people who marry one another are more likely to divorce. Effective functioning, as coordination or efficiency, derives from either similarity of the components of the system, which may consist of members of a family unit, parts of an operating system, players on a basketball team, or peacekeeper tasks involving multiple missions. Our interest in compatibility stems from an expectation that a compatible combination of missions is more likely to lead to an effective peace operation. This expectation derives from an assumption that compatibility facilitates the coordination needed for smooth functioning or reduces the chances for disagreement within an operation. Peace operation missions can be considered compatible when one mission enhances or at least does not diminish the performance of another. Compatibility for peacekeeping most noticeably comes from similarities in an operation's characteristics.[12]

One of similarities is that the different missions envision the same roles in the conflict. For example, some missions have peacekeepers participate in the conflict directly in ways that are related to the disputants themselves (primary parties), whereas others have peace operations that are external to the core conflict (third parties), so-called robust operations in which peacekeepers use offensive military force are indicative of the former, whereas supervising elections reflects the latter. Other aspects include orientations toward the disputants as being impartial (e.g., protecting humanitarian assistance deliveries) or biased (e.g., the peace operation in Mali clearly favors the government with a mandate that includes the reestablishment of state authority). Missions carried out by the peacekeepers might also be compatible in the sense that peacekeeper activities are similar, such as monitoring tasks in supervising cease-fires and certifying the disarmament of local militias. In a subsequent section, we provide a systematic rendering on how compatibility can be assessed.

How does compatibility matter? The assumption is that compatible missions have reinforcing, positive effects on the success of each other, or at least do not have deleterious effects. In contrast, when the mix of missions places peacekeepers in different roles or emphasizes different processes, they are likely to be incompatible, and therefore are expected to lead to less successful outcomes for all those mission tasks involved. We offer more specific theoretical expectations on this below. This is similar to Rietjens and Ruffa's (2019) concept of coherence. Borrowing from writing on organizational theory, those authors emphasize three dimensions of fit among aspects of peace operations: strategic and organizational, cultural, and operational. They apply these dimensions in an analysis of the United Nations Multidimensional Integrated Stabilization Mission in Mali (MINUSMA).

[12] We choose to highlight the similarity rather than the complementarity of a peace operation's characteristics. This is based on the assumption that these elements are moving in the same direction. Complementarity is defined as contrasting conditions that offset each other's limitations or that together work in a synergistic fashion. This is difficult to conceive in the context of peace operation characteristics or performance. For example, it is hard to imagine how high levels of coordination with the government in one mission would complement lower levels of coordination in another, or how an integrative process would complement a distributive process.

Peacekeepers performing similar missions have the advantage of task performance that requires the same skill sets, and training regimens can be adjusted accordingly; the appropriate mix of "combat" versus "contact" (conflict management and resolution) skills in training and application can be engineered into training prior to deployment (Druckman, Singer, and Van Cott, 1997; Curran, 2017). Working with government authorities, and often the same personnel, is a common feature of several peacebuilding missions—SSR, Rule of Law, and Local Governance. Such ongoing and interconnected relationships can provide for smoother operations across the board.

In contrast, we know that the mechanisms (ways that power is exercised) through which peacekeeping influences outcomes varies—coercion, inducement, persuasion (Howard, 2019)—and does so by mission. Peacekeeping soldiers might find it difficult to shift behaviors in an operation that requires divergent orientations for two missions that are performed simultaneously. For example, actions in a third-party role, such as cease-fire monitoring, are quite different from those in primary party roles in which peacekeepers might need to intervene in the conflict directly, such as Human Rights. Similarly, asking peacekeepers to perform tasks with a biased orientation while remaining impartial in others can create confusion and run the risk that peacekeepers will make errors in missions such as DDR, which is supposed to be applied equally across groups. In addition, the combatants and local population can view peacekeepers in the same fashion and are more likely to cooperate in compatible missions. In contrast, for example, local groups might not consider peacekeepers as impartial in delivering humanitarian aid or supervising an election when those same forces are also employing their military assets against that group in establishing safe zones for displaced persons.

The impacts of compatibility across missions are mediated by success and failure of the missions. That is, if a given mission A is compatible with another mission B, then success in A will enhance the likelihood of success in B, ceteris paribus; the reverse of B affecting A is also expected assuming simultaneity rather than a given sequential order. The same is true for failure—failure begets more failure. Failure in one mission does not help another mission even though it might be compatible with that mission.

Determining the impact of mission compatibility first requires understanding the meaning of compatibility in this context and then how it might be measured. Below, we outline the process of how we measure mission compatibility in peace operations and then apply the measure to seventy UN peace operations over the period 1948–2016. We regard the compilation of indicators as a first step toward developing some expectations concerning compatibility and then evaluating the impacts of mission compatibility on various aspects of peacekeeping effectiveness.

Coding Missions for Compatibility

In moving forward, we drop two of the missions listed in Table 2.1: Preventive Deployment and Pacification. These missions are very rare (appearing only once or twice) and therefore have little utility in understanding interactions among missions. Indeed, the record reveals that these two missions are more hypothetical than actual. The remaining nine peacekeeping missions shown in Table 2.1 are coded in terms of the twelve characteristics in Table 2.4. The missions are coded according to their *ideal* types along the specified characteristics. We recognize that there might be some variation in practice and over time during a particular operation. This potential limitation is reflective of many efforts to identify and code components of such key concepts as democracy, corruption, and judicial independence, but necessary to make cross-case comparisons.

Three independent coders judged each mission type in terms of three categories construed in terms of a high-to-low continuum. For example, the role orientation of peacekeepers is coded as primary, mixed, or third party for each of the missions.[13] The procedure used is a variation of the Delphi method, which is a focus group technique based on systematic expert judgments (Fern, 2001). The goal of this approach is to reach a consensus on decisions. The process consists of several rounds of judgments until the panelists agree on the "best" set. A first step is to select the experts. The three authors served as the panel. This decision captured both inside and outside expertise: two of the authors understood nuances in the ways both the missions and categories were defined; the third author served as an outside expert, having been involved in neither the formulation nor the implementation of the selection of missions or characteristics. The first round consisted of making independent judgments: overall agreement was 77 percent. The highest percentage agreements on the missions

---

[13] The first two characteristics, role orientation and conflict management process, are regarded as categorical rather than ordinal or scaled.

were humanitarian assistance (91%), human rights (85%), and rule of law (85%); the lowest percentage agreement were on traditional (64%) and election supervision (67%). The highest percentage agreements on the mission characteristics were on the distinction between integrative and distributive missions (100%), local population (96%), and primary and third-party roles (89%); the lowest percentage agreements were on ease of exit (37%) and costs (56%).[14]

The second round consisted of distributing the independent judgments to each of the coders. This feedback was a basis of discussions about reasons for the discrepancies, including clarifications about the missions and the characteristics on which they were coded. A third round consisted of revising the codes toward the development of modal judgments. The final coding resulted in 99 percent agreement. The iterations of coding, recoding, and discussions produced a 22 percent improvement in agreements.[15] The revised codes were used for further analyses. They are shown in Table 2.5.

The idea of mission compatibility is conceptualized by the degree to which different missions share the same scores on each of the twelve dimensions. Individual peace operation characteristics do not in themselves raise issues of compatibility; rather, compatibility occurs for a given mission only vis-à-vis at least one other mission, and this can vary according to the characteristics being compared. For example, the Humanitarian Assistance mission differs substantially from the Human Rights one with respect to being a third party (Humanitarian Assistance) versus a primary party (Human Rights). They share, however, the high level of coordination each has with international organizations in carrying out the missions.

Comparing two missions on a single characteristic is conceptually useful but misleading in that the sense that when two missions intersect, they do so with respect to multiple characteristics. Thus, mission compatibility is really an aggregate notion, representing combinations of similarities and dissimilarities across multiple characteristics. Those missions with identical scores on all twelve characteristics can be considered perfectly compatible. The other extreme would be when one mission has all scores at one end of the continuum across those dimensions (all scores = 1 in Table 2.4) and the other

---

[14] The correlations between first round coder judgments are .49 (coders 1 and 2), .57 (coders 1 and 3), and .65 (coders 2 and 3).

[15] No attempt was made to appoint one of us as a final arbiter. The decisions evolved from the iterations of judgment and discussion. In two cases, consensus was not reached and we took the average of the three codings.

Table 2.5 Mission coding across different characteristics

Dimension	Traditional	Humanitarian	Election/ democracy	DDR	Human rights	SSR	Rule of law	Local governance	Reconciliation
						UN missions			
Primary-Third Party	3	3	2	2	1	1	1	1	2
Integrative-Distributive	3	3	2	2	3	3	1	3	1
High-Low Local	2	1	1	1	1	1	1	1	1
Impartial-Biased	1	1	1	2	2	1	1	2	2
Easy-Hard Exit	2	1	2	2	2	2	1.67	1.67	2
Low-High Mission Creep	2	2	2	2	3	3	3	2	3
Low-High IO Coord	1	3	3	2	3	2	3	2	2
Low-High Govt Coord	1	2	3	2	2	3	3	3	3
High-Low Control	1	3	2	2	2	3	3	3	3
Low-High Cost	2	2	3	2	2	3	2	2	3
Short-Long Orientation	1	1	2	2	2	2	3	2	3
Low-High Institutional Change	1	1	3	2	2	2	3	3	3

mission is always at the other end of the continuum (all scores = 3 in Table 2.4). In practice, pairs of missions fall at various points between these two ends or ideal types. We can measure the distance between different missions by considering the distances between different missions on those characteristics in a multidimensional space.

As indicated by the empirical patterns of mission frequency, UN peace operations rarely include all mission types, but they also on average include several more than two missions. Thus, mission compatibility within a given UN operation comes from the number and type of missions performed as well as how they match up with one another on the characteristics in question. For operations with many multiple missions, this can be complex. In the following section, we develop several indicators in an attempt to capture this complexity and measure compatibility in different ways.

One caveat in the analyses above and in the construction of indicators below reflects an implicit assumption: we regard the similarities and differences between all twelve characteristics as being equally important for compatibility and equally so for operational performance. A mismatch on short- and long-term orientations might have a bigger impact on strategies and efficiencies than low versus high cost, but we begin with the idea that the effects are the same. Differences in compatibility effects might also be manifest for some missions versus others. A priori, we do not have rationales for all or even many of the permutations, and these are ultimately empirical questions that we hope will become clearer in our case studies or future research.

Developing Compatibility Indicators for UN Peace Missions and Operations

We have the conceptual framework for understanding mission compatibility, but how can compatibility be assessed across different missions and then a large set of peace operations with different mission profiles? Is there a prima facie case for significant variation in compatibility across operations and therefore an empirical basis for exploring the implications of such?

Our goal was to discern patterns among the nine types of missions based on the coded characteristics. These missions were correlated across the twelve characteristics; we were looking at the degree to which they were similar in those characteristics. The correlations were subjected to a multidimensional scaling (MDS) analysis, a statistical technique that locates cases in a dimensionalized space (Kruskal and Wish, 1990). This allows us to consider more than one characteristic at a time, as well as more than two missions simultaneously. Missions that share the same or similar character-istics are said to be more compatible than those having different characteris-tics, and this is represented by being closer together in the multidimensional space. The coordinates of the missions in the multidimensional space are a basis for calculating distances between each pair of missions.[16]

The scaling was limited to two spatial dimensions for reasons of interpret-ability, ease of use, and stability.[17] A key feature of this analysis is the "good-ness of fit" between the data (correlations among the nine types of missions across the twelve coded characteristics) and the spatial configuration; that is, how well does the spatial arrangement map with the underlying correla-tional associations. This is expressed in terms of a measure referred as "stress" (Kruskal and Wish, 1990). The object is to attain minimum stress and thereby better goodness of fit. A rule of thumb common in MDS applications is that a satisfactory fit is obtained when stress is below 10 percent. Good fit also means that the analyst does not need to search for additional dimensions. In our case two dimensions are sufficient. The final two-dimensional configura-tion is shown in Figure 2.1, with a very desirable goodness of fit attested to by a stress value of 6 percent.

An inspection of Figure 2.1 shows that Traditional Peacekeeping is alone in the lower right-hand quadrant, a significant distance from the other missions examined. This indicates that its characteristics differ considerably from the other missions that UN peace operations now perform. Nevertheless, and perhaps not surprisingly, the most proximate missions to the traditional one are those dealing with security matters: DDR and SSR, each at roughly the same distance from the Traditional Peacekeeping mission. These involve tasks that supplement cease-fire monitoring and stabilization. DDR tends to occur in the early stages of peace operations, most often as part of a peace agreement ending a civil conflict. SSR is a longer-term set of activities, but still designed with similar goals, in part, of limiting violence and providing the mechanisms to ensure law and order.

---

[16] This involves a total of 66 pair-wise comparisons.
[17] We are not naming the horizontal and vertical dimensions. Rather we are examining locations of the missions in the four quadrants. Our interest is the distances in the multidimensional space rather than where the missions align on each of the dimensions.

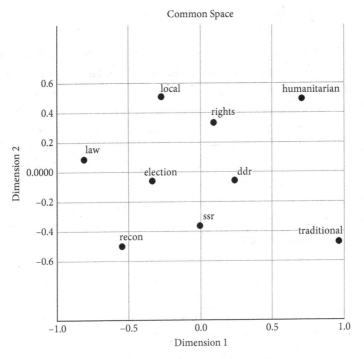

Figure 2.1 Location of missions in the multidimensional space

The Reconciliation mission is also relatively isolated from the others. Unlike the other missions, this one involves the local population directly and is not focused on monitoring or government functions, per se. It is closest to other peacebuilding missions—Local Governance and Rule of Law—which also involve long-term processes and the involvement of agents and stakeholders beyond militarized forces. The remaining spatial configuration suggests some proximity among monitoring missions (Election Supervision/Democracy, DDR, Human Rights), but these are not identical and differ on other characteristics such as mission creep and impartiality.

The bottom line is that the nine missions vary in similarity across the twelve characteristics. This means that peacekeepers are asked to perform actions that might not go well together (e.g., short- versus long-term temporal orientations; biased actions against government interests while other actions require coordination with that host government). The case study chapters in this book examine the impacts of these differing elements on performance.

Alternative Measures of Compatibility

Figure 2.1 arrays the missions vis-à-vis one another in a multidimensional space and provides a visual picture of potential compatibility issues. Nevertheless, particular UN peace operations include various combinations of those individual missions and thus raise case-specific issues of compatibility within those operations. Accordingly, we took the list of missions and codes of their characteristics from above and used them in an analysis of the seventy UN peace operations conducted from 1948 to 2016 and the missions carried out by those operations.

We begin by calculating difference scores between each pair of missions within each given UN operation; operations with one mission are excluded from the analysis, as they do not raise compatibility issues by definition. The resulting score consists of a subtraction between the numerical locations of the missions on the horizontal and vertical axes in the MDS space shown in Figure 2.1. This calculation is done for two missions at a time (e.g., Election Supervision/Promotion of Democracy and Rule of Law). An operation that has four missions produces six difference scores for each of the two dimensions, or a total of twelve scores. For example, four mission operations, such as UNPROFOR (United Nations Protection Force had Traditional Peacekeeping, DDR, Humanitarian Assistance, and SSR) and MINURCAT (the United Nations Mission in the Central African Republic and Chad had Humanitarian Assistance, Human Rights, Rule of Law, and SSR missions), result in six difference scores, and six missions would result in fifteen scores. These mathematical differences are calculated from the coordinates for each of the two dimensions.

There are multiple approaches to translate the difference scores between two missions into aggregate measures of operation compatibility, each with its own underlying logic about the impact on operation success. Our selection of three indicators, among the many options, was guided by several criteria: differentiation in theoretical logics, differentiation in outcome values, having some measures reward mission similarity as well as punish dissimilarity, and variance across operations. We discuss the logic for three indicators before describing the procedures used for calculations.

The logic of the first indicator as a measure of compatibility is related to that of multitasking. Trying to do multiple and divergent things simultaneously or closely connected in time is problematic because attention and resources are stretched thin. For example, protecting civilians in the Human Rights mission can distract peacekeepers from other missions occurring simultaneously (Day and Hunt, 2022). This might complicate the attempt of peacekeepers to do any one task well. Furthermore, the assumption underlying Indicator 1 is that there is always some incompatibility between missions, and there is an additive effect of the problems encountered whenever peacekeepers are asked to do more. This is akin to what foreign policy scholars refer to as "role strain" (Thies, 2010). The International Peace Institute aptly pointed out with respect to MINUSCA that there can be tensions between missions, noting: "If signatories [to the peace agreement] attack or threaten civilians, [the operation] could be torn between responding to the threat and maintaining a positive working relationship between the signatories" for the other goals of the operation (2019:4). Another risk cited there is the possible incompatibility of human rights protection and DDR.

The underlying logic for the second indicator assumes that peacekeepers can multitask, provided that they are not asked to perform tasks that are dramatically diverse. That is, the training, actions, and perceptions of the stakeholders will not change much if the peacekeepers perform similar kinds of missions, such as those involving monitoring functions. Furthermore, there would not necessarily be a substantial shift in attitudes and actions as the peacekeepers move from mission to mission, which could be sequential in some cases rather than simultaneous. Indeed, there could even be a transfer effect because experiences in similar missions might produce a positive transfer as peacekeepers use the skills and lessons from one mission to another that presents similar challenges. For example, DDR might enhance cease-fire monitoring in Traditional Peacekeeping, as has been suggested in the United Nations Mission in the Republic of South Sudan (UNMISS) (International Peace Institute, 2020).

The reasoning for the third indicator is based on the premise that the longer an operation goes, the better able it is to adapt to incompatible missions. Thus, lengthy operations allow for greater changes in mandates, personnel, and strategy to account for problems of incompatibility. These would also facilitate more and better sequencing of missions that might otherwise place peacekeepers in contradictory roles and actions. The possibility of learning over time from multiple mission experiences might also enhance adaptation and performance.

Calculating Three Compatibility Indicators

Following the logics discussed above, we developed calculation procedures for each of the three indicators. In each case, we transformed the final scores to a 0–100 scale for ease of comparison,[18] using a z-transformation. Scores closer to zero indicate greater compatibility. Twelve of the UN peace operations are charged with only a single mission among the 9 examined, and thus have a score of 0. These can be regarded as a baseline to compare multiple mission operations.

Indicator 1

Our first indicator adds the difference scores across the two dimensions for a grand sum. This is designed to signify an aggregate incompatibility score for the operation as a whole, and maps to the logic of multitasking elucidated in the previous section. For example, UNEF I (United Nations Emergency Force I—Traditional Peacekeeping and DDR missions), one of the original peacekeeping operations, with only two missions has a normalized score of only 2.73; in contrast, UNAMID (United Nations African Union Mission in Darfur—Traditional Peacekeeping, Humanitarian Assistance, Election Supervision/Promotion of Democracy, Human Rights, Rule of Law, Local Governance, and Reconciliation), with seven missions, has a score of 65.29. Generally, the more missions that an operation conducts, the higher its (in)compatibility score, ceteris paribus, with some variation according to the particular missions undertaken. The correlation between Indicator 1 and the number of missions is very high (.97), but the measurement does allow a larger range in the scale scores and differentiation between two operations with the same number of missions but different mission profiles. Accordingly, those operations with the most missions have the largest sums; adding more missions, by definition, means creating additional differences even if the new missions are relatively close in space to existing ones. For example, operations at the high end of the scale (score = 100) are those that implement all nine missions, such as UNAMSIL.

---

[18] Note that comparisons on this 100-point scale are valid across cases within each of the three indicators below and not necessarily across different indicators.

Indicator 2

The second indicator consists of taking the sum of difference scores from all mission combinations and dividing it by the number of missions used to produce that sum. Thus, this is the mean distance between pairs of missions in a given operation, reflecting on average how (in)compatible missions are with each other. This is consistent with the logic above that similarity of missions is equated with compatibility, and there might even be positive effects from actions that require the same roles, orientations, and the like. To some extent, comparable missions compensate for incompatible ones in the calculations or at least mitigate the impact of the latter.

Indicators 1 and 2 are related (correlation is .78), but there are some notable differences. Indicator 2 is not a function of the number of missions (correlation is .05); it adjusts for differences in number of missions. Indeed, the highest-scoring mission (100), UNASOG (United Nations Aouzou Strip Observer Group), has only two missions—Traditional Peacekeeping and Rule of Law—but these are the most dissimilar missions among all different mission pairs. The operations discussed above, UNEF I and UNAMID, that had highly divergent scores according to the first indicator are much closer on this indicator—48.95 and 55.67, respectively. Large mission numbers for operations such as UNAMSIL produce outcomes in the middle of the scale (~50) as they entail more and fewer similar missions simultaneously. With this indicator, the range of scores is narrower, primarily from 25.24 to 66.67, with many clustered in the 40–55 range.[19] Thus, this indicator might not produce substantial variation empirically to distinguish between operations in either a statistical or substantive sense, even as the underlying logic suggests clear conceptual differences.

Indicator 3

For a third measure, we experimented with several different calculations. Various combinations of the mean and sum largely produced results that were highly correlated with the number of missions.[20] We eventually arrived at a measure that was statistically distinct and with a different underlying

---

[19] The standard deviation is only 9.34 when excluding the zero cases.

[20] For example, the mean (Indicator 2) weighted by the number of missions produced an indicator with a correlation of +.98 with the sum (Indicator 1) and therefore not distinct from the latter. Various combinations (e.g., additive, multiplicative, weighted) of Indicators 1 and 2 produced similar results.

logic than the previous two measures. Indicator 3 is based on the rationale that peacekeepers and the organizing agents can learn or adapt over time, even in the face of incompatible mission combinations. The measure here is determined by taking the average of the first two indicators and dividing it by the duration of the mission.[21] Importantly, from a statistical vantage point, duration is not correlated with the number of missions (r = −.05). The new measure is also distinct from Indicator 1 (r = +.17) and only moderately correlated with Indicator 2 (r = +.34).[22]

There are several qualifications as to the use of these indicators. They are designed to provide general patterns of compatibility with three different logics. The scores of individual operations are on a relative (to other operations *and* within each indicator) basis rather than definitive and absolute measures of compatibility. Their heuristic value remains to be demonstrated in future chapters. In addition, our indicators are aggregate measures of compatibility for the operation as a whole from a post hoc perspective. In practice, the configuration of missions, and therefore the compatibility, can vary *within* operations depending on the sequencing and simultaneity of missions performed. The case studies in subsequent chapters are designed, in part, to take account of these nuances even as they begin in the directions suggested by our compatibility indicators.

Armed with the knowledge and tools discussed in this chapter, there remains a central question of the book: how do multiple peace missions influence one another? Ultimately, however, our question is one that requires an empirically based answer. Accordingly, the final section of this chapter presents some theoretical expectations about the answers to that fundamental research query. Chapter 3 discusses the approach and evidence to be used in testing those expectations. These efforts serve as a basis for the case studies that follow in Chapters 4, 5, and 6.

---

[21] The duration of the mission is measured in years from the first year of deployment to the year of termination. Sixteen cases are censored as they were ongoing through 2016, the endpoint of the analysis. We also dropped an extreme outlier from the rescaling transformation, as it distorted and compressed all the other scores; after the transformation, we assign 100 to that outlier in the data and 99 to the next highest score.

[22] The data used to calculate the three indicators and a summary file listing the three indicators for each of the UN peace operations are available through Harvard Dataverse at https://dataverse.harvard.edu/dataset.xhtml?persistentId=doi:10.7910/DVN/SBPMDT.

Additional and alternative indicators are possible from our methodology and the spatial configurations in Figure 2.1, although we caution that these should be based on their own plausible or compelling logics rather than what might produce the best fit in a given case or model.

Theoretical Expectations

There have been calls to consider how multiple missions interact with one another (Diehl and Druckman, 2018) and how mandates might be best sequenced (International Peace Institute 2019a, 2019b; United Nations Secretary-General, 2018). Some starting points exist (Diehl and Druckman, 2010) and other analyses comment on limits to different missions carried out by UN peacekeepers (Bellamy and Hunt, 2019), but there is no systematic research to explore their implications. Our pattern analyses indicate that multiple missions are common, and increasingly so over time. Furthermore, we have presented evidence indicating that many of those missions are not compatible with one another as they involve different roles, tasks, and relationships with actors. With such considerations in mind, we develop a series of expectations about how multiple missions influence one another, with attention to two sets of concerns: (1) temporal ordering of missions; and (2) compatibility. Our intention is not to examine an exhaustive list of possible interactions, but given the dearth of prior research and space constraints, we limit ourselves to the most fundamental ones. The concluding chapter raises several possible extensions for future research in light of our findings.

Sequencing, Simultaneity, and Prerequisites

Not all peace missions are designed to occur simultaneously, and indeed that is not possible given the limited number of personnel in UN operations. Some missions implicitly assume the completion of one set of tasks before undertaking others. For example, Reconciliation[23] appears to be an end-stage mission that is put in place when the Rule of Law and Local Governance have been secured. A stable government and established legal institutions facilitate the processes of post-conflict societies dealing with past atrocities and conflict actions.

When a peace operation is authorized, there might be plans that some missions will occur immediately and that others will receive less priority. As mandates are renewed, they can be modified to include new missions

---

[23] Note that Reconciliation assumes that there was a friendly or cooperative relationship between the warring parties in the past. This may not have been the case, especially in countries in which civil wars have recurred. That kind of historical record calls less for renewal of a previous friendship than for a new beginning, and therefore presents a greater challenge for peacekeepers.

and associated tasks. Thus, new missions are added based on the progression (positive or negative) of the operation. Some missions are ongoing in that there is a persistent need for their conduct; cease-fire monitoring in the Traditional Peacekeeping missions is one such example. In contrast, other missions might have fixed time frames. Peace operations that monitor democratic elections and facilitate democratization often do so for the first election following a peace agreement but do not necessarily play a role in subsequent elections.

The patterns discussed above are based on logical orders that might be inferred from the purposes of the different missions as well as sequences reflected in different conceptions of peacekeeping (e.g., liberal model of peacebuilding—see Richmond, 2006, 2021). In practice, temporal order is difficult, if not impossible, to specify fully. Unlike beginning and end dates for the peace operation as a whole, the UN does not necessarily record precise dates for the onset and termination of individual missions. Sometimes this is evident when a new mission is authorized as part of a UN Security Council resolution that reauthorizes the operation as a whole or revises its mandate. More often, however, the same peacekeepers are performing multiple missions simultaneously or moving from sets of tasks associated with one mission to another. Another study has reported that there is no clear pattern across operations regarding the order in which various mandated tasks are performed (Blair et al., 2021). Accordingly, we cannot begin our theoretical expectations with some empirical patterns or heuristic indicators as we do with compatibility.

At a nascent stage of theorizing on these matters, our initial expectation, which we refer to as the "*Security First*" proposition, argues that success in basic security missions—Traditional Peacekeeping and DDR—is a prerequisite for success in other missions. The reverse is also expected to be the case—failure in basic security missions increases the probability of failure in other missions. This is consistent with the UN guidelines for peacekeeping (UN DPKO, 2008), which envision security and stability as initial goals that are segues to peacebuilding efforts in terms of peace consolidation and long-term development for post-conflict societies. Security is also a goal for UN members vis-à-vis so-called fragile states; stabilizing them is a priority and prerequisite for other initiatives (e.g., see US Department of State, 2022).

If disputants do not stop fighting and violence is widespread, the peace operation will be faced with considerable difficulties in carrying out a variety of other missions. Elections will not be free and fair with substantial participation if registration and voting are disrupted by armed conflict. Democratization more broadly is enhanced under conditions of peace rather than war (Blair, Di Salvatore, and Smidt, 2023). Delivering humanitarian assistance has logistical complications under any conditions. When there is active fighting, the challenges are even greater. Food and other supplies become weapons, or their denial becomes a strategy, that disputants use to support their partisans and deny to those of the opposing side. Establishing the rule of law and local governance institutions might be impossible if the political context is not stable. These processes assume some degree of peace and the freedom of movement. Indeed, Blair (2020) argues that UN peacekeeping assists rule-of-law efforts when there is peace to keep; when war is ongoing, however, he finds that peacekeeping has no such positive effect and might even be counterproductive with respect to the rule-of-law efforts.

Similarly, the protection of civilians and threatened populations will fail if war and other significant conflict occurs, especially as these are often directed at civilians. The cessation of hostilities is even relevant as a facilitating condition for constructing a constitution (Johnson, 2020), a fundamental component of the Rule of Law mission. Furthermore, the pursuit of justice and reconciliation might be predicated on establishing peace in the form of limiting violence, as was the case in Liberia (Lieb and Ruppel, 2021). Accordingly, most peace operations have violence abatement and cease-fire monitoring as one of their responsibilities (see Table 2.3).

DDR is also common in the immediate aftermath of civil conflict as the disarming and demobilization of fighters reduces the opportunity for violations of cease-fires. The reduction of arms and armed groups also contributes to the Human Rights mission (Sterio, 2020). The prospective impact of DDR is not confined to the short term. Long-term peacebuilding can be undermined when the three legs of DDR fall short of goals (Goebel and Levy, 2020), as structural reforms could unravel with the renewal of violence and the challenge of armed groups to the new political order. Furthermore, successful DDR fosters trust between political groups and promotes reconciliation as former combatants are reintegrated into society (de Hoon, 2020).

Stabilization actions in Traditional Peacekeeping and DDR missions are usually initiated toward the front end of peace operations, as the most immediate concern in the early deployment period is preventing the renewal of violence. Cease-fire monitoring activities are also an ongoing concern, as progress in initial efforts can unravel if violence recurs later in the peace operation. The outcomes in the basic security missions should, in principle, have downstream consequences for the missions that follow or occur simultaneously. Nevertheless, success in security does not guarantee that later missions will have positive results; other factors will be part of that success equation as well. Thus, we regard success in the basic security missions as likely to be a necessary, but not sufficient, condition for progress in other missions.

The liberal model of peacebuilding (e.g., see Berg, 2020) that guided the UN through much of the post–Cold War era has democratization as one of its core components, along with economic structures for a market economy. Democratic elections are also frequently held in the earlier stages of peace operations and as a result of peace agreements. Brancati and Snyder (2011) contend that the UN and the international community have preferences for early elections to reassure the formerly warring parties; accordingly, the average time for the first election after a civil war has declined to under three years. Some (Paris 2004; see also Brancati and Snyder, 2012; Flores and Nooruddin, 2012; Autesserre, 2021) argue that elections occur too early in the post-conflict period, before the populace is ready for them. Leaving that separate question aside for the moment, we anticipate that failure in Election Supervision and early Promotion of Democracy efforts lessens the likelihood of success in several peacebuilding missions ("*Democracy Matters*"). Looking at it from the other direction, success in elections and democratization lays the groundwork for progress in some other missions. This is the expectation of UN decision makers and perhaps the reason that early elections are preferred, although there is criticism that the UN and its members are also motivated by the prospect of early withdrawal of peacekeeping forces (Diehl, 2022a).

Free and fair elections, as well as accompanying democratization, are supposed to facilitate the development of the rule of law and associated legal institutions. Failure means that the institutions and practices that establish those might never be created. For example, democratic oversight of security forces is one of the core principles of SSR (Perito, 2020; Begayoko and Hutchful, 2022). Equally important, the norms of democratic governance including respect for peaceful conflict resolution and processes must follow from elections that are regarded as legitimate. Establishing the rule of law requires the initial steps of democratic elections for those who will be formulating elements of the rule of law.

Other interactions between missions might also be expected. The cluster of peacebuilding missions—SSR, Local Governance, and Rule of Law—is interconnected in the sense of (re)building local capacity for the proper functioning of society (Perito, 2020). These should move in tandem with respect to progress (or not); success or failure in one should have spillover effects on the others ("*Peacebuilding Synergy*").[24] The policing component of SSR cannot function effectively without well-developed and functioning court and prison systems (Perito, 2020). That said, a priori, we do not have an expectation about which of the three missions has the greatest impact on the others. We leave it to the empirical analysis to offer insights on the relationships involved.

In addition, as alluded to previously, the Reconciliation mission should depend on success in the three peacebuilding missions (in addition to the basic security ones)—this is referred to as the "*Peacebuilding Matters*" expectation. It is hard to conceive that people could put past wrongs behind them in the absence of a functioning government and confidence in the future functioning of society that is effective and legitimate.[25] In particular, a good judicial system built as a foundation in the Rule of Law mission is needed to prosecute war crimes (Trahan, 2020).

Although we cannot always explore this in detail, one might expect a recursive relationship between the early missions and those that follow ("*Recursive Effects*"). That is, there could be feedback from later initiated missions that influence the success of earlier begun missions, providing that the latter are ongoing through most of the life of the mission.[26] Simultaneous interactions might be stronger than sequential ones in our analyses. Specifically, failure in later missions—especially peacebuilding ones—could complicate the ability of peacekeepers to maintain an ongoing cease-fire and prevent the redevelopment of militias, even if they were heretofore successful in those missions. If the payoffs from peacebuilding are not evident, opposition groups might take up arms again to challenge the status quo. This is why some (e.g., Perito,

[24] Although we don't examine this relationship, Day and Hunt (2022) claim that protecting civilians can undermine long-term peacebuilding efforts.

[25] Our focus is on post-conflict societies emerging from civil wars. We do not cover the large number of autocratic societies where the rule of law and democratic governance are challenged on a daily basis and citizens conduct regular protests. Many of these countries have not emerged from civil wars. Peace operations are typically not deployed in these countries.

[26] From a methodological perspective, recursive effects can be construed as a form of post-diction. We are moving back in history, from a recent to a more distant mission. This type of analysis contrasts with attempts to predict future events—here, the success of later missions is conditioned by the outcomes of earlier missions.

2020) argue that DDR and SSR should be carried out together because of their mutually reinforcing effects.

In post–civil war contexts, more than half of civil war peace agreements break down with violence in a short period of time (Caplan and Hoeffler, 2007) and about 40 percent break down over a longer period of time (Collier et al., 2008), even as peacekeeping reduces that failure rate by 70 percent (Mason et al., 2011; see also Quinn, 2007). Accordingly, recursive and reinforcing effects are essential to limit slipping back to violence, and there are numerous interactions that can prevent this. Respect for human rights norms lowers the probability of violence renewal (Sterio, 2020), and human rights protection reinforces the Rule of Law mission (Sterio, 2020). In turn, SSR promotes human rights respect and compliance with the laws, and transitional justice initiatives assist SSR (Sterio, 2020). When peacekeepers are assigned election missions, it lowers the likelihood of electoral violence (Smidt, 2021). Broadly, the logic of the "democratic peace," as applied to internal conflict, predicts that successful democratization lowers the likelihood of violence as disagreements are channeled through representative institutions rather than onto the battlefield (Eizenga, 2022).

Compatibility

A second set of expectations follows from our discussion of the *compatibility* of missions. In a previous section of this chapter, we discussed the concept of mission compatibility, some possible dimensions, and constructed three alternative measures for it. Now we can move the discussion forward to formulate expectations about compatibility.

Most simply, we anticipate that in the aggregate, those peace operations with the most incompatible mission profiles will be the least successful across the board based, in part, on the logics outlined for the different compatibility indicators. Specifically, incompatible roles and differences across all the other dimensions suggest that problems will ensue for the full operation. We know that peacekeeping personnel—both soldiers and commanders—are trained primarily in military tactics and strategy. These skill sets are most applicable to the basic security missions but are not necessarily transferable to other missions, especially peacebuilding ones (Diehl, Druckman, and Wall, 1998). Although training regimens for peacekeeping have improved over time and there are programs specifically dedicated to such training,[27] these are short-term efforts and do not necessarily fill the gaps between skill sets and requirements. Multitasking, in general, produces distractions as workers must deal with multiple and often divergent challenges at one time (Newport, 2016); for peacekeepers, this means having to keep their eyes on different functions in diverse areas when performing multiple missions. In addition, many of the newer peace operation missions involve collaborative relationships with other actors, such as local stakeholders, UN agencies, and NGOs. Such cooperation between diverse actors can produce "collaborative overload" (Cross, Rebele, and Grant, 2016) that leads to institutional bottlenecks and other complications that inhibit efficiency. This is the underlying logic of Indicator 1 of compatibility.

In contrast, highly compatible mission portfolios could have positive and reinforcing effects on one other. This expectation comports with Indicator 2 of compatibility. Here missions with similar skill sets (especially those dealing with conventional military functions) or tasks (e.g., monitoring) could enhance performance across missions, or at least not undermine it. This suggests that fewer and more compatible missions—those closer to one another in Figure 2.1—might be more successful than when the mission profile expands in number and scope. Within operations, even with a large number of missions, there can be positive spillovers between compatible mission subsets embedded within them such as some peacebuilding missions or the basic security missions.

A corollary expectation is that any deleterious properties from incompatibility should dissipate over time as the peace operation adjusts and adapts to the problems encountered. Such an expectation matches the underlying logic of Indicator 3. A priori, we do not have a clear sense of when such learning would take place or which missions would be most affected. Nevertheless, we will be sensitive to this possibility as we proceed through the case studies.

Aggregate measures of compatibility provide an overview of the peace operation, and we anticipate that broad conclusions can be drawn about the outcomes of operations ("*Aggregate Effects*"). Nevertheless, there are also likely to be effects present at a lower level of analysis, specifically between individual missions. These might be hidden within an aggregate

---

[27] United Nations Peacekeeping Resource Hub, https://research.un.org/en/peacekeeping-community/training (last accessed November 26, 2022).

analysis. Accordingly, and as a general expectation, we anticipate missions to have more serious problems when they are paired with other missions that have dissimilar characteristics. That is, in spatial form, the greater the distance between missions in Figure 2.1, the less likely either mission will be successful in operations that include both of them occurring simultaneously or sequentially ("*Individual Effects*"). The inverse is likely also to be the case: compatibility promotes success when similar missions are paired with one another. Given that peace operations are heterogeneous with respect to different combinations of missions, we are not specifying particular pairs or combinations of missions in our theoretical expectations.[28] We address specific combinations of missions in the contexts of the case studies.

Finally, we offer the "*Learning*" expectation postulating that negative effects from incompatible missions will dissipate over the life of the operation for the reasons elucidated earlier and with respect to Indicator 3. That is, the relationship between (in)compatibility and outcomes is stronger earlier in the operation and will be less evident toward the end of operations, especially those with longer durations.[29] The expectation that peace operations and its personnel can and should adapt over time is the underlying basis for the UN Comprehensive Planning and Performance Assessment System (CPAS) (Forti, 2022) and related proposals (de Coning and Brusset, 2018). In those formulations, data are provided on a continual basis so that UN officials and peacekeeping commanders can learn from successes and failures and then adjust strategies and tactics accordingly. For our theoretical interests, we are focused on learning with respect to adaptations to the incompatibility of missions rather than learning and adjustments more broadly or those confined to within individual missions.

A summary of our theoretical expectations is given in Table 2.6.[30]

---

[28] Indeed, there are numerous permutations and some pairs or combinations might have no empirical referents.

[29] The concept of reactive inhibition in scholarly studies is relevant here. Earlier learning dissipates through time even with continuous exposure to the same stimuli, in our case the same combination of missions. The extent to which early learning dissipates depends on the time between early and later assessment. It also depends on the ratio of practice on the same tasks (missions) to external events that shift attention from those tasks. For a treatment of these issues, see Torok et al. (2017). One path for future consideration would be to compare the learning curves for operations with compatible versus incompatible mission profiles.

[30] Our use of the term "expectations" rather than "hypotheses" is meant to suggest that we are not drawing them from a strong theoretical literature.

Table 2.6 Summary of theoretical expectations

Type of expectation	Expectation	Proposition
Sequencing, Simultaneity, and Prerequisites	Security First	The outcome of basic security missions influences the outcomes of other missions in a peace operation. (time-lag)*
	Democracy Matters	The outcomes of Election Supervision and early Promotion of Democracy efforts influence the outcomes of peacebuilding missions. (time-lag)
	Peacebuilding Synergy	SSR, Local Governance, and Rule of Law have synergistic effects and their success or failure are correlated with one another. (association)
	Peacebuilding Matters	The outcome of the Reconciliation mission is correlated with the success or failure of the peacebuilding missions.(association)
	Recursive Effects	Outcomes of later missions influence the success or failure of ongoing missions or those begun earlier. (reverse time-lag)
Compatibility	Aggregate Effects	Effective mission outcomes are more likely from more compatible mission profiles. (time-lag)
	Learning	The relationship between (in)compatibility and outcomes is stronger earlier in the operation and will be less evident toward the end of operations, especially those with longer durations. (time series)
	Individual Effects	The effectiveness of individual missions depends on the compatibility of other missions with which they are paired. (association)

*The parenthetical expressions capture the type of proposition as time lag/time series or association relationships between the variables.

Conclusion

The analyses in this chapter have demonstrated several important things about UN peace operations and the missions they perform. First, there is a variety of missions for peacekeepers beyond the traditional one of cease-fire and related security monitoring, which has been the primary focus of scholarship and policy. Second, UN peace operations regularly perform many of those missions, averaging between four and five of those over the course of the operation. Furthermore, the number of missions per operation has substantially increased in the post–Cold War era along with an increased frequency of UN operations in conflicts with a civil or internal, as opposed to an exclusively interstate, component.

Third, we have shown that peacekeeping missions vary substantially across a dozen relevant dimensions, indicating that the newer missions (and indeed most missions) are substantially different from Traditional Peacekeeping. Fourth, we developed the concept of mission compatibility and postulated how it might influence success and failure in peace operations. Fifth, recognizing mission differences and in light of the compatibility concept, we constructed three quantitative indicators each representing a different theoretical logic about compatibility.

With these empirical patterns in mind, we constructed eight expectations about how missions interact, focused on aspects of timing and compatibility respectively. Chapter 3 lays out our strategy and evaluative criteria for examining those expectations, a prelude to the case studies in the three chapters that follow.

Table 2A.1 Mission profiles of UN peace operations, 1948–2016

UN operation	Operation dates	List of missions
DOMREP	May 1965–October 1966	Traditional Peacekeeping
MINUCI	May 2003–April 2004	Traditional Peacekeeping, DDR, Rule of Law
MINUGUA	January 1997–May 1997	Traditional Peacekeeping, Humanitarian Assistance, Election Supervision/Promotion of Democracy, DDR, Human Rights
MINURCA	April 1998–February 2000	Election Supervision/Promotion of Democracy, DDR, SSR
MINURCAT	September 2007–December 2010	Humanitarian Assistance, Human Rights, SSR, Rule of Law
MINURSO	April 1991–Present	Traditional Peacekeeping, Election Supervision/Promotion of Democracy, DDR, Reconciliation
MINUSCA	April 2014–Present	Humanitarian Assistance, Election Supervision/Promotion of Democracy, DDR, Human Rights, SSR, Rule of Law, Reconciliation
MINUSMA	April 2013–Present	Traditional Peacekeeping, Humanitarian Assistance, Election Supervision/Promotion of Democracy, Preventive, DDR, Human Rights, SSR, Rule of Law, Local Governance, Reconciliation
MINUSTAH	June 2004–October 2017	Humanitarian Assistance, Election Supervision/Promotion of Democracy, DDR, Human Rights, SSR, Rule of Law, Local Governance, Reconciliation
MIPONUH	December 1997–March 2000	SSR, Local Governance
MONUA	June 1997–February 1999	Traditional Peacekeeping, Humanitarian Assistance, Election Supervision/Promotion of Democracy, Human Rights, SSR, Rule of Law, Local Governance, Reconciliation
MONUC	November 1999–June 2010	Traditional Peacekeeping, Humanitarian Assistance, Election Supervision/Promotion of Democracy, DDR, Human Rights, Rule of Law, Local Governance, Reconciliation
MONUSCO	July 2010–Present	Humanitarian Assistance, DDR, Human Rights, SSR

(continued)

Table 2A.1 Continued

UN operation	Operation dates	List of missions
ONUB	June 2004–December 2006	Traditional Peacekeeping, Humanitarian Assistance, Election Supervision/Promotion of Democracy, DDR, Human Rights, SSR, Rule of Law, Local Governance, Reconciliation
ONUC	July 1960–June 1964	Traditional Peacekeeping, DDR, Pacification, SSR
ONUCA	November 1989–January 1992	Traditional Peacekeeping, DDR, SSR
ONUMOZ	December 1992–December 1994	Traditional Peacekeeping, Humanitarian Assistance, Election Supervision/Promotion of Democracy, DDR, SSR
ONUSAL	July 1991–April 1995	Traditional Peacekeeping, Humanitarian Assistance, Election Supervision/Promotion of Democracy, Human Rights, SSR, Rule of Law, Local Governance
UNAMIC	October 1991–March 1992	Traditional Peacekeeping, SSR
UNAMID	July 2007–December 2020	Traditional Peacekeeping, Humanitarian Assistance, Election Supervision/Promotion of Democracy, Human Rights, Rule of Law, Local Governance, Reconciliation
UNAMIR	October 1993–March 1996	Traditional Peacekeeping, Humanitarian Assistance, Election Supervision/Promotion of Democracy, DDR, Human Rights, SSR, Rule of Law, Reconciliation
UNAMSIL	October 1999–December 2005	Traditional Peacekeeping, Humanitarian Assistance, Election Supervision/Promotion of Democracy, DDR, Human Rights, SSR, Rule of Law, Local Governance, Reconciliation
UNASOG	May 1994–June 1994	Traditional Peacekeeping, Rule of Law
UNAVEM I	January 1989–May 1991	DDR
UNAVEM II	May 1991–February 1995	Traditional Peacekeeping, Election Supervision/Promotion of Democracy, SSR
UNAVEM III	February 1995–June 1997	Traditional Peacekeeping, Humanitarian Assistance, Election Supervision/Promotion of Democracy, DDR, Reconciliation
UNCRO	March 1995–January 1996	Traditional Peacekeeping, Humanitarian Assistance, DDR
UNDOF	May 1974–Present	Traditional Peacekeeping, DDR
UNEF I	November 1956–June 1967	Traditional Peacekeeping, DDR

Mission	Dates	Mandate
UNEF II	October 1973–July 1979	Traditional Peacekeeping, DDR
UNFICYP	March 1964–Present	Traditional Peacekeeping, Humanitarian Assistance, SSR
UNGOMAP	May 1988–March 1990	Traditional Peacekeeping, DDR
UNIFIL	March 1978–Present	Traditional Peacekeeping, Humanitarian Assistance, DDR, Human Rights
UNIIMOG	August 1988–February 1991	Traditional Peacekeeping, DDR
UNIKOM	April 1991–October 2003	Traditional Peacekeeping
UNIPOM	September 1965–March 1966	Traditional Peacekeeping
UNISFA	June 2011–Present	Traditional Peacekeeping, Humanitarian Assistance, Human Rights
UNMEE	July 2000–July 2008	Traditional Peacekeeping
UNMIBH	December 1995–December 2002	Traditional Peacekeeping, Humanitarian Assistance, Election Supervision/Promotion of Democracy, Human Rights, SSR, Rule of Law, Reconciliation
UNMIH	September 1993–June 1996	Humanitarian Assistance, Election Supervision/Promotion of Democracy, SSR, Rule of Law
UNMIK	June 1999–Present	Traditional Peacekeeping, Humanitarian Assistance, Election Supervision/Promotion of Democracy, Human Rights, SSR, Rule of Law, Local Governance
UNMIL	September 2003–March 2018	Traditional Peacekeeping, Humanitarian Assistance, Election Supervision/Promotion of Democracy, DDR, Human Rights, SSR, Local Governance, Reconciliation
UNMIS	March 2005–July 2011	Traditional Peacekeeping, Humanitarian Assistance, Election Supervision/Promotion of Democracy, DDR, Human Rights, SSR, Rule of Law, Reconciliation
UNMISET	May 2002–May 2005	Election Supervision/Promotion of Democracy, SSR, Local Governance
UNMISS	July 2011–Present	Traditional Peacekeeping, Humanitarian Assistance, DDR, Human Rights, SSR, Rule of Law, Reconciliation
UNMIT	August 2006–December 2012	Humanitarian Assistance, Election Supervision/Promotion of Democracy, Human Rights, SSR, Local Governance, Reconciliation
UNMOGIP	January 1949–Present	Traditional Peacekeeping

(continued)

Table 2A.1 Continued

UN operation	Operation dates	List of missions
UNMOP	February 1996–December 2002	Traditional Peacekeeping, DDR
UNMOT	December 1994–May 2000	Traditional Peacekeeping, Humanitarian Assistance, Election Supervision/Promotion of Democracy, DDR, Reconciliation
UNOCI	April 2004–June 2017	Traditional Peacekeeping, Humanitarian Assistance, Election Supervision/Promotion of Democracy, DDR, Human Rights, SSR, Local Governance, Reconciliation
UNOGIL	June 1958–December 1958	Traditional Peacekeeping
UNOMIG	August 1993–June 2009	Traditional Peacekeeping, DDR
UNOMIL	September 1993–September 1997	Traditional Peacekeeping, Humanitarian Assistance, Election Supervision/Promotion of Democracy, DDR, Human Rights
UNOMSIL	July 1998–October 1999	Traditional Peacekeeping, Humanitarian Assistance, DDR
UNOMUR	June 1993–September 1994	Traditional Peacekeeping
UNOSOM I	April 1992–March 1993	Traditional Peacekeeping, Humanitarian Assistance, SSR
UNOSOM II	March 1993–March 1995	Traditional Peacekeeping, Humanitarian Assistance, DDR, Pacification, SSR, Rule of Law, Reconciliation
UNPREDEP	March 1995–February 1999	Traditional Peacekeeping, Humanitarian Assistance
UNPROFOR	February 1992–March 1995	Traditional Peacekeeping, Humanitarian Assistance, DDR, SSR
UNPSG	January 1998–October 1998	SSR
UNSF	October 1962–April 1963	Traditional Peacekeeping, SSR
UNSMIH	July 1996–July 1997	Election Supervision/Promotion of Democracy, SSR, Rule of Law, Local Governance, Reconciliation
UNSMIS	April 2012–August 2012	Traditional Peacekeeping

UNTAC	February 1992–September 1993	Traditional Peacekeeping, Humanitarian Assistance, Election Supervision/Promotion of Democracy, DDR, Human Rights, SSR, Reconciliation
UNTAES	January 1996–January 1998	Election Supervision/Promotion of Democracy, DDR, Human Rights, SSR, Local Governance, Reconciliation
UNTAET	October 1999–May 2002	Traditional Peacekeeping, Humanitarian Assistance, Election Supervision/Promotion of Democracy, SSR, Rule of Law, Local Governance
UNTAG	April 1989–March 1990	Traditional Peacekeeping, Election Supervision/Promotion of Democracy, DDR, SSR, Reconciliation
UNTMIH	August 1997–November 1997	Election Supervision/Promotion of Democracy, SSR, Rule of Law, Local Governance, Reconciliation
UNTSO	May 1948–Present	Traditional Peacekeeping
UNYOM	July 1963–September 1964	DDR

3

Research Plan

Introduction

UN peace operations have evolved over time to encompass more numerous and more diverse missions. As we discussed in previous chapters, this could have significant implications for our understanding of peacekeeping success. Nevertheless, this is predicated on establishing the empirical connections between the missions and their resulting impacts on outcomes. This chapter provides the roadmap for these connections, which are then examined in subsequent case studies.

We initially discuss the rationale for the selection of cases for in-depth study. Because our focus is on how mission interaction affects outcomes, we devote a separate section to evaluation standards, extending our previous work on peace operation evaluation (Diehl and Druckman, 2010). The chapter then provides detailed information about the indicators used and the accompanying sources of information available to evaluate our expectations about each of the nine peacekeeping missions.

Case Selection

In an ideal world, we would gather information on the outcomes of all missions carried out by every UN peace operation conducted since 1948. Realistically, however, this would be a Herculean task for what would be almost 300 missions across a broad swath of time. There are also other concerns in coding such outcomes, including that a number of operations are ongoing and that some outcomes can only be assessed in the longer term, even if the operation has been terminated. Accordingly, we have adopted a case study approach, using several criteria for making decisions about case selection. These criteria restrict the kinds of cases to be analyzed.

A first criterion is to consider only operations that involved Traditional Peacekeeping missions; this is the norm for peacekeeping operations, and

When Peacekeeping Missions Collide. Paul F. Diehl, Daniel Druckman, and Grace B. Mueller, Oxford University Press.
© Oxford University Press 2024. DOI: 10.1093/oso/9780197696842.003.0003

success/failure in this mission is a key part of our theoretical argument. Second, the operation needed to be completed by 2016, so that some final outcomes could be assessed. To do otherwise would force us into conclusions for ongoing operations whose results are not fully manifest or that might change before operation termination. In addition, some outcomes and associated indicators of success require an extended period of time to become clear, and some of the missions define success in terms of longer-term effects that are only apparent in retrospect. For example, Reconciliation in post-conflict environments is a long-term process, and truth and reconciliation commissions, prosecution of war crimes, and the like begin during the latter stages of the peace operations and extend beyond force withdrawal. Finally, some of our success indicators are based on existing data, whose information often lags well behind the present date. Although all such data are not necessarily available through 2016, this cutoff provides the best-case scenario for balancing information provision with a suitable sample of cases that have multiple missions.

Third, we considered only those operations with three or more missions; this was necessary to reflect the increasing complexity of contemporary peace operations and to allow the examination of multiple interactions. Fourth, we considered only those operations that lasted more than two years in order to make more reasonable inferences about the impact of peace operations and their missions on long-standing conflicts (we discuss this concern in more detail in a later section). Finally, when multiple peace operations are deployed to a given conflict (e.g., Haiti, Bosnia), we chose to focus on the initial operation or one very early in the sequence of successive operations. An advantage of this decision is that we avoid the problem of path dependency, where later operations may be conditioned by the outcomes of earlier operations. We leave the study of follow-on operations and their interconnections to the future research discussed in Chapter 7.

These criteria narrow the available cases for study. We settled on five cases for intensive examination: United Nations Protection Force or UNPROFOR (Bosnia); United Nations Operation in the Congo or ONUC (Congo); United Nations Transitional Administration in East Timor or UNTAET (East Timor); United Nations Organization Mission in the Democratic Republic of the Congo or MONUC (Congo); and United Nations Mission in Sierra Leone or UNAMSIL (Sierra Leone).

These cases fit the prior criteria and provide suitable variation in missions and geography for us to examine multi-mission interdependence. All five operations included a Traditional Peacekeeping mission, had terminated by the end date of the study (2016), and were the only, first, or an early operation sent to the conflict in question, even as some had successor operations sent to the same conflict. Furthermore, each operation had at least three missions and lasted for a period that extended more than two years. Collectively, the five cases ensure that there are at least two instances of each mission examined.

Most important for our purposes, the number and range of missions in our set of five operations permit a study of many of the different mission interactions and the expectations laid out in Table 2.6. Collectively, the five operations cover the nine missions that are the focus of our analysis, and one (UNAMSIL) includes all nine itself. The range and type of missions represented by the set of cases also have research utility. The variety of conditions and types of conflicts represented by the selected cases provide a robust evaluation of our expectations. Chapter 4 considers two operations (ONUC and UNPROFOR) with a limited number of missions concentrated in the security realm, and these are more compatible (were not as spatially distant—see Figure 2.1) than operations also including peacebuilding missions. Thus, we are able to assess whether Security First and compatibility expectations play out even when small mission numbers and limited incompatibility are at play. Chapters 5 and 6 consider three operations (MONUC, UNTAET, and UNAMSIL) with greater numbers and more complex configurations of missions, each with a substantial peacebuilding component. These provide broader examinations of our expectations.

In addition, and beyond the specified criteria, we selected cases to provide for variation on a series of dimensions. First was geography. Although Africa has dominated operations in the post–Cold War era, we also examine operations in Asia and Europe. From a temporal perspective, we cover a broad range of operations. They include a Cold War operation in the early 1960s (ONUC), one in the early post–Cold War period (UNPROFOR), and the others that reflect more contemporary challenges in post-conflict contexts (UNTAET, MONUC, and UNAMSIL). This allows us to make inferences about multi-missions in various eras of peacekeeping and not be confined to solely Africa-based operations after 1989, which are the focus of many studies, especially those with large data sets. The cases and their missions are summarized in Table 3.1.[1]

---

[1] Recall from Chapter 2 that Pacification and Preventive Deployment are not covered in our analysis because of their infrequency.

Table 3.1 Case studies

UN operation	List of missions
ONUC	Traditional Peacekeeping, DDR, Pacification,* SSR
UNPROFOR	Traditional Peacekeeping, Humanitarian Assistance, DDR, Human Rights
UNTAET	Traditional Peacekeeping, Humanitarian Assistance, Election Supervision/ Promotion of Democracy, SSR, Rule of Law, Local Governance
MONUC	Traditional Peacekeeping, Humanitarian Assistance, Election Supervision/ Promotion of Democracy, DDR, Human Rights, Rule of Law, Local Governance, Reconciliation
UNAMSIL	Traditional Peacekeeping, Humanitarian Assistance, Election Supervision/ Promotion of Democracy, DDR, Human Rights, SSR, Rule of Law, Local Governance, Reconciliation

*not directly covered in the analysis

As with any set of case studies, there are some limitations that come with the trade-offs between in-depth analyses and broad coverage of the phenomena of interest. First are issues of comparability. Shorter operations and those with fewer missions are easier for analysts to isolate effects, given narrower time frames for confounding factors to occur and because of fewer mission interactions. Peace operations with peacebuilding missions, on the other hand, might last longer and by definition involve more missions. Yet it is exactly these kinds of protracted, complex operations that are the focus of our research, and thus a necessary cost to address our research questions. Second, there are contextual or environmental differences (see Druckman and Diehl, 2009) between the five cases, and thus each peace operation begins with a different set of challenges.

Our choice of assessment standard and acknowledgment of causality concerns (see the discussion of these in the following sections) are designed, in part, to mitigate inferences from divergent starting points and conditions. We discuss issues of causality before turning to a discussion of standards for assessment.

Issues of Causality

Various factors, beyond simply the actions of peacekeepers, affect mission outcomes. These include the environmental context of the operation

(Druckman and Diehl, 2009), which encompasses characteristics of the conflict (e.g., underlying disputed issues). Disputant behavior is also a component of context, and the cooperation or resistance of governments and rebel groups, for example, can vary across different missions (Dorussen and Gizelis, 2013) and might be conditioned by their relative strength (Ruggeri, Gizelis, and Dorussen, 2013). Other players might also be involved in some of the missions; such actors include third parties such as international organizations, NGOs, and neighboring states. Their actions, independent of—or in conjunction with—the peace operation have an impact on mission success. A central concern of many studies, and one that readers might raise here, is how much of the praise or blame for mission successes and failure should be attributed to the peace operation as opposed to other influences.

Such a question and associated approaches to deal with it, however, are misplaced in light of our research focus and methodological approach. Our primary research concern is on mission interdependence, namely, how the outcomes of certain missions influence the outcomes of other missions— mission outcomes can be the product of multiple influences including peace operation actions, those of other actors, and contextual factors. Our assessment of the research expectations presented at the end of Chapter 2 does not depend on parceling out the variance associated with each of those other influences on mission outcomes. Our research approach also is not the one typical of large-N studies concerned with causal inference. That said, our discussion of mission outcomes does not ignore actions by peacekeepers and the influence of other factors.

The emphasis on sorting out the responsibility for outcomes from peace operations has led to some problematic approaches. Application of those to our research questions is invalid. One approach in the research milieu has been to focus just on the peace operation and then narrowly, for example, suggesting evaluating peace operations only to the extent that they control outcomes (Johansen, 1994). Yet, generally, analysts should make an evaluation—here on the mission outcomes—on the dimensions specified and not confound that evaluation with determinations of how much influence peace operations had on those outcomes. That is, the measure of the outcome or dependent variable (mission success) should not be confused with or determined by the purported strength of the independent predictor variable (peacekeeper control over missions). Furthermore, it is not clear that any of the peacekeeping missions here are ones in which the peace operation has exclusive control. Peacebuilding missions, in particular, are multifaceted and involve many actors; to exclude them on the basis of lack of peace operation control would eliminate much or most of what peacekeepers do in contemporary operations.

The focus on peace operation impact also raises issues of causal inference, which might not be appropriate or possible in our study. Confidence in the assertion that peace operations lead to reduced conflict or other outcomes depends on two assumptions that can be considered as the sine qua non of causal inference. One is referred to as a time-lagged relationship between the key variables, namely, that the peace operation precedes the measurement of the outcome. This assumption is generally satisfied in our case studies. Another is referred to as controlling other sources of influence on the conflict, such as those noted above. For example, we might want to know how the peacekeeping force contributed to mission outcomes: what portion of the mission outcomes were attributable to the peacekeeping force versus other actors/contexts (except, of course, other missions)? This is difficult to assess with case studies even though progress has been made in developing methodologies that at least increase confidence in attributing causation. Some elaboration about these methods helps to set the stage for the approach taken in this research.

The requisite assumptions in the last paragraph are largely met with the invention of the classical experimental design, usually attributed to Fisher (1935) in the context of agricultural research (see also Edwards, 1962). His distinction between independent (IV) and dependent (DV) variables is the hallmark of causal inference pervasive across the sciences. It has been adopted as well in the nonexperimental sciences with the invention of quasi-experimental designs (Campbell and Stanley, 1963; Cook and Campbell, 1979). Of particular relevance to our work on peacekeeping is the application of causal thinking to the analysis of case studies. This is most evident in the development of focused structured comparisons (George and Bennett, 2005) referred to also as most similar systems designs (MSSD) (Faure, 1994).

Focused comparisons are attempts to satisfy both requirements for causal inference. Time lags between independent and dependent variables are usually easy to establish within cases, although some missions occur simultaneously or in overlapping fashion. Controlling for the effects of other variables, however, is more challenging. This is done by careful matching of the selected cases. An example is Putnam's (1993) study of northern and southern legislatures in two Italian provinces that differed on economic development (the independent variable) and performance (the dependent variable). Another example is Albin and Druckman's (2012) comparison of four peace agreements that differed on procedural justice during the negotiations (the independent variable) and durable peace following the talks (the dependent variable). The plausibility of attributing causation to the relationships found in these studies is based on the extent to which case matching and measurement were successful (for suitability concerns in meeting this purpose, see Braumoeller et al., 2018). Even though there are several peacekeeping operations that share the same number of missions and the same makeup of missions, one cannot argue that they are "matched" cases given the differences in context (geography, time in history, number of troops, and other factors).

Another problem with attributing causal relationships between peace-keeping performance and peace operation outcomes is rooted in analyses of retrospective case studies. The backward-looking approach to causation, referred to as post-diction or retro-diction, contrasts to a forward-looking, predictive perspective taken by experiments and quasi-experiments (Levy, 2008; Druckman, 2002). Analyses of historical case studies are attempts to account for known outcomes that have occurred in the past. This is in the realm of detective work in which investigators piece together "scraps of evidence" in order to assign blame or praise. They have no control over the factors that led to the focal event. Similarly, we are piecing together historical records for evidence that contributes to judgments of mission effectiveness in each case. Ultimately, the quality of these judgments turns on the plausibility of our probes and the quality of information used during the investigative process. With this in mind, our primary objective is to understand the dynamics of multi-mission interactions. Those dynamics are influenced by the peace operation, other actors, and a variety of contextual factors. We are not focused on these other prospective causal effects, but rather on learning how different missions intersect in dealing with conflict to which the peacekeepers are deployed.

Our focus on process dynamics emphasizes synergies rather than the conventional independent-dependent variable relationships. As we have argued, the difficulties in isolating variables and in performing controlled analyses largely preclude making causal inferences in the traditional sense. Furthermore, interactions among missions do not proceed in a linear fashion. This is particularly evident in the Recursive Effects expectation where outcomes of later missions—such as the Rule of Law—influence the success or failure of ongoing missions or those begun earlier—such as Election Supervision/Promotion of Democracy (see Chapter 2). Throughout our discussion of the cases in the chapters to follow, we refer to unexpected twists, concomitant effects, and circularity as in the way missions interact with the broader conflict environment. Although a complex version of multiple causation is conceivable, we prefer an alternative methodological approach.

The approach combines theory, dynamic analyses, and case comparisons. Theoretical concepts are used to organize the analyses of the different cases. This is similar to the research strategy referred to as enhanced case studies (Druckman, 2005), in which concepts play a central role in understanding the way cases unfold through time. The concepts could be part of a framework or, as in this research, a set of expectations derived from relevant literatures. Advantages flow in both directions: the case is understood more broadly in terms of general concepts, and the concepts are evaluated with real-world events that often have important consequences for ending wars or resolving conflicts. It also provides a link between ideographic and nomothetic orientations toward research. Thick analyses of cases in an idiographic tradition are buttressed by application of more general concepts or theoretical expectations in a nomothetic tradition. Rather than to pit case depth and sampling breadth against one another, this approach takes advantage of the strengths of both traditions.

By considering a case as a dynamic unfolding of events and decisions, we recognize that a host of factors influence mission outcomes. Mission interdependence is not the full story about success and failure. Throughout the case studies, we identify a set of other factors (peace agreements, intervention by supportive national armies, conflict characteristics) that enhanced, mitigated, or obviated the connections between missions and conflict outcomes (see also Dorussen, 2022; Walter et al., 2021; Di Salvatore and Ruggeri, 2017, for an overview of the relevant factors). Our holistic approach to analysis includes these factors as additional or synergistic influences on mission outcomes. The emphasis of this approach is on how missions influence and learn from each other. It provides a broad analysis of theory-based relationships similar in some ways to work on dynamical conflict systems (e.g., Coleman, 2011).

The comparative dimension of our research is captured by using the same assessment template on each of the cases. Judgments of outcome effectiveness are made for the same expectations, with a caveat that the number and types of missions vary from case to case. We now turn to a discussion of assessment issues.

Connecting the Dots

In making our holistic judgments about mission outcomes, we rely on numerous and varied indicators and evidence of success/failure. Our theoretical expectations above, however, deal with the interconnection of outcomes across missions. This is a complex analytical process when dealing with case studies. Case studies take a long view on the way events unfold. This facilitates connecting earlier and later processes as posited by several of our expectations. They also allow an investigator to triangulate multiple sources such as archival, interview, and observational information. With these options available, we are able to navigate around the methods landscape for insights that may either support or contradict the expectations. This approach is made possible by the deep-dive probes that we make in the chapters to come. We are operating in the realm of generating ideas, including developing theoretical connections, rather than falsifying hypotheses in a deductive tradition. A detailed discussion of the outcomes from this approach is found in Chapter 7.

The expectations shown in Table 2.6 posit various kinds of relationships among types of mission outcomes. Some are stated in a time-ordered sequence (e.g., Security First, Democracy Matters, Aggregate, and Individual Effects), even suggesting reverse and simultaneous associations as in Recursive Effects. Causal inferences are suggested by these analyses. Without controls for extraneous events or specifying necessary conditions, however, we proceed in this direction with caution, as noted in the section on causality. Others are primarily correlational (Peacebuilding Synergy, Peacebuilding Matters). Learning is apparent in changes over time. The question for us is whether our analyses generally satisfied these expectations.

We begin with the aggregate judgments on success for each mission using a 5-point Likert scale, ranging from Ineffective to Effective, as described in the next section. In determining how two mission outcomes are related to one another, we can look at the paired outcomes and make some initial assessments. The logic underlying our expectations generally assume that success-leads-to-success or that failure-leads-to-failure. Thus, when there is concordance between mission outcomes on the 5-point scale, or nearly so, then this is prima facie evidence for the expectation. For example, problems in DDR and Traditional Peacekeeping (Security First expectation) during the MONUC operation were tied to human rights abuses—something that was uncovered in our detailed case study analysis of this operation. This is reinforced if there is proper temporal ordering between the purported cause (e.g., basic security missions in UNAMSIL) and the anticipated effect (subsequent SSR mission success). Conversely, a mismatch between the outcomes of the missions under scrutiny (e.g., failure in one and success in the other, as in the basic security missions and election supervision in MONUC) provides contrary evidence, especially if the former was characterized as a prerequisite for the latter (e.g., Security First for the other missions). We recognize that temporal ordering can be muddied when two (or more) missions occur/begin simultaneously, thus suggesting there might be concomitant effects or even issues of endogeneity. Nevertheless, taking a case study approach to understanding multiple mission peacekeeping operations, rather than exploring statistical associations, allows us to have a fuller picture of the way the missions are interacting with each other and the broader conflict environment, giving us ample confidence to comment on any causation. From a correlational standpoint, we examine mission outcomes—for example, SSR, Local Governance, and Rule of Law (Peacebuilding Matters)—that are similar for the operations containing some or all of those missions (UNTAET, MONUC, and UNAMSIL). Our case selection facilitates some of this aggregate analysis in that the cases collectively include all missions, at least two of every mission, and, most important, variation in outcomes within and across mission types (see Goertz, 2017, on case selection and causality).

Beyond aggregate analysis, we also tie specific mission actions and outcomes to those of other missions within the same operation. This involves a multifold process. First, the theoretical logic underlying our expectations had to be reflected in the outcomes of the cases; for example, violence from the failures in Traditional Peacekeeping leading to difficulties in delivering humanitarian assistance had to be reflected in the histories of the cases. Indeed, this was evident in MONUC as delivery problems were noted in areas in which active fighting persisted. In contrast, Humanitarian Assistance in UNTAET had no disruption of supplies in areas where basic security was established. With respect to Learning, there needed to be evidence of improvement of performance for coordinating long-standing missions, and that had to fit with adaptations undertaken by the peacekeeping force. For example, there was improvement in the Traditional Peacekeeping mission during

ONUC, but this was a result of earlier pacification efforts and not necessarily learning by peacekeepers. Similarly, foreign military intervention during MONUC and UNAMSIL accounted for some improvements in outcomes rather than peacekeeping adaptations.

Second, there were numerous instances where our sources—reports, narratives, analyses—documented the time-ordered and correlational connections for us. These included evidence such as that failures to establish the Rule of Law were followed by difficulties in the Reconciliation tasks of prosecuting criminals in MONUC. Recursive Effects were documented by analyses that humanitarian assistance efforts lead to retaliation in the form of killing civilians during MONUC and SSR difficulties in UNTAET caused later problems in limiting violence in East Timor.

The above allows us to draw conclusions about whether our expectations were supported, partly supported, or not supported—summarized at the end of each case and collectively at the outset of Chapter 7 and in Table 7.1.

Standards for Assessment

Our central focus is on how multi-mission interaction influences the outcomes of peace operations, specifically the success and failure of those individual missions. In this section, we address a series of issues related to assessment, most notably those dealing with baselines and holistic evaluations.

Baselines

In making judgments about the success or failure of different missions, the choice of a baseline or standard for assessment is critical. Specifically, to what should the outcomes of peace operations and missions be compared (Diehl and Druckman, 2010)? Most analyses implicitly make some choice of baseline, but rarely make that choice explicit or consider alternatives. Yet the choice of baseline could have a profound effect on the assessment of success or failure; what might be viewed as a positive result relative to one standard might be considered a neutral outcome or even a failure from another perspective.

In this section we discuss a number of considerations to be taken into account when devising baselines for evaluation. These include ideal yardsticks, the status quo ante, status quo at the time of deployment, counterfactuals, time frames, and stakeholders.

Ideal Yardsticks

At the outset, we can reject the extreme standard of an "ideal" yardstick against which one can assess peace operations. This would mean different things for various missions, but broadly would include the complete absence of violence after peacekeeping deployment, elimination of all suffering as a result of humanitarian assistance, full integration of former combatants, an efficient government constrained by the rule of law, and more. These can be aspirational goals, but they are wildly unrealistic as ways to evaluate peace operations. No country, whether recovering from conflict or not, whether subject to peacekeeping or not, has ever achieved these "perfect" conditions. Thus, adopting the "ideal" standard will always find peacekeeping missions as falling short and therefore labeled as failures.

Status Quo Ante

A second approach is to make comparisons with the status quo ante, in which the "before" condition is prior to the onset of the conflict and "after" represents conditions at the end of the peace operation. This is more realistic than comparing the situation against an ideal, and it places the comparison in the individual context where the peace operation was deployed. Nevertheless, conflicts can cause dramatic changes in a country, impacting institutions, infrastructure, demography, and attitudes, to name but a few. These changes are especially significant in the face of severe conflict, and it is those severe conflicts that are most likely to have peacekeeping operations (Gilligan and Stedman, 2003). Thus, it might be unrealistic to expect that the status quo ante can be restored by any actions, much less by a peace operation. Thus, although not as high a standard as the ideal, there is the risk that peace missions will be judged automatically as failures. At certain points in our analyses, we use before and after conflict comparisons to make evaluations, but do so selectively when the comparisons are most reasonable and with recognition of the pitfalls therein. Usually, this means assessing whether conditions are moving in the right direction toward the status quo ante rather than whether the status quo ante has been fully restored. There were a few instances in which before/after for the status quo ante comparisons could document correlational associations. Illustrative is the contrast in violence during different elections prior to and following UNTAET deployment in

East Timor or infant mortality rates prior to the war in the Congo and those at the end of the MONUC operation.

Status Quo at Time of Deployment

The primary baseline used in this study is the status quo at the time of deployment, rather than at the start of the conflict. That is, the conditions at the time the peace operation is deployed or begins a particular mission are then compared over time with the same conditions during and following the peace operation. This is based on the relatively simple "before versus after" or pretest-posttest (Druckman, 2005) design, although there are a number of nuances in our application. This is a recommended (de Coning and Brusset, 2018:10) approach for peacekeeping evaluation: "Outcomes are often identified by a change in behaviour, i.e. the difference in behaviour before and after the action taken by the peacekeeping operation." The UN Comprehensive Planning and Performance Assessment System (CPAS) involves a similar process of analyzing trends and how the peace operation affected those trends (Forti, 2022).

The status quo standard will vary somewhat by mission and even within missions. For basic security missions such as Traditional Peacekeeping and DDR, the conditions at the outset of the operation might include a cease-fire and a peace agreement between the disputants. In that case, peacekeepers are assessed on their ability to hold the cease-fire. When deployed during active fighting, peace operations face a different context and are evaluated in terms of their ability to lower the level of violence. Our five cases include both of these success criteria.

With respect to peacebuilding missions such as the Rule of Law, peacekeepers can face differing conditions on which to make progress. A failed state means that the mission must start from square one, whereas other countries have some infrastructure and institutions that can be used as cornerstones for improvement. Reconciliation missions often start without a firm base, especially if legacies of resentment and hostility are strong.

Over the course of peace operations, the status quo shifts in response to changing circumstances and to the effectiveness (or lack thereof) of the peace operation itself. This is most notable in peace operations of long duration. Accordingly, we also pay attention to the status quo at different points of time during the operation, recognizing that mission success can vary in different phases and as conditions change. Although we consider conditions at the end of the mission, we need to be sensitive to the road that got the peace operation there (Stiles and MacDonald, 1992). For example, achieving stability and no violence at the end of the mission is a major accomplishment, but this judgment is tempered if there were substantial casualties during prior parts of the operation.

Using the status quo as the baseline allows us to capture variation across cases and missions. It does mean, however, that such variation will need to be reflected in our assessments, a concern noted also by Heldt and Wallensteen (2006). For example, renewal of violence that results in 300 deaths might be evaluated as a failure when peacekeepers were deployed after a peace agreement and a cease-fire. The same outcome could be considered a qualified success if the peacekeepers were sent to an ongoing and intense conflict and the peace operation was able to reduce the death toll to that level. It also imposes on us a responsibility to consider that different starting points might influence the assessment of success, with better initial conditions expected to produce better peacekeeping outcomes.[2]

The status quo standard most closely matches the perspective of UN and other decision makers. The situation on the ground is the one that they watch and look for improvement in conditions as evidence that the investment in peacekeeping is paying dividends, as well as whether to make mandate changes in reauthorizing resolutions.

Counterfactuals

Another standard for evaluation is to use counterfactuals (e.g., Levy, 2015)— that is, comparing the peacekeeping outcomes with those that would have occurred in the absence of a peace operation. The central purpose of counterfactual analysis is to make causal inferences (Fearon, 1991; Lebow, 2000; Pearl and Mackenzie, 2018), and as we note in an earlier section of this chapter, that is not our purpose. Thus, such analysis cannot be a centerpiece of this study. Yet despite this purpose, we find this approach to be highly speculative and very difficult to use for evaluation in the present context. A major hurdle is to identify an alternative that would have occurred had the peace operation not happened. This requires a plausible choice for that alternative approach. Our approach to counterfactual analysis requires some elaboration, particularly as it has become popular in modern political analysis.

---

[2] In scholarly parlance, this is referred to as a variation of the "selection effect." Peace operations are not deployed to a random set of conflicts, but those with particular characteristics that might make success or failure more likely. Our case studies, however, reflect variation in the initial conditions for deployment.

One strategy for counterfactuals is to consider simply what would have happened had the key factor—here a peace operation—not occurred (Fearon, 1991). This strategy is common in large-N, quantitative analyses in which one holds other variables constant at their means and examines the effect when the key condition is absent or present (often measured in a 0/1 binary fashion). There are a number of problems in these analyses (see King and Zeng, 2007), but merely inferring what would have happened had no peace operation occurred in our cases lacks utility, if not validity. We (Diehl and Druckman, 2010) have criticized this as a "better than nothing" standard, what others label as "absence-based criteria" in the sense of a no-treatment control group (Stiles and MacDonald, 1992). A more sophisticated version is using a simple time series in which actual outcomes are compared to those projected based on past trends, the latter assuming no peacekeeping intervention (Bingham and Felbinger, 2002). In any case, the comparison with no action is fraught with problems. First, it assumes that the UN and other actors do not respond to the conflict with other conflict manage-ment strategies; in practice, this occurs regularly in the form of sanctions, national military intervention, mediation, and other actions. Second, the standard employed could also be too low in that peace operations automat-ically get labeled as successful for any improvement in the situation (Diehl and Druckman, 2010).

If one rejects the "better than nothing" standard, then there needs to be a proper choice of alternative policies. The range of conflict management alternatives is broad, and the individual approaches are not mutually ex-clusive to one another—or to peace operations (Greig, Owsiak, and Diehl, 2019; for some empirical connections, see Diehl, Owsiak, and Goertz, 2021). Which of those, or sets of those, are the appropriate comparison group? There are no clear guidelines on what that choice should be. Furthermore, counterfactuals do not represent the evaluation processes carried out by de-cision makers. Once a peace operation is authorized, alternative policies (the counterfactual standard) becomes much less important, as decision makers cannot go back to square one. Rather, decision makers are more concerned with how well the peace operation is doing according to improving the status quo and meeting goals, rather than retrospectively assessing the operation against "what might have been."

Even if one defines appropriate alternative policies, there still remains the challenge of estimating the impact of those alternatives had they been selected. This is highly speculative. It is extremely difficult to measure, or make a projection based on, a negative—something that did not happen (Menkhaus, 2003). As some peace operations last over a decade and success in our analyses is also assessed in the long term, judging counterfactual alternatives over the course of the operation and beyond lacks validity (Lebow, 2000). In addition, comparisons between peace operations and their alternatives assume that other key factors (e.g., behavior of other actors, environmental context) remain unchanged under the comparison group condition (Fearon, 1991; Lebow, 2000). This is an untestable assumption.

A second counterfactual strategy is to find comparable cases (to the peace operations) in which no peace operation was present (Fearon, 1991). In some quantitative studies, scholars pursue a "matching" strategy (Stuart, 2010) in which cases share similar characteristics except for the key variable(s) of interest. This is referred to earlier as Most Similar Systems Design (MSSD) or a focused comparison. This is not an option for us with case studies, given that it is very difficult to find matched conflicts with the same characteristics that prompted peacekeeping and other alternatives—and we would need to find such matches for each of our five cases, a challenging task.

Perhaps more important, and specific to peace operations, there are few, if any, "no peace operation" cases in which the missions would be the same or similar. The creation of some missions is inherently tied to the deployment of a peace operation. DDR, Rule of Law, and other missions come from a peacebuilding strategy and are not necessarily present in the absence of any peace operations or related to alternatives such as sanctions or adjudication. In addition, many of the success indicators are peacekeeping-specific, and it is not clear whether or how one could devise comparable measures for alternative strategies even if the missions existed in the absence of peace operations. Perhaps primarily with respect to missions and indicators that involved the mitigation of violence (e.g., cease-fire monitoring, protection of civilians) are there possible and valid comparisons.

Despite these considerations, there are instances in which we are able to use certain counterfactuals as a supplement to our core analysis based on the status quo standard. These typically involve comparisons between success and failure *within* a given peace operation mission, rather than between the peace operation and an alternative. We do so judiciously, often with reference to assessments made by secondary sources and analysts that explicitly reference what would have occurred. For example, observers note that the Humanitarian Assistance mission of UNPROFOR might have been more effective had the DDR and Traditional Peacekeeping missions been more successful in Bosnia. This use of counterfactuals can benefit after-action reviews, particularly the discussion of lessons learned from the experience. Discussions of what could have been done better are helped by speculative insights on other ways to tackle certain challenges that were presented. Such an exercise contributes to better performance in future peace operations.

Time Frames

Whatever baselines are adopted, there are several other considerations for making assessments. One is the time frame for evaluation, broadly classified into short- versus long-term evaluations (Diehl and Druckman, 2010). Peace operations and their missions are a mixture of immediate and extended goals. For example, disarmament and demobilization are designed to be achieved in the short term and often with fixed deadlines. Similarly, election supervision is carried out in a concentrated time period, concluding when voting is completed. In contrast, peacebuilding missions are carried out over an extended time frame and tend to have longer-term, if not permanent, effects.

Recognizing the difference in time frames across missions, we adopt varying short- and long-term perspectives on outcomes. We also acknowledge two caveats in doing so. First, short-term successes can be misleading if they are not sustained; for example, disarmament of militias can be followed by rearmament some months later. Accordingly, we will be examining several time points during the operation for mission effectiveness, not relying on single, fixed points. Second, long-term assessments are appropriate for operations with many missions, but the lengthier the time frame from the mission onset or completion to the evaluation observation the greater the risk of intervening or confounding factors affecting the observed outcome. This therefore complicates the attempts to judge impacts of peace operation missions on one another. We recognize and discuss, as appropriate, these considerations as they occur in long-term evaluations.

Stakeholders

Our consideration of multiple missions also means that we consider several stakeholders (Diehl and Druckman, 2010) in our assessments and associated indicators. These include the international community (e.g., whether violence spreads across borders), the disputants (e.g., whether elections were free and fair), and the local population (e.g., whether humanitarian assistance was delivered effectively). The latter addresses some of the weaknesses with past peacekeeping planning and evaluations that ignore the impact on the local population (see Autesserre, 2021). Some missions have outcomes that affect various audiences, such as Reconciliation and Local Security.

We conclude this section by defining our scale of assessment and how we make assessments in a holistic fashion for missions.

Holistic Mission Evaluations

Most studies employ a single indictor to evaluate peace operations (e.g., battle deaths or conflict renewal) and then draw a conclusion about the success or failure of the entire peace operation. This is a myopic view in that there are multiple ways to assess a peace operation; Diehl and Druckman (2010) suggest 140 measures of progress that could be employed. Furthermore, success and failure can vary across different missions, and thus labeling the operation as successful or not is misleading. It obscures underlying processes and outcomes. Because our theoretical focus is on the interaction of missions, we must assess the outcomes of all of the individual missions in an operation in order to determine whether and how success or failure in one mission is associated with the outcomes of other missions.

In our case studies, therefore, we make assessments at the individual mission level rather than for the entire operation. This is necessary to test the expectations in Table 2.6, and reflective of the varied missions and associated tasks that contemporary peace operations perform. This involves indicators and evidence specific to each mission (de Coning and Brusset, 2018), a best practice when there are missions with varying goals and characteristics. We rely on multiple indicators and pieces of evidence in drawing holistic assessments at the mission level. This provides a more nuanced, and we believe valid, way of considering peacekeeping outcomes. In doing so, we avoid narrow and misleading conclusions drawn from a single, and possibly biased, indicator. Multiple indicators also allow us to detect component aspects of success and failure, and thereby tie these to particular aspects of mission interaction. As stated by a UN official, "the different layers of data come together like a mosaic and we see the interlinkages or correlations much better" (quoted in Forti, 2022:10).

Our holistic mission assessments use a Likert scale of outcomes with categories of Effective, Mostly Effective, Mixed, Mostly Ineffective, and Ineffective for each mission within each operation. These are based on the degree to which the mission achieves its specified goals as represented by different indicators and evidence designed to measure progress (goals and indicators/evidence are discussed below for each mission). Broadly, these categories are defined as follows:

Effective: Goals of the mission have been achieved and all or most indicators of outcomes are in the positive direction. Perfection is not required, and there might be some instances in which the operation falls somewhat short in certain achievements. At the same time, minimal progress is not sufficient to be classified in this category; the success must be substantial. Free and fair elections, accepted by all parties and with high levels of participation, would qualify as successful for the Election Supervision/Promotion of Democracy mission, provided there was also similar progress on democratization.

Mostly Effective: Missions in this category follow one of two patterns. One occurs when, across the board, the mission fulfills its goals in part and evidence shows some progress (and some limitations), but not at the level found in the Effective category. A second pattern is strong progress in some indicators, but limited in others. This might be reflected in success in the disarmament and demobilization components of DDR, but limited effects on reintegration.

Mixed: This category is indicative of missions that have clear achievement of some goals, but failures in others. For example, success in constructing a new constitution might be offset by failures in the state's judicial independence and the prison system, all part of the Rule of Law mission.

Mostly Ineffective: Mirroring the Mostly Effective category, such missions might show very limited progress in goal achievement across the board or a few positive outcomes in the face of failure otherwise. For example, successfully delivering humanitarian assistance to (or protecting human rights in) one area of the country but largely failing in others would qualify.

Ineffective: This category shows systematic failure in goal achievement as reflected in all or most indicators. This does not indicate complete lack of improvement, but minimal progress is not enough to move it into the next category. Continued violence with high casualty levels would be indicative of ineffectiveness in the Traditional Peacekeeping mission. Ineffectiveness occurs when conditions deteriorate, but also when they do not improve starting from an undesirable status quo.

Our schematic is similar to the categorizations used in an UN-facilitated study (de Coning and Brusset, 2018) using four outcome categories: "negligible influence," "marginal influence," "average influence," and "strong influence," respectively. Indeed, the UN's own Comprehensive Planning and Performance System Assessment System (CPAS) uses a comparable scale (Forti, 2022): "strong progress," "some progress," "no progress," and "deterioration," respectively, reflecting the status quo baseline adopted in that system and in this study.

We now move from our assessment baselines and strategies to determining specific mission outcomes in the context of our five case studies. The following section provides an overview of the kinds of sources and evidence used to make our assessments. Thereafter, we discuss in detail the evaluation framework for each mission, including key questions about the goals sought and the multiple indicators used to make judgments about success and failure.

Evidentiary Sources and Indicators

Sources

In order to assess the interplay among missions, we first need to make judgments about their outcomes.[3] What kinds of information are needed to make these assessments? In our book on peace operation evaluation (Diehl and Druckman, 2010), we provided an approach to this task. Using a taxonomy of different missions similar to that in Chapter 2, we offered a series of evaluation questions for each mission. This was followed by listing measures of progress, which could be used as quantitative or qualitative indicators, and other evidence of success or failure for each mission. The former might be drawn from existing data collections (e.g., civilian casualties in assessing Human Rights) or could be the result of data collections specific to the peace operation (e.g., surveys of the local population on perceptions of security). These represent data and facts about the conflict context, the host country, and the peacekeeping operation; they are then applied to the evaluation

---

[3] By focusing on the missions from mandates and practice, we do not examine so-called unintended consequences from peace operations, such as incidences of sexual exploitation by peacekeepers or economic distortions (Aoi, de Coning, and Thakur, 2007; Karim and Beardsley, 2017). These are understudied and worthy of examination but beyond the scope of our study.

criteria so that we can make assessments. Other indicators are qualitative, such as the opinions of relevant agencies that deliver humanitarian aid. These can offer specific assessments of peacekeeping effectiveness via expert opinion. They can also provide information and other evidence, albeit not in the same way or with the same precision as quantitative indicators. A discussion of the advantages and disadvantages of sources and associated measures is given in Diehl and Druckman (2010). A continuing theme is that we rely on multiple indicators and pieces of evidence in making our holistic judgments. This makes our assessments less sensitive to the single measures of success and failure that characterize many past peacekeeping studies. It is also reflective of the multiple and somewhat varied goals and desired outcomes embedded in some missions (e.g., the three facets of DDR).

We utilize a wide range of different sources for information about the peace operation missions and their outcomes. This is consistent with the adoption of multiple measures of progress. It also shields us, to some degree, from bias and possible mistakes in assessment stemming from overreliance on only a few indicators from one source.

Most obviously, our evaluation approach draws on previous peacekeeping studies, some of which are specific to a given operation (e.g., ONUC) and others that are more general. Nevertheless, fewer studies have directly addressed some newer missions, although that gap has narrowed somewhat in the last decade. In the concluding chapter of Diehl and Druckman (2010), we considered the Bosnian case, but only in a limited fashion. That chapter includes information and assessments on the UNPROFOR missions. In addition, a special issue of the *Journal of International Peacekeeping* (Druckman and Diehl, 2012) attempted to apply our evaluation template to a series of case studies. Directly relevant here is the article by Braithwaite (2012) on East Timor operations, including UNTAET.

There are also other secondary studies that cover some or all the missions undertaken by individual peace operations. These come in the form of scholarly books, books authored by peacekeeping personnel, journal articles, and book chapters. They provide specific information about an operation and its missions, and in many cases draw conclusions about mission success or failure. We eschew what might be termed "opinion pieces" in favor of analyses by scholars and other experts who have conducted systematic empirical, including field, research. Such assessments can be cross-referenced and integrated with other information. Of further utility are data-based studies about individual missions (e.g., Rule of Law) that provide summary judgments of success for that mission.

Beyond existing studies of peace operations, UN documents and reports for each of the five operations examined provide various details on success or failure in certain missions. These come in the form of UN periodic reports on specific operations, reports to the Security Council, reports by the Secretary-General, reports from UN agencies concerning the peace operation (e.g., United Nations High Commissioner for Refugees [UNHCR]), and Security Council resolutions, among others. Nevertheless, these can be biased in terms of the judgments of success, pointing fingers at various exogenous factors rather than UN operational performance or issues of compatibility for explaining negative results. Yet, one can infer problems from those narratives when UN reports and recommendations involve the need for more troops or shifts in strategy in response to local conditions.

Other organizations also provide information, data, and assessments concerning different peace missions. These include international governmental organizations such as the World Bank and nongovernmental organizations (NGOs) in specialized areas that correspond to particular missions such as Human Rights (e.g., Human Rights Watch) or Election Supervision/ Promotion of Democracy (e.g., the Carter Center). National government institutions—such as the US Agency for International Development (USAID)—provide detailed information and analysis, especially if they were aiding peacebuilding missions. Private foundations also have an interest in peacebuilding outcomes, especially those efforts that have received their support. These can be the source of evidence (e.g., public opinion surveys from the Asia Foundation) that might be unavailable from other sources. Finally, think tank (e.g., RAND) studies on peace operations are akin to some scholarly studies with respect to relying on systematic evidence, but do so with a greater focus on policy application and evaluation.

In making judgments about success and failure, we also rely on data sets that were designed for other purposes (Diehl, 2017) but provide information about outcomes that can be matched with peace operations. For example, data sets on renewal of violence or civilian casualties in a given year in a given country help with assessments on whether the peacekeepers were successful in Traditional Peacekeeping, especially in making "before-after" deployment comparisons. Another example is that progress in the Rule of Law can be measured by data sets that code judicial independence over time.

The specific sources for individual peace operations are given in the case study chapters that follow. These will vary somewhat depending on the peace operation under scrutiny, the particular missions studied, and the availability of information. For example, there is less information on the ONUC operation (begun more than six decades ago) as compared to more recent peace operations; peacekeeping studies, reports by NGOs, and general international attention are much greater since the turn of the twenty-first century than prior to that. As will be evident below, some missions are more difficult to evaluate and information harder to come by than others. Regardless, we rely on multiple indicators of success for each mission evaluated and reach holistic judgments while being transparent on the indicators and other evidence that led us to those conclusions. Beside the improved validity that flows from multiple indicators and assessments, they also reduce limitations and biases imposed by the availability and accuracy of individual sources. This approach gives us confidence in our conclusions even if not conferring the status of causal inferences on them.

Assessment Questions and Evidence

Below we discuss the various assessment questions and measures of progress used in our case studies, following the lead of Diehl and Druckman (2010). This is consistent with the process used by CPAS (Forti, 2022) in specifying objectives and then measuring outputs. The evidence comes from a considerable variety of sources of differential quality. By casting a wide net on the available information, we attempt to provide an expansive picture of the effectiveness of each of the case-relevant missions. For example, the availability of opinion surveys on perceptions augments observational data on events. We conclude the section with a summary of the quality of the different types of information that we used for our holistic evaluations.

Traditional Peacekeeping
Traditional peacekeeping involves monitoring cease-fires where they exist and generally facilitating the end or limitation of violence. This is the mission most identified with UN operations and the one that is the subject of most peacekeeping research. The key general questions are (1) Is violence still present?, and if so (2) Have violence levels decreased? The reference points are the immediate status quo pre- and then post-peacekeeping deployment

as well as over time during the operation. There is also concern for the ability of the peace operation to limit the spread of armed conflict and thus additional evaluation questions are (1) Has the conflict expanded geographically? and (2) Does the conflict include more or fewer actors?

In terms of violence abatement, we consider various pieces of evidence. At the most basic level, we look at the frequency of violent conflict. A high threshold is the top of the severity scale for civil wars, using the Correlates of War (COW) and other data sets on interstate and intrastate wars; the COW threshold of 1,000 or more battle deaths represents severe violence (Sarkees and Wayman, 2010; Dixon and Sarkees, 2015). In assessing Traditional Peacekeeping success, we look to whether such high levels (wars) are renewed during peacekeeping deployment, how long war persists, or when it is terminated should peace operations arrive during active conflict. Reports of cease-fire violations and their scope and severity also suggest problems with the Traditional Peacekeeping mission.

Standard measures of violence are also used, and these are in the form of deaths and casualties of combatants, civilians, and peacekeeping soldiers (e.g., Henke, 2019), especially those that are deemed malicious among the latter group. These can be on a monthly or yearly basis. For example, *The Bosnian Book of the Dead* (Tokača, 2012) chronicles the deaths of almost 96,000 individuals who lost their lives in the Bosnian wars of the 1990s. When available, we also consider the days of active fighting that occur under the watch of a peace operation.

Geographic considerations are also relevant in the assessment. The location of any violent incidents vis-à-vis the peacekeeping force and whether violence is confined to certain areas or regions can signal success or failure. Border violations and the flow of arms across those borders signify problems with this mission. Other pieces of evidence used in our case studies include the number of peacekeeping personnel in relation to geographic and situational demands as well as specific incidents such as the kidnapping of peacekeeping soldiers. For example, the Armed Conflict Location and Event Data Project (ACLED) includes data on "Disorder Involving Peacekeepers," tracking on the political violence and events involving actors directly interacting with peace operations.[4]

Traditional Peacekeeping also includes conflict containment, limiting the spread of any violence to new areas or new actors. Thus, we look for where

[4] ACLED, https://acleddata.com/curated-data-files/#civilian (last accessed November 5, 2022).

any fighting is occurring and whether there is intervention by neighboring states or internal actors, often evident from UN and media reports. The interventions of neighboring states into the Congo wars of the 1990s and beyond would be instances of failures to contain conflict.

Overall, analyzing peace operation outcomes that deal with violence mitigation benefits from a host of available data sets and straightforward indicators. Collectively, they present a set of different kinds of conflict indicators that can offer nuanced assessments of peace operation effectiveness across a range of stakeholders.

Disarmament, Demobilization, and Reintegration (DDR)
Disarmament, Demobilization, and Reintegration (DDR) are, in practice, three interrelated processes even as they are treated as one mission here and in UN classifications. Conceivably, it is possible to have success on one aspect and not the others. Thus, although we make a holistic assessment, we pay attention to the individual components in our analysis. The key assessment questions are (1) Have the combatants disarmed?; (2) Have troops withdrawn from designated zones?; (3) Have the troops demobilized?; and (4) Have ex-combatants been reintegrated into society?

We start with the numbers of weapons collected, troops demobilized, and soldiers reintegrated. These are most useful when there are data or information available about the absolute numbers of weapons, troops, and soldiers, and thus one could determine a success percentage for each. Unfortunately, however, the original baselines required are generally not available, and estimations are especially problematic in post–civil war contexts. The problems are magnified in conflicts that had multiple and more loosely organized groups fighting in civil wars such as Sudan (see Walter and Phillips, 2019).

Without status quo baselines or even precise accounting of weapons surrendered or troops demobilized, analysts are forced to make assessments using indirect methods and sources. Most available are UN field reports and those from other organizations that provide some evidence of effectiveness. For example, if one considers no-fly zones as a form of DDR—albeit during war, rather than following it—UN reports detail hundreds of violations during one month in Bosnia and several thousand in an eighteen-month period. Landmine removal also can indicate a different kind of disarmament in conflicts in which those devices are common.

Troop withdrawal and demobilization of weapons in given geographic areas, rather than in a comprehensive fashion, are easier to detect. For example, the removal of Serbian forces in a 20 kilometer zone around Sarajevo was evident in UN reports, as was a heavy weapons exclusions zone around Gorazde, although not around Sarajevo. The persistence of viable fighting forces outside of UN or government control is direct evidence of some failure in the DDR mission, a concern of the UNTAET operation in East Timor with respect to remaining militia groups loyal to Indonesia. The shift of some former soldiers from the civil war in Sierra Leone to working as mercenaries in the diamond-rich areas of that country is another example of DDR problems.

Other pieces of evidence used to document DDR success or failure are the withdrawal (or not) of foreign forces and the creation of weapons exclusion zones and demobilization camps. The latter two need to exist as signs of progress, but how effective they are might be more important and are sometimes noted in reports and analyses.

Reintegration indicators focus on different elements of the process. Clearly, data on the number of former combatants who join the national military are relevant. Yet the existence and extent of participation in training programs for ex-combatants and civilian employment are also important aspects of reintegration outcomes. Payments to ex-soldiers are part of such programs as well. Furthermore, the amounts distributed and the number of people receiving them in a timely fashion can also be used as supplemental indicators in our holistic assessment.

Traditional Peacekeeping and DDR are security-oriented missions that usually appear for the first time at the onset of peace operations, and in the case of the former often continue for the duration of the operation in some form. In these missions, peacekeepers assume primary and, in some instances, exclusive responsibility for achieving the goals, as opposed to working with NGOs and international organizations. Nevertheless, success depends on the cooperation of the disputants and third-party states; thus, success and failure do not necessarily result from peacekeeper actions alone. The next set of missions discussed are those that can occur at different points of an operation and might have fixed time periods depending upon conditions on the ground.

Humanitarian Assistance

Humanitarian assistance involves taking into account some short-term considerations tied to security; for example, one evaluation question is "Was aid distribution protected?" That reflects one role that peacekeepers have in this mission. More broadly and less directly, peace operations are also supposed to facilitate an improvement in the lives of those who are recipients of humanitarian assistance. This is done by facilitating the delivery of assistance, the first step. Thus, in both the short and long term, we can query: (1) Was human suffering reduced?; and (2) Has the quality of life improved? This is part of what is referred to in scholarly studies and popular discourse as "positive peace" (Galtung, 2011).

Assessing the efforts at humanitarian assistance requires information on both the short- and long-term situations. More immediate concerns involve the amount of aid delivered, a quantitative indicator, and the opinions of key aid agencies, a qualitative assessment. For example, NGOs can provide specific data (e.g., reported in Young, 2001) on a variety of aid indicators; these include tonnage of supplies delivered, funds spent on medical care, and civilians in distress visited. There might also be claims that no one died from hunger or cold during the operations. Some of these data are for the period during the war (e.g., at the time of UNPROFOR deployment) and others after a peace agreement.

Nevertheless, there are at least two problems with relying on these data alone. First, the numbers might not necessarily reflect the full scale of aid delivered. For example, the Bosnia operation involved 250 organizations with UNHCR identity cards, and a full accounting of aid delivered and activities from all these agencies is unavailable. In addition, as was the case with UNAMSIL, some humanitarian aid was provided directly by other states. Thus, when available, we look beyond these data to consider other indicators or information. These include how much of the aid was lost during the deliveries and relatedly what portion was lost from corruption or diverted to the combatants and away from civilian populations.

Second, aid delivery data are not accompanied by baseline information of the demand side of the equation. Without that information, it is difficult to assess whether even large amounts of aid were enough to meet the needs of the local population. This can be mitigated partially by reference to other pieces of data—the number of beneficiaries who receive the aid and the geographic spread of the aid distribution. Aid to specific areas or during specific time periods might be limited; for example, a report to the UN Security Council indicated that aid to Bosnia in December 1993 was only at 10 percent of its regular levels (Young, 2001). Still, there is no panacea to the limited information on need.

Ideally, longer-term impacts could be discerned by reference to various indicators on health, although some data are time-limited. Broadly, the services to and resettlement of refugees and internally displaced persons indicate humanitarian success to two target populations. Varying across cases, we consider several health data and measures, including the availability of health care facilities, schools, and emergency shelters. There are also specific health indicators related to the longer-term impacts of humanitarian assistance, such as life expectancy, frequency of diseases, infant mortality, and infant immunizations. Aggregate indices, such as the Human Development Index, provide us with an overall picture of the human condition across several dimensions.

For longer-term assessments, and depending on the case at hand, indicators can be compared across several periods: prior to the war, during the war, during the peace operation deployment, and during the years following peace operation withdrawal. Our concerns with prewar indicators—the status quo ante standard—was discussed earlier, and thus we lean more heavily on the three other time period observations. We exercise caution in interpreting data too far removed from the peace operation because intervening factors can complicate inferences about the influences on humanitarian assistance during the time of the peace operation. Thus, our strategy of using multiple sources of information and indicators to produce a holistic assessment obviates some of the problems that go with single indicator outcomes. Humanitarian assistance is usually supplied by other agencies, and thus there are limits to what peacekeepers can do beyond facilitating the delivery, directly or indirectly, as well as limits to assessments about the impact of other missions on such aid outcomes.

Election Supervision/Promotion of Democracy
Supervising elections tends to occur relatively early in a peace operation deployment, whereas broader democratization activities go beyond the first elections and can continue for an extended period. The key evaluation question for election supervision concerns whether the election was "free and fair." Quantitative indicators of voter registration and turnout signal the degree to which participation was high; regional, ethnic, and gender breakdowns of participation are useful in considering whether the election was representative of the population as a whole. The baseline for these is the number of eligible voters overall and along these dimensions.

We also consider the peace operation activities surrounding the election, and these include any voter education initiatives and the kind of election day assistance provided by peacekeepers. Ultimately, whether the election can be considered free and fair comes from the absence or limitation of violence and voter intimidation leading up to and including election day. The certification of the election as free and fair by external actors, such as the Carter Center and regional organizations, provides an independent assessment. Still, acceptance or at least acquiescence, indicated by the actions or statements of local groups, opposition parties, and/or segments of the population, is also important in determining election supervision outcomes. For our analyses of operations in Sierra Leone and the Congo, for example, such information is readily available.

The democratization aspects of the mission extend beyond the single event of a given election. Thus, broad political participation by group and geographic location is still a concern. Yet the occurrence and certification of subsequent elections is important for success, even as peacekeepers might not be involved in supervising those later elections. Additional key questions are (1) Is the democratic process stable and regularized over the long term?; and (2) To what degree have democratic attitudes and norms become ingrained in society? There are a number of hallmarks of democratic governance that we consider in the context of the country hosting the peace operation: for example, competitive elections, multiple political parties, and checks and balances across government structures, especially in limiting executive authority (these intersect with indicators for the Rule of Law mission). In aggregate form, these are reflected in summary democracy indices from Polity[5] and Varieties of Democracy (V-Dem) databases.[6]

Human Rights

The protection of civilians is an increasing salient part of UN peace operations, especially in the aftermath of the failure of UN troops to achieve this at Srebrenica during the Bosnian civil war. Prominent peacekeeping studies (e.g., Hultman et al., 2020) have concentrated on how well and under what conditions UN operations achieve this goal. The evaluation questions for

---

[5] Polity Project, https://www.systemicpeace.org/polityproject.html (last accessed October 7, 2022).

[6] V-Dem, https://www.v-dem.net/vdemds.html (last accessed October 7, 2022).

the Human Rights mission begin with a particularly low bar of achieve-ment given the infrequency of the event: Was genocide avoided? More dif-ficult standards to meet are reflected in a series of other concerns: (1) Have human rights abuses been reduced?; (2) Were designated areas protected?; and (3) Were threatened populations such as civilians, women, and refugees protected?

The most obvious indicator of mission success or failure is the number of civilian casualties following peace operation deployment; a before/after de-ployment comparison (see, e.g., the UNAMSIL case) is used when possible to account for trends, especially when abuses were widespread and nu-merous prior to the arrival of the peacekeepers. Yet mass atrocities are not the only kinds of human rights abuses that peace operations are designed to prevent. Thus, there is consideration for the frequency of other abuses including rapes and sexual abuse (including those perpetrated by the peacekeepers), forced dislocations, burning of houses, abductions, forced labor, and other violent actions. Data and other information on such abuses come from a variety of sources. Varying degrees of success are reflected by the degree to which such violations are reduced from pre-deployment levels.

General assessments and information from NGOs, such as Amnesty International, detail specific violations and/or provide an overview of the human rights situation before, during, and after the peace operation deploy-ment. Other actions of the peace operation also factor into the mission eval-uation. These include establishing safe areas and the assistance given by the peacekeepers to international organizations and NGOs engaged in human rights protection. The ability to control the actions of disputants might be limited, but peacekeepers are nevertheless assigned responsibility for doing so.

Security Sector Reform (SSR)

The Security Sector Reform mission has become more prominent in peace operations as peacekeeping agents have begun to emphasize it over other missions and goals. There are short-term and long-term orientations. In the short term, peacekeepers might take a direct role in maintaining law and order. The emphasis is not on the renewal of warfare with respect to combatants, as is the case with Traditional Peacekeeping; rather, it is on lower-level violence, crime, and disorder caused by local gangs and individuals. For the long term, the goal is to develop indigenous capacity to perform the same functions. Thus, peace operations are often involved in training and some-times establishing local police and security forces.

The evaluation questions reflect both temporal orientations: (1) Is there a continuing pattern of violent crime in the post-deployment period?; (2) Is there freedom of movement for the local citizenry?; (3) Do citizens perceive that it is safe to move freely?; and (4) Are local and national police as well as military forces capable of providing local security? The four questions focus on a repeating status quo baseline over the course of the operation. Local security data and information are not generally available during wartime, and in any case would likely indicate more crime and less security than non-wartime periods, with or without peacekeepers.

For local security in the short term, one can look at the number and types of crimes as well as other activity that suggested the breakdown of law and order. The size of operation forces, especially civilian police units (CIVPOL) vis-à-vis geographic and other requirements, also gave signals on whether sufficient capacity was present. For example, CIVPOL units were an important part of UNTAET. Whether certain areas were secured by peacekeepers was also relevant. Reports dealing with whether citizens can carry out such everyday activities as free movement to markets and public opinion surveys about safety perceptions are useful in determining whether the peace operation was able to ensure security for local stakeholders.

Longer-term factors in evaluation centered on whether local infrastructures were developed to handle security matters. Thus, information on the creation, reform, training programs, and personnel recruitment of police agencies was indicative of success, or was useful in identifying problems (these were key elements of the UNAMSIL operation). This went beyond numbers in some cases to include whether those numbers were adequate given the size of the deployment areas and perceived needs. The reported quality of such forces also was considered in assessing outcomes. The existence of security forces itself is a prerequisite for success in SSR, but we also considered: (1) whether such forces had sufficient authority; (2) whether they were free of political bias; and (3) whether alternative and competing security structures, such as militias, existed. Finally, we looked at when and whether security functions were able to be transferred fully from the peace operation to local institutions. Peace operation efforts cannot impose local security over the long run, however, and host country conditions and involvement will also play a role in influencing outcomes.

Rule of Law

Establishing the rule of law in a post-conflict society is a multidimensional set of tasks, especially given that war-torn societies and failed states have had legal institutions displaced or destroyed, if they even functioned effectively prior to the fighting. Thus, a status quo ante standard is probably an unreasonable one. The evaluation questions address a range of considerations: (1) Does a legal framework exist?; (2) Does judicial coverage extend to all areas?; (3) Does the judicial system function fairly, efficiently, and securely?; and (4) Do functioning prison and rehabilitation systems exist? The first and fourth questions are designed to examine the institutional mechanisms for the promotion of the rule of law; these are the de jure requirements for rule of law. Nevertheless, what exists on paper and in reality might differ, and accordingly the second and third queries deal with the de facto elements of the rule of law.

To ascertain the presence and quality of legal frameworks, we first consider whether there is a national constitution, accepted by all relevant parties. For example, constitutional development was a key part of the peace process in both East Timor and the Congo. Other elements considered include the infrastructure needed for rule of law to function—the existence of courts and prisons are two examples. Evidence of problems in some cases revealed more mundane elements such as the lack of computers.

Rule of Law requires detailed laws on which to operate and the willingness of citizens to use legal structures and processes. Accordingly, our evaluation looks at evidence of well-developed legal codes and whether the population is willing to rely on the extant legal institutions and rules, as opposed to alternative processes such as tribal authorities and local customs. Public opinion surveys also signal the extent to which the population is aware and approves of the legal system. Detailed information is sometimes available, as in the case of surveys by the Asia Foundation in East Timor. Summary indicators from democracy data sets (e.g., V-Dem) also reference individual equality before the law.

A significant portion of any rule-of-law evaluation focuses on the judicial system. At a basic level, there must be evidence that courts and legal proceedings exist, tempered by their geographic spread. Evidence of success and shortcomings also comes from the number of judges, prosecutors, and lawyers available to work within the system. How the system operates in terms of efficiency (e.g., speed, accessibility in terms of cost, location, and language) and fairness (e.g., corruption, rules of evidence) is part of coded outcomes. In addition, we look at a measure on "judicial independence" to assess whether the judicial system functions so that it is not politicized and provides a check on the power of the executive or legislature, a hallmark of the rule of law and reflective of de facto practice.

Another key component of the rule of law is the prison system. Reports on prison conditions (e.g., overcrowding, human treatment) indicate how well prisons are run. In at least one instance, surveys of prisoners about those conditions are available and used as another piece of evidence in the evaluation.

Collectively, the Rule of Law mission incorporates many dimensions, and aggregate indicators from organizations such as the World Bank attempt to summarize these. Overall, our holistic judgment relies on a host of different indicators and information depending on the context and availability of evidence for individual cases. Again, the environmental context will offer opportunities and impose limitations on peace operation efforts in this mission.

Local Governance

Another peacebuilding mission involves facilitation in building the structures and provision of services at the local and regional level in post-conflict societies. Most broadly are evaluation concerns that deal with the (re)establishment of government authority: (1) Has local governance been established or restored?; and relatedly (2) Is the governance fully sovereign, having control over all areas and services? The former deals with whether the multiple levels of government provide the variety of food, shelter, health, and other public services that are core to government authority. The latter considers whether it is the official government itself that is the entity in full control of service provision or whether other actors play important roles—foreign powers, militias, alternative government structures (e.g., quasi-states such as Northern Somaliland or local chieftains), and NGOs.

Indicators and sources on governance are heavily dependent on availability in the particular country context as well as the years covered. The presence of local elections or existence of local elected officials, as indicated in various reports, is prima facie evidence that structures are in place. The mere presence of institutions, however, is not enough. Other indicators of success include the number or percentages of administrative posts that have been filled, as local governance cannot function effectively if there is an insufficient number of people present to carry out duties. Beyond sheer numbers, external assessments of the quality of candidates that filled those positions is relevant. World Bank measures of the quality of administration in general provide a macro view of government functioning. The Fragile States Index (FSI),[7] as in the case of MONUC, can be used to detect serious problems with governance and vulnerability to collapse; we particularly focus on the political indicator related to public services.

Tangible evidence on the delivery of government services also helps in assessing governance, as ultimately service delivery to the population is the end goal. Delivery of services success is also conditioned on whether the government reach extends to all areas of the country and by the resources available to carry these out.

As with SSR, success in this mission also includes transferring some functions from the peace operation to local authorities. Thus, as appropriate, our evaluation also looked at the involvement of local authorities in service provision and the timing of authority transfer to them. Peace operations play a role in developing local governance, as do other international actors, but failures might still occur from problems with indigenous contributions and political infighting.

Reconciliation

Finally, we look at one of the long-term missions of peace operation, changing the attitudes and relationships that were a legacy of the conflict such that future armed conflicts are less likely. The applicability of the evaluation framework varies somewhat depending on the circumstances of the conflict in question and the components of any peace agreement. Nevertheless, we generally consider: (1) Have past crimes been addressed?; (2) Do institutions and culture promote conflict resolution?; and (3) Have relations between conflicting parties changed after peace operation deployment and the mission begins? Generally, peace operations start from ground zero on these elements, as the societies and the peace operation have focused on other aspects of peacebuilding first before attempting reconciliation.

Because past conflicts often involved human rights abuses, there is concern about whether those crimes have been acknowledged and that society has dealt with them. There are two general mechanisms under which these occur. First is prosecuting perpetrators through the justice system. Of course,

---

[7] Fragile States Index, https://fragilestatesindex.org/indicators/p2/ (last accessed October 7, 2022).

this might presume the establishment of the rule of law, but the existence of special rules and institutions might be needed for this. Thus, we look for legislation and legal authority for the states involved; peace operations might facilitate this and work with the government, but peacekeepers cannot compel the host state to create processes and institutions for reconciliation. Peacekeepers might be part of the process of documenting such crimes, as was the case in East Timor. The numbers of investigations, trials/prosecutions, and the like provide evidence for the scope of these activities and the prospects for success. Concern is also with whether political leaders accused of atrocities are subject to justice, in addition to lower-level perpetrators.

A second element focuses on promoting healing. The creation of truth and reconciliation commissions (TRCs) that investigate past crimes and provide transparency on what was done and by whom is a first step; such institutions existed in the Congo, Sierra Leone, and East Timor. For effectiveness of these commissions, however, we look beyond their creation. Key evidence for evaluation includes whether hearings are actually held, their number, the number of statements made before the bodies, including the portion that come from perpetrators as opposed to victims, and other outcomes. Indicative of that final category is whether any recommendations from the process are implemented in the future. Public opinion surveys also provide input into the success or failure of TRCs. These are long-term or legacy indicators of the peace operation's effects on reconciliation rather than short-term or direct effects.

Table 3A.1 provides a brief overview of the different missions and examples of the indicators and assessment sources. We also offer summary judgments about the level of confidence we have in making our assessments of particular mission outcomes. The large number and variety of indicators, their match to mission goals, and the variety of sources lead us to have the greatest confidence (rated as "excellent") in the outcome assessments for three of the missions: Traditional Peacekeeping, Election Supervision/Promotion of Democracy, and Human Rights, respectively. For the other missions, our level of confidence is more tempered but still "good," and again the use of multiple indicators and consideration of different dimensions helps mitigate concerns with arbitrary or narrow assessments.

Conclusion

In this chapter, we outlined a research design for assessing how well our expectations from Chapter 2 match the actual dynamics of UN peacekeeping operations over their histories. An attempt is made to develop a methodological approach that guides the analyses of complex cases of peace operations. That approach consists of performing enhanced case studies with cases selected on key dimensions of variation in the tradition of the Most Different Systems Design (see Faure, 1994). Five peace operations were chosen to examine the expectations. Standards of evidence for this investigation, including sources and indicators, are also elucidated. In the next three chapters, we proceed with the case studies, starting with two peace operations that have the fewest number of missions in our data set—ONUC and UNPROFOR, respectively.

Table 3A.1 Overview of mission indicators, sources of information, and levels of confidence

Missions	Examples of indicators/evidence	Examples of sources	Overall confidence for mission outcomes
Traditional Peacekeeping	Frequency of violence, casualties	Correlates of War data; Henke, 2017	Excellent
DDR	Troop withdrawal and demobilization of weapons in given geographic areas	UN reports	Good
Humanitarian Assistance	Amount of aid delivered, the opinions of key aid agencies, health data	NGO reports; UN Human Development Index	Good
Election Supervision/Promotion of Democracy	Changes in democracy scores	Polity, V-Dem datasets	Excellent
Human Rights	The number of civilian casualties following peace operation deployment	Hultman et al., 2020; NGO reports	Excellent
SSR	Training programs and personnel recruitment of police agencies	UN reports, Secondary Assessments	Good
Rule of Law	Levels of judicial independence	Linzer and Staton, 2015 data	Good
Local Governance	Ability of local government to deliver services; corruption reports, GDP growth	UN Human Development Index; World Bank corruption data	Good
Reconciliation	Truth and Reconciliation Commission efforts, local mediation efforts	NGO and TRC reports; Hellmüller, 2018	Good

4

Limited Mission Cases

ONUC and UNPROFOR

Introduction

To begin our case studies, we focus on two of the five cases that were less complex in terms of the number of missions: United Nations Operation in the Congo (ONUC) and United Nations Protection Force (UNPROFOR) in Bosnia, respectively. There are several reasons for choosing these two cases for initial examination. First, they are two of the older UN peace operations, ONUC dating to the early 1960s and UNPROFOR being one of the first post–Cold War operations, formed in 1992. Examining these two cases in tandem allows us to consider whether problems with multiple missions are primarily in the domain of peacebuilding operations in the late 1990s and beyond, or whether the difficulties have been present over the life of UN peace operations.

Second, the limited number of missions in each operation (three in ONUC[1] and four in UNPROFOR) provides a preliminary assessment on whether simply numbers of missions generate complications or whether it is more the incompatibility of those missions that is responsible. Fewer missions also means that analysts have an easier time in tracing the process and understanding the interactions among the different missions.

The case studies proceed in a similar fashion. Initially, we provide the historical and environmental contexts for the conflicts in which the peace operations are deployed. Such discussion includes both the conflict history and the immediate conditions that led to peacekeeping authorization; the former reveals some of the environmental context for the operation and the latter helps establish the status quo baseline for the peacekeeping deployment. We also summarize the different missions carried out by the operation under

---

[1] Recall that ONUC also carried out the pacification mission even as it was not part of the compatibility analysis in previous chapters.

When Peacekeeping Missions Collide. Paul F. Diehl, Daniel Druckman, and Grace B. Mueller, Oxford University Press.

analysis, going beyond simply naming those missions by providing additional details about their implementation. Following these overviews, we divide the sequential analysis of missions roughly according to when those missions were initiated following operation authorization. Our primary focus is on understanding the missions in terms of our theoretical expectations. Accordingly, we usually begin with the Security First missions—Traditional Peacekeeping and DDR. We then consider some other missions that build on these, such as Humanitarian Assistance. Longer-term peacebuilding missions are generally covered in a later section. We conclude our discussion of each mission with a summary assessment of success/failure and document those conclusions using the indicators and evidence presented in the previous chapter as applied to the cases and missions at hand.

United Nations Operation in the Congo (ONUC)

The United Nations Operation in the Congo (abbreviated ONUC for its French name, Opération des Nations Unies au Congo) has been called the first peacebuilding operation, but this is perhaps misleading in light of later definitions (Boutros-Ghali, 1995) and practice. Nevertheless, it was part of an evolution (Hatto, 2013) of UN operations away from traditional peacekeeping to other mandates and actions. It also was one of the few Cold War operations that addressed a conflict with a significant or primary internal conflict component, a characteristic that would become the norm several decades later.

Historical Context and Overview of ONUC

Unlike many civil conflicts and peace operations in later years, the Congo operation had its origins in a colonial transition even as the level of violence would be similar to other internationalized civil wars in Africa. The context, however, shared many similarities with later conflicts in that the country was split along ethnic lines and the administrative machinery of the state—at least the apparatus not developed by colonial authorities—was weak.

Following mounting unrest in the Congo and demands for immediate independence, the Belgian government announced in June 1960 that independence would be granted to the Congo (Boulden, 2015). According to the Treaty of Friendship, which was signed but not ratified by the Congo, it was envisaged that most of the Belgian administrators and technical personnel would continue in their roles after independence (Abi-Saab, 1978). Just days after the Republic of Congo became the Democratic Republic of the Congo (DRC), however, disorder broke out, as Congolese soldiers of the Force Publique (which was in the process of being transformed into the army of the new state: the Armée Nationale Congolaise [ANC]) grew frustrated that no substantial change had occurred in the army ranks (Klinger, 2005). This led to a series of military mutinies, the first taking place in Léopoldville (MacQueen, 2002), which rapidly turned into a general assault against Belgian and other European residents.

Disorder had reached the mineral-rich province of Katanga. To make matters worse, Moïse Tshombe, head of the provincial government of Katanga, who also had strong ties to Belgium, declared Katanga as independent, and the Tshombe administration in Elisabethville (now Lubumbashi) appealed to Belgium for immediate military intervention to restore order. Belgium agreed and sent military reinforcements to both the Kitona and Kamina areas in order to restore order and to protect its citizens and other foreign mercenaries. In short order, there were approximately 10,000 Belgian solders on the ground, a number in excess of that during colonial occupation (MacQueen, 2002). For the newly established Congo government, the Belgian framing of the intervention as humanitarian was insulting (Abi-Saab, 1978).

Under these conditions, the Congolese government, spearheaded by President Kasavubu and Prime Minister Lumumba, asked the UN for military assistance to protect the national territory of the Congo against external aggression from Belgium. In addition to citing the arrival of Belgian troops as a violation of the Treaty of Friendship, their cable to the UN Secretary-General also accused the Belgian government of "having carefully prepared the secession of the [sic] Katanga with a view to maintaining a hold on our country" (S/4382, July 13, 1960).

UN Security Council Resolution 143, adopted on July 14, 1960, established ONUC with an initial mandate to "take all necessary steps" to provide the Congolese government with "such military assistance as may be necessary" until the national security forces are able "to meet fully their tasks" (S/RES/143). The United Nations also tasked ONUC with ensuring that law and order was restored (S/RES/145), what would ultimately be consistent with the pacification mission described in Chapter 2 and an early component of the Security Sector Reform (SSR) mission. With respect to the latter, the expectation was that when order was restored national military and police forces could assume those duties. The force was initially conceived as being impartial, and therefore not favoring any side or group in the political struggles.

According to Dorn (2013), ONUC passed through three main phases: (1) the deployment to restore order (July 1960 to February 1961), per the original mandate; (2) the fight for Katanga (which began with the authorization of S/RES/161 on February 21, 1961); and (3) the endgame in the Congo, which followed the successful defeat of the Katangan secession in January 1963 and ended with the operation's withdrawal in June 1964. The latter two phases reflected changes on the ground and the different orientations of the UN Secretaries-General in the period. The resulting changes in mandates (S/4426, S/4741, and S/5002) and associated missions were very controversial among the UN membership given that the UN operation increasingly adopted a more offensive military posture.

Even though ONUC's original authorization came in response to requests made by President Kasavubu and Prime Minister Lumumba, ostensibly to deal with Belgian intervention and not internal order (Asku, 2003), the situation became profoundly complicated for ONUC at the beginning of September 1960 with the collapse of the central government (MacQueen, 2002). A rift between Kasavubu and Lumumba would ultimately culminate in a constitutional crisis. The situation in the DRC had seemingly been transformed from an *inter*state into an internationalized *intra*state crisis, with peacekeepers caught in the fray.

The UN, therefore, was drawn into the domestic political contestation among leaders representing four distinct power centers, two of which claimed leadership of central government (Kasavubu and Lumumba) and two of which led secessionist movements (Tshombe in Katanga and Kalonji in South Kasai) (Klinger, 2005). Prime Minister Lumumba envisioned ONUC forces as being aligned with him to retake the breakaway Katanga province. President Kasavubu opposed such actions and fired Lumumba, while Lumumba claimed that he did the same to Kasavubu. In the midst of this, the military took advantage of this internal power struggle and staged a coup d'état.

Adding to the complexity were the different approaches taken by two UN Secretaries-General: Dag Hammarskjöld, who believed that the UN should not interfere in Congolese internal politics (but ultimately lost his life on September 17, 1961, on his way to Rhodesia for cease-fire talks with Tshombe), and U Thant, who was far less restrained than his predecessor when it came to using force on these and other challenges for ONUC (see Doss, 2014).

Further confounding ONUC's ability to carry out its missions were the actions of foreign powers, with various states seizing on the crisis for different national interests (Dobbins et al., 2005). The Soviet Union supported the camp under Lumumba and was critical of the Hammarskjöld approach. The United States, United Kingdom, and France backed Kasavubu. The differing political alignments limited ONUC, but they did not prevent some changes in its mandate and missions as circumstances dictated.

ONUC was originally sent to the DRC for security purposes—to restore law and order (SSR)—but the rapidly changing situation on the ground meant that it would then be tasked with the additional responsibilities of DDR and violence abatement, which involved the quelling of civil disturbances that led to civil war. These became the most important missions (S/4741). Restoring law and order ahead of stopping violence and DDR is actually the reverse sequencing of many other UN operations, although it provides us with a window into understanding how important the security missions were to the success of others and vice versa (see Expectation 1, "Security First," and Expectation 5, "Recursive Effects," in Chapter 2); here it is the initial absence, not the failure, of the security missions that provide a critical test. This expansion to include additional missions allowed ONUC to intervene in the civil affairs of the Congo and in the middle of the secessionist conflict in Katanga. The new missions also permitted ONUC to use offensive military force, thereby contravening one of the pillars of the "holy trinity" (Williams and Bellamy, 2021) of peacekeeping practice in the Cold War era: minimum, and usually only defensive, use of military force. The net effect would also violate another of the three elements, namely, impartiality as ONUC was essentially siding with and supporting the central government authority against Katangan rebels.

In this second phase of the operation, ONUC was an active combatant and the object of attack from Katangan forces; these included denying access of certain areas to peacekeepers, firing on their positions, and other hostile acts (Rikhye, 1984). It was in this period that ONUC carried out its mandate and associated missions; most of our evaluation concentrates on this phase. A prospective agreement to end the fighting failed, and ONUC was compelled to secure control of the breakaway province by armed force.

In January 1963, Tshombe announced the end of Katanga's secession and his unconditional acceptance of Secretary-General U Thant's plan for re-unification. This included agreeing to ONUC's entry into the last areas of Katanga under Tshombe's control. Thus, the final phase of ONUC was a roughly eighteen-month period following the agreement in which ONUC monitored the situation and the national government reestablished its au-thority over the whole state. In the month following the peace agreement, the UN began a process of phasing out the peace operation and ONUC was able to withdraw its forces in June 1964. This was generally considered a pe-riod without much controversy (James, 1994), at least relative to the previous three years.

Because the local security element of SSR (the establishment and main-tenance of law and order) in the DRC was the original reason for the UN's intervention, we consider the SSR mission first, and then turn our attention to ONUC's ability to carry out its basic security missions. Nevertheless, DDR and Traditional Peacekeeping went hand in hand with the local security goals. The Pacification mission was dropped from our compatibility analysis, but we will incorporate its elements as they affect the other three missions.

Assessing the ONUC Missions

ONUC is exceptional among our set of cases in that its missions were pri-marily security-related and did not involve those that focused on providing services to the local population (e.g., Humanitarian Assistance) or rebuilding the state (e.g., Rule of Law).[2] This is primarily because the peacekeepers were deployed during active conflict rather than following a peace agreement—following the end of hostilities, the peacekeepers withdrew after a decent interval instead of having an extended mandate that in later years would in-clude peacebuilding missions. International assistance outside the purview of the peace operation occurred during the final phase and after the ONUC withdrawal.

---

[2] Although not necessarily core parts of the mandate, ONUC did perform several actions that are related to what later would be called peacebuilding. ONUC coordinated its efforts to support the civil administration of the Léopoldville regime through the group known as the Consultative Group. This included technical assistance to train Congolese administrators and help with long-term planning of government services. ONUC also provided some food relief to refugees in both the Kasai and Kivu provinces (Dobbins et al., 2005).

Because ONUC was security-oriented, we do not explore the full range of theoretical expectations summarized in Table 3.1. Rather, we focus on the "Security First" and "Recursive Effects" expectations from the set dealing with sequencing and simultaneity. With respect to compatibility, ONUC scores relatively well on all three indicators of compatibility, among the best on the multitasking indicator (Indicator 1) and much better than average on the other two. This is primarily a function of its fewer-than-average number of missions and their focus on security, sharing a number of similarities across multiple dimensions. Most of our expectations concern *in*compatibility, but ONUC offers us an opportunity to ascertain whether highly compatible operations reap benefits for their missions, as well as whether failures have ripple effects across missions with similar profiles.

Our holistic judgment on each of the missions is summarized in Table 4.1, using a Likert scale of outcomes with categories of Effective, Mostly Effective, Mixed, Mostly Ineffective, and Ineffective. The bases for these judgments and details about mission performance for this case are given in the narrative below.

Table 4.1 Holistic judgments of ONUC mission outcomes

Mission category	Mission	Outcome
Basic Security	Traditional Peacekeeping	Mostly Ineffective
	DDR	Mostly Ineffective
Shorter-Term Missions	SSR	Mixed

Security Sector Reform (SSR)

At the beginning of its time in the DRC, ONUC's principal function was to "restore order throughout a vast country that had fallen into widespread lawlessness and chaos" (Dorn, 2013:1401–1402). These conditions arose immediately following the Congo's independence from Belgium on June 30, 1960, when Congolese soldiers mutinied against both the Belgian officers and the Congo's first democratically elected government, which in turn triggered a number of other uprisings against the central government.

Responding to calls for assistance from Congolese leaders, the UN Security Council decided that ONUC should be tasked with providing such assistance until the Congolese government deemed its security forces equal to the task (Asku, 2003). Consequently, ONUC was the first peacekeeping operation to have a police component attached to it—a small Ghanaian police unit deployed in Léopoldville (now Kinshasa) (Williams and Bellamy, 2021). In addition to training and developing a new Congolese Police Service personnel, this thirty-member unit was tasked with supporting the military in assisting in the restoration of law and order, and therefore was a paramilitary entity under military command (Ganiwu, 2018). As a result of the deteriorating security environment, however, this police unit ultimately had to withdraw after a few months (Dobbins et al., 2005). Eventually, a 400-member Nigerian police contingent would replace the original Ghanaian police unit and would stay in the Congo until the end of 1965, more than a year after ONUC had withdrawn (Oakley et al., 1998).

Because the ANC was unable to discharge its internal security responsibilities, ONUC took on many of the normal law-and-order functions of a civilian police force: "apprehending and detaining violators of civilian law, establishing and enforcing curfews, and conducting short- and long-range patrols" (Findlay, 2002:66). Put differently, CIVPOL (Civilian Police) was better trained and more appropriate than a military force to carry out routine law enforcement actions such as traffic control (Chappell and Evans, 1999). Such day-to-day police duties also included to "restore, operate, and when necessary, set up the essential services, air-traffic, telecommunication, customs and immigration offices, health care, education, banking system, monetary foreign exchange and foreign trade control, agriculture, labour and public administration" (Shraga, 1998:69).

Overall, ONUC's performance for this mission can be judged as *Mixed*. Although the return of law and order followed quite quickly in some places after UN troops arrived, the degree of ONUC's success varied substantially across time and geographic area.

Early in the peacekeeping deployment, the peacekeepers were successful in stabilizing much of the country (Fargo, 2006). Coterminous with this was progress in two areas of DDR in its nascent stages. The first was the withdrawal of Belgian troops within the first two weeks. The second was the initial willingness of ANC segments to disarm, which allowed ONUC to collect weapons and secure arms depots (Bloomfield, 1963). This illustrates the synergistic effects of different peacekeeping missions, especially those that are relatively compatible. Here, disruptive forces were removed or disarmed, making the ability to stabilize much of the country easier. The stability facilitated by the establishment of law and order also provided the incentives and assurances to local forces that it was safe to turn in their weapons. This matches our expectations concerning the recursive effects of multiple mission success. More generally, it illuminates the way that multiple missions interact over time.

Local security establishment, however, was not evident in all parts of the country. Even though ONUC's mandate applied to the whole of the Congo, including Katanga, the leader of that province, Tshombe, actively resisted ONUC's efforts and tried to block its entry into that area (Asku, 2003). Accordingly, Katanga became a hotspot and the subsequent focal point for the rest of the operation. Other strategic areas—notably the capital city of the Congo (then Léopoldville, now Kinshasa), the airport, and most refugee camps—were secured at least in the short term (Dobbins et al., 2005). Part of the reason that ONUC was able to achieve success in its capital city can be traced to its decision to take "emergency measures," such as closing the airport and taking control of the radio station. Seizure of the airport also had the effect of mitigating some of the conflict in Katanga, as it prevented Lumumba from using military capabilities in the air against the opposition in the breakaway province (Asku, 2003) and therefore served the purpose of preventing a wider civil war in the country (Boulden, 2015). Thus, peacekeeping actions were able to overcome the difficult environmental context to which the operation was deployed.

Stabilization efforts were primarily confined to chaos in the Katanga region. Some progress was evident, such as in the northern area; nevertheless, this dissipated when ONUC forces were limited in the actions taken. Other areas reverted to disorder after the peacekeeping forces withdrew (Dobbins et al., 2005). The latter can be seen as "a glass half-full or half-empty" in terms of assessment: the presence of the peacekeepers clearly had a positive impact, but their withdrawal was perhaps an error that precipitated a reversion to violence and disorder.

One of the hurdles that ONUC had to overcome was that it was severely limited in the measures that it could take to facilitate law and order. Unlike a traditional police force, ONUC "had no powers of arrest, no jails to detain offenders and no legal authority to try suspects in a court of law," and it was initially "bound by its instructions to use force only in self-defense, which were more restrictive than the use-of-force rules of many police forces" (Findlay, 2002:66). The absence of an established rule of law in the form of detailed legal codes hampered this security-related mission; the Congolese government had yet to develop detailed statutes or even incorporate principles and provisions from Belgian law developed under colonial rule. In these ways, it was not the incompatible intersection of missions on the ground that undermined progress in local security. Rather, it was the *absence* of other, compatible peace missions (e.g., Rule of Law) that were not part of the peacekeeping portfolio at the time. This absence reduced the chances for success.

Beyond directly imposing order on the Congo, ONUC police undertook to carry out another aspect of SSR: assisting in the training and development of a new Congolese police force. Given that Belgian officers had previously been in command of both army and police forces, the need for such training was necessary (Klinger, 2005). Chappell and Evans (1999:85) note that: "No detailed study exists of the overall performance of CIVPOL in ONUC, but the general consensus appears to be that it made a positive contribution to a U.N. mission clouded even today by controversy and debate." The Nigerian military police on duty with ONUC, in particular, have often been heralded for their work in these efforts (Bloomfield, 1963). That this police unit "handled their duties maturely, impartially, professionally and in accordance with the guidelines stipulated by the UN" not only resulted in accolades by the UN, but also in Congolese officials inviting some members of the Nigerian contingents to remain in the Congo under the United Nations Technical Assistance Board (UNTAB) (Oluwafemi, 2020:59). ONUC's attempt to reform the Congolese military, however, was not as successful (Spooner, 2009). This is, in part, attributable to problems with another mission discussed in the next section—DDR.

The SSR mission is one generally conceived as being impartial, although this is difficult in practice when central government authority is challenged by secessionist movements or there are competing factions for control of the central government. As the situation on the ground evolved, ONUC acted in a partial fashion with actions that undermined Lumumba and helped Kasavubu (Abi-Saab, 1978; James, 1994; Boulden, 2015). De facto, ONUC became a primary actor in the conflict and had intervened in the internal affairs of the country, despite initial protestations otherwise. Hobbs (2014:6) bluntly states, "though Hammarskjold publicly spoke of letting 'the African people choose their own way,' the way in which the UN chose both to actively not intervene at certain points and to actively intervene at other points during the Congo Crisis demonstrated the extent to which the UN became an undue influence and failed to fulfill its own ideals by imposing a UN agenda that was directly contrary to the interests of independence for the Congo."

ONUC was, for example, labeled as culpable for not preventing Lumumba's arrest, imprisonment, and death (Findlay, 2002).

Overall, ONUC appears to have been somewhat successful in carrying out its SSR mission, especially given that it was able to restore the breakdown of law and order in the months following ANC's mutiny against its Belgian officers, and later, in its ability to train nascent Congolese police contingents under Nigerian police units. Nevertheless, the sore spot of Katanga remained, and in the short term, local security regressed and it was not until the peace agreement that order was restored.

Basic Security Missions (Traditional Peacekeeping, DDR)
The Traditional Peacekeeping mission in this context was one in which violence abatement by military force occurred in the first three-quarters of the operation, rather than the peace operation serving as an interposition force following a cease-fire. The absence of a cease-fire upon their deployment, in other words, resulted in greater challenges in terms of quelling violence. Furthermore, the additional mission of Pacification therefore complicated its ability to ensure a cease-fire as an *increase* in violence in the short term was the result of a strategy to decrease violence in the long run. Overall, we judge the traditional peacekeeping mission as *Mostly Ineffective*—until the peace agreement, violence levels did not decline, but escalated. With respect to DDR, some early successes were reversed as the war escalated. As with the other ONUC missions, the failures in Katanga prevent a more positive overall assessment; hence, a similar assessment of *Mostly Ineffective* is rendered for DDR.

The traditional and DDR missions complicated the SSR mission and vice versa. One cannot have law and order, by definition, when violence is occurring and groups perpetrating the violence are organized and well-armed. The three security-related missions are relatively compatible with one another on multiple dimensions, but this means that spillover effects can be positive or negative between them. In the case of ONUC, it was primarily negative until the latter stage of the operation.

For the Traditional Peacekeeping mission, in combination with Pacification, fighting began on July 4, 1960 (the day when Congolese soldiers mutinied against their Belgian officers), and ended on January 14, 1963, the day that Tshombe announced the end of Katanga's session and his unconditional acceptance of Secretary-General U Thant's plan for reunification (Sarkees and Wayman, 2010; Dixon and Sarkees, 2015). On the one hand, the termination of the war might be regarded as a success, but that it took almost two and a half years to accomplish and with substantial casualties makes this a qualified success at best.

With a total of 2,550 battle-related combatant fatalities occurring during the First DRC War of 1960–1963, 6,250 occurring during the Second DRC War of 1964–1965, and 4,805 occurring during the Third DRC Rebellion of 1964–1965, the presence of ONUC peacekeepers did not have a lasting impact on reducing casualties involved in the various intrastate conflicts that continued to plague the region (Sarkees and Wayman, 2010; Dixon and Sarkees, 2015). Statistics on peacekeeper casualties also paint a picture of just how deadly this conflict was for those on the ground. According to UN data on peacekeeper casualties, there were a total of 249 peacekeeper deaths between 1960 and 1964—making this peace operation more deadly than our other four case studies (UNPROFOR: 213 deaths; MONUC: 161 deaths; UNTAET: 26 deaths; and UNAMSIL: 192 deaths). Furthermore, 135, or 56 percent, of these peacekeeper casualties were the result of "malicious acts," indicating that ONUC's time in the DRC was especially marked by violence. In many ways, the reason for such high peacekeeper casualties can be traced to two main factors: (1) ONUC's decision to return weapons to the local Congolese army (ANC); and (2) ONUC's increasingly controversial military operations launched to end the secession of Katanga.

When ONUC first arrived in the Congo, there was some success in disarming many ANC troops, and this contributed to early progress at stabilization. This is consistent with our Security First expectation (Dorn, 2013). Similar to a patient that stops taking medicine when symptoms subside, however, ONUC made the serious error amid calm in August 1960 by returning weapons to ANC soldiers. Ironically, this showed the value of DDR for other missions because the effects were significant. First, the decision to return weapons made it possible for the ANC to recapture the capital city of Bakwanga of the secessionist state of South Kasai (Bloomfield, 1963). In the process of requisitioning food and vehicles to aid in their move into Katanga, however, the soldiers turned against the local Baluba, and atrocities soon ensued, with some reports indicating mass imprisonment and dozens of executions (Abi-Saab, 1978; Olivier, 2010). Second, it called into question the UN's ability to discipline indigenous forces effectively, making the possibility of carrying out successful training much less likely (Bloomfield, 1963). Bloomfield (1963:381) raises the counterfactual, "it is a legitimate question whether the continued neutralization of the ANC would not have assisted a speedier political settlement." Lefever (1965:37) answers the question un-equivocally: "Had the ANC been disarmed and kept disarmed, there would have been no domestic military support for contending political factions which continued to tear the country apart. The restoration of order and the creation of a unified national government would have been less difficult."

The perceived view, consistent with evidence of ONUC actions, that ONUC was not impartial and favored the opposition to Lumumba com-plicated DDR efforts and ultimately the other missions as well (Dobbins et al., 2005). Secession crises in Katanga and in another province (Kasai) undermined support and efforts to disarm the ANC. Thus, problems with controlling the violence had negative consequences for DDR. The central government under Mobutu, then chief of staff, was suspicious of ONUC motives in disarming the ANC, even after the latter's mutiny; to support DDR in his view, and that of President Kasavubu, carried with it a risk of having the Congo fall into international trusteeship (Dobbins et al., 2005).

Further complicating DDR efforts were disagreements among military and political officials associated with the operation. Taking a middle ground position was Under-Secretary-General Ralph Bunche, who agreed with the disarmament policy, but only with the consent of the Congolese government (Findlay, 2002); as indicated, this was not to be granted even as the consent requirement was consistent with the classical "holy trinity" requirements at the time for peacekeeping. Consequently, ONUC's modus operandi during the first few months of its operation was to refrain from taking assertive actions because it did not have the liberty to do so under its existing rules of engagement. This proved to be a mistake with substantial consequences.

Upset with ONUC's "passive resistance" and "non-interference" with the ANC, General Alexander (the British head of Ghana's defense force) urged in a letter to the Secretary-General on August 19, 1960, to authorize the use of force against the ANC rather than persuasion (see Howard, 2019, for the distinction between these two forms of exercising power by peacekeepers): "when you are dealing with ill-disciplined soldiers without leadership, persuasion gets nowhere" (S/4445 Annex II:4). Indeed, that was the outcome after initial progress in limiting violence was reversed. Calls for the disarming of Mobutu's ANC were also supported by proximate African countries known as the "Casablanca Group," especially after Mobutu launched a de facto military coup d'état in September 1960 (Abi-Saab, 1978). On January 3–6, 1961, at a conference in Casablanca, six Third World leaders adopted a declaration that, among other things, demanded that Mobutu's solders be disarmed ("Casablanca Powers," 1962). Such measures were originally opposed by Secretary-General Hammarskjöld based on his initial reluctance to become involved in the internal affairs of countries (Asku, 2003). Following Lumumba's death at the hands of ANC in early February 1961, however, Hammarskjöld changed his mind.

In response to the deteriorating situation, the Security Council passed Resolution 161 in February 1961, which in addition to urging that the UN "take immediately all appropriate measures to prevent the occurrence of civil war in the Congo," also included the call for the reorganization of Congolese armed units "under discipline and control" (S/RES/161); the latter is an explicit mandate for a DDR mission. Because this resolution did not specify *how* or *what* this discipline and control would look like, some interpretations regarded this as authorization to use military force to disarm the ANC (Abi-Saab, 1978). This reinforced fears among Congolese leaders and other elites that ONUC was poised to violate Congo's sovereignty, and this galvanized opposition to the peace operation (Abi-Saab, 1978).

Theoretically, we posited that failure in the DDR mission would negatively affect other missions in the operation. Here, however, there is another twist: the presence of the DDR mission, and its perceived mechanisms, undermined the Traditional Peacekeeping and SSR missions. The resistance to Resolution 161 led to increased violence. For example, Katanga soldiers and foreign mercenary supporters clashed several times with ONUC peacekeepers (Boulden, 2015). There were also increased hostile acts and harassment against UN civilian and military personnel, with the most serious incidents taking place in Matadi, Congo's only outlet to the sea; a UN Sudanese detachment ultimately had to evacuate after being outnumbered by the ANC (Abi Saab, 1978).

UN Security Resolution 161 also marked the beginning of the second phase of ONUC (referenced in the last section—Dorn, 2013): the fight for Katanga. In order to achieve the expulsion of foreign mercenaries and political advisers from Katanga, as called for in that resolution, Operation Rumpunch was launched as the first of four offensive operations. Because Operation Rumpunch had the element of surprise, ONUC was able to achieve what it set out to do, as "338 of the 442 European officers in the gendarmerie were rounded up and detained for repatriation" (Spooner, 2009:163)—all without bloodshed (Dobbins et al., 2005). This counts as a success in the mission, but again it was short-lived. The operation was suspended when "UN officials in the Congo agreed to a request from foreign diplomats that they be allowed to complete the deportations themselves" (Boulden, 2015:165). Nevertheless, that these foreign diplomats would soon renege on their commitment to withdraw from Katanga brought ONUC back to the drawing board.

ONUC launched a second operation, known as Operation Morthor (Hindi for "smash"), whose aim was not only to expel the foreign mercenaries but also to end the secession of Katanga (Abi-Saab, 1978); in effect, this combines all the missions of ONUC in one action. Nevertheless, this operation did not run nearly as smoothly as the first, given that it encountered unexpectedly heavy resistance. Irish forces in ONUC surrendered to rebel forces, and an Indian contingent was stalemated against another set of Katanga military forces. A Katangan air force plane also attacked ONUC peacekeepers. UN casualties were low on an absolute (7 dead, 26 wounded) and relative level (Katangan forces and civilians numbered 200 dead and 500 wounded) (Dobbins et al., 2005). Still, this level of violence was quite high and did not mitigate future violence.

Adding to the problems, Secretary-General Hammarskjöld, was killed on September 17, 1961, on his way to Rhodesia, where he had hoped to meet with Katangan leader Tshombe to arrange a cease-fire. Following Hammarskjöld's death, the civilian head of ONUC, Mahmoud Khiari, managed to negotiate a cease-fire with Tshombe on October 13, 1961, but ONUC soon discovered that this was a cease-fire in name only, given that the situation in northern Katanga worsened (Spooner, 2009).

The abduction of Brian Urquhart, UN Representative in Katanga, however, led to another alteration in UN strategy (Doss, 2014). Frustrated with the current status quo, the UN Security Council, led by the new Secretary-General U Thant, passed Resolution 169, which authorized ONUC to "take vigorous action, including the use of the requisite measure of force, if necessary, for the immediate apprehension, detention pending legal action and/or deportation of all foreign military and paramilitary personnel and political advisers not under UN Command, and mercenaries" (S/5002). Unlike his predecessor, Secretary-General U Thant favored a more aggressive posture, including offensive military tactics, even air power, to achieve the outcome (Dorn, 2013). Shortly after the adoption of Resolution 169 (S/5002), ONUC launched Operation Unokat in response to the establishment of roadblocks by Katangan forces, which had hindered ONUC's freedom of movement. After a battle that involved 6,000 ONUC and 3,000 Katangan troops, ONUC would ultimately gain control of the Katangan capital of Elisabethville, but at the cost of many lives lost: ONUC had suffered 10 dead and 34 wounded; the Katangans endured 141 dead and 401 wounded (Dobbins et al., 2005:17).

The first "UN Air Force" played a substantial role in this operation. One of the negative repercussions, however, was extensive collateral damage. Air attacks inadvertently damaged hospitals and other civilian and economic facilities (Dorn, 2013). Furthermore, ONUC's actions, particularly its air campaign, prompted a Katangan aerial buildup as a counterweight (Dorn, 2013). Thus, ONUC violence begat more violence and conflict escalation. In this way, whatever pacification success was achieved came at substantial costs in lives and damage.

Ultimately, ONUC's vigorous actions led to a cease-fire known as the Kitona Declaration, signed on December 21, 1961, which formally recognized the authority of the central government over all of the Congo territory. Ignoring the costs of such an outcome might be regarded at first blush as a step toward success. Nevertheless, during the following year, Tshombe did not follow through on many of his promises, and there is reason to suggest that he repeatedly backtracked on these commitments in order to prepare for another attempt at Katangan independence (Boulden, 2015). This is a classic case of "devious objectives" (Richmond, 1998), in which a disputant agrees to a pause in fighting to rearm or adjust in preparation for renewed fighting later. Indeed, the additional months of fighting that followed seem to confirm this.

ONUC's final offensive against Katanga, Operation Grandslam, began in December 1962. It was launched so that UN troops could regain freedom of movement in the whole of Katanga (Klinger, 2005). Equipped with superior aircraft, including both jet fighters and bombers, ONUC was ultimately able to wipe out the Katangan air force and associated facilities (Findlay, 2002). After being issued an ultimatum by U Thant to surrender, Tshombe and the Katangan ultimately complied on January 14, 1963. Although no UN personnel were killed or injured as a result of the airstrikes that were a part of Operation Grandslam, and there were no confirmed reports on civilian casualties, Dorn (2013) qualifies this positive assessment in that the number of Katangans and mercenaries killed in these attacks is not known.

In the end, ONUC was able to restore law and order in the Congo, but only after significant use of force and lives lost. This leads Pushkina (2006) to ask, "can the UN Operation in the Congo (ONUC) be called successful because its mandate was nearly satisfied and it prevented the recurrence of war, even though violent deaths increased during the mission's deployment and the conflict spread beyond the borders of the Congo?" (Pushkina, 2006:134). Pushkina (2006) identifies "some" spread of conflict from the Congo to other countries in the region during the ONUC operation through contagion—as the fighting spilled across the borders and into neighboring countries.

Findlay (2002:82) argues that ultimately, "ONUC became, through accident and design, involved in military actions that differed little from standard warfare." That ONUC used a variety of weapons, such as "mortars, fighter and bomber aircraft, light armored vehicles, as well as rifles, light automatic weapons and bayonets, and anti-tank and anti-aircraft weapons" is indicative of this (White, 2015:51). That said, Katangan secession was averted through such action (Goulding, 1996). One could argue, however, that ONUC could have avoided being in the situation in which such force was required. Ultimately, ONUC had to use force to solve problems that stemmed from its inaction when it came to disarming ANC troops at the beginning of the operation. Additionally, because the domestic situation in the Congo morphed into an internationalized intrastate conflict, ONUC was left confused about how it was supposed to treat ANC troops. This resulted in increased tensions between ONUC and the host state, culminating in targeted attacks against peacekeepers, which is why the number of peacekeeper deaths from malicious acts was so high.

Summary of the ONUC Case

How does ONUC's experience match our expectations? The results are summarized in Table 4.2. This peace operation carried out two basic security missions (Traditional Peacekeeping and DDR), as well as SSR. Although much of the time, these three missions were done simultaneously, the latter was technically the primary one at the outset. Relative to the full array of peace operation missions, these missions were generally compatible with one another according to all of the three compatibility indicators.

In general, the Security First expectation that those basic missions were essential to other missions was confirmed. The initial absence of effective cease-fires at the outset hampered the ability of the peacekeepers to stabilize the whole country. Furthermore, the reversal of DDR efforts (returning weapons to the ANC) made an unstable situation much worse. The mostly ineffective stabilization and DDR efforts not only complicated the local security tasks of the SSR mission, but they had a deleterious impact on one

Table 4.2 Summary of results vis-à-vis expectations—ONUC

Type of expectation	Expectation	Outcome
Sequencing, Simultaneity, and Prerequisites	Security First	Supported
	Democracy Matters	N/A
	Peacebuilding Synergy	N/A
	Peacebuilding Matters	N/A
	Recursive Effects	Supported
Compatibility	Aggregate Effects	Not Supported
	Learning	Not Supported
	Individual Effects	Supported

another; this meets the Recursive Effects expectation. DDR problems damaged the ability of ONUC to establish and hold cease-fires. Similarly, the continued fighting diminished the willingness of the army and rebel forces to demobilize and lay down their arms.

There are several caveats to the conclusion above. First, the peacekeepers were successful in stabilizing many areas of the country. The failures, as spectacular as they were, were largely confined to breakaway provinces. Second, following the peace agreement, ONUC experienced few problems in maintaining the peace; a balanced assessment, however, would also note that the threat of violence renewal was substantially diminished in that period and that accordingly made ONUC's tasks much easier. Third, as noted in earlier chapters, the impacts from the failures of the basic security missions on each other or the local security efforts were not exclusive or necessarily even primary vis-à-vis other factors. The lack of cooperation from various internal parties and an environment of ongoing civil war made the achievement of those missions very difficult. Nevertheless, peacekeeping actions and inactions exacerbated the contextual problems encountered. Thus, there was an interplay between context and peacekeeper actions that can be construed as a circular relationship among these factors.

Fourth, and perhaps most important, there are the intervening effects from the Pacification mission. In the short term, the extensive use of offensive military force by ONUC increased violence, weakened local security (at least in the secessionist areas), and undermined incentives for DDR.

Peacekeepers performing pacification activities are placed in primary party and biased roles, quite in contrast to those of DDR, and it is perhaps not surprising that performance in the latter mission suffered. After the Pacification mission was successful in defeating rebel forces, however, the stability provided *enhanced* local security and limited violence. Depending on what stage of the operation was considered, there is a case for the Pacification mission as being linked to both the success and the failure of other missions.

Compatibility problems per se were not significant with respect to the three missions examined. Relative to other peace operations, ONUC maintained a portfolio of compatible missions. As we note in the concluding chapter with respect to the Aggregate Effects expectation, one might have anticipated greater success from such an operation with a limited number of largely compatible missions, given that the tasks assigned to peacekeepers are both logistically manageable and similar in their characteristics (except for Pacification). Compatible missions could assist one another, but this was predicated on success in some missions spilling over to other similar missions because of common role orientations among other characteristics. Yet, as indicated, there were limited successes under which such positive spillover could occur. There were Individual Effects, but they were all in the negative direction. Pacification is somewhat incompatible with the other missions in that it involves biased roles and other characteristics in contravention to the other three missions. This unique Pacification mission and its associated military intervention did have negative spillover with the other missions, but its ultimate success produced some positive payoffs only after that mission was completed, not when it was conducted simultaneously with the others. There was no clear evidence in favor of Learning, even as the performance of this short operation improved in the latter stages of its existence.

Overall, what we have is a case in which a few missions—including Pacification—interact throughout the operation and often produce synergetic effects, particularly with regard to the negative spillover of compatible missions. This is an analysis of process dynamics influenced by context; it is not an analysis of linear effects.

United Nations Protection Force (UNPROFOR)

The United Nations Protection Force (UNPROFOR) was one of the first post–Cold War peace operations and represented an unusual foray for peacekeeping into the continent of Europe. It was also the first of several peace operations deployed to the Balkans in response to the Bosnian civil war and proved to be an early test of the new peacekeeping and peacebuilding strategies that accompanied an increased willingness of the UN Security Council and UN membership generally to intervene in civil conflicts, especially those that had been internationalized.

Historical Context and Overview of UNPROFOR

In 1980, the death of Yugoslav President Josip Broz Tito, who had long promoted "brotherhood and unity" among the six republics (Croatia, Slovenia, Bosnia-Herzegovina, Macedonia, Serbia, and Montenegro) and two autonomous regions (Kosovo and Vojvodina), marked in some ways the beginning of the end of the Socialist Federal Republic of Yugoslavia. Subsequently, the League of Communists of Yugoslavia was dissolved, and multiparty elections were held in all six of the republics for the first time, giving the people the opportunity to hold a referendum on independence (for a detailed history on the Bosnia war, see Burg and Shoup, 2000). Slovenia and Croatia were the first two republics to declare their independence on June 25, 1991—marking the initial phase of the dissolution of Yugoslavia (Keil and Kudlenko, 2015). Although the secession of Slovenia from Yugoslavia was relatively short and straightforward following its Ten-Day War with the Yugoslav People's Army (JNA), matters were more complicated for Croatia, given that there were several Serb-dominated areas in the country that received assistance and arms from the JNA. This resulted in a violent six-month internal conflict. As Tardy (2015b:373) explains, "Military confrontation between the nascent Croatian forces on the one hand, the Croat Serbs and the JNA on the other hand, was particularly violent in ethnically mixed areas, with massive international humanitarian law violations and the expulsions of Croats from the Serb-held territories." Eventually, the JNA and the Serb paramilitary forces would go on to control approximately 30 percent of Croatia, and it was in these Serb-controlled areas, such as Eastern Slavonia, that the policy of "ethnic cleansing" first appeared (Lupis et al., 1995). Nevertheless, nascent peace was eventually reached in January 1992, following the Sarajevo cease-fire agreement.

During the following month, the Security Council (S/RES/743) established UNPROFOR with the expectation that it would be an interim force for a period of twelve months and one that would allow for a diplomatic solution to be negotiated for the Balkan Crisis more broadly. Croatia was the locus of deployment following the cease-fire between the Croats and Serbs. UNPROFOR was designed to supervise the cease-fire (Traditional Peacekeeping), facilitate the withdrawal of the Yugoslav People's Army (JNA) (DDR), and set up UN Protected Areas (UNPAs) (Human Rights) where a majority of Serbs resided in Croatia.

A month after the agreement involving Croatia, Bosnia-Herzegovina held its referendum on self-determination, and subsequently proclaimed its independence from Yugoslavia. One indicator that this secession was going to be different from those of Croatia and Slovenia was Belgrade's refusal to recognize the new country, even though the European Community and the United States did so in short order. Violent clashes between Bosniaks (Muslims) and Serbs soon broke out in Sarajevo, which ultimately culminated in its siege by the Bosnian Serbs under the command of Ratko Mladic. Thereafter, conflict quickly spread through the rest of the country, involving three major ethno-religious factions within Bosnia: Bosnian Muslims and Bosnian Croats aligned against the Bosnian Serbs. Further complicating the conflict were national armies supporting the opposing sides; the Croatian army supported the Bosnian Croats, and the Serbian-led federal Yugoslav military provided direct and indirect assistance to the Bosnian Serbs (Schinella, 2019). Arms, from both Croatia and Serbia, flowed into Bosnia as the war in Croatia dissipated and the violent conflict in Bosnia escalated (Beardsley, 2011). Accordingly, UNPROFOR was extended to Bosnia-Herzegovina in June 1992 with the adoption of UN Security Council Resolution 758 (S/RES/758), which assigned peacekeepers to the safe delivery of humanitarian supplies. Three months later, UNPROFOR's mandate would be explicitly enlarged to enable it to provide protection for civilians where and when the United Nations High Commissioner for Refugees (UNHCR) considered protection necessary (S/RES/776).

UNPROFOR began in Bosnia on June 8, 1992—after violent conflict was well underway in the country, stemming from the outbreak of violence in the capital of Sarajevo.[3] After fighting broke out in April 1992, Sarajevo was quickly surrounded, and eventually Bosnian Serb forces would go on

---

[3] Sarkees and Wayman (2010) record April 7, 1992, as the first day of interstate conflict in the war for Bosnian Independence and June 6, 1992, as the first day of intrastate conflict in the region, and Gleditsch et al. (2002) record April 27, 1992, as the first day of conflict.

to occupy nearly 70 percent of the country (Phillips, 2005). One reason that peacekeepers were not deployed in the area sooner can be traced back to disagreements among UN member states about the operation's cost, and Serbian forces exploited this delay to expand their control (Brown, 1993). Deploying peacekeepers in Bosnia was not originally considered by the Security Council; the consensus in April 1992 was that "the present conditions in Bosnia-Hercegovina make it impossible to define a workable concept for a United Nations peacekeeping operation" (S/23836, para. 27).

Over the course of its operation, UNPROFOR would expand to take on many additional responsibilities, described by Secretary-General Boutros-Ghali as "mission creep" (Findlay, 2002). Indeed, between 1991 and the end of 1995, the UN passed eighty-three Security Council resolutions on the Croatian and Bosnian Wars, changing UNPROFOR's mandate in Bosnia rapidly to include Traditional Peacekeeping, DDR, Humanitarian Assistance, and Human Rights missions.

UNPROFOR began to change and ultimately wound down at the end of 1994 with a four-month truce mediated by former US President Jimmy Carter and agreed to by all parties. UNPROFOR was replaced in Croatia at the end of March 1995 with the creation of the United Nations Confidence Restoration Operation in Croatia (UNCRO); that operation was designed as an interim arrangement to promote a negotiated settlement between Serbia and Croatia and to protect different ethnic communities there. At the same time, the UN established the United Nations Preventive Deployment Force (UNPREDEP) in Macedonia to monitor and report any developments in the border areas that could undermine confidence and stability in the former Yugoslav Republic of Macedonia and threaten its territory.

Unlike many future peace operations, UNPROFOR would formally end with the signing of a peace agreement between warring factions rather than beginning after an agreement. The agreement known as the Dayton Accords was the culmination of years of negotiation and was agreed to in November 1995 and signed in December 1995. It included all the major parties (Croat, Serb, and Bosniaks) involved in the Balkan War, as well as key states (e.g., Former Yugoslavia, United States, and several European countries). It provided for recognition of an independent state of Bosnia-Herzegovina, albeit with two sub-political units drawn along ethnic lines: the majority Serb Republika Srpska and Croat-Bosniak Federation of Bosnia and Herzegovina.

The termination of UNPROFOR did not end peace operations in Bosnia-Herzegovina. It was succeeded by the United Nations Mission in Bosnia and Herzegovina (UNMIBH), which took on many of the post-conflict peacebuilding missions that were established by UNPROFOR peacekeepers, specifically Traditional Peacekeeping, Humanitarian Assistance, Election Supervision/Promotion of Democracy, Human Rights, SSR, Rule of Law, and Reconciliation. The Dayton Accords also led to the NATO operation—IFOR, or Implementation Force. The largest peace operation in history (60,000 personnel), IFOR was charged with implementing the military aspects of the Dayton Accords, including the separation of opposing forces and some DDR. After a year, it was replaced by another NATO force—SFOR, or Stabilization Force—which continued many of the same functions and worked to create an environment for full reintegration of society. In addition, the Organization for Security and Cooperation in Europe (OSCE) launched multidimensional peacebuilding efforts, most evident after the peace agreement in 1995, to rebuild Bosnia-Herzegovina, with missions related to human rights, elections, the rule of law, and more (OSCE, 2022; Perry and Keil, 2018). All these efforts indicate that there was much work to be done after UNPROFOR departed and suggest limitations in what that operation was able to achieve during its deployment. Although we limit ourselves to only those missions assigned to UNPROFOR, and therefore not its successors, we raise the research agenda item of interdependence *across* operations and missions in Chapter 7.

Assessing the UNPROFOR Missions

UNPROFOR performed four missions, adaptive to the changing local environment. For much of its existence, it was attempting to perform simultaneously, rather than sequentially, the tasks associated with these missions. Mission interdependence and compatibility are thus relevant concerns for study. UNPROFOR's basic security missions of Traditional Peacekeeping and DDR are similar to ONUC, but its other two missions—Humanitarian Assistance and Human Rights—are different. UNPROFOR's compatibility score on Indicator 1 ("multitasking") is on the lower end of the scale, in part because it had only four missions, below the median, and it lacked long-term peacebuilding missions. Its scores on the other two indicators are closer to average (neither highly compatible nor incompatible) relative to other UN operations.

As done with ONUC, Table 4.3 summarizes our holistic judgment on each of the missions, using a Likert scale of outcomes with categories of Effective,

Table 4.3 Holistic judgments of UNPROFOR mission outcomes

Mission category	Mission	Outcome
Basic Security	Traditional Peacekeeping	Ineffective
	DDR	Ineffective
Shorter-Term Missions	Humanitarian Assistance	Mixed
	Human Rights	Ineffective

Mostly Effective, Mixed, Mostly Ineffective, and Ineffective. The bases for these judgments and details about mission performance in this operation are discussed in the sections to follow.

Basic Security Missions (Traditional Peacekeeping, DDR)

Given that UNPROFOR was deployed during active fighting, it was asked to perform its duties under difficult conditions. UNPROFOR peacekeepers found themselves in the midst of a brutal war, with ethnic cleansing raging around them, with no seeming peace to keep (Cohen and Stamkoski, 1995). Accordingly, it can be judged *Ineffective* in its Traditional Peacekeeping mission.

Traditional Peacekeeping

UNPROFOR was authorized in late February 1992, and most sources—Correlates of War (COW) Project, International Peace Research Institute of Oslo (PRIO), and International Crisis Behavior (ICB) Project—identify the Bosnian civil war as beginning less than a month later. Although one might debate the extent to which the peace operation was responsible for this failure in Bosnia, especially given UNPROFOR's initial deployment in Croatia, it is clear that a failure at conflict management occurred. Furthermore, the resulting civil war lasted until late November 1995 (with the initialing of the General Framework Agreement for Peace in Bosnia-Herzegovina—the Dayton Accords), after over 6,000 days of active fighting (Correlates of War Project, 2020; Brecher et al., 2021).

Despite repeated efforts and implementations, few cease-fires were respected during the period 1992–1995 by warring parties. UNPROFOR was able to negotiate hundreds of cease-fires (Williams and Bellamy, 2021), but that number alone tells us that they did not hold—repeated cease-fires means that their predecessors were broken. Indeed, many lasted less than a day. The initial deployment in Croatia followed a cease-fire, and there were some limited successes. Nevertheless, Serb forces carried out ethnic cleansing in Serb-dominated areas and the Croat military launched offensive military actions that removed any pretense that a cease-fire was in place. Whatever the peace operation did or did not do, the impact on ongoing violence was limited, if not minimal.

Unlike the MONUC and UNTAET peace operations covered in the next chapter, UNPROFOR in Bosnia-Herzegovina was not deployed following a peace agreement but had to facilitate its own (Findlay, 2002). The failure to sustain cease-fires would have downstream consequences, leading to its inability to demilitarize and demobilize (part of DDR) areas in which cease-fires called for such action and in fulfilling other missions. Illustrative of the failure, a Bosnia-wide cease-fire was reached on July 17, 1992, with all sides agreeing to place their heavy weapons under international supervision, but the small UNPROFOR force was inadequate to carry out the task and UN members refused to increase troop strength to the 10,000 personnel level that Secretary-General Boutros-Ghali thought necessary (Findlay, 2002). Recent research (Hultman et al., 2020) establishes the link between troop size and peacekeeping success. Under these conditions, the cease-fire collapsed in short order. As Ashton (1997:783) points out: "The establishment of demilitarized and controlled zones or areas can best be undertaken effectively where the parties are willing to honor their agreements. In the absence of such will, the peacekeeping force's capability to adequately monitor and enforce the agreement becomes the indispensable element of force effectiveness."

The analysis above is not to imply that all cease-fires were ineffective. At the end of March 1994, following a Bosnian Serb offensive against Goražde, which included indiscriminate attacks and civilian casualties, the Security Council called on all parties to respect the safe area fully, in accordance with S/RES/824 (United Nations Security Council, 1993). Indicative of UNPROFOR's inability to defend this safe area and its overall shortage of troops in Bosnia, however, is that when Bosnian Serb forces began to overrun this safe area, there were only eight UNPROFOR military observers present (S/1994/555, paragraph 9). After repeated efforts to arrange for a cease-fire, calls by the Security Council to pull forces back 3 kilometers from the city, and threats to utilize NATO bombings on Bosnian Serb positions, UNPROFOR was finally able to establish a somewhat lasting cease-fire in Goražde on April 23, 1994. Nevertheless, UNPROFOR's overall inability to contain conflict through the adherence of cease-fires far outweighed any success it might have experienced in Goražde, as attacks in other "safe areas" across the country continued unimpeded. In the final months of UNPROFOR deployment, the environment was relatively stable, but this was more a function of the impending peace agreement than of the actions of the peacekeepers. The actions of other actors—specifically threats by NATO—are also part of the story, although it is impossible to parcel out responsibility for outcomes in a precise fashion.

One of UNPROFOR's first steps toward limiting conflict followed from the passage of UN Security Council Resolution 781 (S/RES/781), which banned all military flights over Bosnia and established a "no-fly zone." De facto, this only affected the Serbs, as Bosnia had no aerial capacity (Schinella, 2019); an unintended consequence was that the action strengthened the perception among the Serbs that UNPROFOR was biased against them. In the end, however, this no-fly zone would prove to be anything but effective, given that there would be well over 5,000 no-fly-zone violations (Schinella, 2019). UNPROFOR relied on NATO to enforce the no-fly zones. Yet there was fear among UN and NATO leadership that humanitarian aid shipments might inadvertently be targeted. Accordingly, the rules of engagement were modified by specifying that only verified instances of aircraft engaged in combat could be shot down. Schinella (2019) notes that Bosnian Serb pilots adapted to this rule by flying low and in other ways to avoid radar, and in any case it was difficult to detect and respond quickly to rapid and brief air attacks in multiple locations. We had anticipated that security missions would affect the conduct and success of other missions. Here, however, is a case of the reverse direction consistent with the Recursive Effects expectation: actions taken for facilitating Humanitarian Assistance led to suboptimal performance in one of the basic security missions.

Despite some late successes, there are mostly negative assessments on enforcement of no-fly zones later in the operation. NATO did expand its use of airpower specifically to provide support to threatened UN personnel in UN-designated "safe areas" or to deter Bosnian Serb advances on the ground. Schinella (2019:13) calls these "short, limited engagements" that were dismissed as "pinprick strikes" that did not degrade Bosnia Serb capability. In contrast, a Secretary-General report in 1994 offered a more optimistic and perhaps self-interested conclusion: "the procedures agreed with NATO and executed under Operation Deny Flight have been almost entirely successful in stopping flights by combat aircraft in Bosnia and Herzegovina (S/1994/300, paragraph 24).

What accounts for the failure in the no-fly zones, and in particular the attempt to protect civilians in this fashion? The rules of engagement and Serbian adaptation to them referenced above are only part of the explanation. Effectively subcontracting part of the mission to NATO created or exacerbated command, control, and communication problems between the two organizations as well as with national military commands (Tardy, 2015a, 2015b; see also Findlay, 2002), even as NATO provided the necessary military capability to perform this aspect of the DDR mission. Essentially, the UN peace operation took on part of a mission for which it was ill-equipped to perform. Nor was its reliance on other actors in this case an efficient adaptive strategy.

Casualty figures for peacekeeping soldiers do not reveal much in terms of operational success. Total fatalities for UNPROFOR (United Nations Department of Peacekeeping Operations, 2021) number slightly over 200, but only a minority of these are attributable to malicious intent (as opposed to accident or illness), and there are no secular trends evident. More indicative of the failure outcome are casualty figures of the combatants and civilians in the area of the fighting. Total conflict deaths and missing persons for the period through 1995 are estimated to be 100,000, with about 40 percent of those being civilians (Ball et al., 2007). Among the status quo evaluations of success would be improvements over time. Nettelfield (2011:177) points out that: "Though Srebrenica was the single most horrifying crime of the war, the [RCD's *Bosnian Book of the Dead*] project results illustrated that half of the war's casualties occurred during the first year of the conflict." Battle-related fatalities and civilian-related casualties both peaked in 1992, with 23,297 and 21,813 deaths, respectively, and steadily declined through 1994. In 1995, there was an increase in the number of lives lost, however, in large part from the fall of Srebrenica; the data show that there were 10,538 deaths in July 1995 alone (Tokača, 2012). Improvements were evident in 1994 and 1995, although it is not clear that these can be tied to specific acts by the peace operation. In 1996, following the Dayton Accords that ended the war and *after* the UNPROFOR withdrawal, battle-related fatalities and civilian-related casualties were reduced to fourteen and two, respectively, a result of the peace agreement rather than the end of the UNPROFOR operation or any actions taken therein. The peace agreement enabled the transition to peacebuilding missions following UNPROFOR.

Looking at local data that tie specific peace operation actions to certain areas during the civil war, it is clear that peacekeepers were most active in the areas in which violent conflict was more prevalent (Dertwinkel, 2009). In some sense, this is logical insofar as forces were sent to areas where they were needed most. Nevertheless, local violent events did not necessarily decrease following the deployment of the peace operation troops (Costalli and Moro, 2009). Such local-level data and analysis confirm the conclusions of ineffectiveness drawn from aggregate figures above. Costalli (2014) used disaggregated data from the Peacekeeping Operations Location and Event Dataset (PKOLED) and data from the Research and Documentation of Sarajevo (RDC) to explore UN troop deployment and violence in the Bosnian civil war. He found that although peacekeeping works in the sense that troops are deployed where the most severe violence takes place, "the impact of peacekeeping troops on the severity of violence is shown to be irrelevant during the war" (Costalli, 2014:374) This is echoed by Tardy (2015a:389), who states, "it did not seem that the parties' main war aims were significantly altered by the blue helmets, be it the Serb offensives of 1992, the Croatian siege of Mostar, the Serbian takeover of Srebrenica and Zepa in July 1995 or, more generally, their ethnic cleansing policy, or the Bosnian-Croatian offensives in Western Bosnia over the summer of 1995." Simply put, we perhaps should not expect too much from peace operations employed during war. At best they can facilitate cease-fires, implement the cease-fires, and prepare the way for peace agreements.

A second element of Traditional Peacekeeping, conflict containment, refers to the ability of the peace operation to prevent the spread of the conflict to new geographic areas or to involve additional actors. There are data on those killed and missing by region and by municipality within regions (Research and Documentation Center, 2009). The ability of the peace operation to contain fighting within Bosnia, even in areas of deployment, was limited. Fatality and missing-person figures indicate widespread conflict across and within most regions of the country. Casualties were greatest in Podrinje, a region around Srebrenica, but that city only accounts for about 30 percent of the fatalities and missing persons. UN peacekeepers made a special effort to isolate that city from the worst of the armed conflict. This included expanding demilitarized zones and thereby creating safe havens for civilian populations.

Conflict containment also involves limiting the number of new actors entering the conflict. With respect to Bosnia, this was a clear failure. The former

Yugoslavian state of Serbia played a central role in escalating the Bosnian civil war. It provided arms, funds, and various other kinds of material support to Bosnian Serb forces fighting in the civil war. Until the Dayton Accords and subsequently a change in regime, Serbia was a source of instability and violence that the peace operation was unable to deter or redress. Croatia, which gained its independence a few months before Bosnia (January 1992), was also involved in the fighting, albeit somewhat more sporadically and less seriously than Serbia. Although no other states intervened directly in the conflict, not counting NATO or EU actions, these two instances reveal the failure of conflict containment with disastrous consequences. These failures seem to outweigh any success in preventing the violence from spreading to Macedonia or other areas of the Balkans.

Overall, UNPROFOR's Traditional Peacekeeping mission was a failure. Even though UNPROFOR negotiated hundreds of cease-fires during the war, very few were respected, which resulted in persistent violent conflicts across the country. Concerning conflict containment, UNPROFOR was not able to stop the involvement by neighboring Croatia and Serbia, which supported troops in Bosnia with manpower and military equipment, as well as financial flows to combatants.

DDR

UNPROFOR's DDR mission was a failure on an absolute level, and also in comparison to its successor peace operations in the post-1995 period. Early on, there was some progress in facilitating the withdrawal of JNA forces from Croatia in 1992. Nevertheless, UNPROFOR had set up a number of safe havens in Croatia that were supposed to include demilitarization. These failed to stop ethnic cleansing and military actions within the UNPAs. There were similar problems with weapons exclusion zones in Bosnia. For example, there was supposed to be withdrawal of Serb militia from Srebrenica and weapons exclusion zones around Sarajevo, including the withdrawal of anti-aircraft weapons. Specifically, NATO issued an ultimatum in 1994 against the Bosnian Serbs demanding that they lift the siege and remove heavy weapons from a 20 kilometer exclusion zone around Sarajevo. Even with a cease-fire in early 1995 and some progress in peace negotiations, Serbian forces violated provisions for weapons exclusion zones, and in several instances refused to surrender heavy weapons, prevented peacekeeping access to weapons collection areas, and even moved heavy weapons from those areas to other locations. Only in

September 1995 did Serb forces agree to a withdrawal from the weapons exclusion zone around Sarajevo.

In contrast to UNPROFOR and following the establishment of the Dayton Accords, NATO's Implementation Force (IFOR) experienced much more success establishing a lasting cease-fire. Early in 1996, the latter peace operation successfully created buffer zones separating rival forces. Estimates indicated that there were over 400,000 combatants during the civil war, although some sources put that number lower (Moratti and Sabic-El-Rayess, 2009). In mid-1996, NATO peacekeepers supervised their redeployment and ultimately demobilized 300,000 troops, although no assistance was provided to facilitate this; smaller numbers of troops, in the thousands, were later demobilized, but not necessarily through peace operation efforts. In addition, heavy weapons were placed in containers under international supervision. Bosnia Serb forces did not necessarily give up all the weapons designated in the peace accords, but generally the demilitarized efforts could be judged as a success (Paris, 2004). A related peace operation, UNTAES (United Nations Transitional Authority in Eastern Slavonia), was successful in demilitarizing its assigned area (Doyle and Sambanis, 2006).

Landmine deaths were substantial during the war, numbering almost 3,500 (Landmine Monitor, 2009). These dropped precipitously after the war, and averaged only thirty per year for a period after 2003. Good data on mine clearance are available after 1999 and show limited progress, with relatively small areas surveyed (1244.76 square kilometers) and cleared (49.2 square kilometers) by the end of 2008. By the end of 2008, there were still estimates of 1,683 square kilometers contaminated (Landmine Monitor, 2009). The post-UNPROFOR successes demonstrate that the DDR goals could be achieved, although subsequent operations had the advantage of functioning in a much more permissive environment.

Taken together, security efforts by UNPROFOR can be viewed as *Ineffective*. Peacekeepers cannot be expected to stop all fighting, but UNPROFOR repeatedly failed in supervising cease-fires and limiting violence. With a few exceptions, it was also unsuccessful in DDR activities, in particular with weapons exclusion zones and weapons collections. Indeed, the ineffectiveness of these two missions had recursive and reinforcing effects on one another. The continued fighting decreased the incentives for limiting weapons and troop withdrawals, and the greater availability of weapons and personnel led to further violence. As detailed below, these failures also had negative impacts on UNPROFOR's other missions.

Less Compatible Missions (Humanitarian Assistance and Human Rights Protection)

Humanitarian Assistance

From its beginning, one of UNPROFOR's chief concerns and mandate was to provide humanitarian aid and assistance to those affected by the Bosnian conflict. Our estimation is that despite flaws in the security missions, UNPROFOR was *Mixed* in its Humanitarian Assistance mission.

One of the first courses of action for UNPROFOR in Bosnia was to reopen the previously closed Sarajevo airport for humanitarian purposes (S/RES/758). Specifically, UNPROFOR was tasked with "ensuring the security and functioning of the Sarajevo Airport, assisting in the delivery of humanitarian assistance to Sarajevo and its environs" (Findlay, 2002:136). Working alongside the UN High Commissioner for Refugees (UNHCR), UNPROFOR was able to provide food and shelter to thousands of refugees throughout Bosnia by utilizing this Sarajevo airport, and later on, the Tuzla airport to deliver humanitarian aid (Cohen and Stamkoski, 1995).

The delivery of humanitarian assistance was not simply a logistical problem. The combatants, in particular those on the Serbian side, drove their enemies from their homes and actively sought to prevent assistance from reaching these threatened populations. At one level, the peacekeepers were successful with deliveries. There were almost 13,000 flights carrying aid into Sarajevo from 1992 to 1996 (Andreas, 2008). Estimates of food and other medical supplies delivered often range in the neighborhood of 200,000 tons (Boulden, 2001; Andreas, 2008). In addition, peacekeepers facilitated the work of other aid organizations. Even though UNHCR was the lead humanitarian agency, there were a plethora of other organizations on the ground, as well, including the World Food Programme (WFP), UNICEF, the World Health Organization (WHO), the Food and Agriculture Organization of the United Nations (FAO), UNESCO, the International Committee of the Red Cross (ICRC), and a number of other NGOs, such as Médecins Sans Frontières (Szasz, 1995). It is estimated that some 2.7 million individuals were the beneficiaries of this aid in Bosnia between 1992 and 1995 (Cutts, 1999).

The above might seem to be impressive numbers, but they must be balanced against several other indicators and facts. First, the need for such aid was great. Close to 80 percent of the population (approximately 3.5 million) depended on some form of foreign aid (Doyle and Sambanis, 2006). Viewed in this context, total aid over a four-year period is less impressive. Second, the UN expected to lose at least 30 percent of all supplies en route to final delivery because of malicious interference by enemy combatants, suggesting that convoys were not adequately protected by peacekeepers. Third, much of the peacekeeping strategy in providing assistance was paired with its approach in establishing safe havens (also see the Human Rights mission), but these were economically nonviable and vulnerable to attack, making the need for external humanitarian assistance even greater (Doyle and Sambanis, 2006). Although the failure of basic security missions did not prevent achieving some humanitarian assistance success, it did limit the extent of and locations where such successes could occur. Finally, there was widespread corruption and black-market activity with respect to the humanitarian aid that was delivered. Not only were peacekeepers unable to stop this, but UNPROFOR members were some of the perpetrators (Andreas, 2008).

In addition to delivery of humanitarian aid through air drops, efforts also included delivery via land convoys. These proved more problematic for the peacekeepers, as they were prone to interception by opposing militias. Until 1994, UNPROFOR relied on the consent of the warring parties for movement through the territories they controlled. In particular, Bosnia Serb forces sometimes blocked roads to inspect and regulate the flow of aid to specific areas, and this interdiction could include seizing a portion of the aid or making that a condition of passage (Human Rights Report, 1995). The UN was often hamstrung when denied access, as its interpretation of the mandate was such that it could not use military force in order to guarantee the delivery of aid shipments (Tardy, 2015a, 2015b). One of the ramifications of this approach was that warring parties, in particular the Bosnian Serbs, would take advantage of UNPROFOR peacekeepers. Hillen (1995:4) bluntly put it: "Much of the UN aid, meant for women and children, will end up in the stomachs of gunmen. Fuel for hospitals and power stations will be siphoned into military vehicles. UN provisions will bolster the flimsy economies of all three factions. UN aid is for sale in any town in Bosnia." This raises the question of whether such diversion for military purposes prolonged the fighting (Hillen, 1995). Thus, this could be another instance of a recursive interdependence between missions; here, failure in delivering humanitarian assistance swung back to undermine security missions even as the reverse was also true.

Although it was the responsibility of UNPROFOR to provide security and logistics for other organizations, Cutts (1999) argues that this responsibility could be counterproductive—the mere presence of UNPROFOR escorts sometimes drew fire from Bosnian Serbs, who were hostile toward the peacekeepers after they had called for NATO air strikes. This is another way in which the failure of the basic security missions complicated another mission. It was not until 1994 that the UN decided it would stop requesting permission of local militaries, but merely "inform" them of its intentions to deliver aid (Findlay, 2002). This is perhaps some evidence of learning, but not necessarily that tied to mission coordination. Although UNPROFOR and UNHCR did their best to ensure that aid was delivered, the warring parties were hostile toward their presence and restricted movement; worse, this resulted in having to use bribes for access to various parts of the country. This paints a mixed picture about UNPROFOR's ability to fulfill its humanitarian mandate.

The Traditional Peacekeeping and the Humanitarian Assistance missions are somewhat compatible with each other, particularly relative to peacebuilding missions. Both these missions are spatially distant from all the others in Figure 2.1 but are also somewhat distant from each other. There are commonalities in terms of impartiality, third party, distributive orientations, and other characteristics. DDR and Humanitarian Assistance have less in common, but generally are not at extreme ends of the continuum with respect to the dimensions that we used to characterize missions in Chapter 2. Nevertheless, there were enough differences to cause problems. Baumann et al. (2011:53) highlight the incompatibility issues and consequences:

"Ultimately, the UN mission suffered from the occasional incompatibility of the two broad and lofty purposes that brought it to Bosnia in the first place: to alleviate human suffering and facilitate an end to the war—both, incidentally, within the context of preserving Bosnia-Herzegovina as a sovereign political entity. At times, it was not possible to fulfill the humanitarian mission without being drawn in some measure into the conflict. In turn, assuming the role of the broker of peace without massive military leverage sometimes left the UN appearing confused and ineffectual in protecting civilian noncombatants desperately seeking sanctuary and a means to survive."

Humanitarian Assistance involves more than just emergency aid in the form of food and medical supplies. It also can include assistance with medical care, shelter, and longer-term needs. UNPROFOR encountered a number of challenges because of the destruction caused by the civil war. Almost a third of health facilities were destroyed and nearly 40 percent of emergency clinics as well (Cain et al., 2002). Bosnia also suffered secondary (to direct casualties) health problems. In addition to the psychological traumas that resulted from the war, Bosnians were faced with "lingering health problems due to environmental factors (such as air pollution from metallurgical plants), limited sites for disposing of urban waste, water shortages, and the destruction of infrastructure due to the war" (European Observatory on Health Care Systems, 2002:11). In 1992, it is estimated that the total number of refugees from Bosnia, the first year of conflict, was around 1.8 million, and the number of internally displaced persons was 810,000 (Kačapor-Džihić and Oruč, on behalf of the European Commission DG Employment, Social Affairs and Inclusion, 2012). Kačapor-Džihić and Oruč (2012:20) point out that "refugees faced significant obstacles to exercising rights to work, education, health care, social assistance and documentation including travel documents, while this population also struggled to obtain durable livelihood solutions and obstacles to return and access rights in their pre-war settlements."

Determining the impact of peace operations on these broader challenges is not an easy task. There are a number of quality-of-life indicators to assess the effects of humanitarian assistance, derived largely from the United Nations Millennium Development Goals and World Bank reports (United Nations, 2009; World Bank, 2009a, 2009b), that suggest some progress in goal achievement by the peace operation. Yet appropriate baselines are important to gauge the extent of that progress. Because Bosnia was not an independent state prior to 1992, there are no previous data available on the country, and one cannot generally disaggregate figures for Bosnia from those of Yugoslavia prior to that time. Beginning in 1992 and extending to the end of the major peace operations in 1998 provides a timeline for assessing changes during and immediately following the peace operation. By examining data from a few years after the Dayton Accords, one can detect the effects of policies implemented earlier without complicating the analysis with a host of intervening variables that would come into play over longer time periods.

Not surprisingly, life expectancy for men and women declined during the war but improved substantially thereafter. In 1992, the deadliest year in terms of lives lost to the conflict (RCD, 2007), the estimated life expectancy in Bosnia reached a low of 70.58. Much of the high initial death rate is probably attributed to the fighting itself, a failure of the peace operation to achieve the core goal of violence abatement prior to the Dayton Accords. By 1996 (the year following UNPROFOR's formal departure from Bosnia), however, life expectancy had improved to an estimated prewar level of 72.31 years (United Nations Population Division, 2019). A relatively flat time-series for mortality would have suggested success in humanitarian assistance and violence abatement, but that is not the case. Similarly, there was a decline in the rate of certain diseases after the war, including tuberculosis. There was no change in the availability of safe drinking water over time; rates were generally very high throughout the period, with almost 100 percent access. On this dimension, peacekeepers might have maintained effective protections even as there was little room for improvement.[4]

Human Rights

Among UNPROFOR's first actions in Croatia was to set up UN Protected Areas (UNPAs) for civilian protection. Another milestone in UNPROFOR's mandate was the Security Council's passing of a resolution (S/RES/836) in June 1993, which declared six Bosnian cities and towns (Sarajevo, Tuzla, Bihać, Goražde, Srebrenica, and Žepa) to be "safe areas." Under this resolution, UNPROFOR was authorized to act "in self-defense, to take the necessary measures, including the use of force, in reply to bombardments against the safe areas . . . or to armed incursions into them" (paragraph 9). NATO was authorized to take "all necessary measures" to support UNPROFOR in the performance of this mandate. Although UNPROFOR was carrying out multiple missions in tandem, this represented a shift in emphasis from primarily protecting human assistance deliveries to protecting civilians (Tardy, 2015a, 2015b).

Our previous analysis noted that the ineffectiveness in enforcing a ceasefire in Croatia led to violence and ethnic cleansing in the UNPAs there. This would be repeated several times over in Bosnia, indicative of a lack of learning over time. There were reports already in August 1992 of detention centers, mass deportations of civilians, and other violations of human rights and international humanitarian law. Widespread rape was also something practiced by all parties. An estimated 20,000 women, particularly Muslim women, were raped by Serbian forces (European Community Report, 1993), and the Human Rights Watch (Brown, 1993:82) pointed out that these rapes

---

[4] Some data on hospital admissions and the like are not available for the war period, underlying our contention that certain data are difficult to collect under conditions of active combat and that one cannot rely on external actors to collect the information needed for evaluation (see Diehl and Druckman, 2010, on this point).

often took place before multiple witnesses, "indicating that the perpetrators do not fear punishment." Indiscriminate violence against civilians, such as the attack on the marketplace in Sarajevo in 1994, was also a common occurrence in this civil war.

Problems with the no-fly zones noted under the section on DDR, which were designed in part to protect civilians, also contributed to failures in human rights protection. Casualty figures suggest there was some success with a significant decline by mid-1993, but the most catastrophic failure occurred in July 1995 (Research and Documentation Center, 2009).

UNPROFOR's inability to contain violence can be seen in the atrocity at Srebrenica in July 1995, when over 8,000 Muslim men and boys who had fled from ethnic cleansing elsewhere in Bosnia were systematically killed by Bosnian Serbs, with no attempt of resistance made by the Dutch UNPROFOR contingent there (MacQueen, 2011). Following the mass killing in Srebrenica, the fall of the safe area of Zepa, and another mortar attack on a Sarajevo market (the first market attack occurred on February 5, 1994), UNPROFOR changed its approach to the use of force, ridding itself of previous red tape that hindered it from taking action, and thus was born the offensive campaign "Operation Deliberate Force." On this point, MacQueen (2011:154–155) explains: "NATO's 'Operation Deliberate Force' was pursued without any references to 'dual keys' or inter-agency cooperation." Schinella (2019:11) adds, "after three years of relative inaction, NATO weighed in with an aggressive air campaign, and less than three weeks later the Bosnian Serbs not only acceded to demands to lift the artillery siege of Sarajevo but also proved willing to make key concessions at the negotiating table." Thus, to the extent that progress was achieved, it was NATO actions, not those of UNPROFOR, that were responsible. Furthermore, it was coercive military action and not traditional peacekeeping modalities that accounted for any positive results. As with the early stages of ONUC, putting peacekeepers into the midst of a violent conflict almost guarantees failure.

A Human Rights Watch report harshly summarized UNPROFOR's failures in the human rights mission: "Although the safe areas may have been created with good intentions, in actuality, they became U.N.-administered ethnic ghettos. . . . Thousands of people huddled together, with inadequate food, water and shelter, living in isolation from the rest of the world. Only a few hundred lightly armed peacekeepers and increasingly disingenuous threats of NATO air strikes guaranteed their safety" (Lupis et al., 1995:9). Costalli (2013:375) argues that the creation of safe areas was actually one of the factors that led to *more* civilian involvement in the war, as safe area zones "were exploited by Bosniak forces as bases for their operation and then became the object of Serbian attacks."

Protecting civilians is now a common element of peace operations, as peacekeepers seek to encourage human rights compliance and to protect specifically threatened populations. UNPROFOR is perhaps the most famous example of this mission, but primarily because of a spectacular failure in Srebrenica rather than being a model for how this mission should be conducted. Given that tragedy and other outcomes, we judge UNPROFOR to be *Ineffective* with respect to this Human Rights mission.

UNPROFOR was among the early post–Cold War peace operations launched in an optimistic period for peacekeeping but thrust into an internationalized civil war fraught with ethnic divisions and violence. The scorecard for this operation shows a number of failures. As with ONUC, peacekeepers were sent to a conflict with ongoing violence rather than one in which a peace agreement had been secured and a cease-fire was firmly in place. Although numerous cease-fire agreements were achieved during the course of the peacekeeping deployment, very few held for long. It was not until the Dayton Accords that cease-fires and other goals of the operation were achieved, and these were primarily accomplished under the auspices of successive peace operations.

Summary of the UNPROFOR Case

How does the UNPROFOR experience comport with our expectations? The results are summarized in Table 4.4. With respect to Security First, the failure in the basic security missions had deleterious effects. Being unable to stem the violence undermined efforts at DDR, and vice versa; this negative interaction also fits with the Recursive Effects expectation. Groups were not willing to give up their weapons when there was ongoing fighting; the availability of weapons—most notably heavy weapons and air forces—provided the opportunity to carry out more extensive and deadly attacks.

Problems in basic security missions also complicated other missions, most obviously Human Rights. The ongoing violence and advanced weaponry took a heavy toll on civilians, even those that were in designated safe areas allegedly protected by UN peacekeepers. Ethnic cleansing and other atrocities were pervasive throughout the deployment of the peace operation.

Table 4.4 Summary of results vis-à-vis expectations—UNPROFOR

Type of expectation	Expectation	Outcome
Sequencing, Simultaneity, and Prerequisites	Security First	Supported
	Democracy Matters	N/A
	Peacebuilding Synergy	N/A
	Peacebuilding Matters	N/A
	Recursive Effects	Supported
Compatibility	Aggregate Effects	Not Supported
	Learning	Not Supported
	Individual Effects	Partly Supported

Security failures impacted the protection and delivery of humanitarian assistance, but not to the extent that the latter mission was a complete failure. UNPROFOR was able to contribute to the delivery of assistance and achieve some other humanitarian goals. It might have been even more successful had it been able to limit violence and facilitate DDR. Humanitarian shipments were diverted, stolen, and denied access because they served the interests of groups involved in ongoing fighting.

In terms of compatibility, UNPROFOR was below average in the number of missions performed (four) and slightly better than average in terms of compatibility on all three indicators. This did not enhance outcomes, as anticipated by the Aggregate Effects expectation. Incompatibility was postulated to undermine success, and there was some evidence of this with respect to Humanitarian Assistance vis-à-vis basic security missions working at cross-purposes. Nevertheless, compatibility among missions, alone, does not guarantee success. Indeed, compatibility might only produce positive spillover when there is some success in one of the missions involved, and in particular one(s) earliest in the sequence. Here, the missions were largely simultaneous, and the most compatible missions (DDR and Traditional Peacekeeping) did not experience much initial or even later success; thus, there was no evidence of Learning even as there were some Individual Effects, mostly negative and largely confined to very similar security missions. Indeed, we identified instances of negative spillover between compatible missions when one or both experience problems. Indeed, compatibility might multiply the problems when failures in one mission spill over to another (compatible) mission.

Conclusion

In this chapter, we explored two UN peace operations, one (ONUC) in the relatively early history of peacekeeping and the other (UNPROFOR) that began in the nascent years of the post–Cold War period. Both involved a limited number of missions, centered on basic security missions, and therefore provide the first tests of some, but not all, of the propositions laid out in Chapter 2.

In the next chapters, we explore three more expansive peace operations. These include many more missions for each operation, and therefore allow us to evaluate more of the expectations that deal with democracy, peacebuilding, and incompatible mission profiles. Each of the missions was also deployed following peace agreements, and thus we can assess how important a more secure environment is for peacekeeping and peacebuilding success.

5

Complex Mission Cases

UNTAET and MONUC

Introduction

As peace operations evolved in the post–Cold War era, they assumed more responsibilities and therefore a greater number and more diverse sets of peacebuilding missions. Some of this was a response to the challenges posed by the new environments in which the operations were deployed. The shift to contexts with a civil conflict component (as opposed to exclusively interstate conflicts) became more pronounced, even as a primary or exclusive concern for international peace and security continued. Whereas the previous chapter dealt with older and more traditional peace operations, concentrated on security missions, we shift our attention here to operations with contemporary mission patterns.

We look at two peace operations that have seven and eight missions, respectively. Chapter 6 is an analysis of a peace operation that includes all nine missions used to develop our compatibility indicators outlined in Chapter 2. Collectively, these operations allow us to revisit some of the expectations for security and recursive effects that we considered in the last chapter, but it also affords an opportunity to examine a series of other propositions about democracy and peacebuilding that could not be examined in limited mission operations. Furthermore, our concern with compatibility can be better addressed in that the operations studied in this chapter have significantly more incompatible mission profiles than those in Chapter 4. Peace agreements were critical junctions for ONUC and UNPROFOR, ushering in whatever success those two operations had in their missions. Here, and in the case found in the next chapter, peace agreements occurred at the outset of the operations rather than later, and thus we can determine whether this was an important influence even as the number of missions was greater than those examined in the previous chapter. Thus, we begin with the United Nations Transitional Administration in East Timor (UNTAET), and then proceed in

When Peacekeeping Missions Collide. Paul F. Diehl, Daniel Druckman, and Grace B. Mueller, Oxford University Press.
© Oxford University Press 2024. DOI: 10.1093/oso/9780197696842.003.0005

this chapter to the United Nations Organization Mission in the Democratic Republic of the Congo (MONUC). Chapter 6 addresses the United Nations Mission in Sierra Leone (UNAMSIL).

United Nations Transitional Administration in East Timor (UNTAET)

The United Nations Transitional Administration in East Timor (UNTAET) represents one of the few UN peacekeeping forays into the Asia-Pacific region. In some ways, it was a throwback to earlier times in that East Timor was a dependent territory seeking independence, akin to colonial territories that became states in earlier decades. East Timor became a laboratory for a set of peacebuilding operations, and a good illustration of how short- versus long-term outcomes can differ (Diehl and Druckman, 2010).

Historical Context and Overview of UNTAET

Although it was originally a Portuguese colony (since the early sixteenth century), East Timor had been occupied by Indonesian forces since December 1975—just nine days after East Timor had declared itself independent from Portugal. The twenty-four-year occupation by Indonesia from 1975 to 1999 was characterized by large-scale human rights violations, the deliberate creation of famine as a weapon (MacQueen, 2015), and forced displacement that ultimately resulted in 100,000 to 180,000 deaths (Wassel, 2014). After years of oppression, however, the Asian economic crisis of 1997 led to the replacement of Indonesian President Suharto with B. J. Habibie, whose new government reopened negotiations regarding East Timor's self-determination. Habibie was less nationalistic than his predecessor and more open to accommodation with respect to East Timor. In response to international pressure, he agreed to a popular referendum on the future status of East Timor.

The consultation referendum took place on August 30, 1999, conducted by the United Nations Mission in East Timor (UNAMET). Of the 451,792 registered voters (among the 800,000 in East Timor and abroad), 98 percent showed up to cast their ballots, and 78.5 percent of those voting opted for total independence rather than autonomy within Indonesia as proposed by the Jakarta government (UN Department of Public Information, 2002).

Following the announcement of the results, however, pro-integration militias, supported at times by Indonesia, retaliated by launching a campaign of violence, looting, and arson throughout the country. The aftermath of the Indonesia military's scorched-earth policy was devastating; not only was the country of East Timor in ruins, but the remnants of the population that had not scattered were left frightened and without the resources or experience to organize a recovery effort (Clark et al., 2003). To ensure that violence was abated and that peace was restored, the Australian-led International Force East Timor (INTERFET) stepped into this "security vacuum" in order to bring the situation within East Timor under control, so that conditions were suitable for the re-establishment of a new UN peacekeeping operation (MacQueen, 2015).

On October 19, 1999, just shy of two months after the popular consultation, the Indonesian People's Consultative Assembly finally formally recognized the results of the August 30 popular referendum, and on October 25, UNTAET was officially established through the passing of UN Security Council Resolution 1272 (S/RES/1272). It was tasked with administering East Timor by exercising both legislative and executive authority until its official independence in 2002. UNTAET was entering a country that one local NGO described as a "young, post-conflict, post-colonial, impoverished, traumatized, non-renewable-resource-dependent nation" (Laʾo Hamutuk, 2010:4). Consequently, in addition to dealing with a country in which 70 percent of the infrastructure had been burned and nearly half of its population had been displaced, UNTAET had to build the East Timorese government from scratch, as there was no clear and accepted body of law (Galbraith, 2003; Cohen, 2002). This represents a difficult status quo baseline from which to carry out a peace operation. Nevertheless, given that the Australian-led INTERFET was able to restore security throughout the land and that the East Timorese welcomed peacekeepers with open arms, conditions for UNTAET to carry out its mandated seven missions seemed promising. Not only would UNTAET be operating in a political environment that was relatively favorable (in that the pro-integrationist factions had fled the territory and the vast majority of East Timorese viewed UN intervention as necessary for independence), but UNTAET was also provided with an extraordinary range of powers in order to support capacity building for East Timor's self-government (Goldstone, 2004). Given that UNTAET was granted executive, legislative, and judicial powers until East Timor's independence, the "depth" and "extent" of UNTAET not only created the foundations of the Timorese state (Freire and Lopes, 2013), but it shaped how the Timorese government, itself, would deal with institutional, political, economic, and social issues in the future. These conditions are rarely available to peace missions (Chopra, 2002). With those resources and powers, however, comes the responsibility to succeed, something not shared as broadly as in other operations.

After the INTERFET arrived in September 1999 to put an end to the violence by pro-Indonesian militias that immediately followed the UN-supervised referendum on independence, the security situation in East Timor dramatically improved. UNTAET would arrive shortly after on October 25, and would stay in East Timor through the new nation's first official day as an independent country on May 20, 2002. As described above, UNTAET was established as the temporary governing authority for East Timor (S/RES/1272), and therefore one way to summarize UNTAET is to describe the different phases of increasing participation that the East Timorese experienced. According to Benzing (2005), one can distinguish three distinct phases of increasing local participation, with the fourth and final consequence being independence: (1) the National Consultative Council, which began in December 1999; (2) the First Transitional Government (the National Council and the Cabinet), which began on July 14, 2000; and (3) the Second Transitional Government, which began in September 2001. These governing bodies are described in depth in the discussion of UNTAET's Local Governance mission. A different breakdown of UNTAET's progression, however, is summarized by Smith (2002), who posits that UNTAET was tasked with executing three broad phases: (1) recovery; (2) reconstruction; and (3) transition to independence. Another, more rudimentary, summary is provided by the UN's Joint Inspection Unit (Gonzales et al., 2002), which characterizes the UN response and activities in East Timor as occurring in two main phases: (1) the emergency phase; and (2) the post-emergency phase (JIU/REP/2002/10).

Although UNTAET was hailed by many in the international community as an "outstanding success" (critiqued in Ingram, 2012), the fact that peace and security would collapse in 2006—just four years after UNTAET's end—calls for a more in-depth analysis of UNTAET's ability to carry out its missions. For some, the unraveling of the security situation in East Timor was an indicator that the UN's involvement with East Timor had been scaled back too quickly (see Caplan, 2006). For others (Chopra, 2002), UNTAET's top-down approach to carrying out its missions, which ultimately sidelined

East Timorese from the process of state building, better explains why the East Timor's new institutions proved to be too fragile to maintain law and order in 2006.

Assessing the UNTAET Missions

UNTAET was assigned seven different missions during its existence: Traditional Peacekeeping, Humanitarian Assistance, Election Supervision/Promotion of Democracy, SSR, Rule of Law, Local Governance, and Reconciliation. Because of the number and mixture of different kinds of missions, its scores on the three compatibility indicators are somewhat above average indicating incompatibility, although not as high as the other two operations explored in this and the next chapter. This allows us to assess the three compatibility expectations, and these suggest some problems would occur. Nevertheless, compatibility problems might be mitigated if UNTAET achieves success in basic security (the initial conditions were favorable) and this facilitates favorable spillover into Humanitarian Assistance and Election Supervision, and then there is synergy between the three peacebuilding missions (see the other expectations in Chapter 2).

Table 5.1 summarizes our holistic judgment on each of the missions, using a Likert scale of outcomes with categories of Effective, Mostly Effective, Mixed, Mostly Ineffective, and Ineffective. The bases for these judgments and details about mission performance in this operation are given in the narrative below. We begin by considering the two basic security missions.

Table 5.1 Holistic judgments of UNTAET mission outcomes

Mission category	Mission	Outcome
Basic Security	Traditional Peacekeeping	Effective
Shorter-Term Missions	Humanitarian Assistance	Effective
	Election Supervision/Democracy	Mostly Effective
Longer-Term Missions	SSR	Ineffective
	Local Governance	Mostly Ineffective
	Rule of Law	Mostly Ineffective
	Reconciliation	Mixed

Basic Security Missions (Traditional Peacekeeping)

UNTAET was able to carry out its traditional peacekeeping mission successfully and met the subgoals of violence abatement and conflict containment. Unlike the peace operations analyzed in the last chapter, UNTAET was deployed in a very favorable environment, one characterized by stability rather than ongoing civil war. In large part, this was attributable to INTERFET's laying of a solid security foundation. This assessment is echoed by Secretary-General Kofi Annan, who in January 2000 explained that East Timor's internal security had "greatly improved, owing to the activities of INTERFET" (S/2000/53).

According to UCDP data, fighting between Indonesia and Fretilin (the Revolutionary Front for an Independent East Timor) officially ended on September 22, 1999—almost a month before UNTAET would arrive in East Timor (Pettersson and Öberg, 2020). Disaggregated data on civilian casualties show just how violent things were before the deployment of the peace operation. Indonesia's campaign following East Timor's popular consultation led to a significant jump in the number of civilian deaths, increasing from 26 deaths in August 1999 to 357 in September 1999 (Hultman et al., 2020). In the following month, when UNTAET would finally arrive, civilian casualties were still high at 170 deaths, but that was reduced to zero the following month. This paints UNTAET peacekeepers in a positive light, but there are other considerations that qualify this assessment.

Disaggregating the data to the daily level allows analysts to evaluate more thoroughly the extent to which the peace operation and the Australian military operation were able to abate violence in the mayhem that followed the 1999 popular consultation. Based on data collected by East Timor's Commission for Reception and Reconciliation (CAVR) and raw testimonial evidence (Silva and Ball, 2006), the mass atrocities of September 1999 had largely ended prior to the arrival of INTERFET, with the greatest number of civilian deaths recorded between September 5 and 11, 1999 (Smith and Jarvis, 2018). This suggests that factors other than the arrival of UNTAET were responsible for the rapid decline in one-sided violence by Indonesia. What both Hultman et al. (2020) and Smith and Jarvis (2018) seem to agree on is that the security situation on the ground in East Timor seemed to have been largely under control, which boded well for UNTAET to begin the process of establishing a new political system within East Timor (Fowler, 2016). The withdrawal of Indonesian forces facilitated a more permissive conflict environment, and thus peacekeepers could begin to focus on guaranteeing both internal and external security in East Timor (Hood, 2006). INTERFET would stay in East Timor until the end of February 2000, which meant that it operated alongside UNTAET for a total of four months as a "parallel operation" (Novosseloff and Sharland, 2019). After its formal end date on February 28, INTERFET was "re-hatted" and absorbed into the military component of UNTAET.

Nevertheless, and even given the favorable conditions at the time of its deployment, UNTAET was successful in maintaining the peace during its existence through 2002; the coded outcome is *Effective*. Without knowing the portions of the outcome attributable to early INTERFET intervention versus UNTAET actions, we can nevertheless conclude that the traditional peacekeeping mission was a success. There was no further violence that rose to the level of civil war (Sarkees and Wayman, 2010), and violent incidents were relatively rare. Rounds of conflict between Indonesia and East Timor (CNRT) ceased after September 22, 1999, with the last Indonesian soldiers leaving the territory on October 31. Nevertheless, anti-independence militias were still active throughout 1999 and 2000 in East Timor, which led to lingering acts of one-sided violence against civilians (Gleditsch et al., 2002). Indicative of the change and the subsequent success of the peacekeeping force was the significant decline in one-sided violence that resulted in civilian casualties. There were 914 such deaths in 1999, but in the three years following UNTAET deployment, that number was reduced approximately 95 percent (deaths ranged from thirty-six to forty-nine in those years); the numbers also remained low in the year following UNTAET termination as a new peace operation took over (Gleditsch et al., 2002). There were twenty-six peacekeeper deaths during the UNTAET's deployment; only two of these were classified as "malicious," with the remaining the result of accident or illness, which again speaks to the relatively friendly relations that peacekeepers had with the local population.

One of the reasons security conditions remained stable in East Timor can be traced to UNTAET's successful cantonment (temporary holding or garrisoning) of the Falintil fighters between 1999 and 2001. Through this arrangement, UNTAET was able to ensure that grieving Falintil soldiers were prevented from retaliating against the Indonesian militias who had wreaked so much havoc, while simultaneously giving UNTAET more time to focus on diplomacy. Braithwaite (2012:290) argues that this was central to the success of the operation in its traditional peacekeeping mission and other missions that followed: "all other successes that follow were trivial in comparison."

Although violence stayed at low levels, what remained a challenge for UNTAET throughout its existence was the presence of active militias along the western border (Smith and Dee, 2003). According to the Timor-Leste Armed Violence Assessment (TLAVA) (Small Arms Survey, 2008), in 2000 there was a spike in border incursions by pro-autonomy militia, and this subsequently generated alarm and concerns that militias were armed and growing in number. These attacks and the perceived insecurity they induced spurred the creation of an East Timorese national defense force (F-FDTL). Although Indonesia (TNI) made several attempts to disarm the militias in 2001 and 2002, the effectiveness of such efforts is questionable given that violent attacks continued to take place through 2003 (Small Arms Survey, 2008).

Nevertheless, the peacekeeping force was responsive to these threats and generally successful in dampening them. For example, when militia moved into an area with previous pro-Indonesia ties and no peacekeeping presence, UNTAET responded quickly through diplomacy, coordination with national authorities, increased patrols, redeployment of forces, and the capture of some militia members to meet the threat (Smith and Dee, 2003). Overall, the peacekeepers were able to prevent militias from establishing permanent bases in East Timor, even as those groups continued across the border in West Timor (Smith and Dee, 2003). There was a spike in cross-border incursions in 2000, but with very limited violence and few casualties.

The peace operation also coordinated with Indonesia on border issues in order to minimize the chances for confrontations.[1] This included the establishment of a Joint Border Committee in 2000. Geographic proximity and potentially overlapping jurisdictions raised potential problems, and agreements on arrangements for land, sea, and air did not necessarily resolve all or most issues during UNTAET deployment (Smith and Dee, 2003). Nevertheless, significant incidents were avoided, and the peacekeeping force was able to lessen and then virtually eliminate the risk that an internationalized conflict would break out.

As alluded to above and noted in more detail when discussing SSR, East Timor did not enjoy long-lasting freedom from violence. There were serious

---

[1] There are no militarized disputes between East Timor and Indonesia to report, but this might be because East Timor was not an independent state during the period and therefore any disputes would not be recorded by the Correlates of War Project, which includes only disputes involving a state on each side of the confrontation.

outbreaks of violence in 2006 that undermined much of the progress that had been achieved to date. Nevertheless, the UNTAET operation in terms of traditional peacekeeping had been gone for four years and cannot be held responsible for those problems (Braithwaite, 2012); the same might not be said for its SSR efforts.

Shorter-Term and More Compatible Missions (Humanitarian Assistance and Election Supervision/ Promotion of Democracy)

Based on the success of the Traditional Peacekeeping mission, we would expect that other missions, in particular those most similar to basic security ones, would reap the benefits; both the Security First and compatibility propositions are consistent with these expectations. In the case of UNTAET, these would be the shorter-term missions of Humanitarian Assistance and Election Supervision/Promotion of Democracy. We examine these in turn.

Humanitarian Assistance

Because of the damage and displacement caused by Indonesia's campaign in September 1999, humanitarian assistance became the most pressing crisis facing UNTAET (S/2000/53). There is consensus among aid agencies and observers that the peace operation's efforts in this mission can be judged as *Effective*, even as there might be a few caveats that accompany this assessment (Braithwaite, 2012; Smith and Dee, 2003; S/2000/53; USAID, 2000; Hunt, 2002). Generally, there were substantial improvements from the outset of the peacekeeping deployment through withdrawal; this is the status quo standard.

Among the first priorities was addressing the needs of refugees and internally displaced persons (IDPs). With roughly 250,000 refugees having crossed the border into West Timor and an additional 210,000 displaced internally in East Timor (Wassel, 2014; Martin and Mayer-Rieckh, 2005), emergency relief and repatriation for these populations were paramount. Half of the refugees had been returned by the end of 1999 (Martin and Mayer-Rieckh, 2005), a substantial accomplishment. A few months later (April 2020), the number returned had increased to 161,000 (Hunt, 2002). Much of this was associated with the improvement in the security situation facilitated by the peace operation.

A major element of the Humanitarian Assistance mission for the target populations of refugees and IDPs was the delivery of food and medical aid. UNTAET played the role of coordinating agency among a series of international governmental (e.g., World Food Programme) and nongovernmental (e.g., CARE or Cooperative for American Remittances to Europe) organizations. Massive amounts of aid flowed through these channels, especially in the first critical months. There were also few incidents in the reintegration process, and no deaths related to epidemics or starvation (Martin and Mayer-Rieckh, 2005). This is not to imply that all humanitarian assistance was easy, as bad weather conditions, poor communication, misdirected deliveries, and inadequate supplies of essential commodities complicated UNTAET efforts (Smith and Dee, 2003). Nevertheless, that UNTAET was able to deliver assistance during a time when 80 percent of the population was without means of support (S/2000/53) is worthy of praise.

Limitations to the story of success in helping refugees were the problems encountered in serving those who were in West Timor prior to their repatriation. By the end of UNTAET, there were some lingering 30,000–40,000 refugees remaining in West Timor (Martin and Mayer-Rieckh, 2005). That not all refugees had returned by UNTAET's close was partly a result of continued interference and intimidation by West Timorese militia, which hindered UNHCR efforts to resettle refugees (Smith and Dee, 2003; Martin and Mayer-Rieckh, 2005). Militias still controlled some of the camps and resisted some international efforts to deliver supplies or assist in resettlement. The deployment of UNTAET peacekeepers was confined to East Timor and thus could not redress conditions across the border per se.

Beyond emergency relief, UNTAET and its partner organizations were involved in a series of other activities that supported the health and wellbeing of the local population. Among these efforts, the rehabilitation of East Timor's health sector stands out as a particular success (Rosser and Bremner, 2015). The percentage of the population with access to basic health services within two hours from home improved from 60 percent in June 2001 to 95 percent in June 2003 (World Bank, 2009c). Other kinds of improvements were also evident. By April 2000, 734 of 788 schools had been reopened and 250,000 emergency shelters had been provided. During UNTAET deployment, substantial progress was also made in rebuilding homes and in providing safe drinking water and sanitation (prior to the operation, this was in place for less than half of the population) (S/2000/53).

There was also a steady increase in life expectancy during UNTAET's deployment (United Nations, Department of Economic and Social Affairs, Population Division, 2019). Human Development Index scores, which are calculated on a 0–1 scale using three basic dimensions of human development (a long and healthy life, knowledge, and a decent standard of living), with scores closer to 1 representing "aspirational targets" or "maximum" health, education, and standard of living levels, also show improvement over time. In 2000, East Timor earned a Human Development score of 0.48, but by 2002 that number was 0.50, and by 2010 it had increased to 0.63 (United Nations Development Programme, 2019). Although longer-term data are limited given East Timor's relatively short existence, data from the Human Rights Measurement Initiative (HRMI) show a mixed record for that country. HRMI scores reveal how well the country is doing compared to what is possible at that country's income level, with 100 percent representing a country using their available resources efficiently. Compared with other countries in East Asia, East Timor is performing worse than average on Quality-of-Life rights, whereas it is close to meeting a "fair" benchmark in terms of providing citizens with a right to Education (84.5%). In 2018, its ability to provide Food, Health, Housing, and Work each earned a score of "very bad," with scores of 34.5 percent, 74.9 percent, 70.1 percent, and 42.7 percent, respectively (HRMI, 2021).

There were also some unintended consequences. The local population was divorced from these efforts, not integrated in the short or long run with international agencies and programs. For example, the Interim Health Authority was the only agency that from the outset had created dual leadership by appointing a Timorese doctor as one of its two coordinators (Suhrke, 2001) alongside international aid personnel from the World Health Organization (World Bank, 2000). That local Timorese were not more involved led to alienation and resentment toward the massive international presence (Hunt, 2002). It was exacerbated by the high unemployment rate (Chopra, 2002), especially in comparison to the high living standards of UNTAET international staff (Gorjão, 2002). The failure to build local capacity did not necessarily affect the Humanitarian Assistance mission in the short run, but it did create sustainability problems in services and provision after that international presence diminished.

For our concerns with multiple mission interaction, the expectations of positive spillover from Security First were realized. The stable situation contributed to success in delivering humanitarian assistance. Except for the refugee situation in West Timor, there was no disruption of supplies, and unlike other operations, active fighting did not complicate humanitarian delivery. With INTERFET looking after security in the early months, UNTAET was able to focus on emergency relief. Thus, one of the concerns with multiple missions is that attention and resources are inadequate or diverted from one mission to another. In this operation, the availability of another more traditional military operation assisted the peacekeepers and prevented them from being spread too thinly. Because the food relief stage established the first relationships between UN personnel and the East Timorese, any breakdowns in the food distribution system had the potential to influence early perceptions toward UNTAET (de Coning, 2000). The positive security environment in the early stages of the operation assisted the Humanitarian Assistance mission. Yet because humanitarian assistance and its success came early in the operation, there was feedback to the security mission, which we consider to be a recursive effect in line with our expectations.

Election Supervision/Promotion of Democracy
The second of UNTAET's shorter-term missions was Election Supervision/ Promotion of Democracy. Two major elections were held during UNTAET's deployment, with the hope that these could be repeated successfully by the East Timorese. Combined with progress in broader elements of democratization, UNTAET can be judged as *Mostly Effective* in carrying out this mandate.

To facilitate the elections process, UNTAET created the Independent Electoral Commission (IEC) to oversee all aspects of the two forthcoming elections: the Constituent Assembly Election in 2001 to fill eighty-eight seats, and in 2002, the presidential election. This included a wide range of activities, starting with constructing the guidelines and forms for the election. The IEC also handled the party, candidate, and voter registration processes, as well as certifying domestic and international observers for the election. Furthermore, the IEC provided information about the election to the general public and was charged with vote counting and announcing the results (Carter Center, 2004).

Despite concerns that militias might resurface as a destabilizing force, the presence of UNTAET and CIVPOL during these elections served to dissuade any violent activity. Because security actors maintained a strong presence, the campaign, election day, and post-election period were all calm and free from conflict (Small Arms Survey, 2013); violence and voter intimidation were minimal (Carter Center, 2004). As with providing humanitarian assistance, this illustrates the positive and recursive spillover between Traditional Peacekeeping and the election supervision aspect of the broader Election Supervision/Promotion of Democracy mission.

Broad participation in the elections was also indicative of success. IEC turnout estimates show that 91 percent of eligible voters participated in the Constituent Assembly elections of 2001 (Carter Center, 2001; Hohe, 2002b), and 86.3 percent participated in the presidential election in 2002 (Carter Center, 2004). The 2002 presidential election had 364,780 valid votes cast (S/2002/432/Add1), with an overwhelming majority (82.68%) cast for Xanana Gusmão—the former head of the military wing, Falintil (the Armed Forces for the National Liberation of East Timor). Observers concluded that voters understood the election process; this was a result of civic education efforts under UNTAET and associated organizations that exhibited somewhat varying levels of success (Carter Center, 2004). Demographically, women were active participants in all aspects of the electoral process, including as candidates (Carter Center, 2004). Accordingly, international observers, such as the Carter Center, certified the process and results as "free and fair" (Carter Center, 2004). The participating political parties also accepted the results of the elections. This is not to say that the militias supported the election or its results, but they did generally refrain from challenging it with violence.

The success in these elections stands somewhat in contrast to the electoral experience—the popular referendum—just prior to UNTAET's inception. UNAMET peacekeepers had failed to guarantee safety to those who voted in the 1999 popular consultation, with widespread violence and intimidation, even as other aspects of the election suggested success, namely, broad participation and unambiguous results. The 1999 referendum was also followed by pro-independence troops taking revenge in the days following the voting results (Braithwaite, 2012).

The democratization process, and UNTAET's role in it, involves more than enduring free and fair elections. In this regard, there are a number of short-term indicators of UNTAET and East Timor's success in democratization efforts. First, it was a healthy sign that sixteen different political parties participated in the 2001 elections, as meaningful electoral competition is one of the hallmarks of democracy. Despite concerns that East Timor might become a one-party state, UNTAET's decision for East Timor to adopt a proportional representation model for its Constitutional Assembly election allowed for smaller parties to be represented (Chesterman, 2002). Because Fretilin won fifty-five of the eighty-eight seats in this election, however, it not only became the majority party, but the party to which UNTAET would defer decisions (Simangan, 2019). Thus, one party and then one presidential candidate dominated each election respectively, but this was not manufactured or imposed, but rather the outcome of popular preference. Furthermore, there was progress in the administration of the elections. Compared to the 2001 election, the East Timorese played a much more significant role in the administration of the 2002 presidential election; this is suggestive of indigenous democratic values and institutions gaining a foothold in East Timor during UNTAET's deployment. Other indications of democratization included the peaceful adoption of a constitution (also an important signpost for the Rule of Law mission) by the Assembly chosen in the first election. A caveat, however, is that the constitution allowed the transformation of the assembly into a national parliament without another election, and this allowed the dominant Fretilin group to consolidate its power and pack the first cabinet with its supporters (Richmond and Franks, 2008).

At the time of the termination of the UNTAET operation, most or all signs were positive with respect to elections and democratic processes more generally. As with the Traditional Peacekeeping mission, however, there was a breakdown some years later, albeit not as severe. Institutionally, a dynamic of competition began to emerge between a president with a strong popular mandate, but weak powers under a new constitution, and a new government backed by a strong parliamentary majority (Leach, 2016). This did not provide the kinds of checks and balances or separation of powers that are characteristic of stable democracies. What exacerbated this rift was that security forces would mirror the divisions, with the defense force (F-FDTL) allied with the president and the police (PNTL) aligned with the incoming Minister of the interior, Rogerio Lobato (Leach, 2016), with tensions ultimately boiling over in April 2006. Nevertheless, although the 2007 presidential election was held against a backdrop of persistent insecurity, widespread displacement, and violence in the capital of Dili, the 2,000 observers monitoring both election rounds concluded that the elections were peaceful (Timor-Leste Armed Violence Assessment, 2009; UNDP, 2007).

Aggregate indicators of democracy paint a picture similar to the narrative above. Estimates by the Varieties of Democracy (V-Dem) Project (Coppedge et al., 2021) show improvement in East Timor's deliberative, electoral, participatory, egalitarian, and liberal democracy index scores between 2000 and 2003 (with data on electoral democracy beginning in the year 2002, following its independence). Further improvement over time in its respective democratic indicators is limited, with scores from 2020 not substantially different from those in 2003. Following its independence on May 20, 2002, East Timor's first recorded Polity 5 score was a score of 6—reaching the threshold of democracy (Marshall and Gurr, 2021).[2] In 2006, this number would improve to 7, and by 2012, East Timor would reach an 8 on the −10 to + 10 democracy scale. Therefore, not only has East Timor been labeled as a democracy ever since its independence, but it improved over time and following UNTAET deployment.

Overall, UNTAET successfully delivered its election and democratization mandates (but see Richmond and Franks, 2008, who use this case as evidence of the dangers of early elections before effective political institutions are created). As with Humanitarian Assistance, UNTAET illustrates the positive and recursive spillover between Traditional Peacekeeping and ensuring free and fair elections. The monitoring functions of both missions complemented one another, and the traditional cease-fire supervisions served to limit violence and ensure a peaceful election.

Longer-Term and Less Compatible Peacekeeping Missions (SSR, Local Governance, Rule of Law, and Reconciliation)

Given the success of the traditional peacekeeping mission, and even the shorter-term missions of Humanitarian Assistance and Election Supervision/ Promotion of Democracy, we might expect that this would have downstream consequences for longer-term peacebuilding missions. Nevertheless, the four peacebuilding missions in UNTAET—SSR, Rule of Law, Local Governance, and Reconciliation—are relatively incompatible (see Chapter 2 analyses) with the operation's other missions, suggesting prospective problems according to our compatibility expectations. We also suggested that the first three peacebuilding missions above would have synergistic impacts on one another and that these three would then impact Reconciliation; thus, success or failure might be a uniform pattern rather than variation in outcomes across these longer-term missions.

---

[2] Polity 5's democracy index is derived from coding of competitiveness of political participation, the openness and competitiveness of executive recruitment, and constraints on the chief executive.

In general, UNTAET's success in carrying out its longer-term missions is not as clear-cut as with its short-term ones. Wassel (2014:8–9) articulates this dilemma: "Given the enormous responsibilities to be completed within the two years of its mandate, UNTAET ended up focusing its efforts on putting out fires rather than developing a transition plan which recognized the need for conflict prevention in a post conflict society." That a post-independence UN mission (UNMISET) had to be created to meet the continued need in East Timor for public administration, law and order, and external security (Gorjão, 2002) is itself an indication that UNTAET did not accomplish all it set out to do for East Timorese institutional capacity building. UNTAET had difficulties in all its missions in this section, but its SSR efforts must be deemed *Ineffective* because of the security sector collapse in 2006.

Security Sector Reform (SSR)
Security Sector Reform (SSR) for UNTAET was multifaceted and included developing the East Timor defense force (F-FDTL) and the East Timor Police Service (PNTL), as well as establishing mechanisms for democratic control of both of these security institutions.

UNTAET's original mandate did not make any provisions for a military force as it envisaged that East Timor would instead have security personnel associated with the police, similar to that of the French gendarmerie (Gorjão, 2002). It was not until a team from King's College of London arrived at the cantonment site and encouraged the creation of a defense force that UNTAET approved the establishment of the East Timor Defense Force (F-FDTL)—a modest light infantry force of two battalions (UNTAET Daily Briefing, 2001; Smith and Dee, 2003). Of the two battalions, the first would be recruited exclusively from members of Falintil and the second would be open to all applicants. Problematic was that this first battalion would only have 650 members, even though there were around 1,900 Falintil members in the cantonment. This meant that two-thirds of the soldiers that had previously fought for East Timorese independence would be denied the opportunity to participate in its new military.

Further exacerbating things was the selection process into the first battalion. This was controlled by the Falintil High Command, which resulted in a battalion made up of loyalists of the soon-to-be-elected President Gusmão and dominated by Timorese from the eastern districts—two elements "demarcating the fault lines of the 2006 conflict" (Ingram, 2012:11). Falintil soldiers who were not recruited had to be demobilized through the Falintil

Reintegration Assistance Program (FRAP), which was organized by the International Organization for Migration (IOM), and while reintegration efforts were generally successful, Martin and Mayer-Rieckh (2005) and Ingram (2012) point out that the selection process for both the F-FDTL and the FRAP created resentment among those who were excluded. In his evaluation report on the FRAP, McCarthy (2002) describes that although most of the FRAP recipients were pleased with their packages and assistance, ex-Falintil members that were not recruited—known as the "Forgotten"—were a source of concern in that they were vulnerable to being recruited by issue- or grievance-based security groups, such as the AFC 75 (Association of Former Combatants from 1975).

The creation and recruitment of the East Timor Police Service (PNTL) was also controversial. In a Report of the Secretary-General from September 1999, Kofi Annan called for the development of "a credible, professional and impartial police service"(S/1999/1024). This was a difficult task from the outset as East Timor lacked any indigenous police force covering the whole country at the time of UNTAET. Previously, the Indonesian military (TNI) and the Indonesian National Police (POLRI) were responsible for law and order in the territory. Their withdrawal left a void that was only partly filled by the deployment of UN CIVPOL in early 2000, ultimately numbering 1,600 (Wassel, 2014). UNTAET's recruitment of cadets for the PNTL was marred by several different factors, one being the excessive reliance on former employees of the Indonesian police forces (Hood, 2006; Martin and Mayer-Rieckh, 2005). Despite UNTAET's willingness to take on the politically risky decision to include former Indonesian police personnel in the country's nascent police force, it seemed content with postponing important decisions until a new government was established.

Another problem that plagued the police in East Timor was the highly politicized way it was run. When Lobato became responsible for the police as the Minister for the Interior, he promoted his own partisans, while sidelining others. He embarked upon a progressive militarization of the PNTL (Lemay-Hébert, 2009), which became a dangerous arms race with the military (Braithwaite, 2012). This politicized recruitment often resulted in unqualified police contingents. As Hood (2006:60) explains, "UNTAET's leaders did not engage East Timor's political leaders in PNTL's establishment, creating a force lacking strategic vision, coherent identity, and institutional loyalty." An arrangement for UNMIT to support the PNTL would later be signed in December 2006 (following the outbreak of violence in 2006), and it was aimed at the creation of an autonomous and independent police structure (Freire and Lopes, 2003), but had such efforts been spearheaded under UNTAET's watch, the violence in 2006 might have been avoided or at least limited.

The desired establishment of democratic and institutional control over the security forces was also not manifest. The growing chasm that divided East Timorese leadership between Prime Minister Mari Alkatiri and President Gusmão had dangerous implications for the security sector. In order to compete with Gusmão, who controlled the military (F-FDTL), Alkatiri and his ally Lobato decided to focus their attention on strengthening the police so that it equaled, and later was better armed than, the military (Lemay-Hebert, 2009; Braithwaite, 2012). Under these conditions, the two security forces—military and police—became opposing groups beholden to the political interests of the leaders behind them, rather than the public writ large (Braithwaite (2012). This conflict was not something that the peacekeeping force could manage.

Two other indicators of security offer a slightly more optimistic assessment, but only relative to the failures noted above. Crime rates were generally low during UNTAET deployment, albeit accompanied by an increase in traffic accidents (S/2002/432), two areas that might be directly under UNTAET and CIVPOL purview. Public opinion surveys in 2001 carried out by the Asia Foundation (and reported in Wassal, 2014; Asia Foundation, 2004) indicated that 38 percent of respondents were "somewhat or very concerned" about their safety. On the one hand, this was lower than in subsequent years (50% in 2002; 67% in 2004, and 73% in 2008); this might suggest that on a relative basis, the UNTAET period was better, but it also signals that the groundwork for local security was inadequate for future success.

By East Timor's official independence on May 20, 2002, neither the police (PNTL) nor the military (FTDL) was ready for the full responsibility of public security and external defense (Martin and Mayer-Rieckh, 2005). There are multiple explanations for this shortfall, and indeed the general assessment of *Ineffective*. Attribution for failure of missions can often be laid at the feet of the environmental conditions or other actors, but in the case of UNTAET, it was the (in)action of the operation that receives most of the blame. Poor planning is often cited (e.g., Smith and Dee, 2003; Hood, 2006), and indeed UNTAET never had a strategic plan for setting up a police force in the initial stages of deployment. Poor leadership in CIVPOL driven by political considerations (Hood, 2006) and unprofessional behavior (Braithwaite, 2012) were also complicating factors. The mismatch of external expertise with local conditions (a central point of Autesserre's 2014 and 2021 work) together with language barriers (Smith and Dee, 2003) also produced problems (Braithwaite, 2012). Finally, and consistent with other UNTAET missions, there was little local involvement or ownership in some of the SSR functions; for example, local officials played little or no role in the design or leadership of the national police until independence (Hood, 2006). Overall, Caplan (2006:263) captures these missed opportunities well:

> "An international administration's record by the end of its mandate can also be assessed in relation to what it might have achieved—in terms of opportunities not seized, in other words. Thus, for instance, it seems in ret-rospect that had UNTAET attached a higher priority to the development of public administrative capacity, some of the deficiencies now plaguing East Timor might have been avoided or at least minimised. Similarly, earlier rec-ognition of the need for a strategy of demobilisation and reintegration of the Falintil guerrillas might have led to the development of a more capable defence force by the time of UNTAET's withdrawal."

The problems with security sector reform during UNTAET's deployment manifested themselves in the following years. The structural problems of East Timor's security institutions were not addressed by UNTAET and would ul-timately prove to be a critical factor in explaining the 2006 crisis (Lemay-Hebert, 2009). The deep fissures within and between the military and police, which reflected competing elite interests between East Timor's two senior political leaders, surfaced in May 2006, when East Timorese police and mili-tary took to the streets to fight each other, resulting in the torching of a large number of government buildings, some thirty people killed, and 15 percent of the population being displaced (Schroeder et al., 2014; Ingram, 2012). Although the UN CIVPOL had handed over executive policing authority to PNTL on May 20, 2004 (Wassel, 2014), the UN had to reassume the role of executive police authority in 2006 following the violent clashes and the sub-sequent breakdown in the national police, and it would hold that position until 2011 (Durch and Ker, 2013). Although an Australian-led International Stabilization Force (ISF) and later a new peacekeeping operation (UNMIT) were able to abate violence and restabilize the new democracy, daily gang fighting would persist for an additional two years (Wassel, 2014).

Overall, the 2006 crisis exposed the fractured security sector in East Timor and the hollow police institutions that had been created by UNTAET and its successor UNMISET (Wassel, 2014). Thus, success in the Basic Security and shorter-term missions did not produce positive result in the SSR mission, an outcome that would be repeated in the other peacebuilding missions.

Rule of Law

Overall, our assessment of UNTAET's ability to carry out its Rule of Law mission is *Mostly Ineffective*. There were positive developments, but UNTAET's failure to establish a strong political relationship with the East Timorese people and its slow, cautious "piecemeal" approach to the development of the rule of law resulted in cynicism about East Timor's justice system. The World Bank's aggregate indicator for the rule of law (World Bank, 2022b) shows a sudden improvement in rule of law at the time of deployment of the peace operation, but this is short-lived, as rule of law slips in 2002 and indeed further declines in the aftermath of UNTAET. In addition, scores remain below average globally, and indeed below the 15th percentile when compared to other countries. The breakdown in institutions in 2006 had some of its origins in the weaknesses of the rule-of-law efforts during UNTAET deployment.

Usually when one refers to building institutions in the context of the rule of law, the reference is to processes and personnel to carry out that work. In the case of UNTAET, it was also the physical infrastructure that would house the institutions. At the time of operation deployment, it was estimated that between 60 percent and 80 percent of all buildings had been destroyed by the September 1999 violence, and any preexisting judicial infrastructure had almost been entirely wiped out (Strohmeyer, 2000). Therefore, in order to carry out its Rule of Law mission, UNTAET had to first address the rebuilding of courthouses, police stations, and prisons, effectively creating a judicial system from little existing base (Cohen, 2002). Success in these endeavors, however, is not a substitute for the creation of institutions and processes that underlie the rule of law.

One hallmark of progress, and a prerequisite for establishing the rule of law, is the adoption of a constitution. In East Timor, this followed the election of an assembly and provided the framework under which all laws could be adopted in the pre- and post-independence periods. The constitution drafting process, however, was Fretilin-dominated, with that party's original draft and amendments forming the basis for deliberations. Nevertheless, the constitution was adopted by a substantial majority (72–15–1) and attracted support from delegates beyond those associated with Fretilin (Carter Center, 2004). The constitutional process did not have expansive input from the citizenry (Carter Center, 2004), although there is no clear evidence that this undermined its legitimacy. Judicial constraints on the executive, according to V-Dem measures, were relatively high throughout the period but showed no improvement during or after UNTAET deployment.

Succeeding in the Rule of Law mission was particularly challenging in East Timor. As the country prepared for independence, a new legal system needed to be built from scratch. Yet UNTAET did not have an overall and integrated plan for this, and in any case lacked the necessary funding to make it happen (Martin and Mayer-Rieckh, 2005). Article 165 of the Constitution indicated that Indonesian law would continue, but muddying the waters was at least one judicial ruling that applied Portuguese law as prevailing (Asia Foundation, 2004). There were also rules imposed by international authorities that filled in gaps. With the Assembly still to be elected and then having an initial role of constitutional drafting, East Timor lacked the governmental mechanisms to create its own indigenous legislation.

Rule of law depends on functioning and professional judicial systems, but also on the support from and access for the general public. On these points, the situation in East Timor during the two and a half years of UNTAET deployment fell well short of desired standards.

The establishment of judicial structures and getting them up and running were delayed. The process of selecting and training judges and prosecutors commenced early in 2000. UN officials noted though that poor infrastructure and the dearth of law books created problems in achieving goals (S/2000/53). Judicial proceedings did not begin until May 2000, and even then, these were confined to the capital city Dili. Later that year, the number of judges (25) and prosecutors (13) for the country was still small (Smith and Dee, 2003). Most concerning was that many of those serving in these positions had very limited education and less than two years of experience and training (Smith and Dee, 2003); the number of trained lawyers was also small at the time of independence, even as training programs were in place (Chopra et al., 2009). Furthermore, the courts lacked some of the basic elements to operate effectively. These limitations included only shared computers, no access to the internet, no transportation, limited library collections, and an outdated court management system (Zifcak, 2004). Case backlogs in the early period were also common.

In terms of judicial independence, there was a steady improvement in East Timor's de facto judicial independence: it earned a score of 0.65 in 2000, a score of 0.75 in 2002, and a score of 0.82 in 2004 (with 0 representing no judicial independence and 1.0 representing judicial independence—Linzer and

Staton, 2015). This is not to imply, however, that all courtrooms were fully staffed and up to par, and indeed this was not the case.

Laws, institutions, and procedures are only as good as the extent to which people accept and use them. For East Timor, the balance sheet on these points offers a mixed bag. Public opinion survey results from the Asia Foundation (2004) are revealing. The public exhibited support and general understanding of the national legal system. Furthermore, they recognized the value of formal courts for serious crimes, and supported (about two-thirds) prosecuting rape (note that domestic violence in East Timor generally was a problem—see Olsson, 2009, for the general difficulties the operation had in combating sexual violence). Other indicators, however, are more troubling and suggest peace operation failure to varying degrees and along multiple dimensions. Citizens were not necessarily aware of what laws existed; new laws written in Portuguese were also confusing for many East Timorese, given that Portuguese is only known to 7 percent of East Timorese, even among the literate (Asia Foundation, 2004). Citizens also reported in the survey that they did not know how to bring a legal problem to district courts. Filing fees for civil cases ($75) were also a deterrent to using the formal legal system (Asia Foundation, 2004).

Beyond information shortfalls (which the peace operation could have redressed), East Timorese did not necessarily trust the legal system, and therefore were not willing to rely on it (Asia Foundation, 2004). They expressed uncertainty about whether laws would be upheld by authorities, and especially those related to the rights of the accused. Confidence in the police was the lowest compared to other public officials in the state.[3] Blair (2020) defines, in part, a successful rule-of-law system as one in which citizens rely on state authorities, rather than non-state actors, for addressing crimes and disputes. Yet, the people of East Timor were more inclined to use the traditional *adat* system of dispute management, a system directed by the village head, especially for more minor offenses and issues. Only 9 percent of civil and criminal cases were brought before state courts (Asia Foundation, 2004). Localized institutions involved more than sixty-three different systems throughout the country, varying by location and tradition (Walsh et al., 2019). These also might run contrary to national law, depending on the legal issues involved (Richmond and Franks, 2008). Thus, even though data from

---

[3] From a different perspective, Asia Foundation (2004) does indicate that confidence levels in the police were quite high by international standards. The report also speculates whether this support was attributable to the replacement of hated Indonesian forces with UN officers.

V-Dem indicated strong equality before the law for citizens in terms of rights and access, in practice mistrust and a weak judicial system were not able to ensure such rights were actualized.

Overall, UNTAET was able to establish some elements of rule of law. Nevertheless, the justice sector was slow to get started and the focus of the most serious critiques, especially given that the rule of law impacted CIVPOL and other peacekeeping missions. The problems, however, created difficulties for other missions. Specifically, much of CIVPOL's inability to prevent petty crime could have been averted had UNTAET been able to implement the Rule of Law mission more quickly (Smith and Dee, 2003). Inadequate resources was a severe hindrance (Martin and Mayer-Rieckh, 2005). UNTAET left the territory with few experienced and trained East Timorese judges, public defenders, and prosecutors, as well as limited support services for the courts. The 2006 crisis, which saw the complete breakdown of the rule of law, revealed weaknesses in East Timor's justice system (Chopra et al., 2009).

Local Governance

In terms of local governance, UNTAET was charged with monumental tasks, perhaps greater in scope and depth than any previous peace operation. It had its eye on two broad goals, one short-term and the other oriented more to the future. In the transition to independence, UNTAET had full legislative and executive authority, more akin to a trusteeship role than to one in which peacekeepers and other international actors played only facilitating roles. Thus, UNTAET was tasked with ensuring the macro-level provision of standard governmental services, but it had to do so in a difficult context: most infrastructure was destroyed and half of the population was displaced. At the same time, the operation needed to lay the groundwork for handing over local governance duties to a new East Timor government at the time of independence. The tension between these two goals led to a number of problems for the peace operation. Complicating this further was little guidance about the path to independence, a political timetable for transitions, and the kind and scope of East Timorese participation in these efforts (Martin and Mayer-Rieckh, 2005).

Overall, we score UNTAET's local governance efforts as *Mostly Ineffective*. This is not entirely a rebuke of UNTAET's efforts, but rather a reflection of its inability to accomplish everything during the short duration of the deployment. MacQueen (2015) highlights this dilemma, noting that much of the mission was intentionally deferred to the successor mission—the United

Nations Mission of Support in East Timor (UNMISET). Priority was given to getting East Timor to independence quickly without necessarily having the requisite building blocks in place.

One set of critical decisions involved the administrative organization to achieve the goals of delivering services and facilitating the transition to indigenous rule. One of the first choices that UNTAET made as Transitional Administration was to dissolve the CNRT (the National Council of Timorese Resistance), which had served as an umbrella organization for all Timorese resistance parties since 1998 (Hohe, 2002a). Although the CNRT had elected a Transitional Council to work alongside UNTAET in its tasks, UNTAET instead chose to work with a select group of Timorese leaders chosen along the independent/autonomous axis of the popular consultation to form the National Consultative Council (NCC) (Ingram, 2012). The NCC would be the primary mechanism for consultation about concerns, traditions, and interests of the East Timorese people (Leach, 2016). The dissolution of the CNRT and its district structures, however, was viewed by some East Timorese as one of many examples of UNTAET's nation building as a "high-handed and elite-dominated" process (Leach, 2016). Failing to recognize the CNRT as a local partner for development impeded the development of democracy and effective governance because it led to a contest of authority between the UN and leading political actors (Richmond and Franks, 2008).

UNTAET's primary mechanism for local governance was initially the Governance and Public Administration (GPA), but this unit was the subject of much controversy and criticism from local groups and political figures. The GPA gave way to the East Timor Transitional Administration (ETTA) under the authority of the new Transitional Cabinet. Additionally, a National Council (NC) replaced the NCC and was made up exclusively of East Timorese. Frustrated with the limited powers they could exercise and the unwillingness of international officials to consult with them, the East Timorese members of the NCC threatened to resign over what they saw as UNTAET's failure to share decision-making authority and provide them with adequate resources (Caplan, 2005). Despite the shuffling of organizations, UNTAET retained control of administration and the final say over decisions (Williams and Bellamy, 2021).

Structurally, UNTAET mirrored the subnational configurations used previously by the Portuguese and the Indonesians—thirteen districts with sub-districts below that level. At the lowest levels, however, the provision of services was limited, confined primarily to some policing and very limited staffing. Some offices remained unopened even a year after peace operation deployment (Ingram, 2012). UNTAET tried to address local concerns by creating District Advisory Councils (DACs) to facilitate citizen input in each of the districts. Nevertheless, the DACs were highly variable in impact, plagued by uneven leadership, varying legitimacy, poor accessibility, and other limitations (Ingram, 2012).

The Local Governance mission extends beyond the peacekeepers carrying out services themselves, but also building the process and structures for such services and then integrating local personnel into them; this is a key to long-run success after the peacekeepers depart. Yet, staffing civil service positions, critical for delivering services and providing for a transition to independence, proved to be problematic for UNTAET. After the violence of September 1999, many civil servants left East Timor, resulting in few trained personnel on the ground (Smith and Dee, 2003). The UN failed to plan for such personnel shortages (Smith and Dee, 2003). Even the appointment of a Public Service Commission to assist in civil service selection did not solve all the difficulties. At the end of 2000, fewer than 10 percent of senior positions were occupied by Timorese, and some UN personnel refused to work under Timorese managers (Caplan, 2004). By 2002, the UN acknowledged and documented the persistent problem. Some 11,000 of the 15,000 authorized positions had been filled (almost 75%), but these were primarily at lower levels. Fewer than 50 percent of management positions were filled, owing to what the UN regarded as unqualified candidates combined with "institutional problems" (S/2002/432).

After much frustration and complaints, UNTAET recognized that it needed to engage the East Timorese better, and as a result, there was much more concerted effort by UNTAET at "Timorization"—a term used to describe the process of moving toward the direct participation of the East Timorese. This was essential not only for ensuring functioning bureaucracies when UNTAET left, but also for the legitimacy of governance as viewed by native Timorese. Yet, at the outset, there was no plan or coordination with NGOs that provided for participation by the local population (Harmer and Frith, 2009). East Timorese, especially those at the local level, were often overlooked and barely engaged by UNTAET (Ingram, 2012). There were the aforementioned political decisions aimed at improving Timorization: (1) the replacement of the NCC with the NC; and (2) the replacement of UNTAET's GPA with the ETTA. These efforts were lauded and did help improve Timorese participation (Suhrke, 2001; Smith and Dee, 2003), but some Timorese (the most noteworthy being President Gusmão) and international observers argued that it look too long for UNTAET to make these necessary changes (Mendes and Saramago, 2012), or that these changes were largely cosmetic (Gorjão, 2002). Additionally, the East Timorese servants that were recruited remained highly dependent on the expertise and advice of international personnel, even after two years of UNTAET deployment (Caplan, 2004).

Problems with organization and staffing are relevant, especially for the future, but ultimately the Local Governance mission involves delivery of services in the short term. On this count, however, performance was considered poor (Ingram, 2012). The failures of the government sectors in dealing with justice and security were noted in the discussion of other missions. These problems extended to other areas as well. Perhaps only the health care sector included acceptable functioning levels (Caplan, 2004; Braithwaite, 2012); this was also the only sector led by a Timorese. Thus, not only was UNTAET unsuccessful in providing access to power, but it failed to improve the daily lives for most of the general population (Gorjão, 2002). This was especially the case for individuals living outside the capital in small towns and villages (Ingram, 2012).

Overall, because of UNTAET's inadequate service recruitment and training and its late "Timorization" efforts, the basic infrastructure of a functioning Timorese civil service was not set up by the time UNTAET's mandate ended in May 2002, and that is why, in part, it was shortly followed by UNMISET.

Reconciliation

UNTAET was a relatively short-lived operation (approximately 2.5 years), and thus it is difficult to assess its performance on the Reconciliation mission, which almost by definition requires an extended period of time to come to fruition. Keeping this in mind, but also cognizant of downstream consequences, we code the outcome of this mission as *Mixed*.

Much of the initial focus on reconciliation intersected with the Rule of Law mission and was more backward than forward-looking. Specifically, the focus under UNTAET was in addressing the crimes and human rights abuses during the period of Indonesian occupation. To its credit, UNTAET established the institutional mechanisms to facilitate this first step of holding perpetrators accountable, and thereby provide justice as one of the steps to reconciliation. It created the Serious Crimes Investigation Unit (SCIU) in April 2000 to investigate human rights abuses committed after the August

1999 vote. UNTAET also formed two Special Panels (and a Court of Appeal) of judges embedded within the Dili District Court; they were given exclusive jurisdiction to address crimes against humanity and serious offenses occurring during 1999, generally associated with the referendum and its aftermath (Zifcak, 2004). Most significant under its auspices was the formation of the Commission for Reception, Truth, and Reconciliation (CAVR) in July 2001 to investigate human rights violations against East Timorese during the 1974–1999 time frame. CAVR was assigned to "inquire into human rights violations committed on all sides, between April 1974 and October 1999, and facilitate community reconciliation with justice for those who committed less serious offenses" (CAVR, 2002). The CAVR also sought the return of IDPs, especially those who opposed independence to return to their villages and become reintegrated into community life.

Symbolically, the CAVR was a major achievement; Braithwaite (2012:291) called its creation a "crowning achievement of the peace." Not only did it emphasize the reception, reintegration, and forgiveness of militia leaders who had fled to West Timor, but it welcomed them to return and rebuild their lives. Prior to 2006, there was some repatriation of individuals from West Timor, with few problems in their reintegration (Braithwaite, 2012). CAVR's initiative of Community Reconciliation Process (CRP), which was based on a traditional restorative justice concept called "nahe biti bo'ot" or "spreading of the large mat," was also largely successful (Wassel, 2014). Another positive point was documenting (the "truth" aspect) the abuses that occurred, including the number killed and who was responsible. The CAVR held eight national public hearings and fifty-two local ones, and heard from 7,699 individuals including victims, witnesses, and perpetrators (ICTJ, 2021). This culminated in a massive, five-volume report of the Commission completed in 2005 (Webster, 2018).

The successes above, however, need to be balanced against a number of shortcomings. The SCIU, unfortunately, only made a modest contribution to addressing larger issues of justice and accountability (Human Rights Watch, 2003). One reason was that it was severely underfunded and understaffed (Harmer and Frith, 2009; Smith and Dee, 2003). By 2004, it had filed only 81 indictments with the Special Panel for Serious Crimes at the Dili District Court, with 369 individuals charged (Zifcak, 2004). Of these 369 indicted individuals, however, 281 of them resided in Indonesia, and were therefore beyond the reach of the nation's courts (Zifcak, 2004). According to a report by the Commission of Experts (COE), the judicial process in East

Timor had been "ineffective" due to "Indonesia's lack of political will" and refusal to "comply with any requests for extradition" (Harmer and Frith, 2009:250). Not only was Indonesia stalling East Timorese justice efforts, but its own attempts to provide a credible response to violence resulted in "sham prosecutions" (Human Rights Watch, 2002). Furthermore, there were instances of Indonesian (TNI) officers implicated in atrocities in East Timor being promoted in Indonesia (Human Rights Watch, 2002). By May 2004, half of the 1,422 estimated murders that took place in 1999 remained uninvestigated (Zifcak, 2004). Among those Timorese who were accused of being complicit in human rights violations, few were prosecuted and most of those were low-level individuals rather than the elites responsible for ordering the actions (Cohen, 2002).

The CAVR report included a number of recommendations, but only a few have been implemented (e.g., those on public dissemination of the report and some human rights training). Notably absent have been action on reparations and acceptance of responsibility by Indonesia that might have permitted some closure on past atrocities (ICTJ, 2021). Ultimately, a test for reconciliation in the near term was the maintenance of peace, a reflection of the intersection of the Traditional Peacekeeping and Reconciliation missions. The outbreak of violence and the near collapse of East Timor in 2006 was, itself, an indicator that UNTAET had not paid enough attention to national reconciliation (Williams and Bellamy, 2021), and the process was incomplete.

Summary of the UNTAET Case

UNTAET's operation in East Timor represents a cautionary tale for UN peacekeeping. What was initially hailed as a success in peacebuilding has led to a more sober assessment in light of the 2006 violence and the difficulties thereafter. This peace operation also provides a nuanced view of how different missions intersect with one another. UNTAET had perhaps more control over outcomes than other peace operations given its scope and depth of authority in preparing East Timor for independence.

The results of this case study vis-à-vis our expectations are summarized in Table 5.2. As expected by Security First predictions, the success in Traditional Peacekeeping had positive impacts, but perhaps their reach was less than expected. Keeping the peace during deployment facilitated success

Table 5.2 Summary of results vis-à-vis expectations—UNTAET

Type of expectation	Expectation	Outcome
Sequencing, Simultaneity, and Prerequisites	Security First	Supported
	Democracy Matters	Not Supported
	Peacebuilding Synergy	Supported
	Peacebuilding Matters	Partly Supported
	Recursive Effects	Supported
Compatibility	Aggregate Effects	Supported
	Learning	Not Supported
	Individual Effects	Supported

in delivering humanitarian assistance, supervising elections, and promoting democracy. These were the missions most compatible with Traditional Peacekeeping, and indicative of the Aggregate Effects and Individual Effects expectations. The spillover from basic security success, however, did not extend to peacebuilding missions—SSR, Rule of Law, Local Governance, and Reconciliation. These are the missions least compatible with Traditional Peacekeeping. The relatively negative outcomes for the peacebuilding missions support the expectation that these individual missions would be less successful when paired with less compatible missions.

With respect to the Democracy Matters expectation, we argued that failures in democratization would have downstream consequences for peacebuilding missions. The East Timor case demonstrates that the inverse is not true; that is, success in democratization did not produce better peacebuilding outcomes. Some of the limitations of the democratization efforts by UNTAET—namely problems with respect to incorporating local participation—were mirrored in problems encountered in peacebuilding.

In terms of Peacebuilding Synergy, we anticipated that the three peacebuilding missions of SSR, Rule of Law, and Local Governance would have reinforcing effects on one another, and indeed they did, but not in a positive way. In particular, problems in establishing local security forces and developing rule-of-law institutions influenced one another with negative reinforcing effects and no dominant causal direction. Our expectation that Peacebuilding Matters received only partial support; reconciliation efforts achieved some modest successes even as other peacebuilding missions were mostly ineffective. Nevertheless, problems with the Rule of Law mission, particularly with respect to police and functioning judicial systems, complicated the ability of the various institutions created to hold perpetrators of human rights abuses accountable. Once again, we uncovered little evidence of Learning, as missions did not become more effective over time; adjustments made by UNTAET to local governance and other missions were often inadequate and too late in any case.

United Nations Organization Mission in the Democratic Republic of the Congo (MONUC)

Prototypical of the shift to multiple missions was the United Nations Organization Mission in the Democratic Republic of the Congo (MONUC), which was mandated to perform eight different missions during its decade of existence: Traditional Peacekeeping, Humanitarian Assistance, Election Supervision/Promotion of Democracy, DDR, Human Rights, Rule of Law, Local Governance, and Reconciliation. MONUC also proceeded in distinct phases, with different missions occurring over time. These characteristics allow it to serve as a good case study for analyzing multiple-mission interaction and sequencing.

Historical Context and Overview of MONUC

MONUC's origins can be traced to the Lusaka Ceasefire Agreement in July 1999, a peace agreement between Angola, the DRC, Namibia, Rwanda, Uganda, and Zimbabwe designed to end the so-called Second Congo War, sometimes labeled "Africa's World War" (Lemarchand, 2009; Prunier, 2009). Preceded by several UN Security Council resolutions and the deployment of military liaison personnel, MONUC was authorized in November of that year to monitor the cease-fire and the disarmament of militias, as well as assist in protecting the civilian population and facilitating the withdrawal of foreign forces from the DRC (S/RES/1279).[4]

The civil war in the DRC, which quickly grew into a complicated, interstate conflict, stemmed from a number of different factors. For Doss (2015), the genesis of this conflict lay in the 1994 Rwandan genocide, which resulted

---

[4] For more background on the Congo conflict, see Prunier (2009).

in the exodus of more than one million Rwandans of Hutu origins; many fled to the Kivu regions of eastern Congo (then called Zaire). Unwilling to disarm the armed groups that crossed over from Rwanda, longtime President Mobutu Sese Seko began encouraging anti-Tutsi sentiment in an effort to protect and bolster his political support (Doss, 2015). For Rwanda and its regional allies, such behavior was unacceptable, and as a result, in early 1996, the Rwandan Patriotic Front (RPF), who were responsible for the mass exodus of Hutu into the DRC, began attacking refugee camps in the DRC. By May 1997, the rebel group, the Alliance of Democratic Forces for the Liberation of Congo-Zaire (AFDL), backed by Rwanda and Uganda, was able to overthrow President Mobutu and install Laurent-Désiré Kabila as the president of the Democratic Republic of the Congo (Brecher et al., 2021). Nevertheless, barely one year later, the Ugandan and Rwandan alliance with Kabila broke down, following Kabila's decision to expel all foreign forces out of the country, most of whom were his former Rwandan allies (Council on Foreign Relations, 2018). This, in turn, prompted Angola, Chad, Namibia, Sudan, and Zimbabwe to send troops—with varying degrees of military support—into the DRC to support the Kabila government (Adekeye and Landsberg, 2000). The Lusaka Accord of July 10, 1999, called for an immediate cessation of hostilities, the withdrawal of foreign groups, and the DDR of combatants, among other things (S/1999/815).

Depending on how one categorizes the evolution of the operation, MONUC went through three (Doss, 2015) or four (Tull, 2009) phases. There is consensus that the first phase of the operation lasted through late 2002, with the signing of the Pretoria Accord that established a national unity government. It was dedicated to the missions outlined in the original resolution, namely Traditional Peacekeeping in the form of cease-fire monitoring, DDR, and Human Rights. Because of continued fighting between Rwandan and Ugandan forces around Kisangani, "by the first anniversary of the Lusaka agreement . . . the prospects for the peace process and therefore the UN's peacekeeping role within it were extremely poor" (MacQueen, 2002:92). Although MONUC was mandated to protect civilians under imminent threat of violence during this phase of the operation, peacekeepers often emphasized that they did not have the means to do this with their existing resources. Illustrative of this was the Kisangani massacre that took place in May 2002, when over 100 civilians were killed by Rwandan-backed RCD-Goma troops, despite the presence of roughly 1,000 MONUC troops in that same town (Doss, 2015; Holt et al., 2009).

The second or second/third phases occur in the 2003–2006 period when MONUC was involved in peacebuilding missions, even as its original missions continued. During this phase, MONUC experienced a major turning point in its mandate. In the wake of the establishment of the Transitional Government on June 30, 2003 (Faubert, 2006), MONUC was tasked with a number of missions designed to assist in the re-establishment of the state (S/RES/1493). The new charges included the Rule of Law, Local Governance, and most visibly Election Supervision/Promotion of Democracy. Hindering the peacekeepers' ability to carry out these peacebuilding missions was the continued violence in the eastern provinces of the Congo, particularly along the borders of Rwanda and Burundi. To assist the peacekeepers in abating such violence, a French-led EU interim force—Operation Artemis—was deployed in Bunia for three months in the summer of 2003 to stabilize the security conditions and improve the humanitarian situation. Although the consensus was that this short-term enforcement operation worked, it was of limited duration (three months) and occurred only in a confined area (World Peace Foundation, 2017).

The final phase, in the aftermath of the election and extending through the formal end of the operation in 2010, involved Reconciliation, even as its other missions continued to varying degrees. By early 2007, the Congo was officially at peace (Autesserre, 2016), but violence persisted in the eastern portion of the country. Recognizing that more manpower was needed to push back the belligerents in the South and North Kivu provinces, the Security Council passed Resolution 1856 (S/RES/1856) to increase the strength of MONUC. At its peak, MONUC had 20,586 total uniformed personnel, but for much of 2008 it maintained over 90 percent of its military personnel in the troubled eastern area (Center on International Cooperation, 2009). MONUC was followed by a replacement operation in 2010—renamed the United Nations Organization Stabilization Mission in the Democratic Republic of the Congo (MONUSCO)—that emphasized stabilization to deal with the unresolved problems that lingered following eleven years of MONUC.

Assessing the MONUC Missions

MONUC attempted eight different missions during its decade of existence. Given the mixtures of simultaneity and sequencing associated with them, this case allows us to explore the full range of expectations associated with mission timing and interactions. Because of the number of missions and the long deployment, we also can consider the three expectations related to compatibility. Taken as a whole and relative to all UN peace operations, MONUC had a high incompatibility score on the multitasking-based indicator primarily because of its large number of missions. This suggests that the operation would likely experience problems on multiple dimensions by trying to do too much, although this might be mitigated by some sequencing. Its score based on average compatibility was somewhere in the middle of a tightly clustered pack, signifying that some missions went together better than others; this presages more optimism for outcomes than the multitasking indicator. Because of its decade-plus existence, MONUC's score on the third compatibility indicator—based on learning and adaptation—is on the lower end of the scale (signaling less incompatibility) and suggestive of better performance over time in its missions. Thus, the indicators present three contrasting expectations about mission interdependence.

Table 5.3 summarizes our holistic judgment on each of the missions, using a Likert scale of outcomes with categories of Effective, Mostly Effective, Mixed, Mostly Ineffective, and Ineffective. The bases for these judgments and details about mission performance are given in the narrative below for this operation. We begin by considering the two basic security missions.

Table 5.3 Holistic judgments of MONUC mission outcomes

Mission category	Mission	Outcome
Basic Security	Traditional Peacekeeping	Mostly Ineffective
	DDR	Ineffective
Shorter-Term Missions	Humanitarian Assistance	Mostly Ineffective
	Human Rights Protection	Ineffective
	Election Supervision/Democracy	Mostly Effective
Longer-Term Missions	Local Governance	Ineffective
	Rule of Law	Ineffective
	Reconciliation	Ineffective

Basic Security Missions (Traditional Peacekeeping and DDR)

We begin with the traditional peacekeeping and DDR missions. Sequentially, these were the first missions that MONUC undertook. Theoretically, success or failure in these security-related efforts was expected to have consequences for the other missions that would follow. Initially, we examine the success of MONUC in maintaining the cease-fire and abating violence.

Traditional Peacekeeping

Analysts offer several assessments of the Traditional Peacekeeping mission. On the more positive end, Tull (2009:217) concludes that "MONUC's role was limited but effective. Its thinly spread personnel, 455 military observers and 3,595 soldiers (as of October 2002), verified cease-fire violations and the eventual withdrawal of foreign armies." Yet this positive assessment seems to be based, in part, on what was accomplished with a limited number of personnel; that is, the analysis confounds a factor impacting success (force size) with the success evaluation. In contrast, Eriksen (2009:657) argues that "Even after the signing of the [Lusaka] peace agreement and the official withdrawal of foreign forces, various militias fought for control over different parts of the territory, some with assistance from or close links to governments in neighboring countries." In this regard, although MONUC limited some violence between the DRC and Rwanda and Uganda (external actors), it was less effective in terms of dealing with the militia groups that rose to power in the place of Rwandan and Ugandan troops. Putting it all in perspective leads analysts to conclude that MONUC was limited in its achievements; Holt et al. (2009:242) note that even though various agreements were signed, which ultimately led to the formal withdrawal of most foreign forces by the mid-2000s, "the complex conflict dynamics that had been unleashed by nearly a decade of nearly continuous conflict, and the state collapse that had preceded it continued to drive low-intensity violence punctuated by occasional crises."

Looking at multiple indicators of success confirms the assessments of analysts above, leading us to the overall judgment that the mission was *Mostly Ineffective*. The cease-fire established by the Lusaka Accords was short-lived, owing to the large number of different militias and foreign armies in the DRC and the relatively small number (5,000) of MONUC troops assigned to keep the peace. Over the course of the eleven-year deployment, various cease-fires were achieved and broken. Even as success was accomplished in some areas, violence shifted to other parts of the country; thus, the peacekeeping force was unable to contain the conflict. The Second Congo War began prior to MONUC's deployment (1998) and continued for several years after the peacekeeping force's arrival in the Congo. Throughout the deployment period, there were numerous conflict incidents that met the twenty-five-death threshold designated as serious conflict (Pettersson and Öberg, 2020). Such events extended beyond the MONUC operation, even as it was replaced by its successor MONUSCO. More specifically, ACLED (2022) Data on Disorder Involving Peacekeepers identified 209 incidents during MONUC deployment, 135 of which were battles or what can be considered armed clashes.

At the most fundamental level, MONUC was a failure in stopping or deterring large-scale violence. This was especially the case in the DRC's eastern provinces (Sud-Kivu, Nord-Kivu, and Orientale), where mortality rates were significantly higher compared to those in the rest of the country (Mobekk, 2009) because of the presence of foreign and local militias (Raeymaekers, 2013). Recognizing that regional violence threatened the whole peace process, MONUC transferred 92 percent of its troops to these eastern provinces, but Tull (2009:226) states that "even then MONUC lacked resolve to take robust action, as renewed conflict in North Kivu demonstrated."

More positive are some changes in trends with respect to different kinds of fatalities before and after peacekeeping deployment. Battle-related fatalities peaked in 1997 with 4,457 deaths (before MONUC) and declined significantly after 1999, with a drop to 1,294 fatalities in 2000 and down to zero for several years starting in 2002; thereafter, battle deaths occurred in some years, but never more than 550. Civilian casualties (Eck and Hultman, 2007; Pettersson and Öberg, 2020) also show a downward trend, but hardly disappear during MONUC's deployment. These were well over 30,000 civilian deaths in 1996 with a drop below 1,000 in 2000, although they spike up again in 2002 and 2003. Illustrative was when over 100 civilians were killed by Rwandan-backed RCD-Goma troops in Kisangani while roughly 1,000 UN troops and military observers were in that same town. Although Operation Artemis, which was launched in 2003 to stabilize the area of Bunia, is an example of a successful enforcement operation that directly addressed the needs of civilians, it proved to be "a one-off" (Reardon et al., 2012), and at least sixteen massacres occurred outside Bunia during Artemis' three-month deployment (Holt et al., 2006). Short of deaths, other atrocities continued against civilians, especially in 2006 and 2007; this included widespread rape and the displacement of almost a million people (Mobekk, 2009). Peacekeepers themselves were not immune from violence, with 161 fatalities during their deployment, which is on the higher end relative to other UN peace operations.

DDR

Part of the strategy designed to complement cease-fire monitoring was DDR. DDR efforts began in June 2001, following UN Security Council Resolution 1355, which authorized MONUC "to assist, upon request, and within its capabilities, in the early implementation, on a voluntary basis, of the DDRR of armed groups" (S/RES/1355). In 2003, it was agreed that MONUC would assist the national army (the FARDC) in observing the disarmament and de-mobilization process at orientation centers (S/RES/1493). It was not until November 2004, however, that the National DDR Programme (PNDDR) was initiated, developed in coordination with the UNDP, MONUC, and Belgium (Onana and Taylor, 2008). According to the national DDR plan, troops were given the choice of staying in the national army (the FARDC) or demobilizing and returning to civilian life. Accordingly, the DDR process was in some sense a voluntary one left in the hands of individual combatants (Onana and Taylor, 2008). The results were uneven (Amnesty International, 2006). Implementation included limited military assistance by MONUC to the FARDC for enforced demobilization (Center on International Cooperation, 2009). As an incentive to encourage more combatants to turn over their weapons to the government, those who opted for demobi-lization were given a monetary sum called a "filet de sécurité" or a "safety net" of $110 and a promise of a further $25 monthly allowance for one year. Nevertheless, reports suggest that this process was widely abused (Amnesty International, 2006). In addition, delays in repatriation have been judged by analysts as disappointing and agonizingly slow (Tull, 2009). The "miserable" and "squalid" living conditions of the DDR orientation centers resulted in many ex-combatants giving up on waiting for demobilization, and then they joined other armed groups (Mobekk, 2009; Amnesty International, 2006). Even those who were demobilized often found that securing employment was a very difficult task, despite being provided training by the UNDP and its partners (Hellmüller, 2016). Because a large number of groups chose not to participate in the process, it was necessary for a second attempt at demobili-zation known as "mixage," but that would ultimately fail to disarm groups in the east. This incomplete DDR process is partly responsible for the spike in violence that occurred in the eastern provinces of North and South Kivu in the latter part of 2008 (Center on International Cooperation, 2009).

Indicators and evidence for DDR are consistent with this negative assessment, and therefore we judge the mission as *Ineffective*. One can point to large numbers of combatants participating in DDR; by December 2009, a total of 208,438 combatants had been processed in the DDR program since November 2004, and a total of 110,921 of these individuals had opted for demobilization rather than army integration (Small Arms Survey, 2013b). Nevertheless, there were significant exceptions, with several militias not disbanding and indeed remaining as active participants in fighting in certain areas. Even the large numbers of soldiers participating in DDR could be misleading, as some reports had soldiers demobilizing, accepting payments, and then joining new militias. MONUC might have been somewhat more successful supervising the withdrawal of foreign forces, but as late as 2007 some 6,000 rebels reportedly remained (Tull, 2009), and all foreign troops were not withdrawn until much later.

Similarly, large caches of weapons were collected (during the five-year period of DDR, 118,548 weapons were collected) (Small Arms Survey, 2013b), but there are no accurate aggregate totals of weapons that needed to be or should have been collected, so it is hard to assess whether the actual collection represents substantial progress. Furthermore, many demobilized ex-combatants handed in one weapon while burying others (Van Puijenbroek et al., 2008), and the disarmament outcome was ascribed as "insufficient" (Hellmüller, 2016).

Perhaps most disappointing were the results of reintegration of fighters into the FARDC, the national army. The integration of Congolese armed groups into the FARDC, particularly from the rebel group (CNDP), has been described as "ad hoc" (Center on International Cooperation, 2010:45). Davis (2009:17) indicates that some expert observers suggest that "the way in which DDR was carried out encouraged the worst elements of each militia to stay in the army rather than demobilize." Onana and Taylor (2008:512) conclude that "the Congolese army, superficially unified . . . remained politicized, unprofessional and poorly equipped—victimizing rather than protecting the population." As a result, Wilén's (2016:98) study of reintegration across multiple dimensions concludes that "FARDC scores were unsurprisingly low on all accounts of the key variables of integration." Without a truly integrated national army, the Congo's capacity to fight rebel groups that continued to challenge the state's control over parts of the country remained severely limited (Eriksen, 2009). Even more discouraging, the FARDC was the source of human rights violations during this period, suggesting that even if the dismantling of militias and the repatriation of foreign fighters were successful, the security purposes of DDR would not have addressed many of the sources of the underlying problems.

Overall, basic security efforts by MONUC can be judged as failures. Using the period immediately preceding the peacekeeping deployment as a baseline almost necessarily produces a positive trendline for any action, and thus some progress in violence abatement was inevitable. Nevertheless, the results fell far short of expectations, especially with respect to the DDR mission. According to our Security First expectation, these problems should have deleterious, downstream consequences for the other missions performed by MONUC. Our other expectations posited that as MONUC added more incompatible missions, difficulties would ensue as well.

Short-Term and More Compatible Missions (Humanitarian Assistance, Human Rights, and Election Supervision/ Promotion of Democracy)

We now move to the success/failure of those MONUC missions that are most closely tied to the success (failure) of the two security missions above, namely Humanitarian Assistance, Human Rights, and Election Supervision/ Promotion of Democracy, respectively. Peacekeepers play somewhat similar roles and have orientations related to those in Traditional Peacekeeping and DDR. They are not identical, but these three missions are closer in terms of compatibility and involve short-term actions as compared to the three peacebuilding missions that are examined in the subsequent section. If well-armed militias are actively using violence, the ability to deliver assistance will be very difficult, and indeed such violence will likely encourage many human rights abuses.

Humanitarian Assistance

Perhaps the mission most closely tied to the Security First logic is Humanitarian Assistance, in which peacekeepers facilitate the delivery of food and medical aid to civilian populations. By 2006, there were still nearly 1.7 million displaced persons, with 1,200 individuals dying daily from causes directly attributive to the conflict. "In a country where 80 percent of the population lives with less than US $1 a day, where 71 percent suffer from food insecurity, where 57 percent have no safe water and 54 percent cannot benefit from basic health services, relief assistance indeed remains highly necessary" (Faubert, 2006:13). Intervention by international agencies and MONUC tried to alleviate the most acute consequences of the war by providing food, shelter, and health services to vulnerable civilian populations, but it was difficult to deliver assistance or provide protection for NGOs doing the same when active fighting occur red and disputants used such assistance as a weapon against areas under the control of their enemies.

In general, MONUC's Humanitarian Assistance can be judged as *Mostly Ineffective* and falling well short of needs and goals. Despite extensive assistance from the UN and other NGOs, failures could be largely tied to the inability to stop militia activity and violence; this was acute and evident in the areas around of North Kivu where aid access was restricted and violence was prevalent (UNICEF, 2008). These outcomes are consistent with our Security First expectation that failures in establishing a safe and secure environment have negative consequences for other missions. Furthermore, MONUC efforts to ensure humanitarian access led to several civilian massacres by militia in retaliation (Holt and Berkman, 2006). This comports with the Recursive Effects expectation (here, the Humanitarian Assistance mission undermined Traditional Peacekeeping as well as vice versa and also had an impact on Human Rights).

Available data document some progress from wartime levels and limited success at best thereafter. Violent conflict and its collateral damage on infrastructure contributed to the deaths of an estimated 5.4 million Congolese between 1998 and 2007 (Coghlan et al., 2007, mortality survey quoted in US Department of State, 2010). Early on, less than half of internally displaced persons (IDPs)—the primary targets of aid—were receiving humanitarian assistance (UN Digest, January–March 2001) and 70 percent of the population as a whole had inadequate access to health care (UN Digest, August–October 2001). Data analyzed through 2008 show an inverse correlation between the number of IDPs and the number of peacekeepers (Tull, 2009), but data extending through 2018 (see Raleigh et al., 2010, as well as Tull, 2018) paint a more sobering picture as IDPs jumped dramatically[5] even as MONUC was replaced with another peace operation.

---

[5] The humanitarian situation significantly deteriorated in 2015, when the total number of IDPs in the Congo was an estimated 2.8 million (Ishizuka, 2016).

Peacekeepers worked with various organizations, indigenous and international, to improve the human condition. Aggregate changes in various health indicators, both short- and long-term, provide outcomes of such efforts; these are joint outcomes of different actors, rather than ones primarily or directly attributable to the peace operation, but they do provide information about mission achievement as a whole. UN Human Development Index scores similarly show a steady increase over the course of MONUC's mandate; in 2000, the score was 0.35, but by 2010, that had climbed to 0.44 (United Nations Development Programme, 2019). Despite this improvement, the DRC was given the rank of 168 out of 169 countries in the HDI ranking for 2010 (United Nations Development Programme, 2010). That said, infant mortality rates returned to prewar levels in areas that did not have active fighting (Holt and Berkman, 2006) and life expectancy in the aggregate climbed during MONUC and beyond (United Nations, Department of Economics and Social Affairs, Population Division, 2019). Both of these results can be attributed, in part, to the peace agreements and some decline in fatalities from violence. Nevertheless, areas of militia activity experienced serious problems on a host of indicators, including nutrition and health care. In other cases, a variety of health indicators remained flat during the peace operation, and aid efficiency measures in general fell below goals (Reardon et al., 2012).

Human Rights
The Human Rights mission also requires violence abatement and DDR, and the former is more compatible (see the analysis in Chapter 2) with security missions than is Humanitarian Assistance, although protecting civilians means placing peacekeepers in primary combat roles and possibly necessitating "robust" uses of military force. Novosseloff et al. (2019:22) argued that for every crisis that peacekeepers had to face—Bunia in 2003, Bukavu in 2004, Goma in 2008, and further crises after MONUC's departure—"each crisis led to massive displacements of populations, gross violations of human rights, and numerous deaths among civilians." Figures on civilian deaths and IDPs, given above, are therefore a direct consequence of the failure to limit violence. Other human rights abuses occurred, in part, because of the problems with the basic security missions. Some abuses were the result of failure or neglect, including inadequate resources and failure in DDR (Murphy, 2016).

Illustrative of human rights failures was the incident in which 200 women were raped near a UN peacekeeping base (Global Policy Forum, 2010).

MONUC and its successor MONUSCO had substantially greater rates of sexual exploitation and abuse than other peace operations, 275 incidents from 2007 to 2013 (Karim and Beardsley, 2016). More broadly, sexual and gender-based violence were routinely utilized as weapons of war by combatants on all sides during this conflict, with some victims as young as two years old (US Department of State, 2010). Toward the end of MONUC's mandate, the UN Population Fund (see Human Rights Watch, 2009b) reported over 15,000 incidents of sexual violence in one year, and the Human Rights Watch reported a substantial increase in 2009, with the majority (65%) of the cases committed by the national army (Afoaku, 2010). Despite foreign assistance efforts, however, observers report that impunity was often the norm for perpetrators (Kippenberg, 2009; Arieff, 2014).

In addition to unlawful killings, disappearances, torture, rape, and arbitrary arrests, the US State Department also warned of the following major problems: abuse of journalists and human rights advocates, life-threatening prison conditions, widespread official corruption, the use of child soldiers, forced labor, and human trafficking (Arieff, 2014). Abuses were also most common in areas where fighting persisted and militias remained active, most often during the various crises that MONUC failed to prevent or stop.

Other failures in protecting civilians were unrelated to security or compatibility concerns per se. MONUC actions made the operation complicit in, and in some cases directly responsible for, abuses. Joint operations with the national army backfired as those troops committed atrocities against civilians, even as they succeeded in reducing rebel activity. As MONUC began preparations to withdraw, there were serious concerns over the national army's capacity to protect civilian populations, given that a number of its troops had been implicated in human rights violations. Although MONUC had provided training to Congolese army units in human rights and international humanitarian law, Iqbal (2010) states that "it is questionable whether further training can alleviate the proclivity of some DRC soldiers to commit heinous acts of violence." Summarized by one report, "for every rebel combatant disarmed during the operation, one civilian has been killed, seven women and girls have been raped, six houses burned and destroyed, and 900 people have been forced to flee their homes" (Human Rights Watch, 2009b).

That the mandate of MONUC's successor operation, MONUSCO, was expanded to permit the use of "all necessary means, within the limits of its capacity and in areas where its units are deployed, to carry out its protection mandate" (S/RES/1925)—including the civilians and humanitarian personnel—speaks to the violence that took place under MONUC's watch (Murphy, 2016).

During MONUC's mandate (1999–2010), the Congo's human rights record fluctuated between improving and worsening; even though there was slight improvement in human rights scores (Fariss, 2019) in the period 2000 to 2005, these slowly declined between 2005 and 2008. There was again a slight improvement from 2009 to 2011, but scores would dip in the following years, which again speaks to fragility of the state's ability to suppress violence. When considering how the Congo fared compared to its regional neighbors, the DRC's human rights scores lag dismally behind, both in terms of aggregate performance and in terms of relative improvement over time (Fariss, 2019). Overall, MONUC's Human Rights mission can be considered to be *Ineffective*, the result at least in part because of the way that this mission interacted with the earlier and contemporary basic security missions.

Election Supervision/Promotion of Democracy
Contrary to expectations based on the Security First logic and despite some systematic differences in role and orientation with those missions (e.g., working with other actors), election supervision and promoting democracy in the DRC was *Mostly Effective*, with more success on the electoral aspect than on long-term democratization. The constitutional referendum of 2005 and the parliamentary and provincial elections in 2006 were negotiated in the Global and All-Inclusive Agreement on Transition signed in 2002. To ensure that things ran smoothly, the UN Security Council passed Resolution 1592, which authorized MONUC "to deter any attempt at the use of force to threaten the political process" (S/RES/1592). Although substantial violence preceded the voting and indeed afterward, numerous actors certified the elections as free, fair, or credible: African Union, European Union, South Africa, and the Carter Center, among others.

Indicators of election supervision success are strongly positive for the DRC elections. An estimated 28 million citizens were eligible to vote and approximately 25 million were successfully registered (Carter Center, 2006), and MONUC is given credit for its logistical and political support (Tull, 2009). Equally impressive was the 70+ percent and 65+ percent turnouts for the two rounds of voting in 2006. Even though turnout was lower in some violence-prone areas (e.g., East Kasai), the aggregate numbers indicate success despite limitations in promoting a fully secure environment.

Following the election, democratization stalled somewhat in the Congo. The newly elected President Kabila[6] and his allies took actions to limit democratic reforms and suppress his opponents specifically by using violence and intimidation to eliminate political opponents (Van Woudenberg, 2008). Although provincial assembly elections of 2007 took place peacefully, they were marred by credible allegations of vote buying (US Department of State, 2010). Local elections, originally scheduled for 2008, were not held until 2011.

Aggregate indicators of democracy are consistent with the positive results of the election and the limited progress thereafter. In the period between 2005 and 2007, the V-Dem indicates that the Congo's deliberative, electoral, participatory, egalitarian, and liberal democracy index scores all experienced growth—coinciding with the national elections that took place in 2006. Nevertheless, such improvement in democratization did not continue, as scores as recent as 2019 barely show improvements from those in 2007. The improvement in democratization under MONUC's watch is also reflected in Polity 5 scores, which show that after interregnum and transition periods between 1992 and 2005, in 2006, the Congo earned a polity score of 5—an open anocracy and on the verge of the threshold score (6) that many analysts used to designate a democracy. Nevertheless, democratization would remain stagnant, and indeed there was backsliding in the longer term with the score dropping to –3 in 2016, indicating a reversion toward authoritarianism.

Longer-Term and Less Compatible Peacekeeping Missions (Rule of Law, Local Governance, and Reconciliation)

We next move to those missions whose primary functions were generally implemented later in the peace operation deployment as well as being much further away from the basic security missions in terms of compatible roles, orientations, and other characteristics. MONUC was charged with the interrelated missions of Rule of Law and Local Governance, respectively, as well as facilitating Reconciliation. Compared to the basic security missions, these involve roles for peacekeepers that are less impartial, more primary rather than third party, require more coordination with governing authorities, and have longer-term orientations; in these ways, they can be

---

[6] He had previously been president, albeit under a nondemocratic regime.

considered different and less compatible than the ongoing basic security missions.

Local Governance

The second phase of the MONUC operation beginning in 2003 constituted the first steps in facilitating local governance and indirectly in promoting the rule of law. MONUC's initial role was to provide security for the transitional government that was ushered in following the Pretoria Accord in 2002; MONUC soldiers were redeployed to the capital Kinshasa for this purpose. Although MONUC did assist in the development of the transitional government, the reach of that government did not extend to large swaths of the country where active fighting continued; the latter directly ties failure in the security missions to problems in the Local Governance mission.

A year following the conclusion of the MONUC mission, the picture that emerges from a USAID report and from other organizations is one of systemic failures of local governance (Tetra Tech, 2012). The Fragile States Index (2021) includes a component that rates countries in terms of state capacity to carry out basic government functions. The DRC finished second to last (only Somalia was worse) among all the countries in the world in 2012; most relevant is the dimension on providing services, in which the DRC scored 9.2 on a scale in which 10 is complete failure. Specific problems included systematic power failures (even in the capital) and problems in the water supply (USAID, 2012). Governance at all levels experienced revenue shortfalls well below what was needed to function adequately. Problems at the local level were particularly crippling, as the model of governance depended substantially on decentralized structures (Tetra Tech, 2012).

The World Bank offers an equally dismal assessment (World Bank, 2010). Considering elements such as public sector management and quality of administration and accountability among others in the public sector, in 2010 the DRC ranked 177th out of 183 in terms of ease of doing business relative to other countries. At the national level, redeveloping the national army was a key element in supporting government structures. As noted previously, however, the national army was the source of violence and human rights abuses, at times in conjunction with the peacekeepers.

The general conclusion on governance and state-building efforts by MONUC is one of failure, and thus we code UNTAET in this mission as *Ineffective*. Erikson (2009) offers four reasons for such failure, namely

limited resources, poor adaptation to local conditions and needs, the contrary interests of local actors, and flawed models of state-building generally.
The second and fourth are perhaps somewhat related to issues of compatibility and trying to perform functions with a peace operation designed for
other purposes.

Rule of Law

Governance at the local level intersects with the Rule of Law mission, and
failures in one reinforced failures in the other. On the one hand, during
MONUC's deployment, the DRC had constitution and law-making processes
that were a substantial improvement over those during the reign of President
Mobutu. Nevertheless, these proved to be a veneer under which substantial failure in establishing the rule of law existed. Even when laws existed,
there was a notable disconnect between the letter of the law and its actual
application (Tetra Tech, 2012). For example, human rights protections were
included in the 2006 constitution, but enacting or implementing domestic
legislation (e.g., defining torture) was not forthcoming (Afouaku, 2010).
Congolese constitutional protections of speech and of the press were not
necessarily respected, indicated by one local press watchdog reporting 110
attacks on freedom of expression in 2008 alone (Journaliste en Danger, 2009,
reported in Afoaku, 2010).

Blair (2020) compiled measures of the rule of law from multiple sources
and across several dimensions. With respect to the DRC, the aggregate
indicators for rule of law generally paint a discouraging picture. World Bank
scores find the DRC significantly below average and with minimal improvement for the period of MONUC deployment. Freedom House figures place
the DRC at the bottom of their scale, with no meaningful change over time.
V-Dem scores for the dimensions of equality before the law and judicial
constraints on the executive, respectively, show a similar pattern: low scores
and no improvement over time. Accordingly, performance in this mission
was *Ineffective*.

Widespread corruption undermined attempts to facilitate the rule of law.
USAID (Tetra Tech, 2012) reported that 81 percent of companies said that
they had to pay bribes for contracts. Government anti-corruption campaigns
were designed more to punish political enemies than to redress endemic corruption (International Crisis Group, 2010). Complicating this was strong executive power that was largely unchecked by clear separation of powers or
checks and balances (USAID, 2012).

Another notable element is the establishment of a police force. In the middle of the MONUC operation, Mobekk (2009:276) characterized these efforts as "the police force remains largely inefficient, poorly trained, without unified and accountable command structures, lacking equipment and plagued by endemic corruption." This is a result of many factors, but MONUC had not devoted enough attention to police reform, as compared to military reform efforts, and was not able to integrate its efforts with other actors (Mobekk, 2009), an orientation required by these peacebuilding missions, but not similar to its security missions. Not enough attention was paid to creating the legal frameworks that would be the foundation for the security apparatus of the state (Boshoff et al., 2010).

Part of the Rule of Law mission was MONUC's efforts to provide "advice, training, and material support . . . to the Ministry of Justice to promote judicial and penal reform" (Doss, 2015:666). Those results have been mixed at best. The electoral supervision success of the peace operation facilitated the successful constitutional referendum in 2005. This is one instance in which democratization efforts assisted the Rule of Law mission, but this did not extend to other parts of the latter mission. Other reforms lagged. During that same year, the detention and judicial systems were so inadequate that MONUC was requested to confine suspects and ensure humane conditions (United Nations Digest, July–September 2005). Two years later, only a third (out of 180) of initial courts in the system existed and half of those did not function (Mobekk, 2009).

MONUC did post officers to correction facilities to provide advice, and the peace operation held training seminars for the Ministry of Justice. Nevertheless, poor conditions and other problems remained widespread with respect to prisoners (Mobekk, 2009). There were several hundred political prisoners being held at any given time, and observers and others were often denied access to them (US State Department, 2010). Defendants were de facto presumed guilty in trials and often not given legal counsel. Disappearances also became more common, presumably at the behest of authorities (US State Department, 2010).

The rule of law depends substantially on an effective judiciary as a backstop to abuses of power within the government and society more broadly. In the DRC, this protection was not present. A hallmark of the rule of law is judicial independence, or the ability of the judicial branch to provide legal checks on the legislative and executive branches as well as render independent and fair judgments. The 2006 constitution removed executive appointment power over magistrates and judges (consistent with judicial independence). Appointment of these officials was made the responsibility of the Supreme Council of the Judiciary, but this body was not functional as of mid-2009 (Afoaku, 2010). Focusing on de facto (rather than that existing merely on paper) judicial independence, Linzer and Staton (2015) reported that the DRC's scores were extremely low prior to and in the early years of the peace operation (all <.05 on a scale of 0–1). Thereafter, there is a slow, steady climb in the judicial independence score to above .20 at the end of MONUC's deployment; nevertheless, this is still very low on the scale and low relative to most other states in the world, even those with authoritarian governments. (Tetra Tech, 2012:20) provides an apt summary of the limits of the judicial system: "the judiciary itself suffers from deep structural limitations, such as a lack of administrative and technical capacity, few resources, and weak infrastructure, which limit the effective recourse to adjudication by courts available to Congolese citizens. As a result, Congo operates in a context of widespread impunity."

Reconciliation

MONUC's efforts at reconciliation in the DRC were *Ineffective*. The centerpiece of reconciliation efforts was supposed to be a truth and reconciliation commission (TRC) created in 2004 and modeled after the one in South Africa. A survey of the Congolese population (Vinck et al., 2008), found that 88 percent of the population regarded the revelation of truth as necessary for the future of the state. Nevertheless, the TRC in the Congo was an abject failure. One observer (Ngoma-Binda, 2008) argued that truth was not necessarily a priority, and the commission was only designed to be a bridge to the election in 2006 (United States Institute of Peace, n.d.). The TRC mandate expired after the election and its operations were suspended. In its short existence, the commission did not investigate a single case of human rights violations (Aroussi, 2011; Davis and Hayner, 2009). The various Congolese peace agreements also lacked provisions for repatriation of survivors of the war and associated abuses (Aroussi, 2017).

Part of reconciliation is holding abuse perpetrators accountable for their actions. If this does not occur through the acknowledgment and acceptance of responsibility in the context of TRCs, it is left to the criminal justice system, where the focus is on punitive, rather than restorative, justice. The DRC lacked the necessary national legislation, save for military courts, to prosecute such crimes (Diku Mpongola, 2007). Instead, such cases were referred to the International Criminal Court (ICC), but by the provisions of the Rome Statute, that institution only has jurisdiction on cases *following* the date of its entry into force; that date is 2002, meaning that the crimes committed during the heights of the previous civil wars are not under ICC purview.

Although restoration and reconciliation were mostly failures, this does not mean that MONUC and other peacebuilding actors did not initiate such efforts, especially at the local level. Hellmüller (2018:1) notes that in at least one province, "[t]hey created networks to join forces, mediated local conflicts, conducted sensitization activities, brought people from different ethnic groups together in joint activities, started to engage communities with the past and created local peace structures." Nevertheless, the lack of coordination between local and national authorities undermined the effectiveness of the attempts at reconciliation (Hellmüller, 2016).

Summary of the MONUC Case

Overall, many of our expectations found support in this case; the results are summarized in Table 5.4. Our expectations on Security First were generally met. Serious problems in facilitating and sustaining a cease-fire, especially in certain regions in the country, along with failure on DDR, had downstream consequences in complicating the ability of peacekeepers and other agents in delivering humanitarian assistance and protecting human rights. The relative compatibility of the three short-term operations did not overcome the problems with the security missions. The one exception to the anticipated pattern was that election supervision was successful despite the deteriorated security situation; nevertheless, election participation was best in areas that were stabilized and more problematic in regions with continued militia activity and violence. Yet, further democratization efforts did not proceed as smoothly as the elections that began the process. Any success in the Election Supervision/Promotion of Democracy mission, however, did not have a spillover to Humanitarian Assistance or Human Rights despite some similarities and compatibility in skill sets, roles, and orientations, as would have been suggested by our associated measure of compatibility (Individual Effects expectation). Problems with inadequate resources, something characteristic of multitasking, was suggested as being partly responsible for some of the difficulties encountered.

Table 5.4 Summary of results vis-à-vis expectations—MONUC

Type of expectation	Expectation	Outcome
Sequencing, Simultaneity, and Prerequisites	Security First	Supported
	Democracy Matters	Not Supported
	Peacebuilding Synergy	Supported
	Peacebuilding Matters	Supported
	Recursive Effects	Supported
Compatibility	Aggregate Effects	Supported
	Learning	Not Supported
	Individual Effects	Supported

How did the Election Supervision/Promotion of Democracy mission have some success when the Traditional Peacekeeping and DDR missions experienced serious problems? This was surprising, especially as elections are mostly successful only in the context of generally effective operations, evidenced by other multi-mission analyses (e.g., Braithwaite, 2012; Farrall, 2012); the exception here, however, is consistent with Cambodia (Whalan, 2012).

One factor directly related to peacekeeping might have been the deployment of a peace operation supplemental to MONUC. EUFOR RD (European Union Military Operation in the Democratic Republic of the Congo) was installed in 2006 to assist with stabilizing the country during the election process that year. It was effective in limiting violence and in offering an information campaign designed to counter propaganda and disinformation efforts (Williams and Bellamy, 2021). A similar European effort, Operation Artemis, was launched in 2003 and was also effective in stemming violence. In both cases, the operations were short-term (less than 1 year) and were more effective than MONUC. The difference was that the election supervision activities only required short-term impact, as elections occur on a fixed date and were time-limited; the longer-term democratization outcomes were less impressive. Limiting violence is an ongoing concern, and short-term impacts will be insufficient in long-term goal achievement. We posited that Democracy Matters in that success/failure in elections and democratization would lead to similar outcomes in the peacebuilding missions. In MONUC's case, success in supervising free and fair elections did not lead to later success in promoting the rule of law and other longer-term missions.

Our expectations also included two related interconnections of peacebuilding missions. The first (Peacebuilding Synergy) was that some of those missions would have a synergistic impact on one another, here in particular those concerned with Local Governance and Rule of Law. There should have been some synergistic effects from their compatibility, given their commonalities. Instead of positive effects, however, the impact was negative. This was confirmed in the MONUC operation as persistent problems in establishing government authority produced dysfunction and corruption and vice versa. A second expectation (Peacebuilding Matters) was that Reconciliation would struggle in the face of other ineffective peacebuilding missions. This proved to be true, in particular with failures in rule-of-law efforts undermining bringing criminals to justice and facilitating healing in society.

Our second group of expectations centered on the compatibility of missions. Among UN peace operations, MONUC was tasked with a relatively large number of missions (eight), and sets of these were quite different from one another on various dimensions. Generally, MONUC's problems were consistent with those associated with this kind of incompatibility. Most notable were MONUC's difficulties in achieving peacebuilding goals. The MONUC force was designed primarily for security missions; it was not well suited for efforts directed at Reconciliation, Local Governance, and the Rule of Law. We found evidence for both the Aggregate Effects of incompatibility—all the peacebuilding missions were ineffective—as well as Individual Effects—various missions had negative impacts on other incompatible missions. There was, however, no evidence of Learning over the course of this long operation (ten years); incompatible missions did not improve performance over time and there were few signs of adaptation that enhanced outcomes.

The *absence* of additional mission mandates can also have deleterious effects, as economic reform was not among the international efforts in the DRC and that omission helped fuel the conflict and undermine other missions. Furthermore, reforms take a long time to encourage the investments needed for economic recovery following civil wars (O'Reilly, 2014).

Comparing UNTAET with MONUC, as shown in Tables 5.1–5.4, reveals both differences and similarities. The differences are in the short-term missions in which UNTAET missions were more effective than those of

MONUC. Both, however, were consistent with the Security First expectation. In UNTAET, traditional peacekeeping had downstream effects on humanitarian assistance and election supervision followed by progress toward democratization. In MONUC, failure in traditional peacekeeping set the stage for failures in other short-term missions, except for monitoring elections. We accounted for this anomaly, but note that long-term democratization did not eventuate.

Both peace operations were largely ineffective in their peacebuilding tasks. In both cases, we observed a synergy between the three peacebuilding missions; failure in one mission coincided with failure in the others. Clearly, it takes more than success in security missions to pull off the more complex institutional changes required to rebuild war-torn societies. Above all, perhaps, is meeting the challenges posed by a need to coordinate the efforts of peacekeepers, NGOs, and various civil society groups (for more on this see Cuhadar and Druckman, 2023, on the role played by inclusive commissions in post–civil war societies).

6

The United Nations Mission in Sierra Leone (UNAMSIL)

Introduction

The United Nations Mission in Sierra Leone (UNAMSIL) rates as the most multifaceted peace operation in this study, including all nine of the missions that we identified for scrutiny and compatibility in Chapter 2. These missions were: Traditional Peacekeeping, Humanitarian Assistance, Election Supervision/Promotion of Democracy, DDR, Human Rights, Rule of Law, Local Governance, SSR, and Reconciliation, respectively. Although UNAMSIL is atypical in having so many missions, it does provide a laboratory for examining all the interactions between missions.

Historical Context and Overview of UNAMSIL

The crisis in Sierra Leone was a direct spillover of Liberia's complex civil war, which began in 1989 (Brecher et al., 2021). Civil war came to Sierra Leone in 1991 when members of the Revolutionary United Front (RUF), aided by Liberia's National Patriotic Front for Liberia (NPFL), attacked a town in eastern Sierra Leone, along the border of Liberia. Although Sierra Leone President Joseph Saidu Momoh was in power at the time, he would be deposed the following year by soldiers of the Sierra Leone army, led by Captain Valentine Strasser. Strasser's government perpetrated numerous and varied human rights abuses, including the torture and murder of political opponents (Lincoln, 2011).

Diamond laundering during this tumultuous time also became highly profitable (Keen, 2005). One reason rebel forces were able to last as long as they did in Sierra Leone was the external support they received from neighboring states, who had a vested interest in their lucrative diamond fields in the east, over which the rebel groups had control (Adebajo and Landsberg,

When Peacekeeping Missions Collide. Paul F. Diehl, Daniel Druckman, and Grace B. Mueller, Oxford University Press.
© Oxford University Press 2024. DOI: 10.1093/oso/9780197696842.003.0006

2000). Liberia and Burkina Faso, specifically, were accused of resupplying the RUF with weapons that were purchased using money from "blood" or "conflict" diamonds (Almuslem, 2020; Adebajo and Landsberg, 2000; Fanthorpe, 2001).

By 1995, the RUF rebels had threatened the capital city of Freetown, and Strasser was unable to divert state resources to the war effort because of debts owed to external creditors; thus, he was unable to muster an army capable of defeating the RUF (Williams, 2004). In 1996, Strasser was ousted in another military coup led by his deputy, Brigadier Julius Maada Bio, and subsequently Bio decided to return the government back to civilian rule in a peaceful fashion. Ahmad Tejan Kabbah of the Sierra Leone People's Party became president after winning the majority of the votes in the 1996 election, but peace was short-lived, as he was overthrown in 1997 in yet another military coup, one led by Johnny Paul Koroma and the Sierra Leonean military. After declaring himself head of the state and chairman of the Armed Forces Revolutionary Council (AFRC), Koroma invited the RUF to rule alongside him (Lincoln, 2011; Williams, 2004).

In an effort to restore order, Kabbah recruited assistance from ECOWAS (the Economic Community of West African States) and other external actors. To supervise and complement the ECOWAS Ceasefire Monitoring Group's (ECOMOG) activities in Sierra Leone, the Security Council authorized the United Nations Observer Mission in Sierra Leone (UNOMSIL) to monitor the military and security situation in Sierra Leone, facilitate the disarmament and demobilization of former combatants, and assist in monitoring respect for international humanitarian law (S/RES/1181). Even though ECOMOG, with the backing of UNOMSIL, was successful in restoring the government of Sierra Leone in March 1998, it was ultimately unable to re-establish order. Indicative of this was when UNOMSIL and ECOMOG forces could not prevent the brutal attack on Freetown in January 1999, in which rebel fighters of AFRC and RUF destroyed the capital city's infrastructure while committing horrific atrocities against civilians (Martin-Brûlé, 2012; Boege and Rinck, 2019).

According to data on one-sided violence, the month that this siege took place—January 1999—was the most violent one of the civil war, with 870 civilian casualties and 2,054 battle-related deaths (Pettersson and Öberg, 2020; Hultman et al., 2020), not to mention the forced amputations, recruitment of children, and sexual violence that were used as "strategies" by warring factions during their Operation No Living Thing (Brast, 2015;

Olonisakin, 2008). Other estimates of civilian casualties from RUF's campaign in Freetown, however, are much higher, ranging between 5,000 and 6,000 (Lincoln, 2011; Carter Center, 2013).

Although the Freetown offensive of January 1999 resulted in the evacuation of UNOMSIL personnel to Conakry, ECOMOG troops were ultimately able to retake the capital, forcing the AFRC/RUF government from power, and committing the belligerents to a six-month transition period for Kabbah's restoration (UN Department of Public Information, 2000; Martin-Brûlé, 2012).

Negotiations between the government and the rebels began in May 1999, and by July 7, all parties to the conflict signed an agreement in Lomé, Togo. International and public pressures on the Kabila government to negotiate with the RUF to end war provided the impetus for a diplomatic solution (Olonisakin, 2015). Although this peace agreement was welcomed by Sierra Leoneans, there were provisions that left many uncomfortable—blanket amnesty to all combatants and a power-sharing arrangement that included former rebel factions (Olonisakin, 2015; Rizvi, 2017). The UN also objected to this amnesty clause of the peace agreement, with Secretary-General Kofi Annan asserting that amnesty should not apply to international crimes of genocide, crimes against humanity, war crimes, or other serious violations of humanitarian law (S/2000/915). The Lomé Agreement further proved to be flawed, in that although it had been signed by all parties, it did not result in a cessation in fighting, particularly on the part of RUF (Bernath and Nyce, 2002; S/2000/1055). The expectation had been that the agreement was signed by key parties who had a sincere desire to end the fighting, an assumption not borne out by subsequent events (Williams and Bellamy, 2021).

The same day that UNOMSIL's mandate ended (October 22, 1999) was the first day of the United Nations Mission in Sierra Leone (UNAMSIL) (S/RES/1270). In one conception (Porter, 2003), UNAMSIL proceeded through three phases up to and including 2002. The first period from deployment to May 2000 was the operation's most difficult one and was characterized by substantial problems in all its missions. The second phase (over the next year until March 2001) was significantly better, as the operation was enhanced with a larger force and supplemented by a military operation carried out by the United Kingdom. The kidnapping of UN peacekeepers in May 2000 (more on this in a later section) was, in large part, the impetus for the increased troop strength to 13,000 (S/RES/1299). The timeline of these two phases is roughly reflected in O'Flaherty (2004), who titles the first phase as "the adoption of the Lomé Agreement to the Attacks on UNAMSIL" and the second phase as the "reestablishment of control to the Abuja Agreement"—a cease-fire agreement in which the RUF committed to returning to the provisions to the Lomé Agreement that they had previously disregarded. Phase 3 (until October 2002) ushered in a period of relative stability, and the focus of the operation was on DDR and other more advanced missions. These scholars end their analysis in late 2002, but one could justify a fourth phase thereafter in which peacebuilding missions (e.g., Local Governance, Reconciliation) were introduced or received greater attention. UN peacekeepers also transferred responsibility for the security sector to the Sierra Leone government during this phase (Gbla, 2006; Bell, 2005). UNAMSIL remained in Sierra Leone through December 31, 2005, and over the course of the operation, it was able to restore peace and security throughout the entire country.

Assessing the UNAMSIL Missions

UNAMSIL attempted nine different missions during its existence. As with MONUC, there was some mixture of simultaneity and sequencing associated with them, and thus we can test the full range of expectations on timing, interactions, and compatibility. Because it had so many missions, UNAMSIL had the maximum incompatibility score on the multitasking-based indicator. This suggests that the operation would likely experience problems on multiple dimensions by trying to do too much, although this might be mitigated by some sequencing. Its score based on average compatibility is close to the median because the mission profile contains some missions that are very compatible and others that are not. Finally, the propensity for learning was somewhat above average given its 5+ years in existence.

Table 6.1 summarizes our holistic judgment on each of the missions, using a Likert scale of outcomes with categories of Effective, Mostly Effective, Mixed, Mostly Ineffective, and Ineffective. As with all other operations, the bases for these judgments and details about mission performance are given in the narrative below.

Our scoring of the UNAMSIL missions produces the most successful operation overall among our case studies. Nevertheless, such success was not foreseen, especially early in its existence. In May 2000, the operation nearly collapsed when RUF forces destroyed UNAMSIL's DDR camps in Makeni

Table 6.1 Holistic judgments of UNAMSIL mission outcomes

Mission category	Mission	Outcome
Basic Security	Traditional Peacekeeping	Mostly Effective
	DDR	Mostly Effective
Shorter-Term Missions	Humanitarian Assistance	Effective
	Human Rights Protection	Mostly Effective
	Election Supervision	Mostly Effective
Longer-Term Missions	Local Governance	Mixed
	Rule of Law	Mixed
	Security Sector Reform	Mostly Effective
	Restoration/Reconciliation	Mostly Effective

and Magburaka and kidnapped nearly 500 UN peacekeepers, breaching the cease-fire. Not only was this UNAMSIL's "darkest hour" (Olonisakin, 2015), but it severely damaged the peacekeepers' reputation among Sierra Leoneans. The problems in the initial period of deployment had a negative impact on all the missions in place at that time. Nevertheless, the reversal of fortune during 2001 had the opposite impact—general success across the different missions and the basis for our more optimistic assessments.

Overall, UNAMSIL was lauded as the UN's most successful multidimensional peacekeeping operation, in large part because it was able to adapt its mandate and its approach after May 2000. As Olonisakin (2015:629) concludes, "the adversity experienced earlier in the operation turned into an opportunity to transform UN peacekeeping." With the in-country support of the United Kingdom, UNAMSIL was able to salvage the operation, utilize its Chapter VII powers to engage in the protection of civilians, and get a head start on the peacebuilding missions that followed earlier missions.

Basic Security Missions (Traditional Peacekeeping and DDR)

UNAMSIL was mostly effective at carrying out its basic security missions, a judgment echoed by the 2000 Brahimi Report (Durch et al., 2003). The creation and sustainment of a cease-fire combined with DDR efforts to lay the groundwork for a series of other missions. A consistent thread in our assessments here, and later, is that early problems were followed by success and sustaining that performance by the end of deployment in 2005.

Traditional Peacekeeping

UNAMSIL was deployed in an environment that was preferable to one characterized by ongoing war, but somewhat less than ideal in terms of having all forms of violence halted. On the one hand, the Lomé Peace Agreement was signed before UNAMSIL forces arrived in Sierra Leone, and this post-agreement conflict phase (Diehl and Balas, 2014) often portends success as disputing parties are committed to peace. On the other hand, there was a history of very deadly conflict and a past record of cease-fire violations. As one Human Rights Watch director stated in 1999, "This is not a war in which civilians are accidental victims. This is a war in which civilians are the targets" (Human Rights Watch, 1999a). Although the RUF and AFRC (the group of the Sierra Leone army that had allied itself with the RUF to oust the Kabbah government) were the original parties that committed violence against civilians, atrocities against civilians were being committed by all sides in the latter stages of the conflict, including government soldiers, ECOMOG forces, and Civil Defense Forces (Lincoln, 2011).

The initial outcomes at facilitating and monitoring a cease-fire were not promising. Prior to 2001, the operation faced significant challenges to its military capacity and commitment, the most significant of these occurring in May 2000, when rebel forces kidnapped nearly 500 UN peacekeepers after overtaking a DDR camp (Hazen, 2007). This is a stark illustration of how the compatible basic security missions were intertwined. The crisis in May 2000 revealed a gap between the mandate and the available resources, given the inadequate and ill-equipped UNAMSIL force (Yamashita, 2008). Liberia's Charles Taylor played a key role in the release of the UN peacekeepers (Olonisakin, 2008), but meanwhile sentiment about the UNAMSIL's competence worsened among Sierra Leoneans, with many calling the peacekeepers "U-Nasty" or "Beach-keepers" (Gberie, 2005). UN updates from early 2000 reveal a sense of desperation facing peacekeepers in a security situation that was described as "tense and volatile" (PK mission update, January–March, 2000). Rebel forces maintained particular strongholds over the northern and eastern provinces of Sierra Leone—the areas with concentrated diamond fields (the Kono region and the Mano River basin region). They were also able to move freely throughout much of the western and southern provinces (Olonisakin, 2008; Almuslem, 2020; Adebajo and Landsberg, 2000). What also stood in the way of UNAMSIL's ability to abate violence was the RUF's staunch opposition to UNAMSIL's presence—particularly in the eastern parts of the country.

Both the COW (Dixon and Sarkees, 2015) and UCDP (Gleditsch et al., 2002) data sets designate March 1991 as the start date of the conflict, but their end dates to the conflict vary, most likely because of their differing thresholds for fatalities. Nevertheless, each has the conflict as restarting or ongoing during the first part of UNAMSIL deployment. According to COW data, the first Sierra Leonean War began on March 23, 1991, and ended on April 23, 1996, and the Second Sierra Leonean War began on February 6, 1998, and ended on July 7, 1999, only to resume in May 2000 and finally end on November 10, 2000. According to UCDP data, the conflict in Sierra Leone began on March 23, 1991, and ended on December 20, 2001. Thus, by 2002, a couple of years after UNAMSIL's deployment, the operation had turned things around and violent conflict in Sierra Leone had for the most part been eradicated. Had the peacekeeping operation ended in 2001, one might have judged the mission as mostly ineffective. Considering the progress made thereafter, however, we can code the traditional peacekeeping results as being *Mostly Effective*.

By 2002, UNAMSIL had made tremendous strides in accomplishing its core mission of providing security throughout Sierra Leone (Malan, 2003). Looking at disaggregated monthly data on one-sided violence, after the peacekeepers' arrival in Sierra Leone in October 1999, there would be an additional 528 total civilian casualties, but by July 2001, civilian causalities had ended (Hultman et al., 2020), implying that peacekeepers also had a positive impact on reducing one-sided violence, even if such an effect was not immediate. There was also a significant reduction in the number of battle-related deaths after the arrival of UNAMSIL peacekeepers. In 1998 and 1999, there were more than 3,000 deaths per year; by 2000, however, that number had dropped to 382, and by 2001—the last year of recorded conflict—there were just 48 deaths (Gleditsch et al., 2002). One can contrast the situations during the civil war with those at the end of UNAMSIL deployment. During the former, there were rebel forces, renegade soldiers, mercenaries, and foreign troops operating in the country; by 2005, only the official government armed forces of Sierra Leone were present. ACLED (2022) records 159 incidents of "Disorder Involving Peacekeepers," but, in contrast to MONUC, most were nonviolent and armed clashes were a minority (<16%). These data reflect well on the effectiveness of the peacekeeping operation.

As time went on, UNAMSIL was slowly able to increase its fragile presence in the interior parts of the country (Brattberg, 2012). Following UNAMSIL's strengthened mandate after the May 2000 crisis, it was decided not only that there should be an increase in the mission's military strength,[1] but also that troops should be progressively deployed "in sufficient numbers and density at key strategic locations and main population centers" in order to "further stabilize the situation progressively throughout the entire country" (S/RES/ 1313). Consequently, although peacekeepers were bound to the capital at the outset of the mission, the increase in UNAMSIL troop strength allowed it to expand its scope of operations to towns throughout the countryside (e.g., Lunsar, Makeni, Magburaka, Mano Junction, and Koidu), as well as the diamond-producing regions of the east (PK Update, January–March 2001). This increased presence throughout Sierra Leone greatly contributed to UNAMISL's ability to carry out its mandated tasks. Throughout the entire operation, there were 192 peacekeeper fatalities, but the majority of these deaths were a result of accident (41.12%) or illness (45.31%), rather than malicious acts of violence on the part of rebel actors.

What accounted for the reversal of fortunes and the subsequent success of UNAMSIL in stabilizing the situation? First was a change in troop levels, moving from 6,000 to 11,000, and ultimately to 17,500. The size of peace operations is associated with its success in limiting violence, especially violence directed against civilians (Hultman et al., 2021). Changes in peace operation leadership and tactics also allowed UNAMSIL to address the security situation better.

In addition, and perhaps most significantly, the intervention and assistance from UK troops were critical to UNAMSIL's success in restoring security throughout Sierra Leone. It was not until UK troops assisted UNAMSIL in disarming armed groups and used military force to help the government retake control over RUF-controlled areas that the RUF's stronghold on Sierra Leone slowly was weakened (Carter Center, 2013). In addition to allowing UNAMSIL to reassert its authority on the ground, the United Kingdom's bilateral military assistance also restored confidence in the UN operation among peacekeepers and the people of Sierra Leone alike (Brattberg, 2012). The United Kingdom's "over-the-horizon" offshore firepower demonstrations were particularly effective at deterring rebels from re-entering Freetown

---

[1] At its peak in 2002, UNAMSIL was the largest and most expensive UN mission on the ground, with over 17,000 troops (Olonisakin, 2015).

(Curran and Woodhouse, 2007). UNAMSIL assisted in these military operations, but it is questionable whether the positive outcomes would have occurred without UK involvement or by sticking with traditional peace-keeping rules of engagement.

Among the sources of violence in the civil war was the support of outside forces and states, especially in the diamond-rich areas. For the most part, UNAMSIL was able to minimize the cross-border diamond smuggling and the support of such efforts by neighboring states. This took away some of the impetus for violence, and as new areas came under government and UNAMSIL control, the geographic scope of the violence narrowed until it disappeared.

After 2001, the peace process faced few serious challenges, with the exception of localized protests and demonstrations over rising economic difficulties, but none of these uprisings seriously threatened the security of the state of Sierra Leone as a whole (Hazen, 2007). Most important, the biggest threat to peace—RUF—was essentially defunct by end of UNAMSIL's term.

DDR

The initial problems with DDR were evident in the violence incident previously noted—when RUF forces destroyed DDR camps and kidnapped UN peacekeepers. Some of the tension between the RUF and the UN stemmed from misplaced worries that UNAMSIL would forcibly disarm them (Sloan, 2010). As a result, UNAMSIL's disarmament process was described as "spotty" at the outset of the peace operation (Gberie, 2005:165). As with the traditional peacekeeping mission, this would change dramatically in short order and in a positive direction. Thus, we have judged the DDR mission to be *Mostly Effective*, although success was greater in the first two elements of the DDR acronym (disarmament and demobilization) than the third component (reintegration).

Early in the deployment period, only approximately half of the fighters had entered demobilization camps, and some of these were then rearmed in order to fight the RUF. Payments to demobilized troops lagged, and international contributions fell short of what was needed for such payments (Adebajo and Landsberg, 2000). Nevertheless, incentives did prove attractive to many former fighters in this impoverished environment. The cash payments and supplies provided to those that chose to disarm, together with potential for skills training, were important incentives, better than the alternatives in farming or diamond mining (Hoffman, 2005).

As of January 17, 2002, the UN reported that the disarmament process was officially complete (UN Digest, February–April 2002). Combatants from three factions made up the bulk of those participating in DDR efforts: (1) members of the RUF; (2) members of the AFRC (the former state army personnel who staged a coup in 1997 under the leadership of Johnny Paul Koroma); and (3) members of the Civil Defense Forces (CDF)—an umbrella organization of pro-government, ethnically based community militias that arose to protect local communities from RUF/AFRC attacks (Hoffman, 2005; Lincoln, 2011). Disarming the latter group might not seem obvious, as they fought alongside the Sierra Leone army during the civil war. Nevertheless, the civilian militia of the CDF were not blameless when it came to atrocities committed in the name of war. It often dealt harshly with the civilian population, especially when it suspected individuals to be RUF-sympathizers, resulting in numerous abuses, such as forced recruitment, looting, rape, and executions (Baker, 2005; Lincoln, 2011).

By 2002, 72,490 combatants had been disarmed, and a total of 42,000 weapons and 1.2 million rounds of ammunition had been collected (Gberie, 2005; see also Hoffman, 2005). By early December 2002, the government of Sierra Leone declared that elements of the former Sierra Leone army and the AFRC had also been disarmed (UN Department of Public Information, 2005). Among the ex-combatants disarmed, an estimated 20,000 were former child soldiers that had been recruited by various rebel parties during the war (Bell, 2005). In addition to the weapons collected from former fighters, the Sierra Leone police and UNAMSIL also conducted a program for the voluntary collection of illegal arms held by civilians. Those efforts, as of January 2002, had produced 8,536 weapons and 33,968 rounds of ammunition (UN Digest, February–April 2002)—moving Sierra Leone one step closer to a day when individuals could return to a sense of normalcy.

A major objective of the disarmament process was to encourage RUF to transform itself into a political party (RUFP) to pursue its interests in a non-violent, democratic fashion, and by all assessments, after the DDR process, the military structures of the RUF had crumbled (S/2002/987). The RUF did attempt to participate in the formal political system, although its efforts were not productive, as it garnered less than 2 percent of the vote in the presidential and parliamentary elections of May 2002 (Brast, 2015). Gberie (2005:193) notes that the RUFP presidential candidate actually received fewer votes than the number of RUF combatants who had handed in weapons—a "reflection of the fact that a large number of the ex-combatants were still below the minimum voting age of 18" or of its lack of broad support. Its poor performance at the polls also meant that it did not meet the threshold of 12.5 percent to win a single parliamentary seat (Carter Center, 2003).

Even as UNAMSIL was able to experience success in its disarmament and demobilization efforts, there is consensus that it was not as successful in its reintegration efforts (Gbla, 2006). On the one hand, more than 55–56,000 former combatants (more than 80% of the total) registered for reintegration, and many did receive training. Of the 55,000 ex-combatants that had registered for reintegration, by June 2003, 46,000 of them had been reached with some form of assistance, leaving approximately 9,000 unaccounted for (Durch et al., 2003). That number then shrank to an outstanding caseload of 6,000 (United Nations, 2003). As Secretary-General Kofi Annan stated in his Fifteenth Report on UNAMSIL, "the disarmament and demobilization cannot be considered a success until the reintegration process . . . is completed" (S/2002/987). Reintegration was so important because without it, it would leave ex-combatants as "easy prey" to be lured into other conflicts, thus increasing the potential for future conflicts (Gbla, 2006; S/2002/987; S/2002/1417). Poor economic conditions made it difficult to place ex-combatants in the local economy. Indeed, some ex-combatants not reached by the reintegration program chose to migrate to Sierra Leone's diamond-rich areas, which subsequently led to clashes with local groups, or they were recruited as mercenaries for the neighboring wars in Côte d'Ivoire and Liberia (Nitzschke and Studdard, 2005). That 3,000 Kamajor—one of the militia elements of the CDF—fled to Liberia with the threat of an imminent return presented a serious security challenge to Sierra Leonean national intelligence agencies (Baker, 2005; UN Digest, May–July 2003).

Although all ex-combatants were given the option to seek entry into Sierra Leone's armed forces, only a small minority (2,500–3,500) from various groups (RUF, SLA, AFRC, and CDF) decided to do this (Nilsson and Kovacs, 2013; Gbla, 2006). The Military Reintegration Program (MRP), however, had other alternatives for ex-combatants, and of the 72,490 that passed through this program, 29,000 received vocational training and 12,000 received assistance with formal education (Hoffman, 2005). By March 2004, all former soldiers had been reintegrated, thus marking the closure of UNAMSIL's DDR program (Van Pottelbergh, 2010).

There were a number of factors that accounted for the ultimate success of the DDR efforts. As with traditional peacekeeping, the UK's sustained and visible military presence throughout Sierra Leone contributed to RUF's cooperation with the UNAMSIL's DDR efforts (Gberie, 2005). The provision of additional troops and resources to UNAMSIL by the Security Council also helped change the course of the mission. In addition, some elements particular to the RUF promoted greater cooperation with the peace operation. One was a change in its leadership to someone more willing to cooperate. The RUF also agreed to disarm because it had run out of options as a result of military and diplomatic actions, such as the "Kambia formula" of May 2001—a concerted military offensive by the Guinean forces and the Sierra Leone army to target a large concentration of RUF fighters in the Western Kambia district, while the UN and local militias focused on the eastern districts (Olonisakin, 2008; Brast, 2015). This effort was "integral in revitalizing the UN's stalled DDR process" (Kaplan, 2013:100), as it ultimately "opened the floodgate to all sorts of compliance by the RUF" (Olonisakin, 2008:104). Because of the careful negotiations and diplomatic measures taken by Special Representative of the Secretary-General Oluyemi Adeniji, the disarmament of these RUF fighters took place with no reports of violent flare-ups (Adolfo, 2010; Olonisakin, 2015).

Unlike some of the other operations covered in this study, UNAMSIL's basic security missions (Traditional Peacekeeping and DDR) were mostly successful, even after an inauspicious start. The success of the two missions illustrates their interconnection. They are compatible with one another and thus have the potential to influence each other positively—our Individual Effects expectation. Yet there was also a cascading synergy as success in DDR, especially in disarmament and dissolution of RUF as a fighting force, lessened the chances for violence and made the Traditional Peacekeeping mission successful. Conversely, keeping the peace lessened the incentives for the RUF to continue its armed challenge to the government. Thus, the DDR process and the Traditional Peacekeeping mission involving violence abatement had a synergistic effect on one another. The military defeat of the RUF made the group more willing to cooperate in disarmament efforts, and in turn successful disarmament lessened the threat from the RUF. Indicative of these interrelated processes were negotiations involving the RUF that brought about two agreements—the Abuja Ceasefire Agreement (Abuja I) in November 2000 and the Abuja Ceasefire Review Agreement (Abuja II) in May 2001, respectively (Brattberg, 2012).

The relative success of the basic security missions is posited to have positive downstream consequences for other missions. As a hint of this, the dissolution of the RUF and the disarmament of the CDF militias are purported to have created an environment in which SSR could occur (Brast, 2015). This, and other connections, are examined empirically in the following sections.

Short-Term Missions (Humanitarian Assistance, Human Rights Protection, and Election Supervision /Promotion of Democracy)

UNAMSIL carried out three shorter-term missions—Humanitarian Assistance, Human Rights, and Election Supervision/Promotion of Democracy. The success of the basic security missions augured well for the prospective outcomes of each. Indeed, indicators paint a positive picture for all three missions.

Humanitarian Assistance

Overall, UNAMSIL was *Effective* in carrying out its humanitarian assistance mission. A decade of violent civil conflict had left Sierra Leone devastated—killings, looting, and the destruction of property were widespread, resulting in the displacement of a third of the population (Tavakoli et al., 2015). Delivering humanitarian assistance was a major undertaking for the peacekeepers. Furthermore, prior to the disarmament and demobilization of rebel groups, it was not uncommon for opposition groups to interfere with humanitarian assistance, particularly in RUF-controlled areas (PK Update, January–March 2000; PK Update, January–March 2001).

Concordant with the improvements in basic security outcomes, humanitarian access was broadened and greatly improved after the wider deployment of UNAMSIL peacekeepers throughout the territory, opening up the door for refugees to return to previous RUF strongholds (PK Update, May–July 2001). Indeed, Porter (2003) states that two main forces affected humanitarian action in the early stages of UNAMSIL: (1) access into RUF areas; and (2) the deployment of peacekeepers throughout the country. The deployment of the Sierra Leone army in Kambia and the presence of UNAMSIL troops in Koinadugu and Kono, for example, enabled UN agencies and NGOs to initiate programs in the most critical sectors (PK Update, August–October, 2001). Still, some 200,000 Sierra Leonean refugees remained in asylum countries in 2001. In early 2002, the UNHCR began concerted efforts to repatriate refugees from Liberia, who were eager to return to their home country so they could vote in the upcoming elections (Olonisakin, 2008). UNICEF, for example, had a number of wide-ranging projects in the sectors of education, health, reintegration, water, and sanitation that specifically benefited returning internally displaced persons (IDPs), among others (Norwegian Refugee Council, 2003). Thus, there was an unexpected and indirect connection between the humanitarian assistance and election supervision actions.

December 2002 marked the completion of the final phase of the national program to resettle IDPs, as some 222,000 had been resettled since efforts began in April the year before (S/2002/1417). At a joint conference with the World Bank, UNDP, the government of Sierra Leone, and its humanitarian partners, humanitarian efforts were specifically credited for a number of improvements. Most clear and direct for this mission was the rise of infant immunization rates from 33 percent in 2000 to 70 percent in 2002. Humanitarian assistance and repatriation of refugees also had some indirect effects on other sectors of society—the relatively quick upturn in macroeconomic stability, economic growth, and improved public reforms. For example, Sierra Leone's GDP growth rates went from 2.8 percent in 2000 to 5.4 percent in 2001, and primary school enrollment rose from 42 percent in 2001 to 59 percent in 2002.

To support humanitarian efforts on the ground in Sierra Leone, external support and funding from the international community was needed. UNAMSIL's success was aided by such support. Not only did aid pour in through bilateral assistance from countries such as the United Kingdom and the United States, which pledged $120 million and $37 million respectively, but a number of other NGOs, UN initiatives, and international organizations similarly contributed to efforts (Norwegian Refugee Council, 2003). The World Food Programme, for example, launched its Vulnerable Group Feeding (VGF) and Mother and Child Health (MCH) Programmes to meet the needs of the most vulnerable (UN Office for the Coordination of Humanitarian Affairs, 2003). UNAMSIL efforts were not divorced from IO and NGO distribution though. Indeed, peacekeepers were often ahead of such organizations and were central to the distribution. Porter (2003:46) points out that "the speed with which UNAMSIL was deploying around the country meant that aid agencies struggled to keep up." As a result, UNAMSIL contingents found themselves having to provide humanitarian assistance directly to the local population. For some analysts (e.g., Olonisakin 2008), however, that UNAMSIL military contingents had to do humanitarian work on their own is instead a reflection of the "disjointedness" between UNAMSIL and the humanitarian community. NGO refusal to use UNAMSIL helicopters to deliver essential commodities such as food aid is one such example of this disconnection. It was not until the appointment of Alan Doss as the deputy special representative of the secretary-general (DSRSG) that relations between the UN and NGOs started to improve after 2001 (Porter, 2003).

Longer-term and lagging indicators of health and prosperity support the conclusion that UNAMSIL was effective in its humanitarian mission, even as it continued to compare poorly with other countries in the world and given that its humanitarian efforts might not be felt immediately during UNAMSIL's deployment. During the civil war and at its lowest point (1995), life expectancy for Sierra Leoneans was 37.1 (UN Department of Economic and Social Affairs, Population Division, 2019)—the second lowest in the world, just above Rwanda. One year after UNAMSIL's departure (2006), life expectancy had risen to 45.5 years, and five years after its departure (2011), it was even higher at 50.2 years. The UNDP's Human Development Index also shows subtle improvement over time in Sierra Leone's ability to facilitate long and healthy lives, access to knowledge, and a decent standard of living for its citizens. Prior to the arrival of UNAMSIL and during the early years of the operation (1998–2002), Sierra Leone was at the bottom of human development rankings. In the years following the departure of UNAMSIL, although not in last place anymore, Sierra Leone hovered in the bottom five of HDI rankings, indicating that even as improvement occurred, it was still one of the poorest and least developed countries. By 2011 (five years after UNAMSIL's departure), however, Sierra Leone had moved out of the bottom five (180th/ 187), but would not see much improvement in the following years.

The ultimate successes of the basic security missions provided the necessary environment for success in UNAMSIL's Humanitarian Assistance mission. Early difficulties with security correlated with problems in aid distribution but then largely disappeared when violence decreased and DDR was implemented. A similar story is evident in the next two missions.

Human Rights

In the same way that UNAMSIL had much to accomplish to deliver humanitarian assistance, it also faced challenges in its Human Rights mission. During the civil war, the mutilation and amputation of civilians were widespread (Lincoln, 2011; Newman, 2002). In general, UNAMSIL made huge strides in reducing the atrocities and human rights abuses facing civilians, and thus we judged it to be *Mostly Effective* in this mission. The qualified endorsement, rather than calling this a full success, is a function of two limitations: (1) early struggles with curbing abuses; and (2) alleged sexual misconduct by UNAMSIL peacekeepers with respect to the very citizens—including children—they were supposed to protect.

Priority for the peace operation in the early phases was given to defeating the RUF and stabilization, rather than necessarily providing direct protection (Yamashita, 2008). Thus, to implement its human rights mission, UNAMSIL concentrated on three areas, each involving indirect support of human rights efforts rather than direct protection of threatened populations (as was the case in Bosnia): (1) monitoring the human rights situation; (2) reporting; and (3) providing technical cooperation to civil society and the government (O'Flaherty, 2004). Peacekeepers worked in the context of and supported a number of protection programs of the United Nations Children's Fund (UNICEF), the United Nations High Commissioner for Refugees (UNHCR), the United Nations Office for the Coordination of Humanitarian Affairs (OCHA), and an International Committee of the Red Cross delegation.

At the beginning of UNAMSIL's deployment, violence and abuses remained commonplace. This problematic performance paralleled the early difficulties of the other peace operation missions. For example, IDPs were often abducted, raped, and forced into labor by RUF and AFRC (ex-SLA) forces, and approximately 25 percent of CDF, AFRC, and SLA combatants were child soldiers—under the age of eighteen, with some as young as seven years old (PK Update, April–June 2000). As many as 50,000 to 64,000 internally displaced women may have been subjected to sexual violence as a result of the civil war, and when adding extrapolated data for other types of victims, that number jumps to as many as 215,000 to 257,000 Sierra Leonean women and girls (Physicians for Human Rights, 2002—report in conjunction with the UNAMSIL Human Rights Section). The harassment and abduction of civilians continued throughout 2001, as there continued to be "serious breaches" of international humanitarian law against civilians (PK Update, May–July 2001).

By early 2002, however, there was a general improvement in the human rights situation in Sierra Leone, with the exception of atrocities in the east (which had only been revealed after increased access for peacekeepers) (PK Update, February–April 2002). The Mass Atrocity Endings project by the World Peace Foundation (2015) describes that from 2000 to 2002, "the intensity of atrocities decreased to 'more sporadic' levels of violence."[2] The human

---

[2] Taken from https://sites.tufts.edu/atrocityendings/2015/08/07/sierra-leone/ (last accessed December 9, 2022).

rights situation had improved in 2002 (also noted by Human Rights Watch, 2005), owing in large part to the successfully completed disarmament and demobilization of ex-combatants. This improvement in the human rights situation in Sierra Leone by the year 2002 is confirmed by quantitative human rights scores of repression (Schnakenberg and Fariss, 2014; Fariss, 2019). In the years following 1990, there was a dramatic drop in Sierra Leone's human rights scores, with 1998 representing the worst year for individuals. After 1998, the situation slowly improved, and between 2001 and 2002, there was a dramatic jump in scores. Following 2002, Sierra Leone's human rights scores continued to improve slowly until the year 2011 (well after UNAMSIL withdrew), when downward trends became apparent.

Human rights monitoring and reporting were an important part of the efforts to consolidate peace and stability in Sierra Leone. Unlike some other operations, UNAMSIL was focused on past atrocities (pre-deployment, during the civil war), as well as contemporary ones. An especially important project of UNAMSIL's Human Rights Section was the establishment of a database of human rights violations, which was handed over to the Truth and Reconciliation Commission (TRC) to help with its proceedings. This demonstrates the interconnection of the Human Rights mission with one of the longer-term missions—Reconciliation. Investigations conducted in 2000 by UNAMSIL's Human Rights Section found that of 733 women randomly selected, 345 reported instances of being raped (PK Update, August–Oct 2001), and 192 reported having been gang-raped (A/56/281). Another investigation analyzed testimonies from over 150 amputees, two-thirds of whom had their limbs forcefully amputated for non-medical reasons (PK Update, May–July 2002; Malan, 2003).

A second qualification to the mission effectiveness concerned allegations of sexual misconduct by UNAMSIL peacekeepers in 2001 and 2002—specifically, allegations of prostitution, abuses of minors, and rape (Nordas and Rustad, 2013); the complaints included reports that uniformed peacekeepers were offering as little as $1 to children for sexual favors (Nduka-Agwu, 2009; Akonor, 2016). Unfortunately, abuse by peacekeepers was not new to those in Sierra Leone, given that in the early 1990s, there was blatant sexual violence against the local population by the ECOWAS Monitoring Group (ECOMOG) that resulted in approximately 6,000 births (Akonor, 2016). Although a UNAMSIL personnel conduct committee was created in March 2002 to respond to such misconduct, UNAMSIL's investigations into sexual exploration and abuse indicate "a lack of appreciation for the seriousness of the problem of sexual violence committed by UNAMSIL military or civilian personnel" (Human Rights Watch, 2003:49). Ultimately, these sexual misconduct charges were dropped by the Office of Internal Oversight Services on the grounds that there was not enough evidence (Fleshman, 2005; Bowers, 2020).

The human rights situation in Sierra Leone was closely tied to the security situation. When civil war was rampant, so were associated war crimes against civilians. The dissipation of violence and the disarmament and demobilization of militias ushered in a period of greater human rights compliance, consistent with our Security First expectation.

Election Supervision/Promotion of Democracy
UNAMSIL was charged with supervising elections in 2002 and 2004 and contributed to laying a foundation for democracy to take root, although its tasks were more limited in the democracy promotion component than the election one. The results of the election and associated actions indicate that UNAMSIL was *Mostly Effective* in this mission.

Ahead of the election in May 2002, UNAMSIL assisted with the voter registration of some 2,276,518 potential voters (which compared well to the 1996 figure of 1,566,000) and some twenty-three political parties (PK Update, February–April 2002). To accomplish this, UNAMSIL conducted massive voter education campaigns (Olonisakin, 2008; PK Update, May–July 2001), and UNAMSIL's Public Information Section utilized UNAMSIL Radio as a medium for disseminating information during its special program called "Election Watch" (Malan, 2003). Security personnel from both the Sierra Leone Police (SLP) and UNAMSIL played a critical role in maintaining order in the months leading up to the election, as they were tasked with providing support to enhance the National Election Commission's (NEC) capacity to organize and conduct the election (S/RES/1389; Carter Center, 2003; PK Update, November 2001–January 2002).

Consequently, the presidential and parliamentary elections of 2002 represented the point of maximum deployment (Van Pottelbergh, 2010). UNAMSIL temporarily deployed 11,000 troops to high-risk areas and assisted the SLP in deploying an additional 4,400 officers (PK Update, May–July 2002). The UNAMSIL military component, for example, was deployed in five sectors across the country, and UNAMSIL's civilian police component (CIVPOL) was strengthened from sixty authorized posts to ninety in order to better support the May 2002 elections (Malan, 2003). Taking things one step further, CIVPOL selected ten of the best SLP police trainers to participate in a two-week course on providing safety and security during elections, with the purpose of training teams of about 100 officers every four days in the runup to the election to ensure sufficient police supervision for the elections (Malan, 2003). When the elections finally rolled around in May 2002, the security situation in Sierra Leone had been effectively improved. The basic security missions and the election supervision mission actions reinforced one another (Recursive Effects), with the net impact benefiting each.

The presidential elections in May 2002 were largely peaceful, with the exception of some clashes between members of the Sierra Leone People's Party and former rebels of the RUF. Observers from the EU and the Commonwealth deemed the 2002 national democratic elections and the 2004 local elections as free and fair (Olonisakin, 2008; Hazen, 2007; Carter Center, 2003). Approximately 1.9 million voters (or 83% of those registered to vote) cast ballots in Sierra Leone's 2002 presidential and parliamentary elections (Carter Center, 2003); these turnout estimates are confirmed by the International Institute for Democracy and Electoral Assistance (IDEA, n.d.).

One cause for concern was that some southern regions had unusually high voter turnout rates (Carter Center, 2003)—as high as 99.4 percent—but NEC officials did not pursue these suspicious anomalies. Consequently, with extensive international support, Sierra Leone conducted two successful democratic elections in 2002 (presidential and parliamentary) and 2004 (local government). Because the 2004 elections were local, there are fewer reports by external agencies, but one report (Commonwealth Expert Team, 2004) found that the election was credible and free and fair, with no signs of intimidation or violence. That said, a local observation group—National Elections Watch (NEW)—estimated turnout as less than 40 percent.[3]

Elections alone are not synonymous with democratization. There is little doubt that progress was evident when comparing 1996 elections with its successors in 2002 and 2004, respectively. Nevertheless, some (Harris, 2014) questioned the sustainability of this progress, especially given the problematic marginalization of the RUF during the 2002 election (which

---

[3] https://www.thenewhumanitarian.org/news/2004/05/24/first-local-polls-32-years-marred-low-turn-out (last accessed December 10, 2022).

ultimately led to the SLPP landslide victory). That was a result of disapprobation from an international community that advocated punishment rather than inclusion. Earning over 70 percent of the presidential vote, President Kabbah won overwhelmingly, and his SLPP also won an absolute majority of 83 seats in the 124-member parliament. This led one NGO to express concern that Sierra Leone was "dangerously close to single party rule" (International Crisis Group, 2002), something suggestive of prospective future problems for democratization as competitive elections are one of the hallmarks of democracy. Furthermore, popular participation in politics among the Sierra Leoneans was often only seen during election periods and that few political parties operated outside of election years was also of concern (Hazen, 2007). This is perhaps why voter turnout in the 2004 local government elections was less than half of that for the 2002 presidential and parliamentary elections.

As a result of one-party control, the Sierra Leone government did not function as a full democracy. There were no checks and balances across different institutions, and indeed the Parliament was a rubber stamp for executive decisions rather than an independent source of authority and representation (Hazen, 2007). Nevertheless, some of the above pessimism might have been premature. The 2007 presidential elections were competitive among multiple parties and resulted in a change of government without violence. Subsequent democratic elections and peaceful transfers of power between different political groups are healthy signs of democracy.

Overall, Sierra Leone's democracy scores show improvement over time. According to Varieties of Democracy (V-Dem) scores, Sierra Leone's deliberative, electoral, participatory, egalitarian, and liberal democracy index scores all jumped significantly after 2001, with the greatest growth in its electoral democracy index scores—Sierra Leone's Electoral Democracy index score in 2001 was 0.23, but that grew to 0.44 in 2002 and 0.57 in 2003, with 0 being "low" and 1 being "high." The Polity 5 Index codes 2001 as a transition period, but following that year, there was steady improvement in its democracy scores: it earned a 5 (open anocracy) during the years 2002–2006, and a score of 7 (democracy) during the period 2007–2018.

Thus far, our expectations about Security First, Individual Effects (from compatibility), and Recursive Effects have been borne out in relation to the basic security and short-term missions. We next turn to the longer-term missions to assess whether the positive interactions persist when UNAMSIL pursues much less compatible missions than its original set of activities.

Longer-Term Missions (Rule of Law, Reconciliation, SSR, Local Governance)

The previous UNAMSIL missions got off to bumpy starts but were able to become steady and successful several years before the end of the deployment. For the peacebuilding missions, this suggests that any problems encountered should also be short-term, and perhaps not present at all if the primary efforts in fulfilling those missions occurred after the initial periods of the security and short-term mission problems. Our theoretical expectations anticipated positive spinoffs from the early missions, but as we move into those missions that are less compatible, concerns arise about how well peacekeepers can perform missions that involve very different roles and skill sets. As evident below, such concerns are reflected by the outcomes associated with each of the missions, with some—SSR—more successful than others—Rule of Law and Local Governance.

Rule of Law

UNAMSIL's Rule of Law and Reconciliation missions were closely intertwined, and therefore are evaluated in consecutive sections. An aggregate measure for rule of law from the World Bank (from Blair, 2020) indicates a 30 percent improvement from 2000 to 2006, roughly reflecting the beginning and ending points of the operation;[4] on a comparative basis, rule of law in Sierra Leone remained below average through 2016, even as there were incremental improvements following the end of the peace operation. Overall, UNAMSIL's performance in its Rule of Law mission was *Mixed*.

The apex of a legal system is a national constitution. Sierra Leone's constitution has undergone several controversial developments since its first version in 1961—the year of national independence, which concomitantly resulted in its inheriting a legal system based on English common law. The One-Party Constitution of 1978 permitted the president to appoint or suspend judges at will (Suma, 2014). The 1991 Constitution, which is the same constitution[5] that Sierra Leone uses today, represented a significant improvement for judicial independence and the administration of the rule of law. Accordingly,

---

[4] Freedom House aggregate measures of the rule of law are only available starting in 2003 and show no change for the last two years of UNAMSIL.

[5] Although the Sierra Leonean Constitution of 1991 is the same constitution the country uses today (after being reinstated in 1996), it has undergone a number of amendments (Constitute Project, 2021).

judicial constraints on the executive increased over the duration of the peace operation (from 0.32 to 0.49 on the 0–1 scale in V-Dem data, as reported in Blair, 2020). Nevertheless, in its final report, the Sierra Leone Truth and Reconciliation Commission (2004) identified a number of lapses in the 1991 Constitution. In particular, it called for including provisions in the constitution about the right to human dignity and the right to human life (TRC Report Volume 2, 2004). Although Sierra Leone's law allows for individuals to initiate legal proceedings if they believe the executive has acted contrary to the interest of the state, "28 years of autocratic rule, punctuated by military governments, has limited the culture, knowledge, and desire for challenging Government in court to a few elite" (Suma, 2014:45). Thus, although there were dramatic improvements in individual equality before the law in a structural sense (from 0.18 to 0.69 on the V-Dem 0–1 scale, reported by Blair, 2020), the results in practice were less because of a number of factors.

A functioning judicial system is a critical piece of a rule-of-law regime. When UNAMSIL turned its attention to assisting the government in rebuilding an impartial, transparent, and independent judiciary in 2002, the extant system was in dire straits. Despite the opportunity to remake the system in whole, there was no comprehensive reform plan (Hazen, 2007). Judicial coverage was extremely limited (S/2002/1417): only five of the fourteen magistrate courts were functioning (PK Update, May–July 2002) and there was a lack of trained personnel (PK Update, November 2002–January 2003). Not only was there a severe shortage of lawyers, but these lawyers remained limited to the capital city, a problem that would persist for many years; of the 100 lawyers nationwide in 2008, 93 of them were based in Freetown (Castillejo, 2009). Although there were impressive efforts to increase coverage of the magistrate's courts throughout the country following the civil war, issues of accessibility remained because courts were only based in the two district capitals and magistrates often had to cover multiple districts (Denney, 2014). Local courts, on the other hand, were much more accessible, with 288 local courts nationwide (Denney, 2014). Another factor hindering accessibility was that the SLP and formal judiciary operated according to formal English law and that proceedings were conducted in English. This privileged Sierra Leoneans living in educated, urban areas, who could afford lawyers and speak English themselves—something that created a perception of a "Freetown bias" (Lincoln, 2011).

Even as the judicial system outside of the capital was hindered as a result of limited trained personnel, the situation in Freetown was also worrisome.

The main court was described as being in "shambles"—with many case files missing and hundreds of people held in overcrowded conditions at the main Pademba Road Prison (Lincoln, 2011). This prison, which was designed to house 350 people, often held more than 1,000 (Human Rights Watch, 2007). Although UNAMSIL worked alongside the Sierra Leone government to build a number of new courts, the lack of personnel (judges, magistrates, and lawyers) to staff these buildings stifled progress, resulting in long waiting periods and a slow legal process (Hazen, 2007). According to a 2010 survey of prisoners in six prisons in up-country Sierra Leone by the Study of African Economics, 6.7 percent of the 890 inmates had experienced more than eleven adjournments (reported in Varvaloucas et al., 2012), which speaks to slow progress of justice in Sierra Leone well after the withdrawal of UNAMSIL Nevertheless, conditions in other areas slowly improved. By mid-to-late 2003, there were reports that the Sierra Leone police were increasingly respecting the time limit for detention and that magistrates had been regularly hearing cases (PK Update, August–October 2003).

As time progressed, there was also a slow, but steady, improvement in judicial independence (Linzer and Staton, 2015). Measuring independence on the 0–1 scale (with 1 indicating full independence), there was a decline during the civil war period from 0.24 at the outset of the war to 0.12 at the lowest point several years later. There was a steady increase in judicial independence associated with the UNAMSIL operation, increasing to 0.44 in 2005, the end of the operation. Equally important, this improvement was sustained in the post-deployment years, reaching 0.54 in 2012.

Because the formal judicial system offered little in the way of efficient, equitable, or timely conflict resolution, however, many individuals felt that it was inaccessible and therefore of little relevance. Exasperated with the court system, individuals sought alternatives, often resorting to local and traditional means of resolving conflict (Hazen, 2007). The reliance upon alternative means for dispute resolution was not necessarily from frustration with the local and national court system, but rather because seeking out chiefs, elders, Mammy Queens, workplace associations, and secret societies was the custom for many Sierra Leoneans (Denney, 2014). Indeed, a 2006 survey indicated that crimes and conflicts were first reported to these traditional authorities (Denney, 2014). This was similar to what was encountered by UNTAET in East Timor, and thus is indicative of failures to meet one of Blair's (2020) standards for effective rule of law. Thus, the average Sierra Leonean—and particularly those in rural communities—was much more likely to rely on chiefly courts or traditional diviners to adjudicate disputes (Millar, 2018), even as the outcomes were not legally binding and did not necessarily comport with established law.

In general, basic security success was a prerequisite for progress in the Rule of Law mission, but Traditional Peacekeeping and DDR could not prompt the essential institutional changes that guaranteed the rule of law. Neither could successful democratic elections. The case provides an example of the difficulties of transitioning from peacekeeping to peacebuilding missions.

Reconciliation

As referenced above, some of the UNAMSIL focus was on dealing with past rule-of-law concerns, namely crimes during the civil war era, in addition to promoting institutional development at the time of deployment. To address the crimes that took place during and after the Sierra Leone Civil War, two judicial mechanisms were established. One was the Truth and Reconciliation Commission (TRC), which was tasked with violations going back to 1991. The purpose of the TRC was to enable a national expression of moral condemnation of the abuses that took place in the civil war and to establish that such abuses should never happen again (Almuslem, 2020). Another established by the Security Council on August 14, 2000, was the Sierra Leone Special Court (SLSC), whose jurisdiction only covered abuses committed after November 1996. The purpose of the latter was to prosecute those "who bear the greatest responsibility" for committing war crimes—a phrase that many found to be vague (Newman, 2002). Although it was envisioned that this would mean those in authority, such as RUF leaders, the people who bore the greatest responsibility in the eyes of the local population were their neighbors—the ones that had carried out the actions (e.g., burning, looting, raping) (Boege and Rinck, 2019). Nevertheless, the purpose of this independent Special Court was to hold individuals accountable for war crimes, so that national reconciliation and the maintenance of peace might begin to take place (S/RES/1315).

Although this "twin approach" to peacebuilding was thought to be an ideal, with the SLSC prosecuting the highest-level perpetrators and the TRC serving as a reparative body designed to facilitate reconciliation, there are some drawbacks to this approach. It is a difficult balancing act to achieve both justice and reconciliation, which can work at cross-purposes. Reconciliation in the context of the TRC involved, in part, perpetrators taking responsibility for their actions. Yet, they are unlikely to do so if their statements might be used against them in criminal prosecutions. Similarly, prosecuting offenders in the judicial system might bring justice in the eyes of victims, but it does not necessarily promote reconciliation between victim and perpetrator. There was an attempt to thread the needle on these two sometimes competing interests, via provisions for amnesty in the Lomé Agreement. Those who committed crimes during the civil war were granted amnesty, setting the stage for possible reconciliation. An exception to the amnesty was that those who had committed war crimes, defined under international humanitarian law, were not covered; thus, those committing the worst crimes could be prosecuted, and this served the need for and interests of justice.

Supplementing the two judicial elements were provisions for reparations, under the auspices of the SLSC. The entire reconciliation process, and even reparations, is not one that can be completed in a short time. Thus, significant reparations came between 2009 and 2013 and were provided to over 32,000 Sierra Leoneans—victims who included forced amputees, victims of sexual violence, severely war-wounded, and orphans and war widows.[6] It is not clear whether these numbers reflect all, a majority, or a minority of those victimized and entitled to compensation.

Most international money and attention in the area of transitional justice were spent on the Special Court, rather than the TRC or local reconciliation measures (Boege and Rinck, 2019). UNAMSIL's role in all of this was to provide logistic, security, and technical support to the Special Court, and at times this meant utilizing UNAMSIL Radio and press to increase awareness of events (S/2002/1417). In October 2002, for example, UNAMSIL handed over to the Special Court a preliminary inventory of war-related killings and grave sites.

One criticism of the SLSC was that its "adversarial" approach to justice—according to Nkansah (2015)—caused more tension than it contributed to peace because "dialoguing" was the preferred approach to dispute resolution among Sierra Leoneans (Almuslem, 2020). In a similar vein, although the TRC was generally helpful in that it served as a way for both victims and perpetrators to voice their grievances so that reconciliation and reintegration into the community might be made easier, the reconciliation aspect received criticism, as hearings were described as "disconnected and culturally inappropriate" (Boege and Rinck, 2019). Shaw (2007) found in field research

---

[6] https://www.iom.int/sites/default/files/migrated_files/What-We-Do/docs/Support-to-the-Implementation-of-the-Sierra-Leone-Reparations-Programme-SLRP.pdf (last accessed December 10, 2022).

that the majority of Sierra Leoneans interviewed expressed a desire to move on from the atrocities, rather than bring back memories of violence and suffering. "Repeating the English expression, 'forgive and forget,' they argued that healing and reconciliation depend on forgetting rather than truthtelling," and this ultimately resulted in some communities refusing to participate in the TRC progress (Shaw, 2007:184).

Local reconciliation that took place under the TRC was limited to "mere ceremonies," as perpetrators were "ceremonially accepted back" by communities that did not want them, which ultimately resulted in many former combatants having to relocate to cities, rather than resettle in their original communities (Boege and Rinck, 2019:232). As one local INGO staff member put it, after the TRC process, "there was truth, but no reconciliation" (quoted in Boege and Rinck, 2019:232). People, instead, preferred to rely on ritual practices such as "sacrifices, prayer, exorcism, funerals, ritual healing, church services" to create "cool hearts" that form the basis for life in a community (Shaw, 2007:195).

Despite these drawbacks, the TRC gathered over 7,000 statements, 10 percent of which were from perpetrators. The TRC was effective in documenting the type and extent of violations during the war. The Commission found that forced displacement, abduction, arbitrary detention, and killing were the most common forms of violations, making up 19.8, 14.8, 12.0, and 11.2 percent of the violations reported to the Commission, respectively. Although forced amputations were not as common a violation, the Commission found that the violations that did occur were so disturbing that "it served to dehumanize the victim and to create grave psychological damage" (SLTRC, Volume 2, Chapter 2:37). The report also describes that although the majority of victims of the war were adult males, "perpetrators singled out women and children for some of the most brutal violations of human rights recorded in any conflict" (SLTRC, Volume 2, Chapter 2:33). Children, girls especially, were often targeted for rape and other forms of abuse, with 4.5 percent (985) of the victims who reported to the Commission under ten years old, and 9.5 percent (2,104) of them under thirteen years old. Even though atrocities were committed by all sides, the TRC found that the RUF was responsible for the largest number of human rights violations (responsible for 60.5% of the violations). The TRC exhibited impartiality in assigning responsibility. Transgressions by the government of Sierra Leone were not ignored, as the Commission argued that it failed to address many human rights violations against civilians that occurred. In addition, the report did not spare UN peacekeepers from derision, pointing to a "poor understanding of the situation" and an inability to "respond timely to the challenges with which they were faced" as the reasons that led to the RUF having "little problem" in kidnapping 500 peacekeepers in May 2000 (SLTRC, Volume 2, Chapter 2:90).

Overall, we judge the mission outcome as *Mostly Effective*. We recognize that UNAMSIL had perhaps the least influence on outcomes in the Reconciliation mission among its other missions, and indeed all the other missions covered in this book.

Security Sector Reform (SSR)

Security Sector Reform under UNAMSIL was multifaceted. It meant reestablishing law and order so that everyday life could resume in a safe environment. SSR also involved training local personnel and establishing processes for the security apparatus to function following the withdrawal of peacekeeping forces. Overall, the outcome of this mission can be considered *Mostly Effective*.

The initial conditions of deployment did not provide the ideal context for UNAMSIL to stabilize the area. Problems with Traditional Peacekeeping and DDR rippled throughout the operation, and early efforts at security were hampered. The defeat of the RUF and the subsequent disarmament of militias, however, created an environment in which SSR reforms could be carried out (Brast, 2015). The security situation had mostly stabilized by 2002, with the exception of some localized protests and cross-border incursions along the Sierra Leone–Liberia border, but none of these violent events seriously threatened the country's stability (S/2002/987; Hazen, 2007). The capital city of Freetown, which previously was deserted, was once more bustling with life. The freedom of movement throughout the country invited the revival of commercial activity, and the return of refugees was one of several indicators that UNAMSIL was able to re-establish order successfully. Public perceptions also reflected a belief that the security situations had improved—a survey conducted in 2005 indicated that 97 percent of respondents agreed with the statement "your security situation has improved" (Curran and Woodhouse, 2007; UN Department of Public Information, 2005).

Despite substantial progress, some crime and security threats continued in certain areas and in several forms. There were hundreds of youth roaming the streets because of lack of opportunity, and there was rampant prostitution among young girls and boys (Olonisakin, 2008; Curran and Woodhouse, 2007). A 2007 report from the UN Peacebuilding Commission, in fact, found that "youth unemployment and disempowerment" was one of the four key areas in which sustained peacebuilding in Sierra Leone was facing serious difficulties (PBC/2/OC/L.1; Curran and Woodhouse, 2007). Most concerning was that these youth were vulnerable to being recruited by "predatory" traders in diamond-producing areas of Sierra Leone, something that the UN Secretary-General acknowledged as contributing to an atmosphere of distrust and tension (S/2002/1417). This is one of the reasons efforts were made by UNAMSIL to help the state to re-establish state control over diamond mining (Hazen, 2007).

With a mostly stable security situation, UNAMSIL turned its attention toward reforming the police force, while the UK-led International Military Advisory and Training Team (IMATT) focused on reforming the Republic of Sierra Leone Armed Forces (RSLAF). The restructuring of Sierra Leone's army followed the reorganization of the Ministry of the Defense, under IMATT leadership. Britain provided most of the funds for restructuring the RSLAF, and 80–90 percent of the IMATT personnel (von Dyck, 2016). One of the first tasks of IMATT was to resume pay for soldiers and implement a Military Reintegration Programme (MRP), which was designed to integrate the various ex-fighters with a view to enhance postwar reconciliation (von Dyck, 2016; Gbla, 2011). To meet the logistical needs of the RSLAF, IMATT provided the army with "75 military land rovers, 25 military trucks, 7 ambulances, 2 helicopter support units and 8 armoured vehicles," as well as communication equipment (Gbla, 2011:133). Although UNAMSIL was able to officially hand over the country's security sector in 2004, IMATT stayed for the years following UNAMSIL's departure. That the reform of the military took longer to accomplish was not worrisome, as SSR can easily require up to a decade or more after a country has achieved peace (Van Pottelbergh, 2010). By 2010, the Sierra Leone armed forces had shrunk by 20 percent to 8,500 (Brast, 2015), leading many to conclude that IMATT was by and large a success story (Boege and Rinck, 2019; Nilsson and Kovacs, 2013). Yet this was a function of the UK program and not UNAMSIL, even as this might be regarded as a success for the SSR mission.

UNAMSIL's task in reforming the police was not easy, given that the Sierra Leone police had experienced long years of neglect under one-party rule, only to then be decimated during the civil war (Baker, 2005). Because of this, a number of other policing bodies or agencies had arisen in Sierra Leone, both approved and unauthorized. As with its Rule of Law and Reconciliation missions, UNAMSIL (and the UK) took a state-centered approach to SSR reform, focusing on the state apparatus to the neglect of the myriad of alternative providers that were more frequently relied upon by Sierra Leoneans (Denney, 2014). Chiefdom police, for example, who were the main providers of security for most Sierra Leoneans, were thus sidelined by government and international reform efforts (Boege and Rinck, 2019). As with the justice system, access to security remained a particular problem for those in rural areas.

In the end, however, UNAMSIL was able to train 3,500 local police personnel and construct (or reconstruct) thirteen police stations, sixty-eight unit barracks, a recruit training school, and four regional training centers in the towns of Bo, Kenema, Makeni, and Jui (United Nations, 2005). At times, peacekeepers ran into challenges in training these new police cadets, particularly because there was only one functioning police training school (PK Update, May–July 2003). The target size (fixed by the government) of 9,500 was supposed to be reached before UNAMSIL withdrew, but as of September 2002, they still needed to find an additional 3,000 cadets. On a comparative basis, police staffing lagged far behind that in other peacebuilding operations. Sierra Leone had only 0.02 police per 1000 inhabitants, six times lower that the next lowest state (Haiti at 0.13) and far below Bosnia, East Timor, and Kosovo (ranging from 1.16–2.20 per thousand) (Dobbins et al., 2005).

Recruitment rates slowly increased over time (Gbla, 2006), and by December 2005—the month when UNAMSIL's mandate ended—the strength of the SLP was close to its goal with 9,019 officers, 15 percent of whom were women (United Nations Department of Public Information, 2005). Although much was achieved in the training of the police force, the UN acknowledged that additional help was needed in the form of vehicles, communication equipment, and office and barracks accommodations. Corruption and mistrust had been problems for the police, and indeed the TRC report referred to the SLP as incompetent, corrupt, and part of state terror during the war. Although corruption remained a problem, public confidence increased—a survey indicated that 46 percent thought that there had been an improvement in police attitudes, whereas only 15 percent believed that things had gotten worse (SLP, 2004)..

By September 2004, the UN peacekeepers were able officially to hand over the country's security sector to Sierra Leone, and in the years that followed, the government did not request any assistance—an indicator of the success in the reforming the security forces (Gbla, 2006). The SSR mission, relative to other peacebuilding missions, is more compatible (closer in Figure 2.1) with the basic security and other shorter-term missions. Accordingly, the positive spillover effects were perhaps felt more with respect to SSR than others in the latter stages of the operation.

Local Governance

Finally, UNAMISL was tasked with carrying out a Local Governance mission, and perhaps this was its least successful venture, with an outcome that we judge as *Mixed*. Once again, the year 2002 signified a turning point for Sierra Leone. With the security situation seemingly under control, peacekeepers turned their attention to decentralization and the empowerment of local communities, focusing on three key areas: (1) the deployment of government officials to the districts; (2) filling the sixty-three posts of Paramount Chiefs that fell vacant during the war; and (3) restoring elected district officials (S/2002/1417). One surface indicator of UNAMSIL performance in the local governance mission was that it transferred government responsibility to local ownership in 2003—just three years after the initiation of international involvement. This might be considered successful, but one might argue that UNAMSIL was too quick in entrusting the task of governing to the local population (Law, 2006).

By mid-2003, the first of these goals was reached (PK Update, May–July 2003), but government officials were hampered by local government structures that still lacked the wherewithal to deliver basic services to the people (PK Update, November 2002–January 2003). Although government institutions existed in form, they had yet to demonstrate that they could function effectively. Local governing councils, who were elected democratically in 2004 for the first time in thirty years, were slow to establish themselves and begin work because of a lack of infrastructure, skilled professionals, and experience (Hazen, 2007). In addition, just six years after the end of the civil war and after the extensive international aid that security sector reform received, UN officials reported that Sierra Leone's government was facing a severe financial crisis, which adversely affected the capacity of the SLP and armed forces (Reno, 2009). As a result, Sierra Leone proved largely incapable of self-governance during the early years following the civil war, as it was heavily reliant on external support. Indeed, state building raises normal development issues for post-conflict nations, given that it necessarily takes longer than the duration of a peace mission (Van Pottelbergh, 2010).

The financial exigency above was debilitating in that national funds are needed for government to function. One promising statistic was the significant increase in licensed mining activities and in official exports of rough diamonds (PK Update, May–July 2003). From $10 million in 2000, government income from diamond exports had soared to $160 million in 2004 (Kreps, 2010), a result of the reforms to the overhaul of the diamond sector that began with Sierra Leone's signing on to the Kimberly Process Certification Scheme to stem the flow of "conflict" or "blood" diamonds. Other sources of revenue came from exports of rutile, bauxite, coffee, and cocoa (United Nations Department of Public Information, 2005).

As with its other missions, however, UNAMSIL was criticized for not seeking out and directly working with the local population. Instead, peacekeepers and other international actors saw the national government as the main point of contact (Boege and Rinck, 2019). This limited the development of many subnational government processes, and the peace operation did not take advantage of existing institutions and mechanisms, including local actors and processes (Boege and Rinck, 2019). This resulted in an apparent gap between what international actors were doing and what locals found relevant, leading to frustration about the priorities and decisions peacekeepers made.

UNAMSIL was not alone in its efforts to restore local governance. It was assisted by a number of other programs, such as the IMF, World Bank, the Department for International Development (DFID), and EU aid programs. By the time of UNAMSIL's end, however, government institutions still lacked the capacity to carry out their duties effectively and to provide essential services (e.g., power, safe water, and proper sanitation) to more than just a few households in urban areas (Curran and Woodhouse, 2007). Thus, UNAMSIL left behind an incomplete mission, even as some improvements were evident. The World Bank's (2021a) government effectiveness indicators do show slow improvement over time following UNAMSIL's departure, but even then, Sierra Leone has consistently lagged behind other low-income countries and other sub-Saharan African countries. One reason for such poor local governance in Sierra Leone can be traced back to the control and power of local paramount chiefs, indicating that local governance structures had not supplanted traditional ones (International Growth Centre, 2013; Acemoglu et al., 2014).[7]

---

[7] Since the re-establishment of local councils in 2004, "the traditional authorities, known as Chiefdom Administrations, have operated side by side with the formal local government structures" (Edwards et al., 2014:3).

The World Bank's (2021b) indicator for control of corruption, which captures perceptions of the extent to which public power is exercised for private gain, is slightly more promising. It shows that Sierra Leone experienced steady improvement following UNAMSIL, and a significant improvement after 2016, when it surpassed the medians of other low-income countries and other sub-Saharan African countries.

Summary of UNAMSIL

UNAMSIL was the most successful of our peace operation case studies and demonstrates that even those operations with a large number of missions, deployed in the context of violent civil wars, can still achieve high levels of success in many of them. To that extent, this suggests that our indicator of multitasking is far from the final word on compatibility; this disconfirms our expectation about Aggregate Effects and the pernicious impact of highly incompatible operation profiles. Sequencing (the security missions being successful early) was important, and there were no obvious examples of learning with respect to adapting to incompatibility, as posited by the Learning expectation.

In reviewing our expectations about simultaneity and sequencing, UNAMSIL confirms most or all of them to varying degrees. Security First was evident insofar as Traditional Peacekeeping and DDR success eased the way for a variety of shorter-term missions—Humanitarian Assistance, Election Supervision/Promotion of Democracy, and Human Rights, respectively. There were also positive Recursive Effects evidenced among these sets of missions. Basic security success might have provided assistance to the later peacebuilding missions, but the impact was neither great nor direct. An exception might be SSR, whose mission profile was more compatible with basic security missions than with other peacebuilding activities.

For Democracy Matters, the results are more uncertain and represent only a partial confirmation. We had anticipated that failure would have downstream consequences for peacebuilding operations. Yet in Sierra Leone, the Election Supervision/Promotion of Democracy mission was Mostly Effective. Negative democratic outcomes might have more impact than positive ones, and successful elections did not necessarily have good consequences; indeed, successful local elections did produce indigenous officeholders and other officials, but resource and other concerns (which cannot be tied to election outcomes) hampered the Local Governance mission.

The interconnection of peacebuilding missions with one another (Peacebuilding Synergy and Peacebuilding Matters) exhibited only partial confirmation. Three of the peacebuilding tasks—SSR, Local Governance, and Rule of Law—did not undermine one another, but dramatic spillover effects were not evident. SSR success did help the other two, but those latter two did not achieve the same level of effectiveness as SSR. Similarly, Reconciliation benefited from a stable security environment but suffered somewhat by a weaker judicial system undergirding the rule of law. Nevertheless, reconciliation efforts produced better outcomes than were obtained by the other three peacebuilding missions.

The results vis-à-vis our expectations are summarized in Table 6.2. There is a disconnect between the Sequencing, Simultaneity, and Prerequisites expectations on the one hand and the compatibility expectations on the other. The former were generally confirmed while the latter were not. This suggests that peace operation missions can be successful even when incompatible missions interact and learning from earlier experiences do not materialize.

Table 6.2 Summary of results vis-à-vis expectations—UNAMSIL

Type of expectation	Expectation	Outcome
Sequencing, Simultaneity, and Prerequisites	Security First	Supported
	Democracy Matters	Partly Supported
	Peacebuilding Synergy	Partly Supported
	Peacebuilding Matters	Partly Supported
	Recursive Effects	Supported
Compatibility	Aggregate Effects	Not Supported
	Learning	Not Supported
	Individual Effects	Partly Supported

7

Conclusions and Implications

Introduction

At the outset of this book, we presented an ambitious agenda for a largely unexplored research focus—how different peacekeeping missions are related to and affect one another. With eight theoretical expectations to guide us, we examined five different peace operations, representing different historical epochs and continents. We can now draw several conclusions that address our central research question and its corollaries.

In this concluding chapter, we initially address our findings in relation to our expectations, in an attempt to judge the degree to which these were met. Following this summary, we delve more deeply into the processes underlying the relationships uncovered in our case studies. We propose a framework for comparing different peace operations in light of our findings. Similar to that used for negotiation (see Druckman and Wagner, 2016) and using the insights gained in previous chapters, our framework includes antecedents (background factors including context, preparation), concomitants (changes in the situation, process dynamics) and consequences (termination decisions, post-operation decisions). The framework allows the analyst to consider different elements of the peace operation at different stages, and it also allows us to offer a series of policy implications that flow from our findings. From a policy standpoint, we discuss some of the emerging trends in peace operation missions and their implications given what we have learned about mission interdependence and compatibility.

In the first chapter, we argued that our study has significant implications for future research on peacekeeping. We can now circle back to those implications. From a scholarly and theoretical standpoint, we assess how our findings prompt reconsideration of what we know about peacekeeping success from extant works. We also lay out a future research agenda on peacekeeping interdependence in light of our findings. In particular, we raise the unexplored question of interdependence between peace operations and their successors; this arrangement has become increasingly common for

When Peacekeeping Missions Collide. Paul F. Diehl, Daniel Druckman, and Grace B. Mueller, Oxford University Press.
© Oxford University Press 2024. DOI: 10.1093/oso/9780197696842.003.0007

peacekeeping with multiple operations occurring in sequence (e.g., Haiti with six UN operations and two others since 1993, at this writing).

Summary of Results on the Expectations

Table 7.1 summarizes the results of the case studies in relation to the theoretical explanations elucidated in Chapter 2. We provide a scorecard for each of the expectations across the five cases and also show how each case performed across the eight expectations. By "support" we refer to meeting the conditions specified by the expectations.[1] The discussion to follow presents the results for each of the expectations.

Security First

The first and perhaps most fundamental expectation about the interdependence of missions was that the outcome of the basic security missions—Traditional Peacekeeping and DDR—would have downstream consequences for all the other missions that a given operation attempted. Success in security missions should enhance the likelihood of success in other missions, and failure would have the opposite effect.

This expectation was examined in all five cases, and strongly supported in each. The ability to establish or monitor cease-fires in particular, as well as the outcomes of DDR missions, influenced the processes and success of the other peacekeeping missions. The relationship held in both specifications, positive and negative; that is, success in basic security missions enhanced success in the other missions, and failure in the former undermined the prospects for success in the latter. The ONUC operation was an illustration of this with initial failures causing problems, giving way to subsequent success after the establishment of stability and the defeat of secessionist forces.

The validation of Security First is not without some qualifications. First, the MONUC operation matches our proposition only in part. Problems in the security area complicated other missions, but successful elections were

---

[1] We do not use the term "confirmation," which is associated with a hypothesis testing tradition. That term would apply if our study consisted of statistical analyses of a large number of cases (see Chapter 3 for a discussion of causality).

Table 7.1 Summary of results vis-à-vis expectations

Expectations/cases	ONUC	UNPROFOR	UNTAET	MONUC	UNAMSIL	Number supported or partly supported
Security First	Supported	Supported	Supported	Supported	Supported	5/5
Democracy Matters	N/A	N/A	Not Supported	Not Supported	Partly Supported	1/3
Peacebuilding Synergy	N/A	N/A	Supported	Supported	Partly Supported	3/3
Peacebuilding Matters	N/A	N/A	Partly Supported	Supported	Partly Supported	3/3
Recursive Effects	Supported	Supported	Supported	Supported	Supported	5/5
Aggregate Effects	Not Supported	Not Supported	Supported	Supported	Not Supported	2/5
Learning	Not Supported	Not Supported	Not Supported	Not Supported	Not Supported	0/5
Individual Effects	Supported	Partially supported	Supported	Supported	Partly Supported	5/5
Number supported or partly supported	3/5	3/5	6/8	6/8	6/8	

conducted despite those difficulties. Second, the impact of the basic security missions seemed to be stronger with respect to those missions that were shorter-term and more compatible with Traditional Peacekeeping and DDR, namely missions such as Humanitarian Assistance. Positive spillover was more limited for peacebuilding missions such as the Rule of Law and Local Governance; security and stability helped those missions, but their overall success was driven by other dynamics.

Democracy Matters

Our second expectation was that the Election Supervision/Promotion of Democracy mission would influence the other missions that followed. Elections usually come early following a peace agreement, so there is ample time to see their effects in the aftermath. Only three of the peace operations that we examined had this mission, and results generally did not match our expectations. Successful elections during the UNTAET and MONUC operations did not translate into positive performances in the peacebuilding operations later on, and thus this expectation was not supported. The most successful of the peace operations—UNAMSIL—was also mostly effective in its democracy-related tasks, but subsequent peacekeeping outcomes saw some slippage in the peacebuilding missions that followed; that is, democracy might have helped, or at least not hindered, peacebuilding, but it did not guarantee positive results in those more complex missions.

Much of the liberal model of peacebuilding is predicated on early elections and the establishment of democracy. That model has long been the subject of intense critique, especially by critical theorists (see Richmond, 2006, 2021; Richmond and MacGinty, 2015). Without the normative underpinnings of those criticisms, our findings are consistent with the skepticism about democratization and early elections as pathways to peacebuilding.

Peacebuilding Synergy

For peacebuilding, we anticipated that there would be reinforcing effects between three missions—SSR, Local Governance, and Rule of Law, respectively. This received full, or at least partial, support across our three relevant operations. For UNTAET, the relationships were in the negative direction. Problems in one mission caused difficulties in others, most notably with respect to SSR and Rule of Law. MONUC was ineffective in all three peacebuilding missions as failure begat further failure, even as the missions were largely compatible.

UNAMSIL represents the only positive directional support for the expectation, but just partly so. Success in the SSR mission helped in the Rule of Law and Local Governance achievements. Yet those two missions experienced other problems that could not be addressed or mitigated by a stable security environment; these included building effective judicial and government institutions, as well as having an adequate financial base.

Peacebuilding Matters

Our fourth expectation about mission interaction focuses on the longer-term peace missions. Reconciliation is posited to be a function of the success or failure of other peacebuilding missions—SSR, Rule of Law, and Local Governance—as these missions could establish a solid foundation that is necessary for healing in a previously conflict-ridden society. This was at least partly supported by all three operations that had these missions. Nevertheless, the connections were not as strong or consistent as the Peacebuilding Synergy expectation. In part, this might be a function of the different orientations of Reconciliation vis-à-vis the other three missions. The process of Reconciliation can be facilitated by peacekeepers, but the resulting attitudinal change (acceptance of truth, forgiveness) does not follow from peace operation actions. Implementation of reconciliation, such as bringing war criminals to justice, ultimately depends on indigenous officials with political interests, and the healing of society is a long-term process, occurring in most cases well after peacekeeping withdrawal.

MONUC illustrated the strongest connections between peacebuilding and Reconciliation. Problems in the Rule of Law mission, in particular, hampered attempts to bring past perpetrators to justice, which was the key component for reconciliation to occur. Thus, the underlying impact was negative. Two cases produced only partial support for our expectations. In UNTAET, progress in Reconciliation actually outpaced that in the other peacebuilding missions. Once again, limitations in the Rule of Law mission had negative downstream consequences for Reconciliation. Similarly, for

UNAMSIL, Reconciliation benefited from successes in the SSR mission but achieved more success than the other two peacebuilding missions, whose outcomes were judged as Mixed.

Recursive Effects

The final expectation with respect to sequencing and simultaneity was that later missions would have a feedback loop back to missions begun earlier, even as there might be impact from those early efforts on later missions (e.g., Security First). This expectation was supported in all five cases.

The presence of recursive effects, however, was not universal, in the sense that not every later mission influenced earlier ones. The relationship was clearest in two formulations. First, feedback was most evident in missions that were temporally proximate to one another. For example, Humanitarian Assistance helped the basic security missions when the former was successful; all tended to come in earlier stages of the peace operation. Second, and somewhat related, recursive effects were evident between missions that had similar profiles, that is, they were relatively more compatible. For example, success in elections assisted Traditional Peacekeeping, as both involved some substantial monitoring activities. It was less clear, if not evident at all, that peacebuilding missions circled back to influence missions begun at the outset of the operations. Some early activities—election supervision, humanitarian aid deliveries—were completed before some peacebuilding missions were undertaken and therefore there was no opportunity for feedback effects. Our findings suggest that although sequencing is important, there are instances of reverse interconnections as well, as when the results of later missions impact the earlier missions that are ongoing. This is an important consideration for both theorizing and policymaking.

Aggregate Effects

Our holistic expectation was that the greater the incompatibility of the missions carried out by a peace operation, the less likely it was to be successful in any or all of its missions. Two operations—MONUC and UNTAET—seem to fit this association. Both had relatively large numbers of missions, scored high on at least the first indicator of incompatibility, and experienced substantial problems in mission performance almost across the board. Nevertheless, the other three operations belie the proposed impact. ONUC and UNPROFOR had relatively compatible mission profiles (and relatively good scores on the first two indicators of compatibility), which theoretically implied that peacekeepers might not experience difficulties carrying out their assigned missions. Yet they experienced significant failures in spite of this. Conversely, the UNAMSIL operation carried out a broad portfolio of missions and was successful in many of them, albeit less so in peacebuilding than more traditional activities. Overall, we must reject the simple proposition that greater compatibility guarantees success and incompatibility is a recipe for failure. This was a useful heuristic for an initial study of peacekeeping compatibility, but it lacked the nuances and varied outcomes for peacekeeping in practice.

Other factors, some out of the peacekeepers' control, may mitigate the expected positive effects of mission compatibility. An example is diversion of resources to militant groups intent on spoiling progress toward peace or undermining peace agreements. Another are difficulties in coordinating with NGOs and other private operations occurring simultaneously. These findings may also have implications for a variety of types of organizations. Multitasking is likely to be facilitated by task compatibility, for example, financial record-keeping and decisions for equitable resource allocation. Nevertheless, other factors often come into play to reduce the positive effects of task compatibility. One of these factors is control over resources by other units in the organizational hierarchy. Another is the need to coordinate with units outside the organization. A third is an organization structure that encourages competition among units. A fourth is the tradeoff between the efficiency of implementing decisions that derives from a vertical organizational hierarchy and the unit creativity encouraged by horizontal structures.

Learning

Our third indicator of compatibility was predicated on the logic that as operations aged, peacekeepers would adapt to the changing environment and to the hurdles inherent in performing incompatible missions. There was little or no evidence that this occurred in any of the five operations, even as they varied substantially in deployment length.[2] Some of this was a function of certain missions ending before others commenced (e.g., DDR and peacebuilding efforts). Thus, incompatibility was less of a problem than might be suggested by our indicators and there was no need to adapt to incompatible tasks. Nevertheless, even as incompatible missions overlapped in time, there was little indication that peacekeeping performance improved over time; ineffectiveness or limited success with missions tended to persist over time. When some improvement did occur, it could not be attributed to learning or adaptation per se. Rather it may have been because of factors out of the peacekeepers' control, such as coordination with NGOs or host nation's cooperation. This finding has clear implications for training programs, which we discuss later in the chapter.

Individual Effects

The final explanation, both broadly and with respect to compatibility, was that individual mission success would be related to its compatibility with other missions to which it was paired. This was supported in all cases to varying degrees, but the effects were not uniform across all pairs or permutations of missions. Compatible missions seemed to have a stronger impact on operation outcomes than incompatible missions, even though aggregate compatibility did not contribute to success.

Some of the clearest individual effects occurred between the relatively compatible Traditional Peacekeeping and DDR missions. When one was unsuccessful, it tended to undermine the other, as was the case for UNPROFOR. One element of the SSR mission—initially establishing local security and stability—was also negatively impacted by the failures in basic security. Still, connections among missions could be positive as well. Success in some missions were tied to progress in others, as UNAMSIL indicated. SSR outcomes, both positive and negative, were tied to other peacebuilding results, as indicated in an earlier section.

---

[2] One might argue that with UNAMSIL, there was some evidence of learning. The kidnapping of 500 peacekeepers by RUF forces in May 2000 (a month in which the operation nearly collapsed) served as the impetus for UNAMSIL's troop strength being increased to 13,000—this allowed for a wider deployment of peacekeepers, which had a positive effect on humanitarian access. Yet such adaptation was not from recognizing the difficulties of incompatible missions per se, but rather from mission-specific problems, even as the result has positive spillover effects across different missions.

In summary, as shown in Table 7.1, five of the eight expectations were wholly or partly supported in our case studies: Security First, Peacebuilding Synergy, Peacebuilding Matters, Recursive Effects, and Individual Effects. Three expectations were not supported for most cases: Democracy Matters, Aggregate Effects, and Learning. Most expectations were supported for the cases, with a rate of either 60 percent (ONUC and UNPROFOR) or 75 percent (UNTAET, MONUC, and UNAMSIL).

A Framework for Analysis with Policy Implications

In Figure 7.1, we present a framework that shows the various elements of peace operations and missions, as well as their relationships in time and to each other. In some sense, it can be considered a holistic depiction of a typical operation. Each time period—considered as antecedents, concomitants, and consequences—contains two boxes. The peace operation is preceded by various kinds of preparation and occurs in a broader context including policy decisions about resources and missions. The operation consists of a variety of challenges and is influenced by conditions on the ground. Outcomes emerge and extend into an uncertain future that might consist of conflict

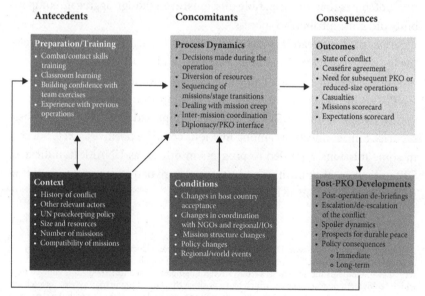

Figure 7.1 A framework for analyzing peace operations

escalation or de-escalation dynamics. In this section, we describe each of the boxes and follow with a discussion of connections among the parts including implications for UN policymakers, especially in light of our findings.

Preparation/Training

In the first box in Figure 7.1, we list several aspects of preparation for deployment. An important distinction exists between developing combat and contact skills. These are quite different and occur in different contexts and missions. Accordingly, such differences are associated with compatibility issues raised throughout this book. The two sets of skills map to the different roles and orientations within missions that have profiles largely distinct from one another.

Combat skills are similar to basic military training and are intended to prepare peacekeepers for the security missions discussed in this book. Many of these are related to monitoring functions in which peacekeepers supervise cease-fires and the first two components of DDR. There are also aspects of election supervision that fit, as peacekeepers are often tasked with serving alongside other security forces to deter or prevent violent activity before and after the election. In addition, protecting humanitarian assistance shipments involves many traditional military skills. The typical peacekeeping soldier receives conventional military training that is applicable to these missions and associated tasks. To the extent that these need modification, it is with respect to how the peacekeeping context differs from that of war. In particular, adhering to the limited use of force (only in self-defense) requirement of the "holy trinity" will run counter to training that emphasizes offensive or more robust military tactics.

Contact skills are those needed for the variety of newer missions intended to (re)build post-conflict societies, notably those associated with peacebuilding. These overlap with the training challenges facing NGOs and other non-UN actors in the conflict theater. Conflict management training is an essential core for the development of such skills. This includes skill sets that incorporate negotiation and mediation. Peacekeepers will not be charged with solving the underlying and remaining causes of the conflict. Rather, they will be dealing with problems at a micro level. These could include negotiating with groups who might want to block aid shipments or resolving disputes between factions in matters of local governance. More senior officers in the peacekeeping forces (and this is plural, as troops are typically organized in national units) might be the primary targets of such training, as opposed to all those who serve in the operation.

Some national armies include such specialized training for those who might serve in peace operations, but it is not clear whether this kind of training is present or uniform across all the militaries whose troops serve in operations—UN peace operations draw on contributions from a diverse and sometimes changing set of countries (for an overview of training, see United Nations Resource Hub, 2021). Other international training programs might be more attuned to contact skills and the different missions of modern UN operations. For example, the Peace Operations Training Institute (2021) offers courses on DDR, Human Rights, Civilian Protection, and Civil-Military Coordination, among others.

Many of the missions also require interaction and coordination with other actors—recall that among the dimensions used to measure mission compatibility in Chapter 2 was the degree of coordination required with the host government and international organizations, respectively. This requires skills and experience that go beyond standard military training. Soldiers sometimes have experience in coordinating actions with other units or agencies, especially related to the Local Security and Security Sector Reform missions. For other peacebuilding missions, such as Reconciliation, the tasks and partners are likely to be quite different than in prior military experience.

The multiple-mission focus of this book calls attention to more complex tasks for peacekeepers, but also the challenges of how to manage transitions from one to another type of mission and associated skill sets. On the one hand, this includes juggling combat and contact skills in ways not conventionally included in training. This might be difficult when the same, even properly trained, peacekeepers need to contribute to different missions simultaneously. The skill sets for Traditional Peacekeeping and Promoting Democracy, respectively, might be very different and require cognitive and practical shifts in behavior. At least equally important, the perceptions of stakeholders—disputants and the local population for example—also need to adapt to the changing actions of the peacekeepers. It might be difficult for others to understand or accept the shifts when they represent divergent roles, such as those that place peacekeepers in impartial positions versus those that might favor other actors (e.g., the host state government). Further complicating this is that peace missions might change in unexpected ways over the course of the deployment. In addition, the security situation on the ground can sometimes change; in ONUC, the collapse of the DRC government transformed the conflict from an interstate one into an intrastate crisis, leaving peacekeepers caught in the middle and unprepared to deal with the altered environment. Mandate renewal in the post–Cold War era has sometimes added missions to the peace operation. Thus, peacekeepers trained for one set of missions at the outset of the operation might be asked to perform new missions with different skill sets for which they have not been trained or have little or no experience.

Our results show rather dismal learning effects within operations for each of the cases examined. Perhaps peacekeepers do not reflect or act on their earlier experiences in the same operation, or at least the sponsoring agencies have not made the necessary adjustments as new missions are added or as the operations progressed in time. The importance of learning at the bureaucratic level, namely UN headquarters, is raised by Howard (2008) as a vital element in the success or failure of operations.

Although adaptations at the planning and administrative levels of the UN have trickle-down effects at the operational level, our concern has been with learning at that second level. There are several concerns. First is whether and how compatibility affects learning for the peace operation. Training protocols might draw on the transfer effects discussed by psychologists in the learning literature (Tornhausen and Buker, 2016). Conceivably, lessons transfer more easily between compatible missions; put another way, reinforcing rather than inhibiting effects are more likely for compatible missions. This training also involves learning about the concept of mission interdependence, which may be best accomplished when peacekeeping training includes exercises involving the design of multi-mission operations (Druckman and Ebner, 2017). Second, specified but left untested by Howard (2008), is so-called second-order learning, in which the UN learns *across* operations. One consideration is that peacekeepers who served in successive operations might be able to draw upon prior experience to improve performance.[3]

Context

Peace operations do not occur in a vacuum. Peacekeepers are placed in a conflict that has been ongoing for some time, often with a long history. There

---

[3] Nevertheless, the UN at the organizational level has not necessarily demonstrated effective learning over time and across operations—see Benner et al. (2011).

is no choice of who the disputants are or what issues led to the armed conflict. Thus, a peace operation is deployed at a moment during an unfolding conflict, as an intervention in a time series of events. In general, the environmental context or conditions (Diehl and Druckman, 2009) set the parameters for the operation and influence the success or failure of its missions.

The peacekeepers have little control over the paths taken by the combatants or whether they are deployed before or after a peace agreement has been signed. Analyses of our cases show that the moment of entering the conflict zone could be critical. ONUC spent the early stages of its operation during an active civil war and experienced significant problems in its basic security mission. In contrast, UNAMSIL was deployed following a peace agreement, creating a far more permissive environment to carry out its initial missions. There is little doubt that the impacts of their actions are path-dependent. The challenge for a peace operation is whether it can change that path or alter the impact of history. Such changes are more likely to occur when the goals underlying Security First are satisfied (see Table 7.1). Sustaining a cease-fire and facilitating DDR as needed lay the groundwork for all the other missions, although it by no means guarantees success for them. Indeed, the Reconciliation mission is predicated on the reality that even successful peacebuilding missions do not redress all the problems that stem from the history of the conflict.

Decisions made about the configuration of an operation are critical. Although we are not privy to discussions leading to the decisions, we can speculate about the concerns. One is a judgment about ambitions for the operation regarding the difference between managing the conflict and contributing to nation building. That assessment primarily determines which missions are deployed, albeit conditioned by contextual factors. Our empirical finding in Chapter 2 revealed there is no set package(s) of mission combinations on which the UN draws. This might be a function of the different contextual factors for each conflict/operation, but it might also reflect the limited conscious planning and the inability to look forward when the operation is initially authorized. The UN is also constrained by the political processes underlying peacekeeping mandates. Security Council members might be reluctant to approve new missions well in advance of their necessity, and the UN Secretariat might be constrained in getting too far ahead of member states in anticipating operational needs.

Another decision deals with the sequencing of missions either as part of an initial plan or in response to developments in the field. Traditional

Peacekeeping and DDR would seem to be urgent as part of the Security First orientation. This could not only be part of the initial operation, but also the priority for implementation, even as other missions might be envisioned or mandated as a consequence of a peace agreement. Sequencing also has implications for the Recursive Effects expectation. Decisions to add missions to the typical basic security collection, especially more short-term ones such as Humanitarian Assistance, can have feedback effects that enhance or mitigate success with a Security First strategy.

A third element deals with mission compatibility, which may not be at the forefront of policy considerations. Contextual factors—for example, a failed state—might dictate operation mandates that lead to incompatible mission profiles. For example, re-establishing local governance and security are necessary for state stability and development in the long run, even as a short-term cease-fire monitored by peacekeepers has its own benefits. Our findings, especially from the UNAMSIL case, indicate that operations can overcome this configuration and still achieve broad success. Nevertheless, there is not the reinforcing effect anticipated from pairing largely compatible peacebuilding missions in the same operation.

Decision makers might seriously consider whether peace operations are the mechanisms to carry out peacebuilding missions that are largely incompatible with their other security-oriented missions. Almost three decades ago, Diehl (1994) argued that peacekeepers were best suited to missions that were closest to their traditional ones in terms of monitoring functions and orientations as impartial third parties. Even when successful, peacekeepers are limited in ensuring that local governance institutions are created and sustained, and reconciliation is achieved. The imperatives of post-conflict civil contexts (as opposed to interstate disputes) might require that peacekeepers be part of peacebuilding processes. Nevertheless, better coordination with other actors and the adoption of improved strategies that go well beyond current practice for the international community will be needed.

A fourth concern is host country acceptance of the operation. UNTAET provides an example of being welcomed by their hosts in East Timor. This is usually negotiated between the responsible UN agency and the incumbent regime, but it may also include other actors such as neighboring countries and local groups. This might also be part of a peace agreement between formerly warring parties. Over time, host state consent has become less of a prerequisite (see Passmore et al., 2022) as peacekeepers respond to calls for "Responsibility to Protect" in civil conflict contexts, including those with limited government capacities.

Initial decisions are revised in response to developments on the ground including casualties, accomplishments, and mission creep. In this book, we call attention to the importance of the dynamics of multiple missions, a concern addressed in the next section.

Process Dynamics

This box is the heart of the framework and contains the processes that are analyzed in this book. Processes are constrained by both preparations and context but also reflect concurrent conditions (which can evolve), as discussed in the next box. The processes in the box are only a sampling of what happens during the course of an operation. Earlier missions usually consist of monitoring the development of the conflict and ensuring some degree of stabilization that facilitates later missions (note in this regard the Security First expectation). A key to overall success is the way that peacekeepers transition from a combat to a contact orientation as humanitarian and electoral concerns become more salient, and then to peacebuilding missions. The ways in which these transitions unfold depend on the goals of the operation and the types of missions deployed. Nevertheless, transitioning to different missions does not necessarily mean abandoning the earlier missions— maintaining a cease-fire tends to be an ongoing set of activities rather than something with a fixed endpoint. The effectiveness of the transitions depends on preparation and resource utilization, particularly whether peacekeepers have specialized or rotating roles.

Another important aspect of process is coordination. There are several types of coordination needed for progress. These include both those within the UN operation and those with other actors. One coordination challenge is among the UN peacekeepers within the operation. This is more challenging with multiple missions, particularly at transition points. It is not clear that peacekeepers can always make that transition, and Blair et al. (2021) indicate that there is some slippage among mandated tasks. This might be the result of incompatible elements, or peacekeepers might merely be overwhelmed with multiple missions and associated tasks. As peace operations add missions, there might need to be a commensurate increase in personnel and perhaps some movement toward specialization (e.g., civilian police already handle many of the duties associated with SSR training) rather than attempting to do more and different things with the same troops.

Another coordination challenge is between the peacekeeping force and diplomatic initiatives. These interactions often depend on some contextual factors. Peacekeepers might be deployed during ongoing fighting (as was the case in ONUC and more recently in Mali with the United Nations Multidimensional Integrated Stabilization Mission in Mali [MINUSMA]), as opposed to following a peace agreement (as was evident in UNAMSIL and UNTAET). With respect to the former, success or failure in peacekeeping can alter the dynamics of the conflict such that a peace agreement is more or less likely (or at least delayed). A peace agreement and an end to the fighting will be a prerequisite to negotiating and implementing election and peacebuilding provisions. In turn, progress at the negotiating table can change the missions, as when a cease-fire or peace agreement alters the mission focus from stabilization to election monitoring.

A third type of coordination is among the UN peacekeepers and various international and nongovernmental organizations, and other actors, with overlapping goals. These relationships might best be conceived in a network fashion (Braithwaite and Campbell, 2020). From our case studies, these other players exercised a significant influence on the outcomes of some missions.

We do not yet know enough about the optimal forms of interaction among the peace operation and other actors. Braithwaite and Campbell (2020) speculate that greater centrality on the part of the peace operation in the conduct of missions will be associated with success, as opposed to when the peace operation has only a peripheral connection or role in peacebuilding. Yet one might expect that this would vary substantially by mission. Those missions more concordant with traditional military skills, such as monitoring, might call for primary or exclusive roles for the peacekeepers. Even mission success in violence mitigation, however, might not have been possible without the intervention of other military forces, on a short-term basis and using more robust rules of engagement. Operation Artemis, the EU force coterminous with MONUC, is reflective of the stabilizing impact that enforcement operations can have.

Other missions involving a mixture of skills and experience, such as Humanitarian Assistance, might best carried out in a shared fashion between the peace operations and other actors. The UN already facilitates such coordination, but relations between different actors have not always been smooth, nor have actions reflected a close partnership (see Weiss, 1998;

Abiew and Keating, 1999; Yamashita, 2012). Finally, peacekeepers seem best suited for secondary or supplemental roles, leaving the more central roles to other actors, in peacebuilding missions. The environmental context (e.g., failed state, renewed civil war) places serious constraints on the peace operations. Even progress in security sector reform and local governance can be reversed in the long run because of indigenous actors and other factors over which peacekeepers have little or no control—especially after forces are withdrawn.

Process dynamics also include a variety of other decisions made during the course of the operation. Among the most critical of these are those associated with renewal and modification of mandates. UN officials and Security Council members need to consider when an operation should be terminated. On the one hand, this can be a function of success in all the missions undertaken by the peacekeepers. That said, our five case studies and a general review of UN operations suggest that it is unlikely that universal achievement of goals will occur even for the best operations. It might be easiest to determine when Traditional Peacekeeping can be ended, but many Cold War operations (e.g., the United Nations Peacekeeping Force in Cyprus [UNIFCYP]) are still in place decades after their initial deployment primarily because the underlying conflict has not been resolved and the substantial risk of war renewal is still present. Many mission goals (e.g., those related to Reconciliation and Local Governance), however, are long-term and subject to influences other than the presence of a peace operation. Thus, it might be difficult to determine at what stage peacekeepers are no longer needed. The experience in East Timor with UNTAET is indicative of what might occur if an operation is terminated prematurely; what appeared to be a successful peace operation at the time of withdrawal proved to be misleading, with the renewal of violence and breakdown of order several years later.

Conditions

During the course of the peace operation, there are changes that occur within the operation and in the larger context of regional and world events. Following research on situational impacts from social psychology and allied fields, it is likely that peacekeepers react more to their proximal environment than to more distal events that occur elsewhere or to the past history of the conflict (Druckman, 2008). Changes in host country cooperation or in the frequency of attacks get their attention quickly. In addition, deteriorated relationships with human rights organizations or sudden changes in the mission structure can also be dramatic. When humanitarian aid is diverted into the hands of militants, peacekeepers need to discourage the flow of funds and supplies in order to avoid tipping the conflict in favor of the opposing forces or militias, as was the case with UNTAET, ONUC, and UNPROFOR.

For our purposes, the key changes are in mission structure, notably when commanders re-evaluate the plausibility of transitioning from security and aid to institutional change. Peacekeepers are likely to be prepared for a transition if the path of the conflict is de-escalatory (fewer skirmishes and casualties through time). More abrupt changes catch them off guard, making mission adjustments difficult. Furthermore, adjustments are easier for compatible missions. Nevertheless, security and humanitarian aid success can be upset by failures in peacebuilding following the logic of the Recursive Effects expectation. How can peacekeepers be prepared to adapt to mission shifts, especially when such change is abrupt? Prior experience helps, but so do simulations during training sessions. Another way of dealing with mission change is through role differentiation. This would entail training peacekeepers for specialized, mission-specific roles. This decision could reduce the challenges of adapting to mission changes in the course of an operation. Thus, if the peacekeeping force is expanded to meet changing needs, troop contributions could be solicited specifically for the new and modified missions rather than for general peacekeeping duty.

Changes during peace operations also occur outside of the day-to-day implementation of the various missions. These changes are usually out of the control of peacemakers. One type of change is world events. The most salient event in 2020 and 2021 was the COVID-19 pandemic. Health restrictions, advocated by the World Health Organization (WHO), can play havoc with travel, coordination, and spread of disease from the troops to the local population and vice versa. Disinformation and rumors about peacekeepers spreading the virus have limited local cooperation and movement for peacekeeping troops (de Coning, 2020; see also United Nations, 2021); some of this is likely a legacy of UN peacekeepers spreading cholera in Haiti during their deployment.

Changing national governments or regimes and accompanying ideologies also has implications for commitment to UN peace operations. Illustrative is the shift in UN support from the Obama internationalist to the Trump isolationist administrations in the United States, the country that makes the largest financial contribution to peace operations, at 28 percent of assessed contributions. A third change is national recruitment. Staffing of operations depends on a willingness of UN member states to support transportation, supplies, personnel, and financial contributions, often over and above their legal obligations under Article 17 of the UN Charter. These are examples of changes in the greater environment that are likely to have direct effects on an operation's process dynamics.

Outcomes

This box provides examples of the state of the conflict when peacekeepers leave and the operation comes to an end. These include measures of overall peace operation success used by researchers: agreements, casualties, and other measures appropriate to the context and missions. In this book, we reiterate earlier arguments for multidimensional indicators of outcomes (see Diehl and Druckman, 2010). Our focus is on mission success. Thus, each mission within an operation can be evaluated both during the course of an operation—part of the process dynamics—and at the end as operation outcomes. For example, mitigating violence might have been achieved, but the rule of law was not firmly established, as was the case with UNTAET. We also provide evaluations of the eight expectations (see Table 7.1). For example, elections could be successfully held, but little progress occurred on institutional change, as illustrated by MONUC. These may be regarded as two scorecards, one on mission progress and another on evaluations of expectations. The former can also be used as a basis for the latter. For example, when progress occurs in developing a rule of law for the country, this could indicate support for the expectation that Peacebuilding Matters.

Outcomes are often a result of termination decisions, which turn on a recognition that peacekeepers can do little more than has been already done. This might be in the face of a success that offers no prospect for building on it or a failure in which there is an understanding that continued deployment might not result in a reversal of outcomes. There might also be political pressure from UN members to end involvement in light of ongoing financial and other burdens. Termination decisions have become more frequent in recent years, and as a result, the average length of peace operation deployment has declined over time, perhaps lasting only a few years (Wright and Greig, 2012). In contrast, Cold War operations with even fewer missions were renewed almost indefinitely (e.g., UNIFCYP).

The choice to continue or end an operation is not necessarily binary. The UN or any other organizing agent can choose to continue an operation but modify the mandate associated with the operation. In the Cold War period, there was a pattern of renewing operations with no change in missions. In the post–Cold War era, however, mandates have been added at the time of renewal in order to reflect changes on the ground and in the evolution of the conflict. For example, MINUSMA moved from a purely security-oriented operation to one that later included civilian protection and human rights. This suggests that greater attention should be paid to sequencing issues. In particular, success in Security First missions would lead decision makers to add other missions in subsequent mandate renewals. It is not problems on the ground that prompt new missions, but laying the groundwork for future efforts at the time and under the conditions that those new missions are likely to be successful.

Terminating one peace operation could be paired with the creation of a new operation in the same conflict. Recall that MONUC ended in 2010 and was immediately followed by another UN operation: the United Nations Organization Stabilization Mission in the Democratic Republic of the Congo (MONUSCO). The latter narrowed its focus to four of the original missions—Humanitarian Assistance, DDR, Human Rights, and SSR. UN operations in Haiti and Bosnia were also followed by successor operations, as well as those by other agents.

Outcomes that occur during the peace operation serve as benchmarks for transitions to another mission. Without violence abatement, democratization and peacebuilding have little chance of succeeding. Unsuccessful attempts to provide elections can rekindle violence, as indicated by the Recursive Effects expectation—see the successive operations in Angola—the United Nations Angola Verification Mission (UNAVEM I and II). Furthermore, peace operations may not be over when the peacekeepers exit. Positive outcomes can unravel and subsequent operations can be initiated. Similarly, negative outcomes can be partially reversed with subsequent operations, as was the case with UNTAET, which was followed by the United Nations Mission of Support to East Timor (UNMISET) and then the United Nations Integrated Mission in Timor-Leste (UNMIT). These long-term developments are discussed in the following section.

Post Peacekeeping Operation Developments

The final box refers to the durability of the operation's outcomes. When peacekeepers exit a conflict that continues to escalate or without a peace agreement (United Nations Emergency Force—UNEF I), the situation is likely to deteriorate further. The chances for durable peace are increased when the violence has receded and DDR has been effective (e.g., UNAMSIL). Nevertheless, post-operation situations shift, particularly when spoiler groups are active. Policy evaluations are ongoing and reinstating an operation may occur (examples include UNEF I and II [1956–1979], United Nations Operation in Somalia—UNISOM I and II (1992–1995), and UNAVEM I, II, and III [1989–1997]). As we have noted in Chapter 3, it is difficult to parcel out the specific impact of peace operations compared to other influences. The impacts of peace operations are more likely to be felt during and in the immediate aftermath of that operation. As time passes, it is more difficult to judge the role played by the operation in the overall dynamics of the conflict. Too many other factors come into play, most notably exogenous or endogenous shocks (e.g., regime change) that are unrelated directly to the peace operation. As many of these are unexpected and unique to context, it is difficult to plan for these or incorporate them in the framework above.

Many peacekeeping agencies have units or processes devoted to "lessons learned" (for some products, see United Nations Peacebuilding, 2021; NATO, 2021) and no shortage of other analyses that seek to draw conclusions from past operations (e.g., Malone, 2001). Nevertheless, there are several limitations to these efforts. One is that learning seems not to occur during the course of an operation. As noted earlier in this chapter, a major hurdle is learning from mistakes and adapting to changed conditions during the operation. Overcoming this hurdle should be a primary focus of the debriefings held during the course of the operation. Our analysis points to mission incompatibility and, to some extent, transitions from the earlier security to later peacebuilding missions. A practical takeaway from these insights is to include these topics in the debriefings, and also to provide opportunities to revisit these dilemmas in the form of role-play simulations. Thus, lessons learned can be applied directly to the conflict at hand, rather than being identified post hoc when the operation is over and their utility is only for future operations.

Second, there is a tendency to draw lessons from single cases, often the most recent one that the organization completed or that is within the interests or purview of the scholar. This carries with it the implicit assumption that future operations will resemble those in the immediate past, with respect to both context and mission profiles. Our analysis of mission profiles in Chapter 2 suggests that although operations are not sui generis, there is considerable variation in the missions that peacekeepers are asked to perform without clear sets of mission packages; as we have demonstrated in our case studies, the interdependence of missions matters, and the addition or subtraction of particular missions from a given operation can alter outcomes. Contextual elements also vary across deployment environments, so lessons from the Congo might not be applicable to Mali.

Connections between the Boxes

The framework in Figure 7.1 provides a holistic view of peace operations. The six parts are arranged in a chronological sequence and connected with arrows indicating directional influence of one set of factors to other sets. A key aspect of the framework, which should be valuable for practitioners, is the connections among the parts and possible recursive effects from later to earlier boxes. The double arrow between preparation and context suggests that training occurs within the constraints imposed by history and decisions made about the resources and scope of an operation. Both preparation and context feed into the way an operation is carried out. Although training is a key to effectiveness, it is also limited by the administrative decisions made about mission structures. The upward arrow from situational changes to process dynamics suggests that peacekeepers must adjust to changes, as well as be prepared to make the adaptations. Outcomes emerge from processes, which are shaped by preparations and constrained by context and situations. Post-operation developments, including debriefings and learning, loop back recursively to the way peacekeepers are prepared for future operations and the flow continues.

This framework captures both the structure and dynamics of peace operations. It calls attention to an interplay among the parts and, in this way, should be a useful way of thinking about an operation as it unfolds as well as in prospect (during preparation) and in retrospect (after the operation).

Limitations

The previous sections contain a number of policy relevant suggestions to enhance the likelihood of mission success for different missions. Nevertheless, there are several constraints in the UN policy process that will make adaptive change difficult. First, the UN is a bureaucratic organization and as such is subject to inertia in its operations. Incremental adaptation to mandate modification is representative of this. Having the organization reorient its process of planning might be difficult, especially as peace operations are organized on an ad hoc basis and rely on precedents that might no longer apply. Nevertheless, the first passage of a UN Security Council (UNSC) resolution on an ongoing conflict is a strong predictor that a peace operation will be authorized in the future (Kathman et al., 2023). This might be the point at which planning for an eventual operation might commence.

UN peacekeeping is also constrained by members of the UN Security Council, who authorize and renew operations, as well as defining its missions. In particular, the permanent five (P-5) members of the Council might be reluctant to expand the range of missions for some operations or authorize more robust operations in certain contexts (see Allen and Yuen, 2020). The P-5 also constrain the UN bureaucracy in all its peacekeeping functions from planning to implementation (Allen and Yuen, 2014). Thus, what might be optimal from an organizational standpoint might not be adopted given the necessary and shifting coalitions—sometimes context-specific—within the UNSC to take action.

UN peacekeeping soldiers and police are drawn from member states, with a variety of motivations for doing so (Bellamy and Williams, 2013). Accordingly, contributing states are responsible for training peacekeeping personnel. Indeed, diversity in force composition can be an asset for UN operations, and there are various suggestions for how to achieve that (see Bove et al., 2020, 2022). With that, however, comes a diversity in the quality, type, and depth of training given to peacekeepers. Adjusting training protocols is not something that can be achieved centrally and, as such, change in the right direction is likely to be incomplete, or in some cases nonexistent across the militaries of contributing states. This state of affairs has implications for coordination among peacekeepers within and across the missions. Further research is needed to provide a better understanding of the challenges that arise from asymmetrical national peacekeeping cultures and training approaches.

Extending beyond Contemporary Peacekeeping

The focus of this book has been on multiple missions in the context of historical and recent UN peace operations. In this section, we look to emerging changes in peace operations and the implications from new mission developments.

Several analysts have noted that peace operations are evolving in the direction of so-called stabilization missions (de Coning, 2018; Karlsrud, 2019; Van der Lijn, 2021). What does stabilization mean for peace operations? Peace operations have been under pressure to shift to a scaled-down stabilization model, emphasizing security as an end goal rather than as a means to an end. For example, peacekeeping efforts in the Congo following MONUC (United Nations Organization Mission in the Democratic Republic of the Congo) shifted in focus and appropriately in name to the United Nations Organization Stabilization Mission in the Democratic Republic of the Congo (MONUSCO) and included an explicit authorization for use of military force with the creation of its Force Intervention Brigade. Stabilization operations are designed to strengthen the central government against non-state actors that oppose it and seek to undermine order in the country. Stabilization is characterized by more robust peacekeeping and the offensive use of military force (Helms, 2022). Thus, rules of engagement that were initially restricted to defensive actions and then only in certain missions (protecting civilians) have given way to those that have peacekeeping soldiers increasingly resemble conventional military forces. Stabilization also shifts peace operations from a progressive orientation—the liberal peacebuilding model—that is designed to reform domestic institutions to one that protects and strengthens extant state structures, especially in failing states (Mahmoud, 2020). Connections with issues of justice and legitimacy are de-emphasized in favor of priority given to order (Richmond, 2021).

Stabilization also means taking on new missions that extend well beyond those in the expanded peacebuilding repertoire of the post–Cold War era. In particular, peacekeepers are thrust into conducting anti-terrorism operations (see Neethling, 2019; Karlsrud, 2019), as the operation in Mali has demonstrated. As de Carvalho (2020:2) notes with respect to non-UN operations, peace operations have been recently deployed to contexts of "violent extremism, asymmetric warfare, transnational organized crime, as well as climate change." This is not to say that concern for civilian protection has been abandoned; indeed, it is likely to remain a paramount concern

(Di Razza, 2020). Nevertheless, stabilization perhaps represents a new "generation" of peacekeeping.

Abandoning or at least de-emphasizing peacebuilding missions removes some of the less compatible missions from the basic security orientation of peace operations. Furthermore, it was the peacebuilding missions in our study that were the least successful, and the ones that peace operations seem least able to influence themselves. Nevertheless, the stabilization mission (if indeed one can lump together the disparate activities under any one mission type) introduces tasks and actions that are most similar to pacification, but on a broader scale. This goes beyond Traditional Peacekeeping and DDR, largely third-party roles, to placing the peacekeeping forces as primary parties. The strategy then is not "Security First," but perhaps "Security Only."[4] Thus, security stabilization is designed not to set up other missions, but to replace them. We can speculate that stabilization actions are incompatible with short-term missions such as Election Supervision/Promotion of Democracy and delivering humanitarian aid, but it might not matter if those missions are no longer part of the broader goals of the peace operation. Still, stabilization missions could increase violence against civilians and limit humanitarian access as opposition groups resist the peacekeepers through counterattacks (Sauter, 2022); the effect might be especially strong when stabilization includes anti-terrorism actions, as is evident in Mali (Moe, 2021).

The reduction in the number and range of missions that comes with stabilization has some benefits in terms of training (conventional military training is likely sufficient) and compatibility, but it places peacekeepers in roles more akin to those in traditional military intervention. Accordingly, it is unclear at this writing whether such a transition will be successful in achieving the goals to which it aspires. At least one analyst (Howard, 2019) cautions against blending peacekeeping, which has a good record of success in monitoring cease-fires, with counterinsurgency missions, which have a spottier record. Stabilization also raises more normative questions about whether this shift is desirable and whose interests it serves.

A second concern about future peacekeeping deals with adding a new mission and doing so with the right timing and sequencing. Paris (2004) and others raised the critique that the liberal peacebuilding model gave too much

---

[4] This is not to say that coercive military action is the only part of stabilization even as peacekeepers and national military forces see this as the primary and initial set of military activities. The rule of law, governance, and economic concerns are part of the strategic framework for stability in the long run— see Figure 1 in US Army PKSOI (2022).

emphasis to elections and democratization, and performed these missions too early in the sequence of peacebuilding activities. A similar point is made by Autesserre (2021) in her assessment of UN failures to serve the needs of local populations in peace operations. A common theme is that economic development should be a higher priority; that is, in terms of sequencing, economic efforts should occur prior to some other peacebuilding missions.

The underlying logic of most peace operations is that they can facilitate economic recovery and development by providing the environment in which it can occur—a stable security environment and functioning domestic institutions. Our findings on Security First do not question this orientation, but a functioning democracy in the short run might be less important than progress in ensuring economic security. These two goals may go hand in hand: when economic institutions stabilize, a democratic political system is more likely to develop. O'Reilly's (2014) analysis shows that economic development lags other indicators of post–civil war recovery. It depends on the establishment of stable financial institutions. Building these institutions would not constitute a new mission for peacekeepers, as the tasks and resources needed to accomplish this are not those typically associated with peace operations. Rather, these are best handled by international government and nongovernmental organizations such as the World Bank. Nevertheless, the priority assigned to economic development has implications for the timing of peacekeeping missions and reminds us that peace operations need to be part of a broader strategy of the international community rather than treated in isolation.

Research Implications and Future Agenda

In the opening chapter, we argued that our study would have important implications for research on peacekeeping. In light of our findings, we return to this claim and discuss some of the theoretical and empirical consequences as well as a future research agenda inspired by our results and the broader focus on mission interdependence.

The first implication is that any evaluation of a peacekeeping operation should not be confined to the modal approach of considering only its effectiveness to mitigate violence. In practice, peacekeepers try to accomplish many things, and thus assessments should deal less with the operation as a whole and more with the missions that comprise it. This can occur by focusing on one particular mission beyond Traditional Peacekeeping, as is becoming popular in emerging research (see individual chapters in Dorussen, 2022), or in longer works such as this one, which have a broad focus on a variety of different missions in the same study.

As scholars seek to understand the conditions for success and failure in peacekeeping, there needs to be more done than merely expanding the list of dependent variables or outcomes to include more missions. The other side of the equation—the one containing independent or predictor variables—also needs modification. Conventionally, peacekeeping outcomes have been explained by reference to contextual factors related to the conflict, disputant incentives, and peacekeeping force attributes such as size or gender composition. Our study indicates that the configuration of missions and interdependence effects need to be part of theoretical and empirical analyses. In particular, the strong findings with respect to the Security First expectation indicate that examining the outcomes of certain missions—such as Humanitarian Assistance—requires incorporating the outcomes of basic security missions as influences on the success or failure of those missions. Related adaptations would follow from the Recursive Effects expectation and the interactions among peacebuilding missions. We noted early on that issues of mission interdependence are only part of the overall story about the dynamics of peacekeeping processes and outcomes. Our study demonstrates that they need to be taken seriously, but their relative importance vis-à-vis those other factors is an empirical question for future research that uses other techniques to analyze a large number of cases.

Peacekeeping research, especially in the behavioral tradition, has taken off in the past two decades, and there is a long agenda of new and interesting questions to explore. We will not address all of those concerns here (see Diehl and Richmond, 2022; Diehl, 2022c, for these broader agendas). Rather, we raise items directly related to this study, dealing with operation and mission interdependence.

One priority stems from the observation that many UN peace operations are what might be termed "successors," in that they take the place of previous operations in the same location and often in the same conflict. These might deal with the same underlying roots of conflict, as was the case for the three UN operations in Angola—United Nations Angola Verification Mission I, II, and III. Successor operations might also involve different UN missions and orientations depending on the challenges involved; the six different UN operations in Haiti are indicative of this configuration. Heretofore, peacekeeping studies have treated operations as independent units of analysis or cases. In reality, the outcomes in previous operations will likely influence (1) the kinds of missions authorized in successor operations; and (2) the effectiveness of those successor operations. Just as research on war and international conflict has come to acknowledge that conflict events are related over space and time (see the research on rivalries—e.g., Dreyer and Thompson, 2011), so too could peacekeeping research consider the interdependence of "different" operations. In addition, the learning that was seemingly absent in our study of individual operations might be more evident across operations. The presence of aforementioned lessons learned units or efforts in the UN and national militaries suggests that this is the intention.

A corollary to the previous agenda suggestion is for research to consider how individual missions influence one another across successor operations. Successor operations can have some of the same missions as their predecessors (e.g., UNEF I and II), and this might be a function of problems in the original operations or the continuing need for the mission (e.g., Traditional Peacekeeping). One might speculate that success/failure in the original mission incarnations affects the outcomes of the same missions in later operations in the same conflict. Furthermore, success/failure in some missions from earlier operations could have impacts on different missions in later operations, as is suggested by the Individual Effects, Security First and other expectations. Our study examined mission interdependence *within* the same operations, but a worthwhile endeavor would be to examine mission interconnections *across* operations when they involve the same conflict and in particular when they immediately follow one another (e.g., MONUC and MONUSCO in the Congo or UNAVEM II and III in Angola), as doing so would allow for an in-depth comparison of mission profiles for different operations that share the same environmental context.

This study mirrors most other research in its focus on UN peace operations. Nevertheless, peacekeeping is not the exclusive purview of that organization, as many other agents (e.g., regional organizations, multinational coalitions) conduct such operations. Despite being beset with data limitations, peacekeeping research is beginning to direct attention to these so-called non-UN operations (for a review, see Bara, 2022). Research agenda ideas flowing from our study would deal with those non-UN operations that occur as predecessors (e.g., the African Union Mission in Burundi [AMIB] followed by the UN Operation in Burundi [ONUB]), simultaneous (e.g., overlap of Economic Community of West African States Monitoring

Group [ECOMOG] with UN Observer Mission in Liberia [UNOMIL]; see Balas, 2022), or successors (e.g., Multinational Force and Observers [MFO], which came well after UNEF II in the Sinai) to UN operations in the same host country and conflict. If different UN operations and associated missions in the same conflict can influence each other, it is a reasonable supposition that those from other agents can as well. Theoretically, there might be some differences, as other agents face different experiences and finances and could be viewed as more or less impartial than UN forces. Nevertheless, many of the research concerns elucidated here apply in this context. Compatibility issues arise when different organizations try to coordinate within and between missions.

Several of our cases involved the use of traditional military force in conjunction with peacekeeping missions (ONUC, MONUC, and UNAMSIL). In most instances, it appears that such actions enhanced the success of the peace operation in certain missions, specifically in Traditional Peacekeeping and Election Supervision. As peacekeeping is moving in the direction of stabilization operations, this is a salient concern. Thus, as in contexts such as Mali, research could provide insights into how and when traditional military intervention affects—for better or worse—the various peacekeeping missions. Coordination with conventional militaries is likely to work better for the earlier security-related missions than for later peacebuilding ones. Indeed, military interventions can interfere with nation-building efforts while also creating the stability needed to facilitate those efforts. Exploring these dual effects of military intervention on peacebuilding activities is a worthy research endeavor.

Finally, more research and training should be directed at transitions in the mission-interdependence environments that are the focus of this book. We have discussed the need for adaptations to shifts that occur between the various missions in an operation. We are particularly concerned about the transitions between the security and peacebuilding mission portfolios. This change involves a fundamental shift from one type of skill set to another. Only limited research has been done on conflict management skills in peacekeeping environments. One pathway for examination is whether findings from the more general research literature apply as well to these kinds of security environments. For example, are there roles for integrative bargaining and for facilitative or transformative mediation when trying to settle conflicts among hostile parties? If so, then training should be designed to teach, practice, and debrief applications of these skills. Nevertheless, the training decisions emanate from coordination among policymakers in the UN Department of Peacekeeping Operations (DPKO) and the national governments that support the operations, which is also an exercise in conflict management.

Conclusion

We began the book by noting that peacekeepers are part of a brave new world of international relations. They face a variety of challenges that go well beyond the traditional tasks of sustaining cease-fires and preventing (re)eruptions of violence within or between states. These new tasks include monitoring elections, facilitating transitions to the rule of law, distributing humanitarian aid, and resolving conflicts in civil societies that are undergoing transformation. For the peacekeeper, these changes require multitasking during the course of a peace operation. For the peace operation, these changes necessitate new ways of thinking about operation structures and design. We have addressed challenges at both these levels in this book.

Our systematic exploration of mission interdependence has produced a number of important insights. The theory-testing approach that we used expands the body of knowledge at the intersection of international relations and conflict management. The five case studies provide a useful venue for evaluating the theory-based expectations. Documenting how the peace operations unfold in each of these cases provides useful examples for UN policymakers. Our academic colleagues and practitioners should take away lessons about security, compatibility, learning, and the transition from peacekeeping to peacebuilding. Clearly, security remains the top priority for peacekeepers; it influences the way other missions are carried out. Although security is a necessary condition for performing peacebuilding tasks, it is not a sufficient condition for success. Indeed, the transition to peacebuilding was shown to be difficult for peacekeepers, not least because of insufficient learning or training but also for reasons of mission incompatibility. These insights suggest directions for research and practice.

We close the book on a theme that runs through its chapters. Present-day peacekeepers must manage several types of complexities. These include the multiple missions that we described and the interactions among them that we analyzed. As peace operations unfold, UN peacekeepers move among a variety of roles that draw on both combat and contact skills. An additional layer of complexity comes from a need to coordinate with other actors in the conflict environment, including national peacekeeping forces, humanitarian and other NGOs, the UN bureaucracy, and diplomats. Although often overwhelmed by the tasks at hand, peacekeepers must also keep an eye on how they are doing, referred to as situational awareness, and anticipate transitions from earlier to later missions. Our findings on learning point to problems in both these areas. Understanding how to use the experience gained in earlier missions as lessons for dealing with the challenges of later missions is a priority for researchers and policy practitioners. These are lessons in managing complexity when peacekeeping missions collide.

Bibliography

This is a comprehensive bibliography that includes both cited works and works used by the authors but not cited in the text. By including both types of references we provide the reader with a larger literature that contributed to our concepts and analyses.

Abiew, Francis Kofi, and Tom Keating. (1999) "NGOs and UN Peacekeeping Operations: Strange Bedfellows." *International Peacekeeping* 6(2): 89–111.

Abi-Saab, Georges. (1978) *The United Nations Operation in the Congo, 1960–1964.* Oxford: Oxford University Press.

Acemoglu, Daron, Tristan Reed, and James A. Robinson. (2014) "Chiefs: Economic Development and Elite Control of Civil Society in Sierra Leone." *Journal of Political Economy* 122(2): 319–368.

Adebajo, Adekeye, and Chris Landsberg. (2000) "Back to the Future: UN Peacekeeping in Africa." *International Peacekeeping* 7(4): 161–188.

Adolfo, Eldridge. (2010) *Peace-Building after Post-Modern Conflicts: The UN Integrated Mission (UNAMSIL) in Sierra Leone.* Stockholm, Sweden: FOI Swedish Defence Research Agency.

Afoaku, Osita. (2010) "Democratic Republic of the Congo." In *Countries at the Crossroads: An Analysis of Democratic Governance*, ed. Jake Dizard, Christopher Walker, and Sarah Cook, 125–148. Lanham, MD: Rowman & Littlefield.

Akonor, Kwame. (2016) *UN Peacekeeping in Africa: A Critical Examination and Recommendations for Improvement.* Basel, Switzerland: Springer International.

Albert, Sophie. (1997) "The Return of Refugees to Bosnia and Herzegovina: Peacebuilding with People." *International Peacekeeping* 4(3): 1–23.

Albin, Cecilia, and Daniel Druckman. (2012) "Equality Matters: Negotiating an End to Civil Wars." *Journal of Conflict Resolution* 56(2): 155–182.

Albin, Cecilia, and Daniel Druckman. (2014) "Procedures Matter: Justice and Effectiveness in International Trade Negotiations." *European Journal of International Relations* 20(4): 1014–1042.

Allen, Susan Hannah, and Amy T. Yuen. (2014) "The Politics of Peacekeeping: UN Security Council Oversight across Peacekeeping Missions." *International Studies Quarterly* 58(3): 621–632.

Allen, Susan Hannah, and Amy T. Yuen. (2020) "Action or Inaction: United Nations Security Council Activity." *Journal of Peace Research* 57(5): 658–665.

Almuslem, Abdulaziz G. (2020) "Post Conflict Justice, Peacekeeping, and Civil Conflict Recurrence." *International Peacekeeping* 27(3): 467–509.

Amnesty International. (2006) "Democratic Republic of Congo: Children at War, Creating Hope for the Future." Accessed September 27, 2021. https://www.amnesty.org/en/documents/afr62/017/2006/en/.

Andreas, Peter. (2011) *Blue Helmets and Black Markets.* Ithaca, NY: Cornell University Press.

Aoi, Chiyuki, Cedric de Coning, and Ramesh Thakur, eds. (2007) *Unintended Consequences of Peacekeeping Operations*. Hong Kong: United Nations University Press.

Arieff, Alexis. (2014) "Democratic Republic of Congo: Background and U.S. Policy." *Congressional Research Service*. Accessed October 5, 2021. https://sgp.fas.org/crs/row/R43166.pdf.

Armed Conflict Location and Event Data Project (ACLED). "Disorder Involving Peacekeepers." Accessed November 5, 2022. https://acleddata.com/curated-data-files/#civilian.

Aroussi, Sahla. (2011) "'Women, Peace and Security': Addressing Accountability for Wartime Sexual Violence." *International Feminist Journal of Politics* 13(4): 576–593.

Aroussi, Sahla. (2017) "From Colombia to the Democratic Republic of Congo: Exploring the Untapped Potential of Restorative Justice. A Response to Annette Pearson." *Restorative Justice* 5(2): 313–318.

Ashton, Barry. (1997) "Making Peace Agreements Work: United Nations Experience in the Former Yugoslavia." *Cornell International Law Journal* 30(3): 769–788.

Asia Foundation. (2004) "Law and Justice in East Timor: A Survey of Citizen Awareness and Attitudes Regarding Law and Justice in East Timor." Washington, DC: US Agency for International Development.

Asku, Esref. (2003) *The United Nations, Intra-State Peacekeeping and Normative Change*. Manchester, UK: Manchester University Press.

Autesserre, Séverine. (2014) *Peaceland: Conflict Resolution and the Everyday Politics of International Intervention*. Cambridge: Cambridge University Press.

Autesserre, Séverine. (2016) "The Responsibility to Protect in Congo: The Failure of Grassroots Prevention." *International Peacekeeping* 23(1): 29–51.

Autesserre, Séverine. (2021) *The Frontlines of Peace: An Insider's Guide to Changing the World*. New York: Oxford University Press.

Bagayoko, Niagale, and Eboe Hutchful. (2022) "Peacebuilding via Security Sector Reform and Governance?: The Case of West Africa." In *Routledge Handbook of African Peacebuilding*, ed. Bruno Charbonneau and Maxime Ricard, 44–56. London: Routledge.

Bakaki, Zorzeta, and Tobias Bohmelt. (2021) "Can UN Peacekeeping Promote Environmental Quality?" *International Studies Quarterly* 65(4): 881–890.

Baker, Bruce. (2005) "Who Do People Turn To for Policing in Sierra Leone?" *Journal of Contemporary African Studies* 23(3): 371–390.

Balas, Alexandru. (2022) *Sharing the Burden of Peace: Inter-Organizational Cooperation in Peace Operations*. New York: Peter Lang.

Balcells, Laia, and Patricia Justino. (2014) "Bridging Micro and Macro Approaches on Civil Wars and Political Violence: Issues, Challenges, and the Way Forward." *Journal of Conflict Resolution* 58(8): 1343–1359.

Ball, Patrick, Ewa Tabeau, and Philip Verwimp. (2007) *The Bosnian Book of Dead: Assessment of the Database (Full Report)*. Households in Conflict Network. Accessed September 25, 2021. https://www.hicn.org/wp-content/uploads/sites/10/2012/07/rdn5.pdf.

Bara, Corinne. (2022) "UN and Non-UN Peacekeeping." In *Handbook on Peacekeeping and International Relations*, ed. Han Dorussen. 102–117. Cheltenham, UK: Edward Elgar.

Barnett, Michael, and Martha Finnemore. (2004) "The Power of Liberal International Organizations." In *Power in Global Governance*, ed. Michael Barnett and Raymond Duvall, 161–184. Cambridge: Cambridge University Press.

Bartoli, Andrea. (2013) *Negotiating Peace: The Role of Non-governmental Organizations*. Dordrecht, Netherlands: Republic of Letters.

Baumann, Robert F., George W. Gawrych, and Walter E. Kretchik. (2011) *Armed Peacekeepers in Bosnia*. Fort Leavenworth, KS: Combat Studies Institute Press.

Beardsley, Kyle. (2011) "Peacekeeping and the Contagion of Armed Conflict." *Journal of Politics* 73(4): 1051–1064.

Beber, Bernd. (2022) "Peacekeeping and the Geographic Containment/Diffusion of Conflict." In *Handbook on Peacekeeping and International Relations*, ed. Han Dorussen, 196–209. Cheltenham, UK: Edward Elgar.

Belgioioso, Margherita, Jessica Di Salvatore, and Jonathan Pinckney. (2021) "Tangled Up in Blue: The Effect of UN Peacekeeping on Nonviolent Protests in Post–Civil War Countries." *International Studies Quarterly* 65(1): 1–15.

Bell, Udy. (2005) "Sierra Leone Building on a Hard-won Peace." *UN Chronicle* 42(4): 42–43.

Bellamy, Alex J., and Charles Hunt. (2019) "Benefits of Paring Down Peacekeeping Mandates also Come with Risks." IPI Global Observatory. Accessed September 28, 2021. https://theglobalobservatory.org/2019/03/benefits-paring-down-peacekeeping-mandates-come-with-risks/.

Bellamy, Alex J., and Paul D. Williams. (2012) "Local Politics and International Partnerships: The UN Operation in Côte d'Ivoire (UNOCI)." *Journal of International Peacekeeping* 16(3–4): 252–281.

Bellamy, Alex J., and Paul D. Williams, eds. (2013) *Providing Peacekeepers: The Politics, Challenges, and Future of United Nations Peacekeeping Contributions*. New York: Oxford University Press.

Benner, Thorsten, Stephan Mergenthaler, and Philipp Rotmann. (2011) *The New World of UN Peace Operations: Learning to Build Peace?* Oxford: Oxford University Press.

Bennett, Andrew, and Jeffrey T. Checkel, eds. (2015) *Process Tracing: From Metaphor to Analytic Tool*. Cambridge: Cambridge University Press.

Bennett, Christopher. (2016) *Bosnia's Paralyzed Peace*. Oxford: Oxford University Press.

Benson, Michelle, and Colin Tucker. (2019) "UN Security Council Resolutions and Peacekeeping Operations in Civil Conflicts, 1946–2015." Paper presented at the FBA-UNIGE Research Workshop "State of the Art? The Future of Peacekeeping Data," Genoa, Italy, June 2019.

Benson, Michelle, and Colin Tucker. (2022) "Naming Names: UN Security Council Resolution Sentiment in Civil Wars." In *Handbook on Peacekeeping and International Relations*, ed. Han Dorussen, 74–87. Cheltenham, UK: Edward Elgar.

Benzing, Markus. (2005) "Midwifing a New State: The United Nations in East Timor." *Max Planck Yearbook of United Nations Law Online* 9(1): 295–372.

Berg, Louis-Alexandre. (2014) "From Weakness to Strength: The Political Roots of Security Sector Reform in Bosnia and Herzegovina." *International Peacekeeping* 21(2): 149–164.

Berg, Louis-Alexandre. (2020) "Liberal Peacebuilding: Bringing Domestic Politics Back In." In *Peacebuilding Paradigms: The Impact of Theoretical Diversity on Implementing Peace*, ed. Henry Cary, 77–93. Cambridge: Cambridge University Press.

Bernath, Clifford, and Sayre Nyce. (2002) *A Peacekeeping Success: Lesson Learned from UNAMSIL*. Washington, DC: Refugees International.

Bingham, Richard D., and Claire L. Felbinger. (2002) *Evaluation in Practice: A Methodological Approach*. 2nd ed. New York: Chatham House Publishers/Seven Bridges Press.

Blair, Robert A. (2020) *Peacekeeping, Policing, and the Rule of Law after Civil War*. Cambridge: Cambridge University Press.

Blair, Robert A. (2022) "Rule of Law and Peacekeeping." In *Handbook on Peacekeeping and International Relations* ed. Han Dorussen, 134–147. Cheltenham, UK: Edward Elgar.

Blair, Robert A., Jessica Di Salvatore, and Hannah Smidt. (2021) "When Do UN Peacekeeping Operations Implement Their Mandates?" *American Journal of Political Science* 66(3): 664–680.

Blair, Robert A., Jessica Di Salvatore, and Hannah Smidt. (2023) "UN Peacekeeping and Democratization in Conflict-Affected Countries." *American Political Science Review*, 1–19. doi: 10.1017/S0003055422001319.

Bloomfield, Lincoln P. (1963) "Headquarters-Field Relations: Some Notes on the Beginning and End of ONUC." *International Organization* 17(2): 377–389.

Boege, Volker, and Patricia Rinck. (2019) "The Local/International Interface in Peacebuilding: Experiences from Bougainville and Sierra Leone." *International Peacekeeping* 26(2): 216–239.

Boshoff, Henri, Dylan Hendrickson, Sylvie More, and Thierry Vircoulon. (2010) *Supporting SSR in the DRC: Between a Rock and a Hard Place*. The Hague: Clingendael Institute.

Boulden, Jane. (2001) *Peace Enforcement: The United Nations Experience in Congo, Somalia, and Bosnia*. Westport, CT: Greenwood Publishing.

Boulden, Jane. (2015) "United Nations Operation in the Congo (ONUC)." In *The Oxford Handbook of United Nations Peacekeeping Operations*, ed. Joachim A Koops, Norrie MacQueen, Thierry Tardy, and Paul D Williams, 160–170. Oxford: Oxford University Press.

Boutros-Ghali, Boutros. (1992) "An Agenda for Peace: Preventive Diplomacy, Peacemaking and Peace-Keeping." *International Relations* 11(3): 201–218.

Boutros-Ghali, Boutros. (1995) "Democracy: A Newly Recognized Imperative." *Global Governance* 1(1): 3–11.

Bove, Vincenzo, Chiara Ruffa, and Andrea Ruggeri. (2020) *Composing Peace: Mission Composition in UN Peacekeeping*. Oxford: Oxford University Press.

Bove, Vincenzo, Chiara Ruffa, and Andrea Ruggeri. (2022) "Kinds of Blue? How Does the Composition of Peacekeeping Operations Matter?" In *Handbook on Peacekeeping and International Relations*, ed. Han Dorussen, 60–73. Cheltenham, UK: Edward Elgar.

Bowers, Devon. (2020) "Disturbing the Peace: UN Peacekeepers and Sexual Abuse." The Hampton Institute. Accessed September 26, 2021. https://www.hamptonthink.org/read/disturbing-the-peace-un-peacekeepers-and-sexual-abuse.

Braithwaite, Jessica Maves, and Susanna P. Campbell. (2020) "Who Keeps the Peace? Reconceptualizing Peacebuilding through Networks of Influence and Support." Accessed October 12, 2021. https://www.kpsrl.org/sites/default/files/2020-12/Braithwaite_Campbell_112020.pdf.

Braithwaite, John. (2012) "Evaluating the Timor-Leste Peace Operation." *Journal of International Peacekeeping* 16(3–4): 282–305.

Brancati, Dawn, and Jack L. Snyder. (2011) "Rushing to the Polls: The Causes of Premature Postconflict Elections." *Journal of Conflict Resolution* 55(3): 469–492.

Brancati, Dawn, and Jack L. Snyder. (2013) "Time to Kill: The Impact of Election Timing on Postconflict Stability." *Journal of Conflict Resolution* 57(5): 822–853.

Brast, Benjamin. (2015) The Regional Dimension of Statebuilding Interventions. *International Peacekeeping* 22(1): 81–99.

Brattberg, Erik. (2012) "Revisiting UN Peacekeeping in Rwanda and Sierra Leone." *Peace Review* 24(2): 156–162.

Braumoeller, Bear F., Giampiero Marra, Rosalba Radice, and Aisha E. Bradshaw. (2018) "Flexible Causal Inference for Political Science." *Political Analysis* 26(1): 54–71.

Brecher, Michael, and Jonathan Wilkenfeld. (2000) *A Study of Crisis.* Ann Arbor: University of Michigan Press.

Brecher, Michael, Jonathan Wilkenfeld, Kyle Beardsley, Patrick James, and David Quinn. (2021) *International Crisis Behavior Data Codebook, Version 14.* Accessed September 28, 2021. http://sites.duke.edu/icbdata/data-collections/.

Brown, Cynthia, ed. (1993) "Former Yugoslavia." In *The Lost Agenda: Human Rights and UN Field Operations*, 75–106. New York: Human Rights Watch.

Burg, Steven L., Paul S. Shoup, and John Fraser. (2000) *The War in Bosnia-Herzegovina: Ethnic Conflict and International Intervention.* Armonk, NY: M. E. Sharpe.

Caddick-Adams, Peter. (1998) "Civil Affairs Operations by IFOR and SFOR in Bosnia, 1995–97." *International Peacekeeping* 5(3): 142–154.

Cain, Jennifer, Antonio Duran, Amya Fortis, Elke Jakubowski, and World Health Organization. (2002) *Health Care Systems in Transition: Bosnia and Herzegovina.* Copenhagen: European Observatory on Health Care Systems 4(7). Accessed October 30, 2021. https://www.euro.who.int/__data/assets/pdf_file/0018/75132/E78673.pdf.

Campbell, Donald T., and Julian C. Stanley. (1963) *Experimental and Quasi-Experimental Designs for Research.* Boston: Houghton-Mifflin.

Caplan, Richard. (2004) "Partner or Patron? International Civil Administration and Local Capacity-Building." *International Peacekeeping* 11(2): 229–247.

Caplan, Richard. (2005) *International Governance of War-Torn Territories: Rule and Reconstruction.* Oxford: Oxford University Press.

Caplan, Richard. (2006) "After Exit: Successor Missions and Peace Consolidation." *Civil Wars* 8(3–4): 253–267.

Caplan, Richard, John Gledhill, and Maline Meiske. (2022) "Peacekeeping Operations— the Endgame." In *Handbook on Peacekeeping and International Relations*, ed. Han Dorussen, 343–359. Cheltenham, UK: Edward Elgar.

Caplan, Richard, and Anke Hoeffler. (2017) "Why Peace Endures: An Analysis of Post-Conflict Stabilisation." *European Journal of International Security* 2(2): 133–152.

Carter Center. (2001) "Postelection Statement on East Timor Elections." Accessed September 22, 2021. https://www.cartercenter.org/news/documents/doc253.html.

Carter Center. (2003) *Observing the 2002 Sierra Leone Elections—Final Report.* Atlanta, GA: Carter Center Democracy Program. Accessed October 20, 2021. https://www.cartercenter.org/documents/1349.pdf.

Carter Center. (2004) *The East Timor Political and Election Observation Project: Final Project Report.* Atlanta, GA: Carter Center Democracy Program. Accessed October 20, 2021. https://www.cartercenter.org/documents/1691.pdf.

Carter Center. (2006) *International Election Observation Mission to Democratic Republic of Congo 2006 Presidential and Legislative Elections Final Report.* Atlanta, GA: Carter Center Democracy Program. Accessed October 20, 2021. https://www.cartercenter.org/resources/pdfs/news/peace_publications/election_reports/drc-2006-final-rpt.pdf.

Carter Center. (2013) *Observing Sierra Leone's November 2012 National Elections—Final Report.* Atlanta, GA: Carter Center Democracy Program. Accessed October 20, 2021. https://www.cartercenter.org/resources/pdfs/news/peace_publications/election_repo rts/sierra-leone-final-101613.pdf.

"Casablanca Powers." (1962) *International Organization* 16(2): 437–439. http://www.jstor.org/stable/2705397.

Castillejo, Clare. (2009) "Building Accountable Justice in Sierra Leone." Fundación para las Relaciones Internacionales y el Diálogo Exterior (FRIDE) Working Paper, Madrid. Accessed December 4, 2022. https://gsdrc.org/document-library/building-accounta ble-justice-in-sierra-leone/.

Center on International Cooperation. (2009) *Annual Review of Global Peace Operations 2009.* Boulder, CO: Lynne Rienner.

Center on International Cooperation. (2010) *Annual Review of Global Peace Operations 2010.* Boulder, CO: Lynne Rienner.

Chandler, David. (2005) "From Dayton to Europe." *International Peacekeeping* 12(3): 336–349.

Chandler, David. (2017) *Peacebuilding: The Twenty Years' Crisis, 1997–2017.* Cham, Switzerland: Palgrave Macmillan.

Chappell, Duncan, and John Evans. (1999) "The Role, Preparation and Performance of Civilian Police in United Nations Peacekeeping Operations." *Criminal Law Forum* 10(2): 171–271.

Chesterman, Simon. (2002) "East Timor in Transition: Self-Determination, State-Building and the United Nations." *International Peacekeeping* 9(1): 45–76.

Chopra, Jarat. (2002) "Building State Failure in East Timor." *Development and Change* 33(5): 979–1000.

Chopra, Tanja, Susan Pologruto, and Timóteo de Deus. (2009) *Fostering Justice in Timor-Leste: Rule of Law Program Evaluation.* Washington, DC: US Agency for International Development.

Clark, Jeffrey, Ann von Briesen Lewis, and Lia Juliani. (2003) *Final Evaluation: The OTI Program in East Timor.* Arlington, VA: Development Associates, Inc.

Clayton, Govinda, Laurie Nathan, and Claudia Wiehler. (2021) "Ceasefire Success: A Conceptual Framework." *International Peacekeeping* 28(3): 341–365.

Coghlan, Benjamin, Pascal Ngoy, Flavien Mulumba, Colleen Hardy, Valerie Nkamgang Bemo, Tony Stewart, Jennifer Lewis, and Richard Brennan. (2007) *Mortality in the Democratic Republic of Congo: An Ongoing Crisis.* New York: International Rescue Committee. Accessed September 25, 2022. https://www.rescue.org/sites/default/files/document/661/2006-7congomortalitysurvey.pdf.

Cohen, Ben, and George Stamkoski, eds. (1995) *With No Peace to Keep: United Nations Peacekeeping and the War in the Former Yugoslavia.* London: Grainpress.

Cohen, David. (2002) *Seeking Justice on the Cheap: Is the East Timor Tribunal Really a Model for the Future?* Honolulu, HI: East-West Center.

Coleman, Katharina P. (2022) "Financing Peacekeeping Operations." In *Handbook on Peacekeeping and International Relations,* ed. Han Dorussen, 27–45. Cheltenham, UK: Edward Elgar.

Coleman, Peter. (2011) *The Five Percent: Finding Solutions to Seemingly Impossible Conflicts.* New York: Public Affairs.

Collier, Paul, Anke Hoeffler, and Måns Söderbom. (2008) "Post-Conflict Risks." *Journal of Peace Research* 45(4): 461–478.

Commission for Reception, Truth and Reconciliation in East Timor. (2002) "Mandate." Accessed June 18, 2021. http://www.easttimor-reconciliation.org/mandate.html.

Commonwealth Expert Team. (2004) "Sierra Leone Local Government Elections." Accessed September 26, 2021. https://aceproject.org/ero-en/regions/africa/SL/sierra-leone-final-report-local-elections.

Constitute Project. (2021) "Sierra Leone's Constitution of 1991, Reinstated in 1996, with Amendments through 2008." Accessed September 26, 2021. https://www.constitute project.org/constitution/Sierra_Leone_2008.pdf?lang=en.

Cook, Thomas D., and Donald T. Campbell. (1979) *Quasi-Experimentation*. Boston: Houghton-Mifflin.

Coppedge, Michael, John Gerring, Carl Henrik Knutsen, Staffan I. Lindberg, Jan Teorell, Nazifa Alizada, David Altman, Michael Bernhard, Agnes Cornell, M. Steven Fish, Lisa Gastaldi, Haakon Gjerløw, Adam Glynn, Allen Hicken, Garry Hindle, Nina Ilchenko, Joshua Krusell, Anna Luhrmann, Seraphine F. Maerz, Kyle L. Marquardt, Kelly McMann, Valeriya Mechkova, Juraj Medzihorsky, Pamela Paxton, Daniel Pemstein, Josefine Pernes, Johannes von Römer, Brigitte Seim, Rachel Sigman, Svend-Erik Skaaning, Jeffrey Staton, Aksel Sundström, Ei-tan Tzelgov, Yi-ting Wang, Tore Wig, Steven Wilson and Daniel Ziblatt. (2021) "V-Dem [Country–Year/Country–Date] Dataset v11.1" Varieties of Democracy Project. Accessed October 7, 2022. https://www.v-dem.net/vdemds.html.

Cordone, Claudio. (1999) "Police Reform and Human Rights Investigations: The Experience of the UN Mission in Bosnia and Herzegovina." *International Peacekeeping* 6(4): 191–209.

Correlates of War Project. (2020). Accessed October 30, 2021. https://correlatesofwar.org.

Costalli, Stefano. (2014) "Does Peacekeeping Work? A Disaggregated Analysis of Deployment and Violence Reduction in the Bosnian War." *British Journal of Political Science* 44(2): 357–380.

Costalli, Stefano, and Francesco F. Moro. (2009) "A Local-Level Analysis of Violence and Intervention in Bosnia's Civil War." Paper presented at the *Workshop on Localized Effects of and Impacts on Peacekeeping in Civil War*. University of Essex.

Council on Foreign Relations. (2018) "The Eastern Congo." Accessed September 22, 2021. https://www.cfr.org/eastern-congo/#!/?cid=soc-at-interactive-the_eastern_congo_in foguide-121015.

Cross, Rob, Reb Rebele, and Adam Grant. (January–February 2016) "Collaborative Overload." *Harvard Business Review*, 74–79. Accessed September 24, 2021. https://hbr. org/2016/01/collaborative-overload.

Cuhadar, Esra, and Daniel Druckman. (2023) "Let the People Speak!: What Kind of Civil Society Inclusion is Best for Durable Peace?" *International Studies Perspectives* (forthcoming).

Curran, David. (2017) *More than Fighting for Peace?: Conflict Resolution, United Nations Peacekeeping, and the Role of Training Military Personnel*. New York: Springer.

Curran, David, and Tom Woodhouse. (2007) "Cosmopolitan Peacekeeping and Peacebuilding in Sierra Leone: What Can Africa Contribute?" *International Affairs* 83(6): 1055–1070.

Cutts, Mark. (1999) "The Humanitarian Operation in Bosnia, 1992–95: Dilemmas of Negotiating Humanitarian Access." UNHCR. Accessed September 20, 2021. https://www.unhcr.org/en-us/research/working/3ae6a0c58/humanitarian-operation-bosnia-1992-95-dilemmas-negotiating-humanitarian.html.

Dallas, Elizabeth, and Tyler Beckelman. (2020) "Humanitarian Action." In *Research Handbook on Post-Conflict State Building*, ed. Paul Williams and Milena Sterio, 304–317. Cheltenham, UK: Edward Elgar.

Davis, Laura. (2009) *Justice-Sensitive Security System Reform in the Democratic Republic of Congo*. Brussels, Belgium: Initiative for Peacebuilding.

Davis, Laura, and Priscilla Hayner. (2009) *Difficult Peace, Limited Justice: Ten Years of Peacemaking in the DRC.* New York: International Center for Transitional Justice.

Day, Adam, and Charles Hunt. (2022) "Distractions, Distortions, and Dilemmas: The Externalities of Protecting Civilians in United Nations Peacekeeping." *Civil Wars* 24(1): 97–116.

De Carvalho, Gustavo, and Priyal Singh. (2020) "Looking Back, Looking Forward: South Africa in the UN Security Council." *ISS Africa Report 2020* 22: 1–23.

de Coning, Cedric. (2000) "The UN Transitional Administration in East Timor (UNTAET): Lessons Learned from the First 100 Days." *Journal of International Peacekeeping* 6(2–3): 83–90.

de Coning, Cedric. (2018) "Is Stabilization the New Normal? Implications of Stabilization Mandates for the Use of Force in UN Peacekeeping Operations." In *The Use of Force in UN Peacekeeping*, ed. Peter Nardin, 85–99. London: Routledge.

de Coning, Cedric. (2020) "Examining the Longer-Term Effects of COVID-19 on UN Peacekeeping Operations." Accessed October 20, 2021. https://nupi.brage.unit.no/nupi-xmlui/bitstream/handle/11250/2684680/de+Coning+2020+Examining+the+Longer-Term+Effects+of+COVID-19+on+UN+Peacekeeping+Operations+-+IPI+Global+Observatory.pdf.

de Coning, Cedric, and Emery Brusset. (2018) "Towards a Comprehensive Results-based Reporting and Performance Assessment Framework for UN Peacekeeping Operations." Oslo: Norwegian Institute for International Affairs. Accessed December 11, 2022. https://www.nupi.no/en/publications/cristin-pub/towards-a-comprehensive-results-based-reporting-and-performance-assessment-framework-for-un-peacekeeping-operations.

de Hoon, Marieke. (2020) "Transitional Justice." In *Research Handbook on Post-Conflict State Building*, ed. Paul Williams and Milena Sterio, 162–182. Cheltenham, UK: Edward Elgar.

Denney, Lisa. (2014) "Overcoming the State/Non-state Divide: An End User Approach to Security and Justice Reform." *International Peacekeeping* 21(2): 251–268.

Dertwinkel, Tim. (2009) "The Effect of Local Peacekeeping on Different Forms of Violence During the Bosnian Civil War." Paper presented at the Workshop on Localized Effects of and Impacts on Peacekeeping in Civil War, University of Essex.

Diehl, Paul F. (1994) *International Peacekeeping.* Rev. ed. Baltimore: Johns Hopkins University Press.

Diehl, Paul F. (2016) "Exploring Peace: Looking beyond War and Negative Peace." *International Studies Quarterly* 60(1): 1–10.

Diehl, Paul F. (2017) "Peacekeeping Research with Non-Peacekeeping Data." *International Peacekeeping* 24(1): 38–43.

Diehl, Paul F. (2022a) "Breaking the Conflict Trap: The Impact on Peacekeeping on Violence and Democratization in the Post-Conflict Context." In *What Do We Know about Civil War?* 2nd ed., ed. Sara Mitchell and David Mason, 205–235. Lanham, MD: Rowman & Littlefield.

Diehl, Paul F. (2022b) "Conceptual Evolution of Peace Operations." In *The Palgrave Encyclopedia of Peace and Conflict Studies*, ed. Oliver Richmond and Gëzim Visoka. London: Palgrave Macmillan. doi: 10.1007/978-3-030-11795-5_30-1.

Diehl, Paul F. (2022c) "State of the Art Research on Peacekeeping." In *Handbook on Peacekeeping and International Relations*, ed. Han Dorussen, 360–372. Cheltenham, UK: Edward Elgar.

Diehl, Paul F., and Alexandru Balas. (2014) *Peace Operations*. 2nd ed. Cambridge, UK: Polity Press.

Diehl, Paul F., and Daniel Druckman. (2010) *Evaluating Peace Operations*. Boulder, CO: Lynne Rienner.

Diehl, Paul F., and Daniel Druckman. (2018) "Multiple Peacekeeping Missions: Analysing Interdependence." *International Peacekeeping* 25(1): 28–51.

Diehl, Paul F., Daniel Druckman, and James Wall. (1998) "International Peacekeeping and Conflict Resolution: A Taxonomic Analysis with Implications." *Journal of Conflict Resolution* 42(1): 33–55.

Diehl, Paul F., Andrew Owsiak, and Gary Goertz. (2021) "Managing International–Civil Militarized Conflicts (I-CMC): Empirical Patterns." *Civil Wars* 23(3): 343–370.

Diehl, Paul F., and Oliver Richmond. (2022) "The Changing Face(s) of Peace Operations: Critical and Behavioral Paths for Future Research." *Journal of International Peacekeeping* 25(2): 205–235.

Diku Mpongola, Dieudonné. (2007) "République Démocratique du Congo." In *Dealing with the Past—Series: La justice transitionnelle dans le monde francophone: État des lieux*, ed. Mô Bleeker and Carol Mottet, 105–114. Bern, Switzerland: Political Affairs Division IV, Swiss Federal Department of Foreign Affairs.

Di Razza, Namie. (2020) "UN Peacekeeping and the Protection of Civilians in the COVID-19 Era." IPI Global Observatory. Accessed March 28, 2021. https://theglobal observatory.org/2020/05/un-peacekeeping-protection-of-civilians-in-covid-19-era/ May 22.

Di Salvatore, Jessica. (2022) "Peacekeeping and Post-War Violence." In *Handbook on Peacekeeping and International Relations*, ed. Han Dorussen, 286–299. Cheltenham, UK: Edward Elgar.

Di Salvatore, Jessica, Magnus Lundgren, Kseniya Oksamytna, and Hannah M. Smidt. (2022) "Introducing the Peacekeeping Mandates (PEMA) Dataset." *Journal of Conflict Resolution* 66(4–5): 924–951.

Di Salvatore, Jessica, and Andrea Ruggeri. (2017) "Effectiveness of Peacekeeping Operations." In *Oxford Research Encyclopedia of Politics*, ed. William R. Thompson. Oxford University Press. doi: 10.1093/acrefore/9780190228637.013.586.

Dixon, Jeffrey S., and Meredith Reid Sarkees. (2015) *A Guide to Intra-state Wars: An Examination of Civil, Regional, and Intercommunal Wars, 1816–2014*. Thousand Oaks, CA: CQ Press.

Dobbins, James, Seth G. Jones, Keith Crane, Andrew Rathmell, Brett Steele, Richard Teltschik, and Anga R. Timilsina. (2005) *The UN's Role in Nation-Building: From the Congo to Iraq*. Santa Monica, CA: RAND Corporation.

Donais, Timothy. (2006) "The Limits of Post-Conflict Police Reform." In *Bosnian Security after Dayton: New Perspectives*, ed. Michael A. Innes, 173–190. London: Routledge.

Dorn, Walter. (2013) "The UN's First 'Air Force': Peacekeepers in Combat, Congo 1960–64." *Journal of Military History* 77(4): 1399–1425.

Dorussen, Han, ed. (2022) *Handbook on Peacekeeping and International Relations*. Cheltenham, UK: Edward Elgar.

Dorussen, Han, and Marian de Vooght. (2022) "The Local Perception of Peacekeepers." In *Handbook on Peacekeeping and International Relations*, ed. Han Dorussen, 314–326. Cheltenham, UK: Edward Elgar.

Dorussen, Han, and Theodora-Ismene Gizelis. (2013) "Into the Lion's Den: Local Responses to UN Peacekeeping." *Journal of Peace Research* 50(6): 691–706.

Doss, Alan. (2014) "In the Footsteps of Dr Bunche: The Congo, UN Peacekeeping and the Use of Force." *Journal of Strategic Studies* 37(5): 703–735.

Doss, Alan. (2015) "United Nations Organization Mission in the Democratic Republic of the Congo (MONUC)." In *The Oxford Handbook of United Nations Peacekeeping Operations*, ed. Joachim A. Koops, Norrie MacQueen, Thierry Tardy, and Paul D. Williams, 656–670. New York: Oxford University Press.

Doyle, Michael, and Nicholas Sambanis. (2006) *Making War and Building Peace: United Nations Peace Operations*. Princeton, NJ: Princeton University Press.

Druckman, Daniel. (2002) "Case-Based Research on International Negotiation." *International Negotiation* 7(1): 17–37.

Druckman, Daniel. (2005) *Doing Research: Methods of Inquiry for Conflict Analysis*. Thousand Oaks, CA: Sage.

Druckman, Daniel. (2006) "Time-Series Designs and Analyses." In *Methods of Negotiation Research*, ed. Peter Carnevale and Carsten de Dreu, 61–78. Leiden, Netherlands: Martinus Nijhoff.

Druckman, Daniel. (2008) "Situations." In *Conflict: From Analysis to Intervention*, 2nd ed., ed. Sandra Cheldelin, Daniel Druckman, and Larissa Fast, 120–146. New York: Continuum.

Druckman, Daniel, and Paul F. Diehl. (2009) "Dimensions of the Conflict Environment: Implications for Peace Operation Success." *Journal of International Peacekeeping* 13(1–2): 6–44.

Druckman, Daniel, and Paul F. Diehl. (2012) "Revisiting the Framework: Extensions and Refinements." *Journal of International Peacekeeping* 16(3–4): 343–353.

Druckman, Daniel, and Paul F. Diehl, eds. (2013) *Peace Operation Success: A Comparative Analysis*. Leiden, Netherlands: Martinus Nijhoff.

Druckman, Daniel, and Noam Ebner. (2018) "Discovery Learning in Management Education: Design and Case Analysis." *Journal of Management Education* 42(3): 347–374.

Druckman, Daniel, Jerome E. Singer, and Harold P. Van Cott, eds. (1997) *Enhancing Organizational Performance*. Washington, DC: National Academy Press.

Druckman, Daniel, and Lynn M. Wagner. (2016) "Justice and Negotiation." *Annual Review of Psychology* 67(1): 387–413.

Druckman, Daniel, and Lynn M. Wagner. (2019) "Justice Matters: Peace Negotiations, Stable Agreements, and Durable Peace." *Journal of Conflict Resolution* 63(2): 287–316.

Druckman, Daniel, and James Wall. (2017) "A Treasure Trove of Insights: Sixty Years of JCR Research on Negotiation and Mediation." *Journal of Conflict Resolution* 61(9): 1898–1924.

Durch, William J., Victoria K. Holt, Caroline R. Earle, and Moira K. Shanahan. (2003) *The Brahimi Report and the Future of UN Peace Operations*. Washington, DC: Henry L. Stimson Center.

Durch, William J., and Michelle Ker. (2013) *Police in UN Peacekeeping: Improving Selection, Recruitment, and Deployment*. New York: International Peace Institute.

Eck, Kristine, and Lisa Hultman. (2007) "One-Sided Violence against Civilians in War." *Journal of Peace Research* 44(2): 233–246.

Edwards, Allen L. (1962) *Experimental Design in Psychological Research*. New York: Holt, Rinehart and Winston.

Edwards, Benjamin, Serdar Yilmaz, and Jamie Boex. (2014) "Local Government Discretion and Accountability in Sierra Leone." Urban Institute Center on International Development and Governance. Accessed September 26, 2021. https://www.urban.org/

sites/default/files/publication/22546/413101-Local-Government-Discretion-and-Accountability-in-Sierra-Leone.PDF.

Eizenga, Daniel. (2022) "Peacebuilding and Democracy in Africa." In *Routledge Handbook of African Peacebuilding*, ed. Bruno Charbonneau and Maxime Ricard, 155–168. London: Routledge.

Eriksen, Stein Sundstøl. (2009) "The Liberal Peace Is Neither: Peacebuilding, State Building and the Reproduction of Conflict in the Democratic Republic of Congo." *International Peacekeeping* 16(5): 652–666.

European Community Investigative Mission into the Treatment of Muslim Women in the Former Yugoslavia. (1993) *Warburton Report, E/CN.4/1993/92, Women Living under Muslim Laws, Compilation of Information on Crimes of War against Women in Ex-Yugoslavia.*

Fanthorpe, Richard. (2001) "Neither Citizen nor Subject? 'Lumpen' Agency and the Legacy of Native Administration in Sierra Leone." *African Affairs* 100(400): 363–386.

Fargo, Sofia. (2006) *An Analysis of the United Nations: Two Peace Operations in the Congo.* Tampa: University of South Florida.

Fariss, Christopher J. (2019) "Yes, Human Rights Practices Are Improving over Time." *American Political Science Review* 113(3): 868–881.

Farrall, Jeremy. (2012) "Recurring Dilemmas in a Recurring Conflict: Evaluating the UN Mission in Liberia (2003–2006)." *Journal of International Peacekeeping* 16(3–4): 306–342.

Faubert, Carrol. (2006) *Case Study Democratic Republic of the Congo Evaluation of UNDP Assistance to Conflict-Affected Countries.* New York: United Nations Development Programme.

Faure, Andrew M. (1994) "Some Methodological Problems in Comparative Politics." *Journal of Theoretical Politics* 6(3): 307–322.

Fearon, James D. (1991) "Counterfactuals and Hypothesis Testing in Political Science." *World Politics* 43(2): 169–195.

Fearon, James D. (1995) "Rationalist Explanations for War." *International Organization* 49(3): 379–414.

Fern, Edward F. (2001) *Advanced Focus Group Research.* Thousand Oaks, CA: Sage.

Fetherston, Anne Betts. (1994) *Towards a Theory of United Nations Peacekeeping.* London: Palgrave Macmillan.

Findlay, Trevor. (2002) *The Use of Force in UN Peace Operations.* Solna, Sweden: Stockholm International Peace Research Institute.

Fisher, Ronald A. (1935) *The Design of Experiments.* London: Collier Macmillan.

Fleshman, Michael. (2005) "Tough UN Line on Peacekeeper Abuses." Africa Renewal. Accessed September 26, 2021. https://www.un.org/africarenewal/magazine/april-2005/tough-un-line-peacekeeper-abuses.

Flores, Thomas Edward, and Irfan Nooruddin. (2012) "The Effect of Elections on Postconflict Peace and Reconstruction." *Journal of Politics* 74(2): 558–570.

Forti, Daniel. (2022) "UN Peacekeeping and CPAS: An Experiment in Performance Assessment and Mission Planning." New York: International Peace Institute.

Fortna, Virginia Page. (2003) "Inside and Out: Peacekeeping and the Duration of Peace after Civil and Interstate Wars." *International Studies Review* 5(4): 97–114.

Fortna, Virginia Page. (2008) *Does Peacekeeping Work? Shaping Belligerents' Choices after Civil War.* Princeton, NJ: Princeton University Press.

Fowler, Andrew H. (2016) *Stability Operations in East Timor 1999–2000: A Case Study.* Carlisle, PA: US Army War College Peacekeeping and Stability Operations Institute.

Fragile States Index. (2021) "Country Dashboard: Congo Democratic Republic." Accessed September 23, 2021. https://fragilestatesindex.org/country-data/.

Franke, Volker C., and Andrea Warnecke. (2009) "Building Peace: An Inventory of UN Peace Missions since the End of the Cold War." *International Peacekeeping* 16(3): 407–436.

Freire, Maria Raquel, and Paula Duarte Lopes. (2013) "Peacebuilding in Timor-Leste: Finding a Way between External Intervention and Local Dynamics." *International Peacekeeping* 20(2): 204–218.

Galbraith, Peter. (2003) "The United Nations Transitional Authority in East Timor (UNTAET)." *Proceedings of the Annual American Society of International Law Meeting* 97, 210–212. doi: 10.1017/S0272503700060110.

Galtung, Johan. (2011) "Peace, Positive and Negative." In *The Encyclopedia of Peace Psychology*, ed. Daniel J. Christie. New York: Wiley.

Ganiwu, Yahaya. (2018) *Assessing the Ghana Police Service's Participation in International Peacekeeping Operations as a Modern Tool of Foreign Policy: Challenges and Prospects.* Accra: University of Ghana.

Gberie, Lansana. (2005) *A Dirty War in West Africa: The RUF and the Destruction of Sierra Leone.* Bloomington: Indiana University Press.

Gbla, Osman. (2006) "Security Sector Reform under International Tutelage in Sierra Leone." *International Peacekeeping* 13(1): 78–93.

George, Alexander L., and Andrew Bennett. (2005) *Case Studies and Theory Development in the Social Sciences.* Cambridge, MA: MIT Press.

Gilligan, Michael, and Stephen Stedman. (2003) "Where Do the Peacekeepers Go?" *International Studies Review* 5(4): 37–54.

Gleditsch, Nils Petter, Peter Wallensteen, Mikael Eriksson, Margareta Sollenberg, and Håvard Strand. (2002) "Armed Conflict 1946–2001: A New Dataset." *Journal of Peace Research* 39(5): 615–637.

Global Policy Forum. (2010) "Two Hundred Women Gang-Raped near UN Base." Accessed September 23, 2021. https://archive.globalpolicy.org/security-council/index-of-countries-on-the-security-council-agenda/democratic-republic-of-congo/49415.html?itemid=868.

Goebel, Christopher, and Jessica Levy. (2020) "Disarmament, Demobilization, and Reintegration." In *Research Handbook on Post-Conflict State Building*, ed. Paul Williams and Milena Sterio, 117–144. Cheltenham, UK: Edward Elgar.

Goertz, Gary. (2017) *Multimethod Research, Causal Mechanisms, and Case Studies.* Princeton, NJ: Princeton University Press.

Goldstone, Anthony. (2004) "UNTAET with Hindsight: The Peculiarities of Politics in an Incomplete State." *Global Governance* 10(1): 83–98.

González, Armando Duque, Francesco Mezzalama, and Khalil Issa Othman. (2002) *Evaluation of United Nations System Response in East Timor: Coordination and Effectiveness.* Geneva, Switzerland: United Nations Joint Inspection Unit, JIU/REP/2002/10.

González Peña, Andrea and Herrara, Dylan. (2022) "Demobilization, Demilitarization and Reintegration in Peacekeeping." In *Handbook on Peacekeeping and International Relations*, ed. Han Dorussen, 118–133. Cheltenham, UK: Edward Elgar.

Gorjão, Paulo. (2002) "The Legacy and Lessons of the United Nations Transitional Administration in East Timor." *Contemporary Southeast Asia* 24(2): 313–336.

Goulding, Marrack. (1996) "The Use of Force by the United Nations." *International Peacekeeping* 3(1): 1–18.

Greig, J. Michael, Andrew Owsiak, and Paul F. Diehl. (2019) *International Conflict Management.* Cambridge: Polity Press.

Harinck, Fieke, Carsten K. W. De Dreu, and Annelies E. M. Van Vianen. (2000) "The Impact of Conflict Issues on Fixed-Pie Perceptions, Problem Solving, and Integrative Outcomes in Negotiation." *Organizational Behavior and Human Decision Processes* 81(2): 329–358.

Harmer, Andrew, and Robert Frith. (2009) "'Walking Together' toward Independence? A Civil Society Perspective on the United Nations Administration in East Timor, 1999–2002." *Global Governance* 15(2): 239–258.

Harris, David. (2014) *Civil War and Democracy in West Africa: Conflict Resolution, Elections and Justice in Sierra Leone and Liberia.* London: I. B. Tauris.

Hatto, Ronald. (2013) "From Peacekeeping to Peacebuilding: The Evolution of the Role of the United Nations in Peace Operations." *International Review of the Red Cross* 95(891–892): 495–515.

Hayner, Priscilla B. (2011) *Unspeakable Truths: Transitional Justice and the Challenge of Truth Commissions.* New York: Routledge.

Hazen, Jennifer M. (2007) "Can Peacekeepers Be Peacebuilders?" *International Peacekeeping* 14(3): 323–338.

Hegre, Håvard, Lisa Hultman, and Håvard Mokleiv Nygård. (2018) "Evaluating the Conflict-Reducing Effect of UN Peacekeeping Operations." *Journal of Politics* 81(1): 215–232.

Heldt, Birger, and Peter Wallensteen. (2006) *Peacekeeping Operations: Global Patterns of Intervention and Success, 1948–2004.* 2nd ed. Sandoverken, Sweden: Folke Bernadotte Academy Press.

Hellmüller, Sara. (2016) "Timing and Sequencing of Post-Conflict Reconstruction and Peacebuilding Efforts in DR Congo." In *Building Sustainable Peace—Timing and Sequencing of Post-Conflict Reconstruction and Peacebuilding,* ed. Armin Langer and Graham K. Brown, 243–261. Oxford: Oxford University Press.

Hellmüller, Sara. (2018) *The Interaction between Local and International Peacebuilding Actors: Partners for Peace.* London: Palgrave Macmillan.

Helms, Emily. (2022) "Mandating Peacekeeping Operations and International Law." In *Handbook on Peacekeeping and International Relations,* ed. Han Dorussen, 12–26. Cheltenham, UK: Edward Elgar.

Henke, Marina E. (2017) "UN Fatalities 1948–2015: A New Dataset." *Conflict Management and Peace Science* 36(4): 425–442.

Hillen, John F., III. (1995) "Killing with Kindness: The UN Peacekeeping Mission in Bosnia." Cato Institute. Accessed September 28, 2021. https://www.cato.org/foreign-policy-briefing/killing-kindness-un-peacekeeping-mission-bosnia.

Hobbs, Nicole. (2014) "The UN and the Congo Crisis of 1960." Harvey M. Applebaum '59 Award. 6. Accessed September 28, 2021. http://elischolar.library.yale.edu/applebaum_award/6.

Hoffman, Danny. (2005) "West-African Warscapes: Violent Events as Narrative Blocs: The Disarmament at Bo, Sierra Leone." *Anthropological Quarterly* 78(2): 329–353.

Hohe, Tanja. (2002a) "The Clash of Paradigms: International Administration and Local Political Legitimacy in East Timor." *Contemporary Southeast Asia* 24(3): 569–589.

Hohe, Tanja. (2002b) "'Totem Polls': Indigenous Concepts and 'Free and Fair' Elections in East Timor." *International Peacekeeping* 9(4): 69–88.

Holt, Victoria K., and Tobias C. Berkman. (2006) *The Impossible Mandate?: Military Preparedness, the Responsibility to Protect and Modern Peace Operations.* Washington, DC: Henry L. Stimson Center.

Holt, Victoria K., Glyn Taylor, and Max Kelly. (2009) *Protecting Civilians in the Context of UN Peacekeeping Operations: Successes, Setbacks and Remaining Challenges.* New York: United Nations.

Hood, Ludovic. (2006) "Security Sector Reform in East Timor, 1999–2004." *International Peacekeeping* 3(1): 60–77.

Hopmann, P. Terrence. (1995) "Two Paradigms of Negotiation: Bargaining and Problem Solving." *Annals of the American Academy of Political and Social Science* 542(1): 24–47.

Howard, Lise Morjé. (2008) *UN Peacekeeping in Civil Wars.* Cambridge: Cambridge University Press.

Howard, Lise Morjé. (2019) *Power in Peacekeeping.* Cambridge: Cambridge University Press.

Hultman, Lisa, Jacob Kathman, and Megan Shannon. (2013) "United Nations Peacekeeping and Civilian Protection in Civil War." *American Journal of Political Science* 57(4): 875–891.

Hultman, Lisa, Jacob Kathman, and Megan Shannon. (2014) "Beyond Keeping Peace: United Nations Effectiveness in the Midst of Fighting." *American Political Science Review* 108(4): 737–753.

Hultman, Lisa, Jacob Kathman, and Megan Shannon. (2020) *Peacekeeping in the Midst of War.* Oxford: Oxford University Press.

Hultman, Lisa, Jacob Kathman, and Megan Shannon. (2022) "Peacekeeping and the Protection of Civilians." In *Handbook on Peacekeeping and International Relations,* ed. Han Dorussen, 210–224. Cheltenham, UK: Edward Elgar.

Human Rights Measurement Initiative. (2021) "Rights Tracker: Timor-Leste—How Well Is Timor-Leste Respecting People's Human Rights?" Accessed September 24, 2021. https://rightstracker.org/en/country/TLS.

Human Rights Watch. (1999a) "Shocking War Crimes in Sierra Leone: New Testimonies on Mutilation, Rape of Civilians." Accessed September 26, 2021. https://www.hrw.org/news/1999/06/24/shocking-war-crimes-sierra-leone#.

Human Rights Watch. (1999b) "Sierra Leone: Getting Away with Murder, Mutilation, Rape—New Testimony from Sierra Leone." Accessed September 26, 2021. https://www.hrw.org/reports/1999/sierra/.

Human Rights Watch. (2002) "Justice Denied for East Timor: Indonesia's Sham Prosecutions, the Need to Strengthen the Trial Process in East Timor, and the Imperative of U.N. Action." Accessed September 24, 2021. https://www.hrw.org/legacy/backgrounder/asia/timor/etimor1202bg.htm.

Human Rights Watch. (2003) *"We'll Kill You If You Cry": Sexual Violence in the Sierra Leone Conflict.* New York: Human Rights Watch.

Human Rights Watch. (2005) *World Report 2005: Events of 2004.* New York: Human Rights Watch.

Human Rights Watch. (2007) "Letter to H.E. Ernest Bai Koroma: Recommendations Following the 2007 Presidential Elections." Accessed September 26, 2021. https://reliefweb.int/report/sierra-leone/letter-he-ernest-bai-koroma-sierra-leone.

Human Rights Watch. (2009a) "DR Congo: Civilian Cost of Military Operation Is Unacceptable." Accessed September 25, 2021. https://www.hrw.org/news/2009/10/13/dr-congo-civilian-cost-military-operation-unacceptable#.

Human Rights Watch. (2009b) "Q&A: DR Congo—Dossier for Hillary Clinton's Visit." Accessed September 24, 2021. https://www.hrw.org/news/2009/08/10/q-dr-congo-dossier-hillary-clintons-visit.

Hunt, Janet. (2002) "The East Timor Emergency Response." Humanitarian Practice Network. Accessed September 24, 2021. https://odihpn.org/magazine/the-east-timor-emergency-response/.

Ingram, Sue. (2012) "Building the Wrong Peace: Reviewing the United Nations Transitional Administration in East Timor (UNTAET) through a Political Settlement Lens." *Political Science* 64(1): 3–20.

Innes, Michael A., ed. (2006) *Bosnian Security after Dayton: New Perspectives*. London: Routledge.

International Campaign to Ban Landmines. (2009) *Landmine Monitor Report 2009: Toward a Mine-free World*. Ottawa, ON: Mines Action Canada. Accessed September 9, 2009. http://archives.the-monitor.org/index.php/publications/display?url=lm/2009/.

International Center for Transitional Justice. (2021) "After 10 Years, CAVR Report Still Resonates in Timor-Leste and around the World." *ICTJ*. Accessed June 18, 2021. https://www.ictj.org/news/10-years-cavr-report-timor-leste-truth.

International Crisis Group. (2002) "Sierra Leone after Elections: Politics as Usual?" ICG Africa Report No. 49. Accessed September 20, 2021. https://www.crisisgroup.org/africa/west-africa/sierra-leone/sierra-leone-after-elections-politics-usual.

International Crisis Group. (2010) "Congo: A Stalled Democratic Agenda." Africa Briefing No. 73. Accessed September 24, 2021. https://www.crisisgroup.org/africa/central-africa/democratic-republic-congo/congo-stalled-democratic-agenda.

International Growth Centre. (2013) "Local Governance and Development in Sierra Leone." Accessed September 26, 2021.https://www.theigc.org/wp-content/uploads/2015/07/Acemoglu-Et-Al-2013-Policy-Brief.pdf.

International Institute for Democracy and Electoral Assistance (IDEA). (n.d.) "Sierra Leone." Accessed December 12, 2022. https://www.idea.int/data-tools/country-view/267/40.

International Organization for Migration. (n.d.) "Support to the Implementation of the Sierra Leone Reparations Programme (SLRP)." Accessed September 26, 2021. https://www.iom.int/sites/g/files/tmzbdl486/files/migrated_files/What-We-Do/docs/Support-to-the-Implementation-of-the-Sierra-Leone-Reparations-Programme-SLRP.pdf.

International Peace Institute. (2019) "Prioritizing and Sequencing Peacekeeping Mandates in 2019: The Case of MINUSCA." Accessed August 29, 2020. https://www.ipinst.org/2019/10/prioritizing-and-sequencing-peacekeeping-mandates-in-2019-the-case-of-minusca.

International Peace Institute. (2019) "Prioritizing and Sequencing Peacekeeping Mandates in 2019: The Case of UNMISS." Accessed August 29, 2020. https://www.ipinst.org/2019/02/prioritizing-and-sequencing-peacekeeping-mandates-the-case-of-unmiss.

International Peace Institute. (n.d.) "Providing for Peacekeeping." Accessed July 15, 2021. https://www.ipinst.org/publications/series/providing-for-peacekeeping.

Iqbal, Zareen. (2010) "Democratic Republic of Congo (DRC): MONUC's Impending Withdrawal." International Institute for Justice and Development. Accessed September 24, 2021. http://iijd.org/news/entry/drc-monucs-impending-withdrawal.

Ishizuka, Katsumi. (2016) "The History of Robust Peacekeeping and Peace Enforcement in the DRC: The Limitations of the Pursuit of Negative Peace." Paper presented at the 2016 Annual Meeting for the Academic Council on the United Nations System.

Jacobson, Harold K. (1964) "ONUC's Civilian Operations: State-Preserving and State-Building." *World Politics* 17(1): 75–107.

James, Alan. (1994) "The Congo Controversies." *International Peacekeeping* 1(1): 44–58.

Jenkins, Robert. (2013) *Peacebuilding: From Concept to Commission*. London: Routledge.

Johansen, Robert. (1994) "UN Peacekeeping; How Should We Measure Success." *Mershon International Studies Review* 38(2): 307–310.

Johnson, Darin. (2020) "Post-conflict Constitution-making." In *Research Handbook on Post-Conflict State Building*, ed. Paul Williams and Milena Sterio, 6–29. Cheltenham, UK: Edward Elgar.

Journaliste en Danger. (2009) "Rapport Annual 2008." News alert, 3–94. December 10, 2009.

Kačapor-Džihić, Zehra, and Nermin Oruč. (2012) *Social Impact of Emigration and Rural-Urban Migration in Central and Eastern Europe: Final Country Report—Bosnia and Herzegovina*. European Commission DG Employment, Social Affairs, and Inclusion.

Kaplan, Josiah. (2013) "'Reading' British Armed Humanitarian Intervention in Sierra Leone, 2000–2." In *The History and Practice of Humanitarian Intervention and Aid in Africa*, ed. Bronwen Everill and Josiah Kaplan, 93–119. New York: Springer.

Karim, Sabrina, and Kyle Beardsley. (2016) "Explaining Sexual Exploitation and Abuse in Peacekeeping Missions: The Role of Female Peacekeepers and Gender Equality in Contributing Countries." *Journal of Peace Research* 53(1): 100–115.

Karim, Sabrina, and Kyle Beardsley. (2017) *Equal Opportunity Peacekeeping: Women, Peace, and Security in Post-Conflict States*. New York: Oxford University Press.

Karim, Sabrina, and Kyle Beardsley. (2022) "Sexual Abuse by Peacekeepers." In *Handbook on Peacekeeping and International Relations*, ed. Han Dorussen, 256–269. Cheltenham, UK: Edward Elgar.

Karlsrud, John. (2019) "United Nations Stabilization Operations: Chapter Seven and a Half." *Ethnopolitics* 18(5): 494–508.

Kathman, Jacob, Michelle Benson, and Paul F. Diehl. (2023) "Punching before the Bell Rings: UN Signaling and Pre-Deployment Violence in Civil Wars." *International Studies Quarterly* (forthcoming).

Kaufmann, Daniel, Aart Kraay, and Massimo Mastruzzi. (2010) "The Worldwide Governance Indicators: Methodology and Analytical Issues." World Bank Policy Research Working Paper No. 5430. Accessed September 24, 2021. http://papers.ssrn.com/sol3/papers.cfm?abstract_id=1682130.

Keen, David. (2005) *Conflict and Collusion in Sierra Leone*. Oxford: James Currey.

Keil, Soeren, and Anastasiia Kudlenko. (2015) "Bosnia and Herzegovina 20 Years after Dayton: Complexity Born of Paradoxes." *International Peacekeeping* 22(5): 471–489.

Khadka, Prabin, and Arun Phayal. (2022) "The Political Economy of Peacekeeping: Unemployment, Violence and Trust toward Peacekeepers." In *Handbook on Peacekeeping and International Relations*, ed. Han Dorussen, 327–342. Cheltenham, UK: Edward Elgar.

King, Gary, and Langche Zeng. (2007) "When Can History Be Our Guide? The Pitfalls of Counterfactual Inference." *International Studies Quarterly* 51(1): 183–210.

King, Jeremy A., Walter Dorn, and Matthew Hodes. (2002) *An Unprecedented Experiment: Security Sector Reform in Bosnia and Herzegovina*. London: Saferworld.

Kippenberg, Juliane. (2009) *Soldiers Who Rape, Commanders Who Condone: Sexual Violence and Military Reform in the Democratic Republic of Congo.* New York: Human Rights Watch.

Klinger, Janeen. (2005) "Stabilization Operations and Nation-Building: Lessons from United Nations Peacekeeping in the Congo, 1960–1964." *Fletcher F. World Affairs* 29(2): 83–102.

Knight, W. Andy. (2008) "Disarmament, Demobilization, and Reintegration and Post-Conflict Peacebuilding in Africa: An Overview." *African Security* 1(1): 24–52.

Koneska, Cvete. (2016) *After Ethnic Conflict: Policy-Making in Post-Conflict Bosnia and Herzegovina and Macedonia.* London: Routledge.

Koops, Joachim, Joachim Alexander Koops, Norrie MacQueen, Thierry Tardy, and Paul D. Williams, eds. (2015) *The Oxford Handbook of United Nations Peacekeeping Operations.* Oxford: Oxford University Press.

Kreps, Sarah E. (2010) "Why Does Peacekeeping Succeed or Fail? Peacekeeping in the Democratic Republic of Congo and Sierra Leone." In *Modern War and the Utility of Force*, ed. Jan Angstrom and Isabelle Duyvesteyn, 90–118. New York: Routledge.

Kroeker, Evgenija, and Andrea Ruggeri. (2022) "Peacekeeping and Conflict Resolution." In *Handbook on Peacekeeping and International Relations*, ed. Han Dorussen, 182–196. Cheltenham, UK: Edward Elgar.

Kruskal, Joseph B., and Myron Wish. (1990) *Multidimensional Scaling.* Newbury Park: Sage.

Kudlenko, Anastasiia. (2018) *The Impact of the EU on Security Sector Reform in the Western Balkans.* Canterbury, England: Canterbury Christ Church University.

La'o Hamutuk: Timor-Leste Institute for Development Monitoring and Analysis. (2010) "Letter to UN Security Council, February 2010." Accessed September 20, 2021. https://www.laohamutuk.org/Justice/10LHtoUNSC22FebEn.pdf.

Law, David M. (2006) "Conclusion: Security Sector (Re)Construction In Post-Conflict Settings." *International Peacekeeping* 13(1): 111–123.

Leach, Michael. (2016) *Nation-Building and National Identity in Timor-Leste.* London: Routledge.

Lebow, Richard Ned. (2000) "What's So Different about a Counterfactual?" *World Politics*, 52(4): 550–585.

Lefever, Ernest W. (1965) *Crisis in the Congo: A United Nations Force in Action.* Washington, DC: Brookings Institution.

Leib, Julia, and Samantha Ruppel. (2021) "The Dance of Peace and Justice: Local Perceptions of International Peacebuilding in West Africa." *International Peacekeeping* 28(5): 783–812.

Lemarchand, René. (2012) *The Dynamics of Violence in Central Africa.* Philadelphia: University of Pennsylvania Press.

Lemay-Hébert, Nicolas. (2009) "UNPOL and Police Reform in Timor-Leste: Accomplishments and Setbacks." *International Peacekeeping* 16(3): 393–406.

Levy, Jack S. (2008) "Case Studies: Types, Designs, and Logics." *Conflict Management and Peace Science* 25(1): 1–18.

Levy, Jack S. (2015) "Counterfactuals, Causal Inference, and Historical Analysis." *Security Studies* 24(3): 379–402.

Lincoln, Jessica. (2011) *Transitional Justice, Peace and Accountability: Outreach and the Role of International Courts after Conflict.* London: Routledge.

Lindberg Bromley, Sara. (2022) "The Hazards of Peacekeeping: Peacekeepers as Targets of Violence." In *Handbook on Peacekeeping and International Relations*, ed. Han Dorussen, 300–313. Cheltenham, UK: Edward Elgar.

Linzer, Drew A., and Jeffrey K. Staton. (2015) "A Global Measure of Judicial Independence, 1948–2012." *Journal of Law and Courts* 3(2): 223–256.

Lloyd, Gabriella. (2021) "New Data on UN Mission Mandates 1948–2015: Tasks Assigned to Missions in Their Mandates (TAMM)." *Journal of Peace Research* 58(5): 1149–1160.

Lupis, Ivan, Laura Pitter, Ivana Nizich, and Holly Cartner. (1995) *The Fall of Srebrenica and the Failure of UN Peacekeeping: Bosnia-Hercegovina.* New York: Human Rights Watch.

MacQueen, Norrie. (2002) *United Nations Peacekeeping in Africa since 1960.* London: Routledge.

MacQueen, Norrie. (2011) *Humanitarian Intervention and the United Nations.* Edinburgh: Edinburgh University Press.

MacQueen, Norrie. (2015) "United Nations Transitional Administration in East Timor (UNTAET)." In *The Oxford Handbook of United Nations Peacekeeping Operations*, ed. Joachim A Koops, Norrie MacQueen, Thierry Tardy, and Paul D Williams, 642–655. Oxford: Oxford University Press.

Maertens, Lucile. (2019) "From Blue to Green? Environmentalization and Securitization in UN Peacekeeping Practices." *International Peacekeeping* 26(3): 302–326.

Maertens, Lucile, and Mathilde LeLoup. (2022) "The Material Impact of Peace Missions on the Environment and Cultural Heritage." In *Handbook on Peacekeeping and International Relations*, ed. Han Dorussen, 270–285. Cheltenham, UK: Edward Elgar.

Mahmoud, Youssef. (2020) "Whatever Future Holds for Peace Operations, Peacebuilding Must Be More Local and Plural." Accessed March 28, 2021. https://theglobalobservatory.org/2020/09/whatever-future-holds-peace-operationspeacebuilding-must-be-more-local-plural/.

Mahoney, Robert, and Daniel Druckman. (1975) "Simulation, Experimentation, and Context: Dimensions of Design and Inference." *Simulation & Games* 6(3): 235–270.

Malan, Mark. (2003) "UNAMSIL after the Elections." Accessed September 26, 2021. https://www.researchgate.net/profile/Mark-Malan/publication/238770093_UNAM SIL_AFTER_THE_ELECTIONS/links/0046352d70c51ef79e000000/UNAMSIL-AFTER-THE-ELECTIONS.pdf.

Malone, David M., and Ramesh Thakur. (2001) "UN Peacekeeping: Lessons Learned?" *Global Governance* 7(11): 11–17.

Marshall, Monty G., and Ted Robert Gurr. (2020) "Polity 5: Political Regime Characteristics and Transitions, 1800–2018." Center for Systemic Peace. Accessed September 8, 2021. http://www.systemicpeace.org/inscr/p5manualv2018.pdf.

Martin, Ian, and Alexander Mayer-Rieckh. (2005) "The United Nations and East Timor: From Self-determination to State-building." *International Peacekeeping* 12(1): 125–145.

Martin-Brûlé, Sarah-Myriam. (2012) "Assessing Peace Operations' Mitigated Outcomes." *International Peacekeeping* 19(2): 235–250.

Mason, David T., Mehmet Gurses, Patrick T. Brandt, and Jason Michael Quinn. (2011) "When Civil Wars Recur: Conditions for Durable Peace after Civil Wars." *International Studies Perspectives* 12(2): 171–189.

McCarthy, John. (2002) *FALINTIL Reinsertion Assistant Program (FRAP)—Final Evaluation Report.* Geneva: International Organization for Migration.

McGinty, Roger, and Oliver Richmond. (2013) "The Local Turn in Peace Building: A Critical Agenda for Peace." *Third World Quarterly* 34(5): 763–783.

Mearsheimer, John J. (1994–1995) "The False Promise of International Institutions." *International Security* 19(3): 5–49.

Mendes, Nuno Canas, and André Saramajo. (2012) *Dimensions of State-Building: Timor-Leste in Focus.* Saarbrücken, Germany: LAMBERT Academic Publishing.

Menkhaus, Ken. (2003) "Measuring Impact: Issues and Dilemmas." InterPeace (previously War-Torn Societies Project-International), Geneva, Occasional Paper Series.

Millar, Gearoid. (2013) "Expectations and Experiences of Peacebuilding in Sierra Leone: Parallel Peacebuilding Processes and Compound Friction." *International Peacekeeping* 20(2): 189–203.

Miller, Kenneth, Jasmina Muzurovic, Gregory Worthington, and Susannah Tipping. (2002) "Bosnian Refugees and the Stressors of Exile: A Narrative Study." *American Journal of Orthopsychiatry* 72(3): 341–354.

Mobekk, Eirin. (2009) "Security Sector Reform and the UN Mission in the Democratic Republic of Congo: Protecting Civilians in the East." *International Peacekeeping* 16(2): 273–286.

Moe, Louise Wiuff. (2021) "The Dark Side of Institutional Collaboration: How Peacekeeping-Counterterrorism Convergences Weaken the Protection of Civilians in Mali." *International Peacekeeping* 28(1): 1–29.

Moratti, Massimo, and Amra Sabic-El-Rayess. (2009) *Transitional Justice and DDR: The Case of Bosnia and Herzegovina.* New York: International Center for Transitional Justice.

Mullenbach, Mark. (2013) "Third-Party Peacekeeping in Intrastate Disputes, 1946–2012: A New Data Set." *Midsouth Political Science Review* 14(1): 103–133.

Murphy, Ray. (2016) "UN Peacekeeping in the Democratic Republic of the Congo and the Protection of Civilians." *Journal of Conflict and Security Law* 21(2): 209–246.

Nadin, Peter. (2014) "An Argument for More Focused UN Peacekeeping Mandates." Our World. Accessed October 20, 2021. https://ourworld.unu.edu/en/an-argument-for-more-focused-un-peacekeeping-mandates.

Neethling, Theo. (2019) "The Entanglement between Peacekeeping and Counterterrorism, with Special Reference to Peacekeeping Operations in Africa." *African Journal on Conflict Resolution* 19(2): 57–84.

The New Humanitarian. (2004) "First Local Polls in 32 Years Marred by Low Turn Out." Accessed September 26, 2021. https://www.thenewhumanitarian.org/news/2004/05/24/first-local-polls-32-years-marred-low-turn-out.

Nduka-Agwu, Adibeli. (2009) "'Doing Gender' after the War: Dealing with Gender Mainstreaming and Sexual Exploitation and Abuse in UN Peace Support Operations in Liberia and Sierra Leone." *Civil Wars* 11(2): 179–199.

Nettelfield, Lara J. (2011) "Research and Repercussions of Death Tolls: The Case of the Bosnian Book of the Dead." In *Sex, Drugs, and Body Counts: The Politics of Numbers in Global Crime and Conflict,* ed. Peter Andreas and Kelly M. Greenhill, 159–187. Ithaca, NY: Cornell University Press.

Newman, Edward. (2002) "'Transitional Justice': The Impact of Transnational Norms and the UN." *International Peacekeeping* 9(2): 31–50.

Newport, Cal. (2016) *Deep Work: Rules for Focused Success in a Distracted World.* New York: Grand Central Publishing.

Ngoma-Binda, P. (2008) *Justice transitionnelle en RD Congo.* Paris: L'Harmattan.

Nilsson, Desirée, and Mimmi Söderberg Kovacs. (2013) "Different Paths of Reconstruction: Military Reform in Post-War Sierra Leone and Liberia." *International Peacekeeping* 20(1): 2–16.

Nitzschke, Heiko, and Kaysie Studdard. (2005) "The Legacies of War Economies: Challenges and Options for Peacemaking and Peacebuilding." *International Peacekeeping* 12(2): 222–239.

Nkansah, Lydia A. (2015) "The Dance of Truth and Justice in Postconflict Peacebuilding in Sierra Leone." *African Journal of International and Comparative Law* 23(2): 199–225.

Nordås, Ragnhild, and Siri Rustad. (2013) "Sexual Exploitation and Abuse by Peacekeepers: Understanding Variation." *International Interactions* 39(4): 511–534.

North Atlantic Treaty Organization. (2021) *Lessons Learned in Peacekeeping Operations.* Accessed October 20, 2021. https://www.nato.int/docu/peacekeeping_lessons/peace keeping-lessons-eng.pdf.

Norwegian Refugee Council. (2003) *Profile of Internal Displacement: Sierra Leone: Compilation of the Information Available in the Global IDP Database of the Norwegian Refugee Council.* Geneva: Norwegian Refugee Council/Global IDP Project.

Novosseloff, Alexandra, Adriana Erthal Abdenur, Thomas Mandrup, and Aaron Pangburn. (2019) *Assessing the Effectiveness of the United Nations Mission in the DRC/MONUC-MONUSCO.* Oslo: Norwegian Institute of International Affairs.

Novosseloff, Alexandra, and Lisa Sharland. (2019) *Partners and Competitors: Forces Operating in Parallel to UN Peace Operations.* New York: International Peace Institute.

Oakley, Robert B., Michael J. Dziedzic, and Eliot M. Goldberg. (1998) *Policing the New World Disorder Peace Operations and Public Security.* Washington, DC: National Defense University Press.

O'Flaherty, Michael. (2004) "Sierra Leone's Peace Process: The Role of the Human Rights Community." *Human Rights Quarterly* 26(1): 29–62.

Oksamytna, Ksemiya. (2022) "Public Information and Strategic Communication." In *Handbook on Peacekeeping and International Relations,* ed. Han Dorussen, 148–162. Cheltenham, UK: Edward Elgar.

Oksamytna, Ksemiya, and Magnus Lundgrun. (2021) "Decorating the 'Christmas Tree:' The UN Security Council and the Secretariat's Recommendations on Peacekeeping Mandates." *Global Governance* 27(2): 226–250.

Olivier, Lanotte. (2010) "Chronology of the Democratic Republic of Congo/Zaire (1960–1997)." Accessed September 24, 2021. https://www.sciencespo.fr/mass-violence-war-massacre-resistance/en/document/chronology-democratic-republic-congoza ire-1960-1997.html.

Olonisakin, Funmi. (2008) *Peacekeeping in Sierra Leone: The Story of UNAMSIL.* Boulder, CO: Lynne Rienner.

Olonisakin, Funmi. (2015) "United Nations Mission in Sierra Leone (UNAMSIL)." In *The Oxford Handbook of United Nations Peacekeeping Operations,* ed. Joachim A. Koops, Norrie MacQueen, Thierry Tardy, and Paul D Williams, 629–641. Oxford: Oxford University Press.

Olsson, Louise. (2009) *Gender, Equality, and United Nations Peace Operations in Timor-Leste.* Leiden: Martinus Nijhoff.

Olsson, Louise. (2022) "Protecting Women in Peacekeeping." In *Handbook on Peacekeeping and International Relations,* ed. Han Dorussen, 242–255. Cheltenham, UK: Edward Elgar.

Oluwafemi, Buhari Lateef. (2020) "A Historical Review of the Nigeria Police Force's Involvement in Some Selected United Nations Peacekeeping Missions in Africa." *African Journal of Social Sciences and Humanities Research* 3(1): 56–67.

Onana, Renner, and Hannah Taylor. (2008) "MONUC and SSR in the Democratic Republic of Congo." *International Peacekeeping* 15(4): 501–516.

O'Neill, J. T. (2002) "EYEWITNESS—The Irish Company at Jadotville, Congo, 1961: Soldiers or Symbols?" *International Peacekeeping* 9(4): 127–144.

O'Reilly, Colin. (2014) "Investment and Institutions in Post–Civil War Recovery." *Comparative Economic Studies* 56(1): 1–24.

Organization for Security and Cooperation in Europe (OSCE). (2022) *Factsheet: OSCE Mission to Bosnia and Herzegovina.* Accessed 14 November 2022. https://www.osce.org/files/f/documents/4/1/356601_1.pdf.

Paris, Roland. (2000) "Broadening the Study of Peace Operations." *International Studies Review* 2(3): 27–44.

Paris, Roland. (2004) *At War's End: Building Peace after Civil Conflict.* Cambridge: Cambridge University Press.

Passmore, Timothy, Johannes Karreth, and Jaroslav Tir. (2022) "Consent in Peacekeeping." In *Handbook on Peacekeeping and International Relations*, ed. Han Dorussen, 46–59. Cheltenham, UK: Edward Elgar.

Peace Operations Training Institute. (2021) "Our Courses." Accessed November 6, 2021. https://www.peaceopstraining.org/courses/.

Pearl, Judea, and Dana MacKenzie. (2018) *The Book of Why: The New Science of Cause and Effect.* New York: Basic Books.

Pemstein, Daniel, Kyle L. Marquardt, Eitan Tzelgov, Yi-ting Wang, Juraj Medzihorsky, Joshua Krusell, Farhad Miri, and Johannes von Römer. (2021) *The V-Dem Measurement Model: Latent Variable Analysis for Cross-National and Cross-Temporal Expert-Coded Data.* 6th ed. Gothenburg, Sweden: Varieties of Democracy Institute, University of Gothenburg.

Perito, Robert. (2020) "Security Sector Reform." In *Research Handbook on Post-Conflict State Building*, ed. Paul Williams and Milena Sterio, 145–161, Cheltenham, UK: Edward Elgar.

Perry, Valery, and Soeren Keil. (2018) "The OSCE Mission in Bosnia and Herzegovina: Testing the Limits of Ownership." *Nationalities Papers* 41(3): 371–394.

Pettersson, Therése, and Magnus Öberg. (2020) "Organized Violence, 1989–2019." *Journal of Peace Research* 57(4): 597–613.

Phillips, R. Cody. (2005) *Bosnia-Herzegovina: The US Army's Role in Peace Enforcement Operations 1995–2004.* Washington, DC: US Army Center of Military History (CMHD), US Department of the Army.

Physicians for Human Rights. (2002) "War-Related Sexual Violence in Sierra Leone: A Population-Based Assessment." Accessed September 26, 2021. http://www.peacewomen.org/sites/default/files/Disp-Health-VAW_WarSexSierraLeone_PHR_2002_0.pdf.

Pietz, Tobias. (2006) "Overcoming the Failings of Dayton: Defense Reform in Bosnia-Herzegovina." In *Bosnian Security after Dayton: New Perspectives*, ed. Michael A. Innes, 155–172. London: Routledge.

Porter, Toby. (2003) *The Interaction between Political and Humanitarian Action in Sierra Leone, 1995 to 2002.* Geneva: Centre for Humanitarian Dialogue. Accessed September 26, 2021. https://sites.tufts.edu/jha/files/2011/04/a117.pdf.

Prunier, Gerard. (2009) *Africa's World War: Congo, the Rwandan Genocide, and the Making of a Continental Catastrophe.* Oxford: Oxford University Press.

Pugh, Michael. (2004) "Peacekeeping and Critical Theory." *International Peacekeeping* 11(1): 39–58.

Pushkina, Darya. (2006) "A Recipe for Success? Ingredients of a Successful Peacekeeping Mission." *International Peacekeeping* 13(2): 133–149.

Putnam, Robert. (1993) *Making Democracy Work: Civic Traditions in Modern Italy.* Princeton, NJ: Princeton University Press.

Quinn, J. Michael, T. David Mason, and Mehmet Gurses. (2007) "Sustaining the Peace: Determinants of Civil War Recurrence." *International Interactions* 33(2): 167–193.

Raeymaekers, Timothy. (2013) "Post-war Conflict and the Market for Protection: The Challenges to Congo's Hybrid Peace." *International Peacekeeping* 20(5): 600–617.

Rahman, Nayem, Navneet Kumar, and Dale Rutz. (2016) "Managing Application Compatibility during ETL Tools and Environment Upgrades." *Journal of Decision Systems* 25(2): 136–150.

Raleigh, Clionadh, Andrew Linke, Håvard Hegre, and Joakim Karlsen. (2010) "Introducing ACLED: An Armed Conflict Location and Event Dataset." *Journal of Peace Research* 47(5): 651–660.

Ramet, Sabrina P. (2013) "Bosnia-Herzegovina since Dayton—An Introduction." In *Bosnia-Herzegovina since Dayton: Civic and Uncivic Values*, ed. Ola Listhaug and Sabrina P. Ramet, 11–48. Ravenna, Italy: Longo Editore.

Reardon, Meghan Kathryn, Marianne Nørgaard Jensby, Jens Boesen, Mengxi Tian, and Stepan Malinak. (2012) "Aid Effectiveness in the Democratic Republic of Congo: A Case Study Investigating the Factors Influencing Ineffective Aid." *Interdisciplinary Journal of International Studies* 8(1): 59–73.

Reeder, Bryce, and Marc Polizzi. (2021) "Transforming Zones of Exclusion to Zones of Inclusion?: Local-Level UN Peacekeeping Deployments and Educational Attainment." *International Studies Quarterly* 65(4): 867–880.

Reno, William. (2009) "Understanding Criminality in West African Conflicts." *International Peacekeeping* 16(1): 47–61.

Richmond, Oliver. (1998) "Devious Objectives and the Disputants' View of International Mediation: A Theoretical Framework." *Journal of Peace Research* 35(6): 707–722.

Richmond, Oliver P. (2006) "The Problem of Peace: Understanding the 'Liberal Peace'" *Conflict, Security, and Development* 6(3): 291–314.

Richmond, Oliver P. (2021) *The Grand Design: The Evolution of the International Peace Architecture*. Oxford: Oxford University Press.

Richmond, Oliver P., and Jason Franks. (2008) "Liberal Peacebuilding in Timor Leste: The Emperor's New Clothes?" *International Peacekeeping* 15(2): 185–200.

Richmond, Oliver P., and Roger Mac Ginty. (2015) "What Now for the Critique of the Liberal Peace?" *Conflict and Cooperation* 50(2): 171–189.

Rietjens, Sebastiaan, and Chiara Ruffa. (2019) "Understanding Coherence in UN Peacekeeping: A Conceptual Framework." *International Peacekeeping* 26(2): 383–407.

Rikhye, Indar Jit. (1984) *The Theory and Practice of Peacekeeping*. London: Hurst.

Rizvi, Ferzana. (2017) "UN Peacekeeping Mission in Sierra Leone: Pakistan's Role." *Journal of Pakistan Vision* 18(1): 57–75.

Rosser, Andrew, and Sharna Bremner. (2015) "The World Bank's Health Projects in Timor-Leste: The Political Economy of Effective Aid." *International Peacekeeping* 22(4): 435–451.

Ruggeri, Andrea, Theodora-Ismene Gizelis, and Han Dorussen. (2013) "Managing Mistrust: An Analysis of Cooperation with UN Peacekeeping in Africa." *Journal of Conflict Resolution* 57(3): 387–409.

Sambanis, Nicholas, and Michael Doyle. (2007) "No Easy Choices: Estimating the Effects of United Nations Peacekeeping (Response to King and Zeng)." *International Studies Quarterly* 51(1): 217–226.

Sandler, Todd. (2017) "International Peacekeeping Operations: Burden Sharing and Effectiveness." *Journal of Conflict Resolution* 61(9): 1875–1897.

Sarkees, Meredith Reid, and Frank Wayman. (2010) *Resort to War: 1816–2007*. Washington DC: CQ Press.

Sauter, Melanie. (2022) "A Shrinking Humanitarian Space: Peacekeeping Stabilization Projects and Violence in Mali." *International Peacekeeping* 29(4): 624–649.

Schinella, Anthony M. (2019) *Bombs without Boots: The Limits of Airpower*. Washington, DC: Brookings Institution.

Schnakenberg, Keith E., and Christopher J. Fariss. (2014) "Dynamic Patterns of Human Rights Practices." *Political Science Research and Methods* 2(1): 1–31.

Schroeder, Ursula C., Fairlie Chappuis, and Deniz Kocak. (2014) "Security Sector Reform and the Emergence of Hybrid Security Governance." *International Peacekeeping* 21(2): 214–230.

Shaw, Rosalind. (2007) "Memory Frictions: Localizing the Truth and Reconciliation Commission in Sierra Leone." *International Journal of Transitional Justice* 1(2): 183–207.

Shraga, Daphna. (1998) "The United Nations as an Actor Bound by International Humanitarian Law." *International Peacekeeping* 5(2): 64–81.

Sierra Leone Truth and Reconciliation Commission (SLTRC). Accessed September 27, 2021. https://www.sierraleonetrc.org/index.php/view-the-final-report/table-of-contents.

Silva, Romesh, and Patrick Ball. (2006) "The Profile of Human Rights Violations in Timor-Leste, 1974–1999." A Report by the Benetech Human Rights Data Analysis Group to the Commission on Reception, Truth and Reconciliation. Accessed September 24, 2021. https://www.hrdag.org/content/timorleste/Benetech-Report-to-CAVR.pdf.

Simangan, Dahlia. (2019) "A Case for a Normative Local Involvement in Post-Conflict Peacebuilding." *International Peacekeeping* 27(1): 77–101.

Sloan, James. (2010) "Peacekeepers under Fire: Prosecuting the RUF for Attacks against the UN Assistance Mission in Sierra Leone." *The Law & Practice of International Courts and Tribunals* 9(2): 243–293.

Small Arms Survey. (2008) "Timor-Leste Armed Violence Assessment—Dealing with the Kilat: An Historical Overview of Small Arms Availability and Arms Control in Timor-Leste, October 2008." Accessed September 24, 2021. http://www.genevadeclaration.org/fileadmin/docs/focus-countries/Issue_Brief_1_-_Dealing_with_the_kilat.pdf.

Small Arms Survey. (2009) "Timor-Leste Armed Violence Assessment—After the Guns Fall Silent: Sexual and Gender-based Violence in Timor-Leste." Accessed September 24, 2021. http://www.smallarmssurvey.org/fileadmin/docs/K-Timor-leste-ava/SAS-Timor-Leste-AVA-IB5-ENG.pdf.

Small Arms Survey. (2013a) "Timor-Leste Armed Violence Assessment—Electoral Violence in Timor-Leste: Mapping Incidents and Responses." Accessed September 24, 2021. http://www.smallarmssurvey.org/fileadmin/docs/K-Timor-leste-ava/SAS-Timor-Leste-AVA-IB3-ENG.pdf.

Small Arms Survey. (2013b) "Demobilization in the DRC: Armed Groups and the Role of Organizational Control." Accessed September 24, 2021. http://www.smallarmssurvey.org/fileadmin/docs/G-Issue-briefs/SAS-AA-IB1-DDR-in-the-DRC.pdf.

Smidt, Hannah. (2021) "Keeping Electoral Peace?: Activities of United Nations Peacekeeping Operations and Their Effects on Election-Related Violence." *Conflict Management and Peace Science* 38(5): 580–604.

Smidt, Hannah. (2022) "Peacekeeping and Electoral Violence." In *Handbook on Peacekeeping and International Relations*, edited by Han Dorussen, 225–241. Cheltenham, UK: Edward Elgar.

Smith, Alastair, and Allan C. Stam. (2003) "Mediation and Peacekeeping in a Random Walk Model of Civil and Interstate War." *International Studies Review* 5(4): 115–135.

Smith, Anthony L. (2002) "Timor Leste, Timor Timur, East Timor, Timor Lorosa'e: What's in a Name?" In *Southeast Asian Affairs*, ed. Daljit Singh and Anthony Smith, 54–77. Singapore: Institute of Southeast Asian Studies.

Smith, Claire Q., and Tom Jarvis. (2018) "Ending Mass Atrocities: An Empirical Reinterpretation of 'Successful' International Military Intervention in East Timor." *International Peacekeeping* 25(1): 1–27.

Smith, Michael Geoffrey, and Moreen Dee. (2003) *Peacekeeping in East Timor: The Path to Independence*. Boulder, CO: Lynne Rienner.

Spooner, Kevin A. (2009) "Just West of Neutral: Canadian 'Objectivity' and Peacekeeping during the Congo Crisis, 1960–61." *Canadian Journal of African Studies / Revue Canadienne des Études Africaines* 43(2): 303–336.

Srna, Shalena, Rom Y. Schrift, and Gal Zauberman. (2018) "The Illusion of Multitasking and Its Positive Effect on Performance." *Psychological Science* 29(12): 1942–1955.

Sterio, Milena. (2020) "Human Rights." In *Research Handbook on Post-Conflict State Building*, ed. Paul Williams and Milena Sterio, 260–278, Cheltenham, UK: Edward Elgar.

Steele, Jonathan. (2002) "Nation Building in East Timor." *World Policy Journal* 19(2): 76–87.

Stiles, Kendall, and Maryellen MacDonald. 1992. "After Consensus, What?: Performance Criteria for the UN in the Post–Cold War Era." *Journal of Peace Research* 29(3): 299–311.

Strohmeyer, Hansjoerg. (2000) "Building a New Judiciary for East Timor: Challenges of a Fledgling Nation." *Criminal Law Forum* 11(3): 259–285.

Stuart, Elizabeth. (2010) "Matching Methods for Causal Inference: A Review and a Look Forward." *Statistical Science* 25(1): 1–21.

Suhrke, Astri. (2001) "Peacekeepers as Nation-builders: Dilemmas of the UN in East Timor." *International Peacekeeping* 8(4): 1–20.

Suma, Mohamed. (2014) *Sierra Leone: Justice Sector and the Rule of Law*. Dakar, Senegal: Open Society Initiative for West Africa.

Svensson, Isak. (2009) "Who Brings Which Peace? Neutral versus Biased Mediation and Institutional Peace Agreements in Civil Wars." *Journal of Conflict Resolution* 53(3): 446–469.

Szasz, Paul C. (1995) "Peacekeeping in Operation: A Conflict Study of Bosnia." *Cornell International Law Journal* 28(3): 685–699.

Tardy, Thierry. (2015a) "United Nations Protection Force (UNPROFOR—Bosnia-Herzegovina)." In *The Oxford Handbook of United Nations Peacekeeping Operations*, ed. Joachim A. Koops, Norrie MacQueen, Thierry Tardy, and Paul D Williams, 383–394. Oxford: Oxford University Press.

Tardy, Thierry. (2015b) "United Nations Protection Force (UNPROFOR—Croatia)." In *The Oxford Handbook of United Nations Peacekeeping Operations*, ed. Joachim A Koops, Norrie MacQueen, Thierry Tardy, and Paul D Williams, 371–382. Oxford: Oxford University Press.

Tavakoli, Heidi, Ismaila B. Cessay, and Winston Percy Onipede Cole. (2015) "Substantial but Uneven Achievement: Selected Success When Stars Align. Public Financial Management Reforms in Sierra Leone." *International Peacekeeping* 22(4): 337–353.

Tetra Tech ARD. (2012) *Democracy, Human Rights, and Governance Assessment of the Democratic Republic of the Congo—Final Report*. Washington, DC: US Agency for International Development.

Thies, Cameron. (2010) "Role Theory and Foreign Policy." In *Oxford Research Encyclopedia of International Studies*, ed. Robert A. Denemark, vol. X, 6335–6356. West Sussex, UK: Wiley-Blackwell. doi: 10.1093/acrefore/9780190846626.013.291.

Thompson, William, and David Dreyer. (2011) *Handbook of International Rivalries 1494–2010*. Washington, DC: CQ Press.

Thoms, Oskar N. T., James Ron, and Roland Paris. (2010) "State-Level Effects of Transitional Justice: What Do We Know?" *International Journal of Transitional Justice* 4(3): 329–354.

Tokača, Mirsad. (2012) *The Bosnian Book of the Dead. Human Losses in Bosnia and Herzegovina 1991–1995*. Sarajevo: Research and Documentation Center.

Tonhäuser, Cornelia, and Laura Büker. (2016) "Determinants of Transfer of Training: A Comprehensive Literature Review." *International Journal for Research in Vocational Education and Training* 3(2): 127–165.

Török, Balázs, Karolina Janacsek, David G. Nagy, Gergő Orbán, and Dezso Nemeth. (2017) "Measuring and Filtering Reactive Inhibition Is Essential for Assessing Serial Decision Making and Learning." *Journal of Experimental Psychology* 146(4): 529–542.

Trahan, Jennifer. (2020) "Judicial Reform and Rebuilding." In *Research Handbook on Post-Conflict State Building*, ed. Paul Williams and Milena Sterio, 245–259. Cheltenham, UK: Edward Elgar.

Tull, Denis M. (2009) "Peacekeeping in the Democratic Republic of Congo: Waging Peace and Fighting War." *International Peacekeeping* 16(2): 215–230.

Tull, Denis M. (2018) "The Limits and Unintended Consequences of UN Peace Enforcement: The Force Intervention Brigade in the DR Congo." *International Peacekeeping* 25(2): 167–190.

UNICEF. (2008) "Continued Insecurity Hinders Aid to Displaced Families in DR Congo." Accessed September 25, 2021. https://reliefweb.int/report/democratic-republic-congo/continued-insecurity-hinders-aid-displaced-families-dr-congo.

United Nations. (1960a) "Cable Dated 60/07/12 from the President of the Republic of the Congo and Supreme Commander of the National Army and the Prime Minister and Minister of National Defence Addressed to the Secretary-General of the United Nations." UN document S/4382, 13 July 1960. Accessed September 16, 2021. https://digitallibrary.un.org/record/619887?ln=en.

United Nations. (1960b) "Report by Major-General H. T. Alexander, DSO, OBE, Chief of Defense Staff." In *Exchange of Messages between the Secretary-General and the President of Ghana*. UN document S/4445 Annex II, 19 August 1960. Accessed September 16, 2021. https://digitallibrary.un.org/record/620173?ln=en.

United Nations. (1992) "Report of the Secretary-General Pursuant to Security Council Resolution 749." UN document S/23836. Accessed September 16, 2021. https://digitallibrary.un.org/record/143263?ln=en.

United Nations. (1993a) "Report of the Secretary-General Pursuant to Security Council Resolution 844." UN document S/1994/55, 9 May 1994. Accessed September 16, 2021. https://digitallibrary.un.org/record/186754?ln=en.

United Nations. (1993b) "Report of the Secretary-General Pursuant to Security Council Resolution 871." UN document S/1994/300, 16 March 1994. Accessed September 16, 2021. https://digitallibrary.un.org/record/185141?ln=en.

United Nations. (1995) "Letter Dated 95/11/29 from the Permanent Representative of the United States of America to the United Nations Addressed to the Secretary-General." UN document S/1995/999. Accessed September 27, 2021. https://digitallibrary.un.org/record/201746?ln=en.

United Nations. (1999a) "Letter Dated 99/07/23 from the Permanent Representative of Zambia to the United Nations Addressed to the President of the Security Council", UN document S/1999/815, 23 July 1999. Accessed September 25, 2021. https://digitallibrary.un.org/record/276965?ln=en.

United Nations. (1999b) "Report of the Secretary General on the Situation in East Timor." UN document S/1999/1024. Accessed September 25, 2021. https://digitallibrary.un.org/record/286642?ln=en.

United Nations. (2000a) "Peacekeeping Mission Updates: January–March 2000." *International Peacekeeping* 7(3): 137–147.

United Nations. (2000b) "Peacekeeping Mission Updates: April–June 2000." *International Peacekeeping* 7(4): 207–217.

United Nations. (2000c) "Report of the Secretary-General on the Establishment of a Special Court for Sierra Leone." UN document S/2000/915. Accessed September 25, 2021. https://digitallibrary.un.org/record/424039?ln=en.

United Nations. (2000d) "Report of the Secretary-General on the United Nations Administration in East Timor." UN document S/2000/53. Accessed September 25, 2021. https://digitallibrary.un.org/record/406631?ln=en.

United Nations. (2001a) "Peacekeeping Mission Updates: January–March 2001." *International Peacekeeping* 8(3): 125–135.

United Nations. (2001b) "Peacekeeping Mission Updates: May–July 2001." *International Peacekeeping* 8(4): 147–157.

United Nations. (2002a) "Digest of Operations (August–October 2001)." *International Peacekeeping* 9(1): 172–183.

United Nations. (2002b) "Digest (November 2001 to January 2002), Documentation (Security Council Resolution 1389 (2002) on the Role of the UN in Assisting Elections in Sierra Leone, Abstracts, Notes for Contributors." *International Peacekeeping* 9(2): 222–238.

United Nations. (2002c) "Digest of Operations (February–April 2002) Documentation—Security Council Resolutions 1397, 1402, 1403 and 1405 (2002) on the Situation in the Middle East, Including the Palestinian Question." *International Peacekeeping* 9(3): 129–139.

United Nations. (2002d) "Digest." *International Peacekeeping* 9(4): 145–156.

United Nations. (2002e) "Fifteenth Report of the Secretary-General on the United Nations Mission in Sierra Leone." UN document S/2002/987. Accessed September 25, 2021. https://digitallibrary.un.org/record/473453?ln=en.

United Nations. (2002f) "Report of the Secretary-General on the United Nations Transitional Administration in East Timor." UN document S/2002/432. Accessed September 25, 2021. https://digitallibrary.un.org/record/462761?ln=en.

United Nations. (2002g) "Report of the Secretary-General on the United Nations Transitional Administration in East Timor: Addendum." UN document S/2002/432/Add.1. Accessed September 25, 2021. https://digitallibrary.un.org/record/463270?ln=en.

United Nations. (2002h) "Seventh Report of the Secretary-General on the United Nations Mission in Sierra Leone." UN document S/2000/1055. Accessed September 25, 2021. https://digitallibrary.un.org/record/426095?ln=en.

United Nations. (2002i) "Sixteenth Report of the Secretary-General on the United Nations Mission in Sierra Leone." UN document S/2002/1417. Accessed September 25, 2021. https://digitallibrary.un.org/record/482729?ln=en.

United Nations. (2003a) "Digest of Operations (November 2002–January 2003)." *International Peacekeeping* 10(2): 119–126.

United Nations. (2003b) "Digest." *International Peacekeeping* 10(4): 129–137.

United Nations. (2004) "Digest." *International Peacekeeping* 11(1): 213–222.

United Nations. (2005) "Digest." *International Peacekeeping* 13(2): 269–274.

United Nations. (2009) "UN Statistics Division: Millennium Development Goals Indicators." Accessed September 17, 2021. http://mdgs.un.org/unsd/mdg/Resources/Static/Products/Progress2009/MDG_Report_2009_En.pdf.

United Nations. (2010) *Second Generation Disarmament, Demobilization and Reintegration (DDR) Practices in Peace Operations: A Contribution to the New Horizon Discussion on Challenges and Opportunities for UN Peacekeeping.* New York: United Nations Department of Peacekeeping Operations.

United Nations. (2021) "Peacekeeping Resource Hub." Accessed July 21, 2021. https://research.un.org/en/peacekeeping-community/training.

United Nations. (n.d.) "Department of Peace Operations." Accessed July 15, 2021. https://peacekeeping.un.org/en/department-of-peace-operations.

United Nations. (n.d.) "What Is Peacekeeping." Accessed June 10, 2020. https://peacekeeping.un.org/en/what-is-peacekeeping.

United Nations Department of Economic and Social Affairs, Population Division. (2019) "World Population Prospects 2019." ST/ESA/SER.A/423. Accessed September 24, 2021. https://population.un.org/wpp/.

United Nations Department of Peacekeeping Operations. (2008) "United Nations Peacekeeping Operations Principles and Guidelines." Accessed 28 October 2022. https://peacekeeping.un.org/sites/default/files/capstone_eng_0.pdf.

United Nations Department of Peacekeeping Operations. (1996) "Former Yugoslavia—UNPROFOR: Background." Accessed January 17, 2019. https://peacekeeping.un.org/mission/past/unprof_b.htm.

United Nations Department of Peacekeeping Operations. "MONUC: United Nations Organization Mission in the Democratic Republic of the Congo." Accessed September 24, 2021. https://peacekeeping.un.org/mission/past/monuc/.

United Nations Department of Peacekeeping Operations. (2001) "Republic of the Congo—ONUC Background." Accessed March 25, 2019. https://peacekeeping.un.org/mission/past/onucB.htm.

United Nations Department of Peacekeeping Operations. "Sierra Leone—UNAMSIL—Background." Accessed September 27, 2021. https://peacekeeping.un.org/mission/past/unamsil/background.html.

United Nations Department of Peacekeeping Operations. (2021) "Total Fatalities since 1948." Accessed September 17, 2021. https://peacekeeping.un.org/en/fatalities.

United Nations Department of Public Information. (2002) "East Timor—UNTAET—Background." Accessed September 20, 2021. https://peacekeeping.un.org/sites/default/files/past/etimor/UntaetB.htm.

United Nations Department of Public Information. (2005a) "UNAMSIL Fact Sheet 3: Human Rights and Rule of Law—Respect for Human Rights and Rule of Law Brings Stability." Accessed September 26, 2021. https://peacekeeping.un.org/mission/past/unamsil/factsheet3_HRRL.pdf.

United Nations Department of Public Information. (2005b) "UNAMSIL Fact Sheet 4: Economic Recovery and Development—Diamond Exports Set to Jump Start Economic Recovery." Accessed September 26, 2021. https://peacekeeping.un.org/miss ion/past/unamsil/factsheet4_ERD.pdf.

United Nations Development Programme. (2007) "Timor-Leste: Presidential Election, Round 2—Status of Electoral Observers Groups at Saturday 5th May 2007." Accessed September 24, 2021. https://www.etan.org/etanpdf/2007/Presidential%20Round%20 2%20%20Status%20of%20Electoral%20Observers.pdf.

United Nations Development Program. (2010) *Human Development Report 2010. The Real Wealth of Nations: Pathways to Human Development.* New York: United Nations Development Program.

United Nations Development Program. (2019) "Human Development Index (HDI)." Accessed September 24, 2021. http://hdr.undp.org/en/indicators/137506.

United Nations Office for the Coordination of Humanitarian Affairs. (2003) "Sierra Leone: Humanitarian Situation Report." Accessed September 26, 2021. https://apps. who.int/disasters/repo/11318.pdf.

United Nations Peacebuilding. (n.d.) "Policy Issues and Partnerships." Accessed October 20, 2021. https://www.un.org/peacebuilding/policy-issues-and-partnerships/policy/ lessons-learned.

United Nations Peacebuilding Commission. (2007) "Provisional Report on the Work of the Peacebuilding Commission." UN document PBC/2/OC/L.1. Accessed September 26, 2021. https://digitallibrary.un.org/record/603210?ln=en.

United Nations Peacekeeping. (2021) "Impact of COVID-19 on Peacekeeping." Accessed October 20, 2021. https://peacekeeping.un.org/en/impact-of-covid-19-un-peace keeping.

United Nations Population Division. (2021) "Life Expectancy at Birth, Total (Years)— Bosnia and Herzegovina." Accessed September 17, 2021. https://data.worldbank.org/ indicator/SP.DYN.LE00.IN?locations=BA.

United Nations Resource Hub. (2021) "Peacekeeping Training Institutions." Accessed November 6, 2021. https://research.un.org/PKTI2020/List.

United Nations Secretary-General. (2018) "Action for Peacekeeping: Declaration of Shared Commitments on UN Peacekeeping Operations." Accessed 28 October 2022. https://peacekeeping.un.org/sites/default/files/a4p-declaration-en.pdf.

United Nations Security Council. (1960a) Resolution 143. Adopted at Its 873rd Meeting on July 14. Accessed September 16, 2021. https://digitallibrary.un.org/record/112 108?ln=en.

United Nations Security Council. (1960b) Resolution 145. Adopted at Its 879th Meeting on July 22. Accessed September 16, 2021. https://digitallibrary.un.org/record/112 109?ln=en.

United Nations Security Council. (1960c) Resolution. Adopted by the Security Council at Its 886th Meeting on August 9. Accessed September 16, 2021. https://digitallibrary. un.org/record/620110?ln=en.

United Nations Security Council. (1961a) Resolution. Adopted by the Security Council at Its 942nd Meeting on February 20–21. Accessed September 16, 2021. https://digitallibr ary.un.org/record/630764?ln=en.

United Nations Security Council. (1961b) Resolution 161. Adopted at Its 942nd Meeting on February 21. Accessed September 16, 2021. https://digitallibrary.un.org/record/112 132?ln=en.

United Nations Security Council. (1961c) Resolution 169. Adopted at Its 982nd Meeting on November 24. Accessed September 16, 2021. https://digitallibrary.un.org/record/112133?ln=en.

United Nations Security Council. (1992a) Resolution 743. Adopted at Its 3055th Meeting on February 21. Accessed September 16, 2021. https://digitallibrary.un.org/record/137965?ln=en.

United Nations Security Council. (1992b) Resolution 758. Adopted at Its 3083rd Meeting on June 8. Accessed September 16, 2021. https://digitallibrary.un.org/record/143774?ln=en.

United Nations Security Council. (1992c) Resolution 776. Adopted at Its 3114th Meeting on September 14. Accessed September 16, 2021. https://digitallibrary.un.org/record/149953?ln=en.

United Nations Security Council. (1992d) Resolution 781. Adopted at Its 3122nd Meeting on October 9. Accessed September 16, 2021. https://digitallibrary.un.org/record/151454?ln=en.

United Nations Security Council. (1993a) Resolution 824. Adopted at Its 3208th Meeting on May 6. Accessed September 16, 2021. https://digitallibrary.un.org/record/166133?ln=en.

United Nations Security Council. (1993b) Resolution 836. Adopted at Its 3228th Meeting on June 4. Accessed September 16, 2021. https://digitallibrary.un.org/record/166973?ln=en.

United Nations Security Council. (1998) Resolution 1181. Adopted at Its 3902nd Meeting on July 13. Accessed September 16, 2021. https://digitallibrary.un.org/record/256788?ln=en.

United Nations Security Council. (1999a) Resolution 1270. Adopted at Its 4054th Meeting on October 22. Accessed September 16, 2021. https://digitallibrary.un.org/record/287753?ln=en.

United Nations Security Council. (1999b) Resolution 1272. Adopted at Its 4057th Meeting on October 25. Accessed September 20, 2021. https://digitallibrary.un.org/record/291410?ln=en.

United Nations Security Council. (1999c) Resolution 1279. Adopted at Its 4076th Meeting on November 30. Accessed September 20, 2021. https://digitallibrary.un.org/record/384901?ln=en.

United Nations Security Council. (2000a) Resolution 1299. Adopted at Its 4145th Meeting on May 19. Accessed September 16, 2021. https://digitallibrary.un.org/record/414570?ln=en.

United Nations Security Council. (2000b) Resolution 1313. Adopted at Its 4184th Meeting on August 4. Accessed September 16, 2021. https://digitallibrary.un.org/record/420042?ln=en.

United Nations Security Council. (2000c) Resolution 1315. Adopted at Its 4186th Meeting on August 14. Accessed September 16, 2021. https://digitallibrary.un.org/record/420605?ln=en.

United Nations Security Council. (2001) Resolution 1355. Adopted at Its 4329th Meeting on June 15. Accessed September 20, 2021. https://digitallibrary.un.org/record/442521?ln=en.

United Nations Security Council. (2002) Resolution 1389. Adopted at Its 4451st Meeting on January 16. Accessed September 16, 2021. https://digitallibrary.un.org/record/456588?ln=en.

United Nations Security Council. (2003) Resolution 1493. Adopted at Its 4797th Meeting on July 28. Accessed September 20, 2021. https://digitallibrary.un.org/record/499 812?ln=en.

United Nations Security Council. (2005) Resolution 1592. Adopted at Its 5155th Meeting on March 30. Accessed September 20, 2021. https://digitallibrary.un.org/record/544 704?ln=en.

United Nations Security Council. (2008) Resolution 1856. Adopted at Its 6055th Meeting on December 22. Accessed September 20, 2021. https://digitallibrary.un.org/record/ 644491?ln=en.

United Nations Security Council. (2010) Resolution 1925. Adopted at Its 6324th Meeting on May 28. Accessed September 20, 2021. https://digitallibrary.un.org/record/683 422?ln=en.

United Nations Transitional Administration in East Timor. (2001) "UNTAET Daily Briefing 01 Feb 2001." Accessed September 25, 2021. https://reliefweb.int/report/ timor-leste/untaet-daily-briefing-01-feb-2001.

United States Agency for International Development. (2000) "USAID Summary Fact Sheet for East Timor Crisis." Accessed September 25, 2021. https://reliefweb.int/rep ort/timor-leste/usaid-summary-fact-sheet-east-timor-crisis.

United States Army Peacekeeping and Stability Operations Institute (PKSOI). (2022) *Defense Support to Stabilization (DSS): A Guide for Stabilization Practitioners.* Accessed December 6, 2022. https://pksoi.armywarcollege.edu/index.php/defense-support-to-stabilization-dssa-guide-for-stabilization-practitioners/.

United States Department of State. (2010) "2009 Human Rights Report: Democratic Republic of the Congo." Accessed September 25, 2021. https://2009-2017.state.gov/j/ drl/rls/hrrpt/2009/af/135947.htm.

United States Department of State. (2022) "United States Strategy to Prevent Conflict and Promote Stability." Accessed 28 October 2022. https://www.state.gov/united-states-strategy-to-prevent-conflict-and-promote-stability/.

United States Institute of Peace. (2003) "Truth Commission: Democratic Republic of the Congo." Accessed October 20, 2021. https://www.usip.org/publications/2003/07/ truth-commission-democratic-republic-congo.

Uppsala Conflict Data Program. Accessed July 15, 2021. ttps://ucdp.uu.se/.

van der Lijn, Jaïr. (2021) "Scenarios for the Future of Peace Operations." *International Peace Institute's Global Observatory.* Accessed May 19, 2021. https://theglobalobservat ory.org/2021/05/scenarios-future-peace-operations/?utm_source=mailchimp&utm_ medium=organic_email&utm_campaign=US_GO_publications_analysis&utm_cont ent=link.

van de Lijn, Jaïr, and Sabine Otto. (2022) "Civilian Components in Peace Operations." In *Handbook on Peacekeeping and International Relations,* ed. Han Dorussen, 163–181. Cheltenham, UK: Edward Elgar.

Van Pottelbergh, Gudrun. (2010) *Handover from International to Local Actors in Peace Missions: Lessons from Burundi, Sierra Leone, and Timor-Leste.* Oslo: Norwegian Institute of International Affairs.

Van Puijenbroek, Joost, Désiré Nkoy Elela, and Eric Mongo Malolo. (2008) "Processus DDR en Ituri: Succès, faiblesses et perspectives." Utrecht: IKV Pax Christi.

Van Woudenberg, Anneke. (2008) *"We Will Crush You": The Restriction of Political Space in the Democratic Republic of Congo.* New York: Human Rights Watch.

Varvaloucas, Alaina, Simeon Koroma, Momo Turay, and Bilal Siddiqi. (2012) "Improving the Justice Sector: Law and Institution-building in Sierra Leone." In *Economic Challenges and Policy Issues in Early Twenty-First-Century Sierra Leone*, ed. O. E. Johnson, 493–528. London: International Growth Centre.

Venigandla, Shilpa A. (2021) "Protection, Justice, and Accountability: Cooperation between the International Criminal Court and UN Peacekeeping Operations." Accessed September 24, 2021. https://www.ipinst.org/wp-content/uploads/2021/05/IPI-E-RPT-Protection-Justice-ICC.pdf.

Vetschera, Heinz, and Matthieu Damian. (2006) "Security Sector Reform in Bosnia and Herzegovina: The Role of the International Community." *International Peacekeeping* 13(1): 28–42.

Von Dyck, Christopher. (2016) *DDR and SSR in War-to-Peace Transition*. London: Ubiquity Press.

Walsh, Barry, Eric Bartz, Benjamin Allen, Kelly Gavagan, Patricia McPhelim, and James Agee. (2019) *Non-State Justice System Programming: A Practitioner's Guide*. Washington, DC: US Agency for International Development.

Walter, Barbara F. (1997) "The Critical Barrier to Civil War Settlement." *International Organization* 51(3): 335–364.

Walter, Barbara F. (2009) "Bargaining Failures and Civil War." *Annual Review of Political Science* 12: 243–261.

Walter, Barbara F., Lise Morje Howard, and Virginia Page Fortna. (2021) "The Extraordinary Relationship between Peacekeeping and Peace." *British Journal of Political Science* 51(4): 1705–1722.

Walter, Barbara F., and Gregoire Phillips. (2019) "Explaining the Number of Rebel Groups in Civil Wars." SSRN: https://ssrn.com/abstract=3477573.

Walton, Richard, and Robert McKersie. (1965) *A Behavioral Theory of Labor Negotiations*. Ithaca, NY: Cornell University Press.

Wassel, Todd. (2014) *Timor-Leste: Links Between Peacebuilding, Conflict Prevention and Durable Solutions to Displacement*. Washington DC: Brookings Institution.

Webster, David. (2018) *Flowers in the Wall: Truth and Reconciliation in Timor-Leste, Indonesia, and Melanesia*. Calgary: University of Calgary Press.

Weiss, Thomas, ed. (1998) *Beyond UN Subcontracting: Task-Sharing with Regional Security Arrangements and Service-Providing NGOs*. New York: St. Martin's Press.

Weller, Marc, and Stefan Wolff. (2006) "Bosnia and Herzegovina Ten Years after Dayton: Lessons for Internationalized State Building." *Ethnopolitics* 5(1): 1–13.

Whalan, Jeni. (2012) "Evaluating Peace Operations: The Case of Cambodia." *Journal of International Peacekeeping* 16(3–4): 236–251.

White, Nigel D. (2015) "Peacekeeping and International Law." In *The Oxford Handbook of United Nations Peacekeeping Operations*, ed. Joachim A Koops, Norrie MacQueen, Thierry Tardy, and Paul D Williams, 43–59. Oxford: Oxford University Press.

Wilén, Nina. (2016) "From Foe to Friend? Army Integration after War in Burundi, Rwanda and the Congo." *International Peacekeeping* 23(1): 79–106.

Williams, Paul D. (2004) "Peace Operations and the International Financial Institutions: Insights From Rwanda and Sierra Leone." *International Peacekeeping* 11(1): 103–123.

Williams, Paul D., and Alex J. Bellamy. (2021) *Understanding Peacekeeping*. 3rd ed. Cambridge: Polity Press.

Williams, Paul D., and Milena Sterio, eds. (2020) *Research Handbook on Post-Conflict State Building*. Cheltenham, UK: Edward Elgar.

World Bank. (2000) "Project Appraisal Document on a Proposed Grant in the Amount of US $12.7 Million Equivalent to East Timor for a Health Sector Rehabilitation Project." Accessed September 24, 2021. https://documents1.worldbank.org/curated/en/604 241468340813111/text/multi-page.txt.

World Bank. (2009a) Health, Nutrition, and Population Statistics: Bosnia and Herzegovina. Accessed September 10, 2021. http://web.worldbank.org/WBSITE/ EXTERNAL/TOPICS/EXTHEALTHNUTRITIO NANDPOPULA TION/EXTDA T AST A TISTICSHNP/EXTHNPST A TS/0,,menuPK: 3237172~pagePK:64168427~pi PK:64168435~theSitePK:3237118,00.html.

World Bank. (2009b) *Implementation Completion and Results Report on Grants in the Amount of US$12.6 Million (TF-51363) and Euro 16.2 Million (TF-51363) to Timor-Leste for a Second Health Sector Rehabilitation and Development Project.* Dili: World Bank.

World Bank. (2009c) Key Development Data and Statistics: Bosnia and Herzegovina. Accessed September 10, 2021. http://web.worldbank.org/WBSITE/EXTERNAL/ DATASTATISTICS/0,,contentMDK:20535285~menuPK:1192694~pagePK:64133 150~piPK:64133175~theSitePK:239 419,00.html.

World Bank. (2010) *Doing Business 2011: Making a Difference for Entrepreneurs.* Washington, DC: World Bank.

World Bank. (2021a) "GovData360—Government Effectiveness." Accessed September 26, 2021. https://govdata360.worldbank.org/indicators/h580f9aa5?country=SLE&indica tor=388&countries=BRA&viz=line_chart&years=1996,2019.

World Bank. (2021b) "TCdata360—Control of Corruption." Accessed September 26, 2021. https://tcdata360.worldbank.org/indicators/hc153e067?country=SLE&indica tor=364&countries=BRA&viz=line_chart&years=1996,2019.

World Peace Foundation. (2015) "Mass Atrocity Endings—Sierra Leone." Accessed September 26, 2021. https://sites.tufts.edu/atrocityendings/2015/08/07/sierra-leone/.

World Peace Foundation. (2017) "United Nations Organization Mission in the Democratic Republic of the Congo (MONUC) / United Nations Organization Stabilization Mission in the Democratic Republic of the Congo (MONUSCO) Short Missions Brief." Accessed September 25, 2021. https://sites.tufts.edu/wpf/files/2017/ 07/Democratic-Republic-of-Congo-brief.pdf.

Yamashita, Hikaru. (2008) "'Impartial' Use of Force in United Nations Peacekeeping." *International Peacekeeping* 15(5): 615–630.

Yamashita, Hikaru. (2012) "Peacekeeping Cooperation the United Nations and Regional Organizations." *Review of International Studies* 38(1): 165–186.

Young, Kirsten. (2001) "UNHCR and ICRC in the Former Yugoslavia: Bosnia-Herzegovina." *International Review of the Red Cross* 83(843): 781–806.

Zanotti, Laura. (2011) *Governing Disorder: UN Peace Operations, International Security, and Democratization in the Post–Cold War Era.* University Park: Pennsylvania State University Press.

Zifcak, Spencer. (2004) *Restorative Justice in East Timor: An Evaluation of the Community Reconciliation Process of the Truth and Reconciliation Commission of East Timor.* New York: Asia Foundation.

Index